FORTUNE'S DAUGHTERS

FORTUNE'S DAUGHTERS

The extravagant lives of the Jerome sisters:
Jennie Churchill, Clara Frewen
and Leonie Leslie

Elisabeth Kehoe

Atlantic Books

LONDON

First published in Great Britain in hardback in 2004 by Atlantic Books,
an imprint of Grove Atlantic Ltd.

1 3 5 7 9 10 8 6 4 2

A CIP catalogue record for this book is available from the British Library.

ISBN 1 84354 158 0

Typeset by Avon DataSet Ltd, Bidford on Avon B50 4JH
Printed in Great Britain by MPG Books, Bodmin, Cornwall

Atlantic Books
An imprint of Grove Atlantic Ltd
Ormond House
26–27 Boswell Street
London WC1N 3JZ

To my sister Jenny, with love and admiration

Contents

Contents

Illustrations

Plates

The author and publishers are grateful to the following for permission to reproduce images:

1, 3, 5, 7, 8, 9, 10, 11, 12, 15, 16, 17, 18, 20, 21, 22, 23, 26, 27, 28, 29, 30, 31, 32, the Leslie Family; 2, 4, 5, 6, 13, 14, 19, 24, 25, 33, Jonathan Frewen

Acknowledgements

In writing this biography I have incurred many debts, and it is a great pleasure to thank all those who have helped me.

I was fortunate to meet many of the Jerome sisters' descendants while researching the book. On the Frewen side, Clara's great-grandson Jonathan Frewen, the holder of Oswald Frewen's diaries as well as of Clara's papers and other family archive material, could not have been more generous. I am grateful to him for all his help, and to him and his wife Anita for inviting me to stay with them while pursuing my research. I would also like to thank Molly Parsons for sharing her memories of Clara. Leonie's descendants, too, the Leslies, were wonderfully helpful. My thanks go to Sammy Leslie, who is at present running the Leslie family seat as a hotel in County Monaghan in Ireland, and of course to her uncle, Sir Jack Leslie, 4th Baronet and to his cousin, Jennifer Leslie. Sir Jack and Jennifer both kindly shared memories as well as letters, photographs, and other mementos during my stays at Castle Leslie. Mark Leslie and Richard Tarka King, Leonie's great-grandsons, were similarly generous with their time, and I am especially grateful to Tarka for allowing me to consult and quote from his archive.

I practically moved into the Irish National Archives building on Kildare Street in Dublin, where the majority of the Leslie papers are now kept, and the archivists there fully deserve my gratitude for their patience and assistance. I would also like to thank the archivists and staff at Churchill College Archives Centre in Cambridge, where Jennie Churchill's voluminous papers are kept, for being so helpful during my visits. I am indebted to the London Library for posting me books and allowing me to keep them for months on end. The staff at Northeast Harbor Library in Maine could not have been kinder in finding books for me throughout the United States, during the summers I spent there working on this book. I would like to thank the following libraries for their assistance: the British Library, the University of London Library, the library at the Institute of Historical Research, and the Public Library in Venice, Florida.

The Earl of Oxford and Asquith kindly copied a letter from Leonie Leslie to Lady Frances Horner and sent it on to me, with permission to quote from it. Mike Jording from the Wyoming State Historical Society sent information on Moreton Frewen. Donald Cameron in Beaufort, Ireland, dug into his library and supplied me with some out-of-print gems. P. Hatfield from Eton College provided me with information on the impact of the First World War on Eton's student body and alumni, as well as on historic fees. Diamond Imaging in Monaghan, Ireland, did a splendid job reproducing old photographs for me. Kevin Kehoe (my brother-in-law) solved many of the technical challenges associated with putting together this manuscript – he deserves and has my gratitude. Professor Sean Kehoe from the John Radcliffe Hospital in Oxford – another talented brother-in-law – shared with me his medical expertise on some of Jennie's illnesses. Giovanna Michelson not only read and critiqued the manuscript, but offered encouragement as well.

I am most grateful to a number of scholars and academics at the University of London. At the Institute of Contemporary British History, my greatest debt is to Professor David Cannadine, who was always willing to provide useful advice and practical help. In addition, he read the manuscript, making corrections and suggestions. Dr Michael Kandiah generously answered many of my questions. At University College London, I would like to thank Kate Quinn who read and fact-checked the manuscript, and Professor Kathy Burke, who over a number of years has offered advice and support.

I am grateful to Toby Mundy at Atlantic Books who believed in me and in this book, and who helped to come up with the idea for the biography. Throughout the research and writing phases he provided constant encouragement, as well as trenchant criticism. My heartfelt thanks go as well to Bonnie Chiang, whose editorial expertise and enthusiasm were much appreciated. My thanks go, too, to Chris Shamwana at Ghost for designing the beautiful book jacket, Celia Levett for copy-editing, Gillian Kemp for proofreading, Richard Marston for text design, Avon DataSet for typesetting, Mike Levett for the index, Jeff Edwards for the family tree and Frances Owen for checking proofs.

I would like to specifically thank those, already mentioned, who read all or parts of the manuscript, including Professor David Cannadine, Kate Quinn, Jonathan Frewen, Sir Jack Leslie, Donald Cameron, and Giovanna Michelson, as well as my editors Toby Mundy and Bonnie Chiang. I am grateful for their comments and corrections, although of course all the remaining errors are mine.

My daughters, Emily and Alice, have been patient in sharing me with Clara, Jennie, and Leonie; I know that now they would like me back. All of my family and friends have been interested in this project (and keen to view the result); I thank them for their enthusiasm. And all roads, in my life, lead to Conor, who is my unfailing rock and my greatest supporter. He deserves my warmest thanks and he has them, along with my love.

Writing and researching this book about sisters has made me appreciate my own sister even more. This book is dedicated to Jenny, because I admire her so much and because I am grateful to have her in my life.

Elisabeth Kehoe
Dublin 2004

Family Tree

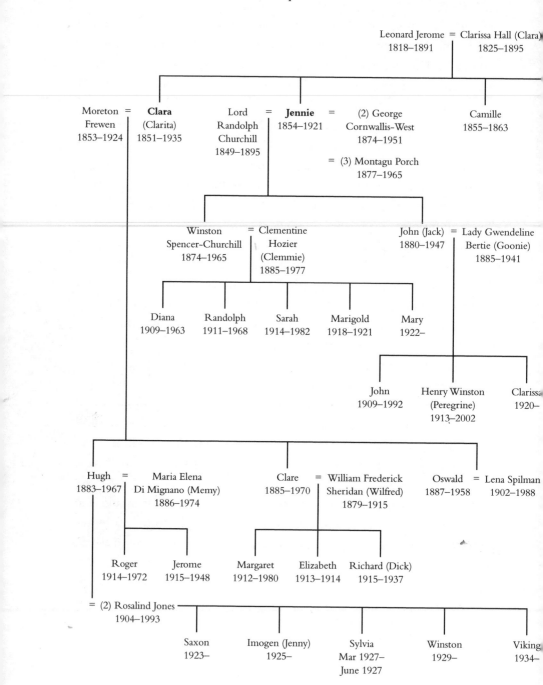

Leonard Jerome = Clarissa Hall (Clara)
1818–1891   1825–1895

Moreton = **Clara**   Lord = **Jennie** = (2) George   Camille
Frewen   (Clarita)   Randolph   1854–1921   Cornwallis-West   1855–1863
1853–1924   1851–1935   Churchill   1874–1951
                 1849–1895

= (3) Montagu Porch
1877–1965

Winston = Clementine   John (Jack) = Lady Gwendeline
Spencer-Churchill   Hozier   1880–1947   Bertie (Goonie)
1874–1965   (Clemmie)   1885–1941
          1885–1977

Diana   Randolph   Sarah   Marigold   Mary
1909–1963   1911–1968   1914–1982   1918–1921   1922–

John   Henry Winston   Clarissa
1909–1992   (Peregrine)   1920–
        1913–2002

Hugh = Maria Elena   Clare = William Frederick   Oswald = Lena Spilman
1883–1967   Di Mignano (Memy)   1885–1970   Sheridan (Wilfred)   1887–1958   1902–1988
         1886–1974   1879–1915

Roger   Jerome   Margaret   Elizabeth   Richard (Dick)
1914–1972   1915–1948   1912–1980   1913–1914   1915–1937

= (2) Rosalind Jones
1904–1993

Saxon   Imogen (Jenny)   Sylvia   Winston   Viking
1923–   1925–   Mar 1927–   1929–   1934–
                       June 1927

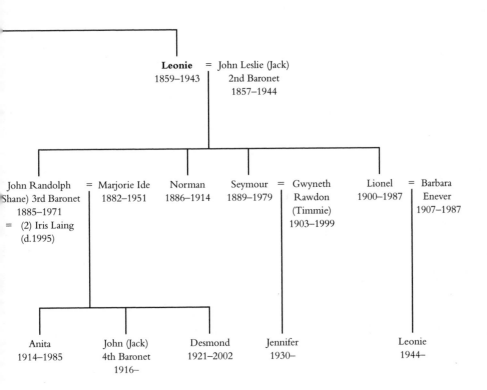

From Manhattan to Mayfair:
A Jerome Family Tree

Introduction

As Lord Randolph Churchill lay dying in the final stages of syphilis, his mind slowly yet inexorably slipping into madness, his wife Jennie wrote letters from the Bay of Bengal to her sisters. In them she described the hellish journey round the world that her sick husband had insisted on taking. 'I am always thinking of you darling & I wd give much to be with you all now,'[1] she wrote to her elder sister Clara. It was 1894 and Jennie Churchill was forty years old. Clara and younger sister Leonie were her confidantes, the only people she entrusted with her deepest feelings of sadness and despair.

Jennie's brilliant marriage in 1873 to the son of the Duke of Marlborough[2] had introduced her sisters, Clara and Leonie, to the aristocratic circles of England. One of the first transatlantic unions, linking American heiresses with members of an increasingly impecunious British aristocracy, it set a trend. By 1914, sixty peers and forty sons of peers had married American women. Although not all were motivated by financial need, there developed a veritable industry for those who were. The American magazine, *Titled Americans: A list of American ladies who have married foreigners of rank*, was published quarterly and revised annually, at a subscription price of $1 per year.

The journal provided details of previous successful transactions and included 'A carefully compiled list of Peers Who are supposed to be eager to lay their coronets and incidentally their hearts, at the feet of the all–conquering American Girl'.[3] The British and American newspapers were not slow to follow, publishing details of these marriages, along with advertisements addressed to lawyers or business representatives of the heiresses. Family lawyers in Britain and on the continent drew up marriage contracts that provided a much–needed injection of funds into empty family coffers. Socially ambitious parents on the other side of the Atlantic, most of them plutocrats, would pay out large sums to secure a prestigious alliance. Daughters were not always consulted on the matter, but many were eager to embrace the entry to high society and status that such a marriage would bring. A French visitor (of aristocratic lineage) to New York in 1897 was astonished at its upper echelons' preoccupation with rank and wrote of Americans' 'secret love of titles'. He observed that there were 'titles galore, among these boastful republicans' who called each other 'Colonel', 'Professor', and 'ex-Attorney-General' so punctiliously, adding wryly that 'these good plain people have societies without number. There are Officers of the Legion of Honor, Comrades of the Grand Army, Sons of the Revolution, Knights of Pythias, Daughters of the Revolution, Colonial Dames, Societies of the Dutch, Societies of New England, the Southern Society, and how many more I know not.'[4] For the socially ambitious, however, there was nothing like a real title, which simply was not to be had in the land of freedom and democracy. To become a 'titled' American meant marrying foreign blue blood.

By the 1870s, the position of the landed aristocracy in Britain was undergoing a significant change. It was slow change, to be sure, but declining revenues from their estates meant that the patrician elite was losing the critical income that had for years supported and consolidated its superior status. The upper classes of Britain had a privileged position predicated on three things: significant wealth generated by land ownership; pre-eminent social status – often manifested by a title; and political power. The aristocrats of Britain were rich, they formed the highest ranks of society, and they were the governing class. In 1880, some 7,000 families owned four-fifths of the land in Britain.[5] Within this group, some 1,000 families were the largest landowners, with estates of over 10,000 acres. Even within this select group, however, it is important to distinguish the various segments of wealth and prestige. At the very top of the pyramid were the great landowning families, numbering some 250, who owned more than 30,000 acres and had incomes of £30,000 per annum.[6] Below them were the 'middling proprietors', a further 750 families who owned properties ranging from 10,000 to 30,000 acres. This group included families such as the Marlboroughs, who owned 23,000 acres and whose revenues from their property in 1878 exceeded £36,000 (over £2.5 million today).[7]

Then there were the titles. In 1880, 580 peers took their seats in the House of Lords, of whom 431 were hereditary.[8] Below these peers were 856 baronets. A baronetage, too, was a hereditary title, and many baronets might later become peers if elevated by the monarch, such as the Dukes of Devonshire and Marlborough.[9] The landed gentry did not have titles, but were recognized by their wealth and privileged position as members of the elite. They also had political power; the majority of Members of Parliament (MPs) were from the landed families, and the upper house of Parliament, the House of Lords, was of course an entirely aristocratic establishment. The judiciary, the army and the Church were also led by members of the same class, while throughout the countryside the landed establishment wielded both official and unofficial power by virtue of their superior, landowning status.

The whole social and governing edifice seemed secure and unassailable. But from around 1873, British farming income began to fall as transatlantic shipment improved, and cheaper, imported food-stuffs became more readily available. Refrigerated meat from the Antipodes, and American wheat, for example, drove down prices for such staples, and British landlords had to reduce rents for their farm-land. As a consequence, the return on investment for land dropped dramatically. For those not in possession of very substantial amounts of acreage, it was becoming more and more difficult to maintain a luxurious lifestyle from the income from land ownership alone. The system of primogeniture, whereby the eldest son inherited the entire estate, had protected the consolidation of family wealth by concentrating family assets in one individual, who then had responsibility for ensuring the continued prosperity of the estate. Upon inheriting, the eldest son was expected to run the properties profitably, generating sufficient income to provide a living for his parents, as well as dowries for his sisters and allowances for younger brothers, not to mention other family members in need. With falling revenues, the pressure increased on eldest sons to ensure sufficient income to run the estate and meet these obligations. The advantages of marrying a wealthy heiress were obvious.

Although the three Jerome sisters could not be described as heiresses, they had no need of advertisements to find desirable husbands. Clara, Jennie, and Leonie Jerome were among the brightest and most beautiful women of their time. Their father, Leonard Jerome, was a Wall Street speculator, who made – and lost – three $1 million fortunes. His passion for music and horses was transmitted to his daughters who became accomplished horsewomen and superb musicians. Their mother, Clarissa Hall, was an orphaned heiress from an old New York family that nevertheless carried the unforgivable stain of reputedly having Iroquois blood. In the 1860s she left Leonard to his horses and his opera and quit New York, taking her daughters to Paris, where they spent their formative years at the court of Napoleon III. It was here that the eldest – blonde, blue-eyed Clara – made her magical debut. However, the war between France and Prussia, and the invasion of Paris by the Prussian army in January 1871, changed everything. Dreams evaporated of balls at the imperial court and marriages to French dukes as Paris came under siege in September 1870. As its population starved, the girls and their mother fled to England.

In 1873 they were living in England, at Cowes. Jennie and Clara caused a sensation at society parties, wearing matching gowns designed by the celebrated couturier Worth and playing duets on the piano after supper. They soon acquired a reputation for wit and beauty. In August 1873, Jennie met and fell in love with Lord Randolph Churchill at a dance given by the Prince of Wales, and three days later the young couple were secretly engaged. Theirs was a turbulent love that would link the entire Jerome family to British high society. Jennie became Lady Randolph Churchill, and both of her sisters would be projected onto a world stage more glamorous than they had ever imagined.

By 1880, their father Leonard had once again lost his fortune and was too old to make another one. Clara and Leonie, like Jennie, married for love and chose well-born men with little discretionary income of their own. Although their mother Clara had spent years drumming into her daughters the necessity to marry well, all three sisters followed their hearts, not their heads, when they made their choices.

In 1881, the eldest – dreamy, fey Clara – married Moreton Frewen, a dashing, handsome sportsman from a distinguished Sussex family. A younger son with no money, he tried relentlessly but unsuccessfully to translate his good looks and riding prowess into a fortune. Instead of making the millions he confidently expected, for a lifetime he endured one failure after another. His family, acquaintances and friends came to know him by his sobriquet, 'Mortal Ruin'. Although he had no title, he was known in Wyoming, where he ran a cattle ranching business, as 'Lord Frewen'. Clara and Moreton had three children. Hugh, Clare, and Oswald all wrote well and became published authors. Clare developed into an artist of considerable repute, sculpting her cousin Winston, as well as Trotsky, Kemal Atatürk, Charlie Chaplin, Gandhi, Lenin, and Mussolini.

The middle sister, Jennie, was the most vivacious of the three. Lord Randolph Churchill determined on the first night they met to make her his wife. She was the mother of two sons, one of whom, Winston, became Britain's most famous prime minister. Jennie lived and loved to the hilt. After the death of her husband from syphilis, she married twice more and had countless affairs in between. She also devoted herself to her sons, Winston (who owed his phenomenal drive to his energetic mother) and his brother Jack. An intimate friend of the Prince of Wales, later Edward VII, she featured in all the society pages – an exciting woman who knew everyone and went everywhere.

In 1883, Leonie, the youngest of the three sisters, married Jack Leslie, a handsome and artistic Anglo-Irishman from a wealthy landowning family in County Monaghan. She spent the season in Ireland and the rest of her time in a townhouse on Great Cumberland Place in London, living the high society life with ever-tightening purse strings, as income from their agricultural estates diminished. A close friend (and probable lover) of Queen Victoria's son, Arthur, Duke of Connaught, she travelled with him in great style on royal tours through India and Egypt. She gave birth to four sons, to whom she was devoted. Her eldest, John, or Jacky (later known as Shane), became a distinguished author who published fifty-three books. Her three other sons, Norman, Seymour, and Lionel, were all talented writers, and all four were deeply indebted to their stylish and intelligent mother.

The three Jerome sisters were not themselves wealthy, nor were they heiresses. In addition to confounding the stereotype of exchanging 'cash for titles', they also married men with dwindling incomes. Their daunting challenge was twofold. First, they married into the world of a patrician elite whose income was shrinking and whose political and social supremacy was threatened as a result. Their marriages, between 1874 and 1884, took place just as this trend was gaining momentum. Second, they each married men with significant character flaws and had to struggle constantly to maintain their social status without the material means with which to do so. What is remarkable is how well they managed, with extraordinary verve, tenacity, and optimism. Their sisterly devotion was lifelong, and it took a practical as well as an emotional form. Americans were not always made welcome in traditional British society, and by believing in themselves and one another, the sisters kept their self-confidence in good repair, as well as offering encouragement and support in times of trouble. In addition to providing a fascinating insight into what it meant to marry into the British ruling class during its decline – but in which standards and status had to be maintained – the story of the Jerome sisters also demonstrates how strong ties of affection can transform lives.

The biography begins in America and ends a century later at Castle Leslie, an imposing old house in the small town of Glaslough in County Monaghan, on the border of the Irish Free State and Northern Ireland.

Through their marriages, the three sisters bridged the gap between the New World and the Old. Although they were American and remained attached to their native land throughout their lives, their homes were in Britain. They experienced the apogee and the twilight of the British Empire, a time that coincided with the profound decline of the British aristocracy. The story reaches its conclusion in the middle of the Second World War, when Britain was facing its supreme challenge and battling for its survival, led by Jennie's son.

CHAPTER ONE

Mrs Astor's New York

Clara and Jennie Jerome spent their childhood in New York. Their father Leonard Jerome began his love affair with the city in 1850, at the age of thirty-two, irresistibly drawn to a place where an ambitious young man could make his mark and his fortune. The company of other like-minded entrepreneurs, who gave themselves wholeheartedly to the pursuit of their dreams, was like a tonic to him. He missed New York when he was away and revelled in everything it had to offer when he was there. It was a city that he made his own from the day in 1850 when he brought his young bride to live in Brooklyn, until the day he left for the last time, in 1890, a sick old man on his way to die in England, where he could once again be in the company of his wife and daughters, who had all chosen to make their homes in Europe.

New York was emblematic of the brash new nation that America was becoming in the nineteenth century; its association with the forces of change and industry made it a target during the American Civil War. By late 1864, the South was losing the war and General William T. Sherman's army had captured Atlanta. In November of that year, a desperate Confederate plot to destroy the city by setting fire to ten hotels was only foiled by the quick action of the hotel employees, and by New York's heroic volunteer firemen who rapidly put out the flames.

The Confederates wanted to destroy New York because it was a symbol of all that they loathed about the North. Bristling and boastful

I

with success, the city encouraged the dynamic creation of riches as well as their ostentatious display. The wealthy of New York were among the wealthiest in America, and in the period leading up to the Civil War many fortunes were made. The war then brought even more prosperity to the city, along with economic speculation. From the 1860s to the turn of the century, millionaires such as Jay Gould, John D. Rockefeller, and Cornelius Vanderbilt cornered markets and influenced politicians, making colossal fortunes. Speculation became the lifeblood of the city and brokerage houses on Wall Street the means to fortune.

Leonard Jerome was born in 1818 on a farm at Pompey Hill, near Syracuse in western New York State. He was the fifth of eight brothers and had a sister, Mary. He was a restless and rebellious youth, much to his parents' distress; they were proud of their Huguenot blood and of their forebears (one of whom had fought with George Washington at Valley Forge), and they encouraged their children to follow their stern, hard-working ways. The Jeromes came from a long line of pioneering ancestors. Timothy Jerome, the first to become an American, was a Protestant who had fled France in 1710 to England and had then sailed from the Isle of Wight in 1717 to settle in Connecticut. His son, Samuel had moved to Massachusetts; his son, Aaron, married Betsey Ball whose grandfather, Revd Elliphant Ball, was a cousin of Mary Ball, George Washington's mother. George Washington had no lineal descendants. Leonard would later write to his wife, explaining the Jerome connection to the Washingtons, exclaiming: 'We are the nearest of kin!'[1] The eldest of Aaron's sons was Isaac, Leonard's father, who was born in 1786 and who married Aurora Murray, a woman of Scottish descent. After the war of 1812–15 against England, they settled at Pompey Hill and raised their family.

Leonard was sent to work in the village store at the age of fourteen, where he honed his commercial skills with the local farmers who paid in trade, rather than ready cash. He then left Pompey Hill to work for his uncle (who had become a judge) in Palmyra, a town sixty miles away. At eighteen, he followed his brothers to Princeton University, where his fees were paid by his elder brother Aaron, who had become a partner in a dry-goods firm. Although Leonard did well at Princeton, he had to leave when Aaron's fortunes took a bad turn and finished his studies at the less expensive Union College, in Schenectady, New York State. Leonard then took up the law, first in Albany where he passed his Bar examinations, and then with his uncle Hiram in Palmyra. In the late 1830s Palmyra was a thriving, busy town with broad streets, many shops, and hotels lining the Erie Canal, with its painted packet boats passing by. Leonard became a partner in his uncle's firm and was also appointed notary public for the county. With his increased prosperity he purchased 170 acres of land.

When Uncle Hiram moved the law practice to Rochester, New York, Leonard and his brother Lawrence, who also worked for the firm as a junior clerk, accompanied him. Rochester had grown into a town of 23,000 inhabitants, made prosperous by its position as a major shipping point for wheat. Its snobbish social elite was much preoccupied with entertainments, and in this milieu Leonard enjoyed an active social life. A Rochester socialite, the daughter of Samuel Wilder, later recorded that the Jerome brothers were 'screamingly funny boys ... very popular with the ladies owing to the dashing manner in which they rode high-spirited horses'.[2]

The brothers became men of importance in the town, and although not wealthy their prospects had improved since their early days. Lawrence married the orphaned heiress Catherine Hall in 1844, and Leonard cast his eye on her younger sister Clara.[3] Like Catherine, Clara was a beauty with dark eyes and an oval face. Their father was the wealthy Ambrose Hall, who had inherited a fortune from his grandfather John Beach. The origins of their mother, Clarissa Wilcox,[4] were shrouded in mystery; tales about her background have become part of family lore. One version has it that Clarissa's mother, Anna Baker, was half Iroquois, something that Clara herself believed, for she later told her own daughters the same story, at a time when mixed blood was socially unacceptable. Her own dark looks and strong facial features suggested such ancestry, especially as she grew older. Clara's other sister Caroline Purdy was, according to Clara Frewen's son

Hugh, 'copper-skinned' and when she visited England in the early 1900s her daughter Kitty Mott kept her hidden 'well behind the curtains'[5] to avoid unfavourable insinuations.

Another account suggested in fact that Clara's grandmother was of African, rather than American Indian, ancestry, which would perhaps explain why these two wealthy Hall heiresses settled for the relatively impecunious Jerome brothers with their risky prospects. Clara's fear of being said to have what were at that time even less acceptable African antecedents might also shed light on why she insisted on her Indian heritage. Most of the speculation about Clara Hall's roots has focussed on the possibility of an Indian and not an African ancestry. However, in November 1912, Norman Leslie wrote to his mother Leonie – Clara Hall's youngest daughter – of an encounter with a man who believed that his first cousin Winston Churchill, had black ancestry: 'There is a gentleman on board who tells me in confidence that Winston isn't half a bad fellow, but that he can't help himself, owing to the black blood that he inherits from his Mother ... he has forgotten whether it was a quadroon or an octaroon, but he knew for certain that it was one of the two.'[6]

Although Anna Baker's family tree has been traced back to her grandparents, her grandmother's maiden name is unknown, as is Anna's date of birth. Two possibilities emerge: either Anna Baker was of mixed race; or she was raped, or had a relationship in Palmyra with either an Indian or an escaped slave that resulted in the birth of her daughter, Clarissa. Of course, it is possible that there is no truth to any of these rumours. None of them can be proved conclusively, but it is instructive to consider what people at the time thought to be true and how it affected their attitudes.

Clarissa Wilcox's daughter, Clara Hall, certainly felt the stigma of the rumours. We also know that Clara's own daughters, their spouses, and their children all believed the story of native American blood to be true. Later generations – including Jennie's son Winston and Leonie's children and grandchildren – thought it was quite exciting. (Her sons-in-law would later refer to her irreverently as 'Sitting Bull'.) What is indisputably clear, however, is that the rumours, whether true or not, help to explain Clara's lifelong obsession with background and rank, and her desire to move among society's highest echelons – an ambition that ultimately she was only able to achieve in Europe. The 'shame' that she might be of mixed race was perhaps the decisive factor in what must have been a difficult decision to leave behind husband, home, and country, and to make a new life, as a single parent, among strangers, in foreign climes.

Clara Hall and Leonard Jerome married in 1849. Soon after, Leonard and his brother decided to leave their uncle's law firm and establish a newspaper. Leonard borrowed $30,000 from his new wife to invest in his new paper, called the *Daily American*, and made it a great success. It was a time of swift development in the newspaper industry in the United States; weeklies and semi-weeklies published chiefly in rural towns expanded quickly, as did the metropolitan dailies. The latter were graphic, multiple (nine to ten editions a day), and hefty (twenty-four to thirty-six pages). In 1800 there were 150 papers; by 1870 this number had dramatically risen to 971, and by 1900 there were 2,226 published daily. The *Daily American* became renowned as a hard-hitting political journal that supported the Whig Party. The Whigs believed in a strong nation, as opposed to strong state control, and they supported national projects such as the building of roads, canals, and railroads. But the formation of the new Republican Party in the 1850s siphoned off many Whigs, and the party was also damaged by the short-lived Native American, or Know-Nothing Party, which was primarily anti-immigrant and anti-Catholic. Until their disappearance in 1856, the Whigs had been especially strong in urban areas, such as Rochester. Sales of the *Daily American* grew rapidly, eventually reaching 3,000, an extraordinary figure for the time. Leonard was able to repay the loan and never again took money from his wife. Encouraged by the paper's commercial success, he then invested in a telegraph company in New York. In order to be close to the new business venture, he sold his interest in the *Daily American* and in 1850 moved with his wife to Brooklyn.

At this time Brooklyn was an independent city, with a population of

120,000. It boasted thirty-five miles of paved and lighted streets. Streetcars would arrive just three years later, in 1853. Leonard rented a fifteen-room, red-brick house in a section later known as Brooklyn Heights, just a block from the East River. It was here that his first child was born on 15 April 1851: Clarita,[7] blonde and blue-eyed, the only one who would physically resemble her father. Leonard's elder brother Addison, who joined him as a partner in the new business, moved in with them, and the two men would set off each morning to cross the river by ferry to work on Wall Street.

Leonard eventually sold the telegraph business to work full time with Addison in stock-market speculation. He called Wall Street 'a jungle where men tear and claw', and threw himself into the work. He was determined to join the city's millionaires – which at that time had been estimated at nineteen. Studies of American wealth (measured in contemporary dollar values) have concluded that there were approximately forty millionaires in the nation some ten years later, in 1860, and that this number grew to 545 in 1870, reaching 5,904 in 1922.[8] Leonard proved successful at making money and achieved a Wall Street reputation for being a man who knew how to get things done.[9] A friend remembered asking him one day how business was and received the reply: 'Oh, dull, confoundedly dull. I have only made $25,000 [$340,000] today.'[10] This was during the 1870s, when the well-known socialite and commentator Ward MacAllister later claimed that 'there were not one or two men in New York who spent, in living and entertaining, over 60,000 dollars [$820,000] a year.'[11]

Leonard's speciality was selling 'short': that is, selling stock that he did not yet own, to be delivered to the purchaser at a specified future date. His calculation was that before that date the price of the stock would drop; he would then buy it at its lower price and make a profit when fulfilling the sale. In addition to the steady nerves and business acumen required for such speculation, Leonard also had wit and exuberance and was well liked. A contemporary recorded that Leonard 'belonged to the city with all its garish brilliance'. No man, he stated, 'ever became more completely a New Yorker'.[12]

Leonard's ambition grew with his income, but his wife, alone in Brooklyn with her young child, became increasingly lonely without his company. She was therefore pleased when he announced in 1852 that he was accepting the position of chief consul in Trieste, a Mediterranean port and at that time a city-state within the Austro-Hungarian Empire, and that she should make preparations for the move. Whilst Leonard often found himself impatient with those who had not 'paid for their own education' and thought it 'more important to think clearly in one idiom than to chatter in five',[13] he loved the opera (a visitor recorded that Leonard had gone to see Verdi's new opera, *Rigoletto*, some thirty times)[14] and also yachting. During their sixteen-month stay, he bought a pair of prize Lipizzaner stallions of which he was extremely proud. Leonard kept busy; he had also insisted that the family bring along one of his operatic protégées, Lillie Greenough, so that she could, he claimed, study Italian singing techniques.

Clara found other amusements and was very taken with the large contingent of Italian nobility in Trieste. She was sorry that their stay was curtailed when Democratic President Franklin Pierce replaced the Whig President Millard Fillmore (the last Whig to hold this office) and Leonard resigned his position. Before leaving Trieste, the couple commissioned the Italian painter, Schiavoni, to paint their portraits, which were shipped to America, along with their collection of art and antiques. That summer, the family crossed Europe by horse-drawn coach, reaching Paris in the autumn, where Clara ordered new gowns from the various couturiers. Paris was being rebuilt by the new Emperor Louis Napoleon, who had commissioned gigantic boulevards, monuments, and columns. Clara loved the glamour and style. Leonard promised her that they would come back, but his eagerness to return to New York was unmistakable. The couple left Europe divided by their desires; Clara lived for the day she would return, while Leonard went home a committed American.

They arrived in New York in November 1853. Leonard was glad to be back in action. He and his brother Addison, whose brokerage firm had failed, bought a house in Brooklyn for their families and threw themselves into the Wall Street fray. Leonard was little interested in cultivating the cream of society, preferring to move within many overlapping circles, focussed on speculating and winning.

Nineteenth-century New York was a modern metropolis of crowded sidewalks and perpetual new building construction. The city's remarkable geographical spread and structural growth accommodated both its nouveaux riches, keen to build mansions on Fifth Avenue, and the steady influx of poor immigrants, who were increasingly confined to the more insalubrious areas. By the 1860s, the wealthy of New York had moved farther uptown from the previously desirable downtown areas. The fashionable world occupied Fifth Avenue from Washington Square to the southern edge of Central Park. The poor, most of whom lived in appalling conditions, were pushed onto the outer rim of the island, along both sides of the river, and in tenements below 14th Street, described by the social commentator Jacob Riis as a 'maze of narrow, often unsuspected passage-ways' where entire communities existed in 'an atmosphere of actual darkness, moral and physical'.[15]

These two communities existed within fifteen minutes' walk of one another, yet they rarely met. The financial speculators, such as Leonard and his brother Addison, made their money downtown, leaving the area at the end of the workday to spend their evenings at the exclusive clubs, restaurants and theatres farther uptown. Leonard loved music and was devoted to concerts and the opera. Clara, however, was not at all musical and rarely accompanied him. Leonard cultivated the operatic world with knowledge and enthusiasm, becoming intimate with some of its most famous singers, one of whom was the Swedish opera star Jenny Lind. Having rarely missed a performance during her concert tour in 1851, he suggested three years later that the new baby, born on 9 January 1854, be called Jenny. 'Just plain Jenny?' queried Clara, clearly unaware of Leonard's friendship. It was indeed just plain Jenny, or Jennie. It was rumoured that another talented singer, Minnie Hauk, who was born at about this time in New York City, was Leonard's daughter from an early romance; certainly he was extremely protective of her and very generous. In 1862, Minnie and her mother returned to

New York from New Orleans where Minnie had begun her musical training. Leonard sponsored her further musical development by paying for her to study under the famous Achille Errani. In September 1866, she made her operatic debut in Bellini's *La sonnambula* at Leonard's private theatre and on 13 October made her public debut in the same opera at the Brooklyn Academy of Music. It was the beginning of a long and successful operatic career. Clara, somewhat surprisingly, welcomed her with good grace, noting on the back of Minnie's photograph:'so like Jennie, but less good-looking'.[16] It was true that the two looked remarkably alike.

Leonard had become very wealthy. He purchased expensive jewellery for Clara, and encouraged her to buy only the finest gowns. In 1855, their third daughter, Camille, was born. Leonard continued to shower his wife with costly gifts and, after a particularly successful period, bought her a diamond necklace from the luxury jeweller Tiffany's. Clara told him how she would love to be taken to a court so that she could show it off.

Moving in the right circles became Clara's ambition. In this city of old families and wealthy nobodies, social climbing was rife, and she was anxious to cultivate the 'right people'. Her family background allowed her admittance to some of New York's elite society, but there was a scramble for the most hallowed circles, and families went to great lengths to gain entrance. The grandest New Yorkers were descendants of the original Dutch settlers, known as the Knickerbockers – named after their ancestors' breeches. One of the most prominent of these was Mrs Astor, born Caroline Schermerhorn of an old Dutch shipping family, who married William Backhouse Astor, Jr, possessor of a more recent fortune. Mrs Astor, helped by the Southerner Ward McAllister, created a system that restricted access of the newly wealthy to the upper levels of society by establishing twenty-five 'Patriarchs' as the leading representative men of the city. The Patriarchs would host parties to which the 'nobs' – those socialites who were already members of the elite – and 'swells' – who had money, and needed access to its highest echelons – could be invited. The result was a list of society's most esteemed members: the 'Four Hundred' (a number that famously described the capacity of Mrs Astor's ballroom).

The Jeromes were not part of the Four Hundred, and Clara felt it deeply. When Leonard lost his entire fortune in 1856 and decided to take a twelve months' sabbatical from speculating in order to study Wall Street psychology, Clara was secretly relieved. They lived quietly for the following year and entertained their friends. These included Leonard's two closest friends, the celebrated financier Henry Clews and August Belmont, with whom he shared a passion for spirited horses and spirited ladies. Belmont was born in Germany and had joined the House of Rothschild Bank at the age of fourteen. (There was a discredited rumour that he was an illegitimate son of that dynasty). Following early success in his career, he was sent to America as the Rothschilds' agent and did so well that he was able, with their blessing, to set up his own banking house in 1837. He became one of the few Jews to enter the portals of elite New York society and firmly secured his place on the social map by fighting a duel in 1841 with Edward Hatward of South Carolina. The slight limp with which he was left, after honour had been satisfied, was a source of pride for the rest of his life. In 1849 he married Caroline Slidell Perry, daughter of a US Navy commodore, and he later rendered sterling service to the North during the civil war. Belmont became known as an art collector, a noted connoisseur of horseflesh, and a 'somewhat rakish man about town'.[17] He was a perfect match for Leonard Jerome; he, together with Clews, William Travers, and Lawrence Jerome, formed Leonard's tight circle. All five men loved playing the financial markets and embodied the spirit of swashbuckling New York.

Clara may have been relieved by a respite from Leonard's absorption in the stock market, but he was not. He suffered privately from the loss of his reputation as one of Wall Street's 'meteors' and the following year threw himself back into the market with his firm Travers Jerome. He was immediately successful, multiplying his capital many times over, and made arrangements to fulfil his dream of owning a racing stud. He also increased the fund he had settled on his wife; built a seaside villa for the family in Newport; and purchased a yacht so he could sail there to visit them. Leonard made so much money that he was able to satisfy Clara's demand for a trip to Europe. The family sailed to France in 1858, renting an apartment in Paris on the Champs Elysées.

Clara fulfilled her dreams of mingling with royalty when she was presented at the court of the Empress Eugénie while Leonard pursued the ladies with golden voices whom he met through operas and concerts. In spite of his amours, he was proud of his beautiful wife and wrote to his brother of her success at the Grand Ball at the Tuileries: 'It was universally acknowledged that Clit [Clara] was the handsomest woman there.' He added that he 'never saw her look so well'.[18] Clara still hoped for a son, but in August 1859, she gave birth to their fourth and last child, a daughter named Leonie.

Clara was delighted with Parisian society. Like most of the French aristocracy, she was unconcerned by Louis Napoleon's war with Emperor Franz Josef of Austria. Determined to emulate his uncle Napoleon I by extending France's influence and frontiers, Louis Napoleon would lead his nation into four wars during the nearly eighteen years he was emperor, but his military achievements were not very impressive. After the Crimean War, he engaged in a conflict with Austria, winning several decisive battles at Magenta and Solferino, but the overall result of this ill-thought-out campaign was not a clear victory for France. It did not seem to matter. In Paris, his court was characterized by frivolity. The aristocracy ignored the military conflicts as well as the hardships of everyday life in France, concentrating instead on their own amusements.

The superficial life suited Clara; she liked being known as 'la belle Américaine' and pleaded with her husband to be allowed to stay in her adopted city. But Leonard was not persuaded. 'Paris is not as agreeable to me as New York,' he had written to his brother, adding that he believed that he would spend his next summer on the Isle of Wight instead.[19] Also, he could not remain away from his business indefinitely and in 1859 the family returned to New York. Leonard's financial touch was once again so sure that he was able to build the six-storey mansion he had long promised his wife on a plot of land in the newly fashionable area of Madison Square and 23rd Street.

By 1860 New York City was the nation's largest city, with a population of some 500,000, yet Fifth Avenue was still unpaved north of 23rd Street, and most of Manhattan was still rolling farmland. But the area was transformed into a desirable address through the addition of Delmonico's chic restaurant, and the building of the magnificent Fifth Avenue Hotel – complete with elevator (a great novelty at the time). Leonard had designed his mansion on the Square to accommodate his passions; it contained a private theatre and an adjacent three-storey stable, built and carpeted and pannelled in black walnut at a cost of $80,000 (an astonishing $900,000 today). Clara, whilst happy with her palatial residence, with its white and gold ballroom and its huge drawing room decorated in flaming red, was nevertheless less pleased by her husband's obsession with horses. More worrying still were the singers whom he indulged with his private theatre, which could seat a staggering 600 people. At the Jeromes' opening ball, champagne flowed from one fountain and reviving eau de cologne from another. One guest present at the magnificent party recorded: 'Invitations were eagerly sought by the 400 of the day, and all the wealth and fashion and beauty of the metropolis took part in the dance ... The front of the theatre was illuminated and the sidewalls covered with crimson tapestry. The Supper must have cost thousands.'[20]

Leonard's energy and high spirits seduced all who knew him. He entertained with panache, financed by his massive stock market earnings. With his friend August Belmont, he took pleasure in a friendly competition to see who could have the best horses, the best dinners, and even the best love affairs. Dinners were celebrated in style, usually at Delmonico's, where William Travers, August Belmont, and Leonard constantly tried to outdo one another. Leonard's gift of a gold bracelet with an attached jewel for each lady at one such dinner was eclipsed by Belmont's platinum favours at the next, but the result was usually judged to be a dead heat all round. Leonard and Belmont also competed for the attentions of Fanny Ronalds, a Boston divorcee with musical talent and good looks. Both men helped her financially; Leonard showed her how to manage horses and put his theatre at her disposal. Belmont and Jerome also shared the honour of each paying – unknown to the other – for a ball given by Fanny that was one of the most spectacular of the season. Their friend Frank Griswold recorded a conversation the two men held some twenty years after the event: '"August," said Jerome, "do you remember Fanny's celebrated ball?"

"Indeed I ought to," replied Belmont. "I paid for it."

"Why how very strange," said Jerome slowly, "so did I."'[21] Mrs Ronalds was also loved by the Jerome girls and became a favourite of the family. Even Clara Jerome was moved to tell her when they first met: 'I don't blame you. I know how irresistible he is.'[22] Jennie and Fanny would remain friends all their lives; she recalled many years later how Fanny had sung to the girls in the evening before bed.

Leonard spent his gains on entertaining lavishly and bought more pieces of jewellery for Clara, which in late nineteenth-century New York City became an increasingly fashionable and ostentatious way to display wealth. By the early 1900s, three Vanderbilt wives owned jewels valued at over $1 million (over $21 million today), as did the daughter-in-law of the wealthy speculator Jay Gould.[23] Clara enjoyed her diamonds and gowns – which were now so numerous that they required an inventory – and turned a dignified blind eye to her husband's many, and indiscreet, affairs. One of Leonard's protégées was the seventeen-year-old singer Adeline Patti, who was often seen riding with him through the city in one of his magnificent carriages.

Although Clara wished to please her husband, it is clear that she had a limited ability to empathize with his interests. Her main preoccupation was with appearances – clothes, accessories, and interiors were what mattered to her – and her ambitions were entirely social. She filled her mind and heart with gossip and social chatter and, with the exception of art, had few passions. She was unmusical, afraid of horses, mistrustful of sport, and disliked boats. Clara loved the European aristocracy – an elite focussed completely on *savoir vivre*, the triumph of sumptuous style over substance. She yearned to return to France, where a glittering social season beckoned. But Leonard would not yield; his home and business were firmly anchored in New York.

The outbreak of the civil war in 1861 brought great opportunities as well as strife to New York City's business community. Along with other rich New Yorkers, the Jeromes were able to maintain their extravagant lifestyle. Although Leonard and his partners were not in any sense profiteers, they, like many Northern businessmen, took a determined supporting stance for Republican President Lincoln. Through their ownership of one quarter of the *New York Times* newspaper, they thundered approval for the Unionist anti-slavery position. Many North-eastern businessmen also supported Lincoln and the war because they believed that the once-dominant power of planter agrarians in the South would be reduced; also that that of the 'captains of industry' in the North would be elevated. The wartime Republican Congress was committed to honouring its business-friendly platform promises made in 1860, which consolidated the interests of North-eastern businessmen and Western farmers. Leonard, was fully committed to the Unionist cause. He became treasurer of the Union Defence Committee and continued his brokerage activities. He also contributed $35,000 to the construction of the warship *Meteor* and acted as an adviser to the government on its proposed National Banking Act, which helped to finance the war as well as creating a uniform system of banking and banknote currency.

The human costs of the war extended beyond the immediate hostilities. In March 1863 there were riots in working-class sections of New York City, in response to the First Conscription Act, which made all men aged between twenty and forty-five liable for military service. Because this service could be avoided by paying a fee or by finding a substitute, it was unfair to the poor and led to violent protests, culminating in the Draft Riots of July 1863. The police could not control the mob which, armed with torches, guns, and pikes, looted the city and terrorized black Americans (whom they blamed for the war). Leonard manned one of the two new machine-guns provided by the army to defend the *New York Times* building. Luckily, the mob turned away when they heard of the guns. Leonard later started a fund to aid the families of those killed and wounded in the Draft Riots, a characteristically generous gesture from this civic-minded man.

Throughout the four bitter years of the conflict, life in New York for society's elite went on much as before, only occasionally troubled by its impact. Clara and the girls spent much of the war in Newport, in the villa Leonard had purchased where the children could, as Jennie later wrote in her memoirs, 'run wild and be as grubby and happy as children ought to be'.[24] Jennie recollected that the great struggle of the civil war had 'passed our nursery unmolested', but that she could remember 'that every little Southerner I met at dancing classes was a "wicked rebel" to be pinched if possible'.[25]

The period following the end of the war was one of reconstruction and reconciliation. The attempt by the Southern states to secede from the Union had failed, and the bloodshed had profoundly shaken the nation. Over 600,000 lives had been lost, and the Southern economy was all but destroyed. The financial cost of the war was estimated at $5.2 billion (over $57 billion in today's money). The South had been battered and humiliated, but American nationalism was triumphant, and 4 million slaves were subsequently freed by ratification of the Thirteenth Amendment in December 1865. On the heels of the victory, President Abraham Lincoln, so closely identified with the cause of the North and the abolition of slavery, was assassinated on 11 April 1865, five days after General Robert E. Lee surrendered to General Ulysses S. Grant at the village of Appomattox, Virginia. The entire city of New York went into public mourning. Jennie recalled that their house was 'draped from top to bottom in white and black', and that the whole city had the appearance of 'one gigantic mausoleum'.[26] Men and women sobbed openly in the streets. On 24 April 1865, even the poorest New Yorkers bought tiny flags, with bits of crêpe attached, to honour their president, who lay in City Hall before being taken to Springfield, Illinois for burial.

New York City had given 15,000 men and $4 million to the Northern cause. Despite these losses, the civil war had stimulated the city's economy and business was booming.[27] This prosperity was under-pinned by New York's rapidly growing immigrant population, which supplied cheap labour, as well as votes for unscrupulous politicians. Corruption scandals followed. City politics were well known to be suspect. One of the most notorious and dishonest offenders, William Marcy Tweed, once famously declared that the corruptness of New York politics was nothing new:

> The fact is that New York politics were always dishonest – long before my time. There never was a time when you couldn't buy the board of aldermen. A politician coming forward takes things as they are. This population is too hopelessly split up into races and factions to govern it under universal suffrage, except by the bribery of patronage or corruption … I don't think there is ever a fair or honest election in New York.[28]

This was almost certainly true. Tweed was an example of how New York's booming economic development, coupled with the population's general lack of interest in the political process, could allow corruption to flourish. He had worked his way up to the New York county board of supervisors, where he established what was known as the 'Tweed Ring'. Every contractor, craftsman or merchant wishing to do business with New York City had to pay Tweed and his henchmen 15 per cent of their total bill before the board of supervisors would grant them a contract. Tweed dominated the board (which was supposedly even-handed because it included six Democrats and six Republicans) by bullying and bribing the other members. He was extraordinarily successful; he 'served' on the board for thirteen years and was elected president four times. 'Boss' Tweed also determined party nominations, while his ward leaders controlled elections through intimidation and bribery. Many voters were Irish or German, and judges who were controlled by Tweed would naturalize thousands of the immigrant population in return for their votes. The Irish voter in particular was targeted, and Tweed's acolytes would go to meet newly arrived immigrants from their ships with promises of citizenship.

The main reason that Tweed's corrupt practices were so successful was that most New Yorkers were simply uninterested in the political process. Making money was what mattered, and merchant capitalism was the ruling creed. By 1869 Tweed was stealing more than $1,000,000 (worth around $13 million in today's money) a month from the city treasury. He was finally arrested in 1871 and, after his trial, was sentenced to a twelve-year prison term. One year later he was released and then rapidly rearrested on further corruption charges. Tweed escaped custody in 1875 and fled to Cuba, then to Spain. He was extradited to the United States in 1876 and died in a New York jail cell in 1878. In all, it was estimated that he and his cronies had stolen about $30 million (about $411 million today) in cash, and when the total loss to the city was calculated – taking into account money paid in bribes, tax cuts for rich men, profit from the rigged sale of franchises, and the sale of other privileges – it was probably more in the region of $200 million (about $2.7 billion in today's values). This was at a time when Tweed's constituents and supporters – recent immigrants and poor, largely unskilled workers – were lucky to earn $10 (equivalent to around $137 today) a week.

Such was the business environment in which Leonard made his millions. Speculation requires information, and gathering information and developing relationships were skills at which Leonard excelled. Consequently, he prospered as a financial investor in New York's swashbuckling atmosphere, where his newly minted money was welcomed and celebrated. Although he was by most accounts an honest man – a rival was once quoted as saying: 'That damn fellow has cashed in on honesty'[29] – he could not have made his fortune without a working relationship with Tweed, which raises doubts as to his financial probity. Leonard and Lawrence (known as Larry) worked closely with the rich and powerful financier Commodore Vanderbilt. In turn Vanderbilt worked with Tweed, as did the Jerome brothers and Leonard's great friend, August Belmont. Indeed, Tweed was Leonard's guest at the 1867 opening of his racecourse. Larry's rather dour and stern wife Catherine once commented disapprovingly that the 'Jeromes seem to have so much sense of honor and hardly any sense of *sin*.'[30]

Leonard's generosity was legendary and he spent with alacrity rather than saving. Yet he was also prepared for losses on the market. Although he was reputed to have made three $1 million fortunes (each worth $13 million today), he also lost as much in speculation.

All three girls adored their successful father, and he set a standard they would each seek in their future husbands. It was a high bench-mark: Leonard's wit, intelligence, and drive were matched by his sporting prowess and his musical talent and appreciation. But his ability to make and lose fortunes with equanimity engendered in his daughters a disregard for wealth that remained with them their entire lives. Leonard had a breezy insouciance about money that gave the girls an unrealistic understanding of the huge cost of maintaining an expensive lifestyle among society's elite. He made finance seem easy and protected his wife from the downfalls of the market by settling a capital sum on her, so she was guaranteed a secure income for life. This was not the case for his daughters, who he believed (as it proved, erroneously) would be provided for by their husbands.

In 1863, the Jeromes suffered the loss of their third daughter, Camille, aged only seven, who died in Newport of a sudden fever.[31] There is little record of this untimely death, and Jennie's own memoirs only include the inaccurate comment that three children returned from Italy to New York in 1853 'one of whom died a year or two later'.[32] (In fact it was only Clarita alone, who travelled with her parents; the other three were as yet unborn.) In an age before penicillin (which would not be discovered until 1928, by the Scottish scientist Alexander Fleming), illnesses such as scarlet fever, meningitis, typhoid, and diphtheria killed thousands. Although there is no record of the family's response to Camille's death, both Leonard and Clara were devoted parents, and this tragedy must have caused them considerable anguish.

Leonard kept busy with work and, increasingly, his great passion for horses. As his fortune grew in the late 1860s and 1870s, much of his income was absorbed by the costs of stabling and horse racing. Belmont also had stables and together, in 1865, they created 'The Coaching

Club', in an attempt to make four-in-hand driving fashionable once more. A reporter noted that Jerome had also trained his horses to 'caper and rear as they turned in the street'. He added:

> Gay and laughing ladies, in gorgeous costume, filled the carriage. Lackeys, carefully gotten up, occupied the coupe behind. Jerome sat on the box and handled the reins. With a huge bouquet of flowers attached to his buttonhole, with white gloves, cracking his whip, and with the shouts of the party, the four horses would rush up Fifth Avenue on towards the Park, while the populace said to one another, 'That is Jerome'.[33]

Organized horse racing was still in its infancy in New York. Although the first American racecourse had been laid out on Long Island in 1665, tracks were few and far between, and were mainly created by the rich to showcase their horses. After the civil war, however, entrepreneurs became involved in the sport and began to develop it as a profit-generating business by establishing public betting on the races. Jerome's business partner, William Travers, and John Hunter founded a racetrack in the popular health resort of Saratoga Springs, in upstate New York. Its inaugural race, run in 1864, was called the Travers and was to become the nation's oldest stakes race.

Encouraged by this success, and no doubt with his competitive juices flowing, Leonard built an elaborate racetrack on his Bathgate estate in 1866 and named it Jerome Park. The Park contained a grandstand that seated 8,000 people, along with a luxurious clubhouse that included a ballroom, dining rooms, guest rooms and additional facilities for such pastimes as trapshooting, polo, sleighing, and skating. The new Park became the headquarters of the American Jockey Club, which was founded by Leonard and Larry, along with Belmont and Travers. Its guiding principles were, according to the founders, to 'promote the improvement of horses, to elevate the public tastes in sports of the turf, and to become an authority on racing matters in the country'.[34] The opening of the track on 25 September 1866 was described by the New York *Tribune* as 'the social event of all time ... a new era in the horse-racing world'.[35] Guests included business associates Boss Tweed and his political agent John Morrissey, as well as friends such as Fanny Ronalds and presidential hopeful Ulysses S. Grant. It was at Jerome Park that the Belmont Stakes, named after Leonard's close friend (who had also helped to finance the Park), was inaugurated on 19 June 1867. This famous race was later transferred to Belmont Park and is the third jewel in the Triple Crown.

Reporters began to call Leonard the 'Father of the American Turf'. In 1884, he founded the Coney Island Jockey Club. He then built a new racecourse called Sheepshead Bay, which opened in 1884. When Jerome Park was pulled down to make room for a reservoir in 1887, Leonard built, with the help of thoroughbred owner and breeder John A. Morris, a new racetrack named Morris Park, which opened in Westchester County in 1889. Leonard passed on to each of his daughters an ability to ride with confidence as well as pleasure. As a girl, Jennie in particular spent as much time as she could in the stables. When budding opera singer Minnie Hauk stayed with the Jeromes in 1865 she was impressed by the sight of Clarita, aged fourteen, and Jennie, aged eleven, on horseback, recollecting in her memoirs: 'Mr Jerome possessed some beautiful saddle-horses and his daughters were in the habit of riding many miles before breakfast. They rode like Amazons.'[36]

The girls also inherited their father's musical ear. Leonard insisted that they learn the piano, and their first teacher was Stephen Heller, a friend of Chopin's. These lessons, along with the excitement of rehearsals in their private theatre, stimulated in them a lifelong love of music. Their musical ability and disciplined practising habits enabled them to play the piano to concert level, a talent that Jennie and Leonie would put to use for charity fund-raising events in London in the 1890s and 1900s. An appreciation of classical music was a highly desirable social skill, one that gave them an entrée into elite European circles.

By the time they reached adulthood, the girls had been meticulously groomed by their mother to enter the top ranks of society. As was the norm, Clarita, Jennie, and Leonie were raised by servants and were taught aristocratic manners in early childhood. They were forbidden to attend many social events with other children. Mrs Jerome's instructions to the nursery prescribed a strict regime that included healthy food, light exercise, and a good night's sleep; she believed that healthy women were beautiful women. The Jerome sisters were blessed with their father's vitality and robust good health, and he approved of vigorous outdoor activities such as skating.

Mama preferred moderation. She taught her daughters that refined manners mattered, and that a harmonious home was the most important attainment for women of their class. She believed in forbearance, as both she and her sister Catherine found their husbands' zest for life somewhat trying. Clara was living proof to her children that in order to hold a man it was necessary to tolerate lapses of conduct with dignity and discretion. She frequently told her girls to never scold a man, lest he should 'go where he is *not* scolded'.[37]

In addition to their mother's social training, Leonard was insistent that his girls be well schooled and took a personal interest in their educational achievements. He encouraged them to study difficult subjects and scrutinized their academic timetables. He wrote to Jennie at her boarding school near Paris in 1868 that he had 'great confidence in your capabilities and if I could have my way I would prescribe a higher order of studies than I fancy you have now. When I come out I shall examine into this.'[38] He urged her to write to him frequently, as it was 'an important branch of education in any body male or female' and 'writing fixes ones ideas more distinctly in the mind and helps them amazingly to be remembered'.[39]

Their father was proud of his daughters' achievements and instigated academic competition between them. He told Jennie that her younger sister Leonie was good at mathematics and had 'just solved the problem of 2 francs and a quarter an hour for 3 hours'; Jennie 'must look out for your laurels', as she had 'a mighty smart sister coming on after you'.[40] All three sisters developed excellent writing skills; Jennie was able to publish her written work later in life, in times of financial necessity, as indeed was her son, Winston. In her memoirs, Jennie described her early childhood days as happy ones, which included 'a few eventful years of lessons, with matinees at the opera "to improve our minds," sleighing and skating for pleasure'. On 'red-letter days' there would be a drive to Jerome Park.[41]

Both Clara and Leonard Jerome, in their very different ways, instilled in their daughters the importance of elevated standards of achievement and self-control. Even in times of difficulty, their public face was to be gracious and decorous. When the Jeromes were not invited to Mrs Astor's balls (Mrs Astor strongly disapproved of new money – the Goulds, the Harrimans, and the Morgans were never invited either), Clara decided to leave for Paris. She ignored Leonard's philandering with dignity. Whilst Mama taught her daughters to be socially ambitious and to overlook marital indiscretions, their father taught them to be high achievers.

Clara was less preoccupied with savouring life's experiences than her husband. Her situation was not easy: first orphaned, then married to a charismatic man whom she was unable to satisfy, and finally rejected by the top echelons of the very society she so desperately wished to join. It is perhaps unsurprising that Clara transferred her ambitions to the marriages of her daughters and sought to achieve through them what she was unable to attain for herself. In spite of a few exciting years of extravagance, Leonard never consolidated the kind of fortune Clara needed to feel truly secure. The really wealthy men of New York City, such as William B. Astor, Alexander T. Stewart, and Cornelius Vanderbilt, had amassed huge wealth from real estate, retailing, and railroads, worth tens of millions. Leonard did well from investing in the stock market, but the money ebbed and flowed, and he was never in their unassailable financial position. In a bad year, such as the New York Stock Market downturn of 1873, many incomes from speculation dropped, including Leonard's, whose assets never really fully recovered.

The closest Clara could get, therefore, to grandeur and unqualified social success would be through her daughters. She became single-minded in her matrimonial ambitions for them and in 1867 decided to move them to Europe. Leonard, who would pay their substantial bills, would be welcome to visit whenever he wished. Thus Clarita, Jennie, and Leonie journeyed with their mother and father (who accompanied them) to Paris and the court of the Emperor Napoleon III at the height of the Second Empire. In Europe, their debuts in the royal courts would earn them a much-envied veneer of social success.

CHAPTER TWO

The Court of Emperor Louis Napoleon

Mrs Jerome claimed that the move to France was necessary because she needed to consult doctors there for her health. Jennie wrote that 'owing to my mother having become ill, we sailed for Europe in order that she might consult the celebrated American physician Dr. Sims, in Paris'.[1] This may be what Mama told the girls, but there is little evidence that Mrs Jerome was in fact ill. The family travelled by sea; by 1867 the ships used for transatlantic journeys were much more comfortable than their predecessors. Since the steam revolution first began in the early 1700s, engineers and shipbuilders on both sides of the Atlantic had sought to use the newly discovered steam power to make ships quicker and more reliable. By 1836, more and more shipping owners had recognized the benefits of steam over sail. The next few years saw remarkable technological advances as well as increased capital investment. The famous P & O and Cunard shipping lines were both established at this time, and from 1839 the British government awarded mail contracts to privately owned steamship companies rather than to the less reliable government sailing packets. Samuel Cunard, a successful Nova Scotia shipping owner and founder of the Cunard Line, was awarded the first British government mail contract across the North Atlantic, providing its first transatlantic service in 1842.

Improvements in maritime technology over the next thirty years resulted in faster and more reliable journey times, eventually reducing the duration of a transatlantic journey from several weeks to five or six days. There was heightened competition for passengers, as rival steamship companies shaved hours off journey times and improved reliability to attract customers. They also invested in more luxurious accommodation on board. This rapidly developing market was driven on the European side by the massive (albeit fluctuating) upswing in steerage traffic as emigrants made their way to America in an increasingly comfortable and more salubrious cabin class.[2] On the return journey, wealthy Americans availed themselves of the elegant first-class accommodation and service provided by newly formed steamship companies competing for their patronage. In 1871 the launch of the White Star Line's first ship, the *Oceanic*, rendered every other ship of its time obsolete in terms of passenger comfort and services. In 1881, Cunard responded with the magnificent *Servia*, which was, apart from Brunel's *Great Eastern*, the largest ship in the world. America's post-civil war nouveaux riches responded enthusiastically, travelling to Europe in great style in ever-greater numbers.

When Clara Jerome, her husband Leonard, and her three daughters, accompanied by Dobbie, their nurse-companion, undertook their transatlantic journey, most European capital cities and resorts were home to long-term American visitors or even a resident American population. Paris in 1867 was everything that Clara dreamed of. The Emperor had transformed the city into a visual delight, building boulevards, designing the Etoile and the Bois de Boulogne, and completing the monumental design of the Louvre Palace. Clara embraced her new life in the French capital, adding French accents to the spelling of Jerome and changing Jennie's name to Jeanette. The family moved into an apartment on the Boulevard Malesherbes, near the Place de la Madeleine in the fashionable 8th arrondissement. After settling his family, Leonard returned home alone.

The Emperor liked Americans, as did his beautiful wife the Empress Eugénie, so Clara Jerome was invited to the court. Aided by her wealth and good taste, she was befriended by Eugénie and welcomed by her entourage. Clara was now forty-two, still very attractive and keen to participate in the imperial social life. 'Never had the Empire seemed more assured,' Jennie later recalled, 'the court more brilliant, the fêtes more gorgeous.'[3]

Life for the wealthy in the capital was centred around the court of the Emperor Louis Napoleon, who was known as Napoleon III. His mother, Hortense, was the daughter of Josephine, Napoleon I's first wife, from her first marriage to the Vicomte de Beauharnais. Hortense was married to Louis, Napoleon I's brother. They had had an unhappy relationship, and there was much speculation as to the true paternity of Louis Napoleon, some even suggesting that Napoleon I himself was the father, although others believed that it was a Dutch admiral. Notwithstanding this speculation, Louis Napoleon was proud of his ancestry and hungry for power. He was constantly plotting ways to rule France and to revive the Napoleonic myth. In 1836, he attempted an unsuccessful coup in Strasbourg against the King, Louis Philippe, who, anxious to be rid of a troublemaker, despatched him to America with a 'gift' of £16,000 in gold. Louis Napoleon returned to France and in 1838, after the death of his beloved mother, went to England, mixing with the upper classes and emphasizing his ambitions to wear the crown of France. He was viewed as an upstart by English society and rapidly acquired an unsavoury reputation as a philanderer and gambler. After another unsuccessful attempt to invade France in 1840, he was arrested and imprisoned for five and a half years in a jail in Ham, south-east of Amiens. He escaped in 1846 to England, where the Prime Minister, Sir Robert Peel, gave him permission to reside, and he spent the next two years indulging in his passion for women and gaming. He believed that he had only to wait for the death of the King, now aged seventy-four and with no heir, to seize power.

His opportunity came in 1848, a year that heralded political unrest throughout Europe and revolution in France. At the by-elections held in June, Louis Napoleon was aided by his supporters who did every-thing possible to promote the Napoleonic legend, using posters, hoardings, pamphlets, handbills, street singers paid to sing songs, and actors bribed to give speeches in support of him on stage. In this way, he gained a seat in the Assembly. He then acceded to office as Prince-President in 1848, placed there by the mass of the people because he was the nephew of the great Emperor and because they recognized his name. In 1851 he ended the Second Republic with a *coup d'état* and became self-proclaimed Emperor the following year, establishing the Second Empire.

Eugénie, whom he married in 1853, had been born at Granada, in Andalusia. Her grandfather was Scottish, a Kirkpatrick of Dumfries, who had left Scotland for Spain – becoming a naturalized American citizen along the way. Eugénie's grandmother, Françoise, was Belgian, the daughter of Baron de Grivegnée, a wine merchant who had also settled in Spain. Her mother, Mañuela, was unhappily married to the Comte de Teba, and the commonly held view in the Second Empire was that Eugénie, Mañuela's second daughter, had been fathered by George Villiers, the British Foreign Secretary (and later the 4th Earl of Clarendon). Eugénie's mother was as ambitious for her daughters as she was promiscuous; in 1834 she left the count and moved with her children to Paris. Their father, by then the Comte de Montijo, had become an extremely wealthy man. When he died in 1839, Mañuela's affairs became flagrant, and her wild behaviour shocked the romantic Eugénie. Mañuela orchestrated her elder daughter's marriage to the Duke d'Alba and then worked hard to ensure that Eugénie would also make a good match. When the Emperor fell in love with her daughter, she was in favour of the marriage, even though it was bitterly opposed by many of the leading nobility of France.

So it was that Eugénie, a foreigner of doubtful antecedents, pushed by her ambitious mother, had married the Emperor Louis Napoleon, a man with a dubious claim to the throne, whose manners and morals were distinctly those of a parvenu. The advantage of such a court, for newcomers such as the Jeromes, was that it presented them with opportunities that might not have been available in a more traditional setting. Here they were warmly welcomed and invited to live among France's elite. 'The Emperor Napoleon III was credited with a great liking for Americans, and he certainly showed his partiality by having

27

many invited to the official festivities',[4] wrote Jennie many years later. The year of the Jeromes' arrival on French shores, 1867, was also that of the Paris Exhibition. Over 52,000 exhibitors and visitors gathered to view exhibits from all over the world. Alongside the ordinary tourists, foreign dignitaries swarmed through the World Fair (of eighty sovereigns and rulers invited, only the Pope and Queen Victoria did not attend). Clara Jerome and her two elder daughters were invited by the American Ambassador, Mr Elihu Washburn, to a reception at the exhibition for American visitors. They then took part in all of the fair's most exclusive festivities; they danced at the ball given for the Tsar of Russia and sat at the table of honour at the gala for German sovereigns: the kings of Prussia, Bavaria, and Württemberg. They met King Leopold of Belgium and the famous Prince Otto von Bismarck, previously the Prussian Ambassador to Paris, who was secretly evaluating French troops, defences, and arms in preparation for his plan to invade France.

Clarita, aged eighteen, made her debut at the court of the Emperor in 1869. This ceremony involved a formal presentation to the Emperor and Empress. After being presented, a young woman had 'come out' and was henceforth included in the social invitations of the court. For Clarita, looking ravishing in a low-cut dress, the occasion was a ball at the Tuileries. After ascending the grand staircase at the palace between the row of Cent-Gardes soldiers, resplendent in their uniforms, she took her place among the assembled guests. The doors were flung open and 'Sa Majesté l'Empereur' was announced, followed shortly by 'Sa Majesté l'Impératrice'. She later described how the 'Emperor and Empress walked round the circle of curtsying and bowing guests, addressing a few words here and there, and then proceeded to the ballroom.'[5] That evening, Eugénie wore green velvet and a crown of emeralds, diamonds, and pearls, which so impressed Clarita that she was able to recount every detail to her eager sister and mother on her return from the glorious evening.

Clarita was extremely attractive – a slender blonde, with a pretty face and agreeable disposition – and she was invited to further dances and other social events. She attended the royal hunt at Compiègne in 1869, the last of these famous parties, where guests joined the Emperor and Empress for hunting, shooting, and dancing. Jennie wrote of Clarita's experiences of the stag hunt, which took place on the first day, describing how 'those who hunted wore the royal colours, the men in green coats and the gold hunt buttons, the ladies in flowing green habits and three-cornered hats'. The evenings were splendid:

> Every night from sixty to one hundred guests sat down to dinner, the Emperor never permitting it to last more than three-quarters of an hour. Sometimes magnificent gold plate adorned the table, sometimes precious *biscuit de Sèvres* [Sèvres porcelain]. Before dinner the company assembled in two long lines. The Emperor took in Princesse Mathilde [his cousin], sitting opposite her at the centre of the table, a few seats of honour being reserved at each side, while the rest placed themselves as they wished, the ladies choosing the gentlemen to take them in, according to the custom of Compiègne. After dinner there was dancing ... At the close of the visit there was a grand lottery, in which all tickets were prizes. The Emperor stood near two great urns, from which the numbers were drawn, and as each guest received one he wished him '*Bonne chance*' ['Good luck'] ... My sister, much to my envy, was given an inkstand shaped like a knotted handkerchief, filled with napoleons [coins], upon which the Emperor remarked, '*Mademoiselle, n'oubliez pas les Napoléons!*' [Mademoiselle, don't forget the Napoleons!'][6]

Clarita was made to please. Leonard's dedication to music and instruction in horsemanship, combined with Clara's social instincts and fashion sense, had given their eldest daughter a solid grounding in the skills required to move gracefully through society. She played the piano wonderfully and danced well. Her horsemanship was excellent – due to Papa's insistence that all his girls should ride well: light hands and graceful in the saddle. As elegant and confident horsemanship was such an important skill, Clarita and her sisters were very lucky in this accomplishment, which in the cities was reserved for the wealthy and the well born.

If the court into which Clarita was introduced was a shade showy, and its manners and morals distinctly shabby, it was undeniably royal. Mrs Jerome had an awed respect for royalty that she transmitted to her daughters. Clarita, mesmerized by the grandeur and wealth that surrounded her, did not question the foundations upon which this magic world was built. She was eighteen and eager to enjoy herself. Mama pushed, Mama encouraged, Mama kept a safe distance, but was always there in the background, hinting at a great marriage – to a wealthy duke if possible.

The Jeromes enjoyed their carefree and light-hearted existence. They were delighted to be well received by monarchs who welcomed Americans, in a court where wealth alone was sufficient for social success. Clarita was particularly taken with 'les Lundis', the smaller, more informal receptions given by the Emperor and Empress on Mondays. More relaxed and intimate than the court balls, they were organized chiefly for the amusement of the Prince Imperial, an only child of twelve, who had attended these receptions from an early age, presumably to gain social confidence. 'All the beautiful and charming women of Paris, including many attractive foreigners were asked,' recollected Jennie. 'Court ceremonial and etiquette were dispensed with, which added greatly to the enjoyment of the evening.'[7] For the rest of her life, Clarita remembered 'les Lundis' at the Tuileries, where she had danced Waldteufel waltzes conducted by the famous composer and court pianist Emile Waldteufel himself.

As well as the Monday-night dances and official balls, Clarita was also invited to soirées given by the Emperor's glamorous cousin, Princesse Mathilde, the daughter of Napoleon I's brother Jerome, King of Westphalia, and his wife, Princess Catherine of Nuremberg. Mathilde's salon had a reputation for wit and style that was known and admired worldwide. When Clarita was invited to Compiègne, she wrote to Mama that she had thrilled to the stag hunt, and that that evening at a cotillion she had worn her white dress with marguerites.

She added that the guests had been asked to lengthen their stay, so 'I shall need another dress. I think I must have it, in fact two if possible, for these ladies dress so much and never appear in the same.'[8]

Mama never refused; she was so pleased at her daughter's success and longed to hear all the details. Every dance, every person Clarita met, every outfit worn, was described at length to Mama, who lived her dreams through her child. The romance was intoxicating – first in the living and then in the constant retelling. Clarita kept an album in which she carefully preserved her memorabilia: invitations, letters, newspaper cuttings. Jennie hung on Clarita's every word and longed for the day when she, too, would be presented at the court and dance with aristocrats.

At the end of 1869, Leonard suffered heavy losses in the stock market. Disheartened and tired, he made his way to his family in Paris. Leonard was no longer a very wealthy man – all he now owned was the magnificent Madison Square mansion, built with such high hopes, which he now let to the Union League Club for $25,000 ($390,000) a year. Jennie was happy to see him, and he was an ideal escort for her. She had always been his favourite, the one most like him, and together they toured Paris. They went riding, attended picnics and parties, the opera, and the theatre. When Leonard's mistress, Fanny Ronalds, arrived in Paris and absorbed most of Leonard's time, Papa asked his friend, the Prince de Sagan, to act as Jennie's escort in his stead. The Prince was a handsome, distinguished companion and he admired Jennie, who was delighted with his company.

Both the blonde blue-eyed Clarita and the dark-haired Jennie, with her flashing blue-grey eyes, were in awe of the celebrated beauties around them. They learned from the imperial court that women should look well and seduce the opposite sex. The Empress loved to surround herself with beautiful noblewomen, such as the bewitching Comtesse de Pourtalès, Princesse Pauline Metternich (wife of the Austrian Ambassador), and the Duchesse de Mouchy, Eugénie's greatest friend. Significantly, the Jerome sisters also saw that affairs were normal, that all men strayed, and that women had to be attractive. In fact, the girls had long ago accepted from Mama that fidelity was not a prerequisite to marital harmony. What was important was dignity and honourable conduct.

In November 1869, Empress Eugénie made a state visit to Egypt to open the Suez Canal. Conditions in France were such that the Emperor himself could not risk leaving the country. The more liberties he granted, such as the freedom of the press and freedom of speech, the more he was criticized. The price of bread had increased, unemployment had risen, and the radical theories of Karl Marx were finding a receptive audience. At the general election in May 1869, the Opposition candidates gained over the imperial ones, and in the large cities there were mass rallies in favour of revolution. Amid all this turmoil, war was on the horizon. Bismarck, who had now become Chancellor, was waiting in Prussia with plans to invade his increasingly troubled neighbour as part of his strategy for the unification of the German states, which were still independent. He calculated that if France were provoked to attack Prussia, he could then invade France, and the southern German states would ally themselves with Prussia against the French Emperor.

In May 1870, Leonard again visited his family and took the two older girls to the South of France. In Nice, where they stayed at a hotel, they arranged a little salon for him, complete with flowers, to make it 'homey', as Clarita reported to her mother. She and Jennie enjoyed themselves, and Clarita wrote to Mama:'I suppose Jennie told you what a charming day we passed at Cannes.'[9] In June, they returned to a new house on the Boulevard Haussman and looked forward to the resumption of the social whirl. Jennie was impatient, longing to make her debut so that she, too, could experience the heady excitement of life at court.

However, in July 1870, the Emperor Napoleon III went reluctantly to war with Prussia. By this time, Louis Napoleon's medical problems, including rheumatism and bladder stone, were very debilitating. Although he had been advised by his doctors that his health was so bad that he could not even ride a horse, let alone take command of an army, he was determined to follow the honourable course. Bismarck engineered a diplomatic insult, through a carefully edited telegram – about a succession crisis in Spain – from the French government to King William of Prussia. The King, not knowing the telegram had been doctored, responded sufficiently stiffly to the French government to precipitate a diplomatic crisis between the two countries. The French were eager to fight the Prussians, and there were outbursts of patriotic fervour from the French crowds. 'À Berlin!' – to Berlin! – became the cry in the streets, and at the opera the audience stood to sing the 'Marseillaise'. The Empress was firmly in agreement with the people and with the many politicians who promoted conflict with inflammatory speeches. She believed that the Emperor, although ill, must do his duty, and when the great surgeon, Germain See, told her that it was 'abominable to place a man in such a condition at the head of an Army', her unsympathetic reply was: '*Le vin est tiré, il faut le boire*' (the wine has been poured, it must be drunk).[10]

Neither the Emperor nor the Empress knew, however, that the French army, contrary to reports, was in a state of total unreadiness. When Louis Napoleon arrived at Metz to take command of the troops with his son, the Prince Imperial, he found staff officers bewildered and unprepared. The Emperor discovered that one third of the regular troops had been on leave when war was declared, and that many of the cavalry horses had been loaned to farmers. Instead of the expected 385,000 troops mustered along the Rhine, Louis Napoleon found only 220,000. He telegraphed his wife that nothing was ready and that he considered the war lost before it began. To gratify the eager hordes in Paris, however, on 2 August he ordered the invasion of Saarbrücken, a town two miles across the frontier in Germany. This was to be his only victory. Two days later, Crown Prince Frederick William marched into France. Although the 'thin red line' of French troops fought bravely, they had little support. Entire villages were deserted by civilians terrified by reports of German cannibalism. Discarding their rifles and badges, the beaten troops escaped into the surrounding countryside.

Meanwhile, in Paris, the Empress was becoming very uneasy. She acceded to the suggestion that a professional soldier, Marshal Bazaine, should assume command of the French army instead of her increasingly sick husband. Louis Napoleon wished to return to Paris, which Eugénie refused to contemplate. It was unthinkable that a Bonaparte should retreat. On 15 August, the Emperor and his son had to make a hurried escape from Longueville to Châlons, where they joined the leader of the Alsatian unit, Marshal MacMahon, and his troops. At a council of war held two days latter, attended by the Emperor and high-ranking army staff, it was decided that the Emperor should return to Paris and resume control of the government. Other senior officers shared the responsibility, to help the ailing Emperor; General Trochu was appointed Governor of Paris, and Marshal MacMahon was ordered to march on the capital with his army when it was ready, in order to do battle before the city gates.

Eugénie and her ministers, however, disagreed with these decisions. She insisted that MacMahon should move forward into the field to relieve Bazaine, who was holed up at Metz, rather than retreat to defend Paris. When the Emperor heard of this, he abandoned the agreed plan and instead accompanied MacMahon and his army to Rheims and then to Sedan in an attempt to relieve Bazaine. Here the French troops were surrounded in a disastrous battle. Suspecting a trap, he sent his son to safety with three of his aides and an escort of cavalry. And indeed it was a trap – after three successive defeats, the Emperor had to surrender to King William in person at Sedan in order to avert the massacre of his troops. Paris was unprotected and in a state of panic. Men and boys drilled in the streets; 40,000 oxen and 250,000 sheep were brought in from the countryside to pasture in the Bois de Boulogne. Supplies of food were stored in warehouses as the inhabitants prepared anxiously for a siege.

Most of the foreigners had already left the capital. Clara Jerome and her daughters were, however, reluctant to leave. Mrs Jerome had sprained her ankle and was unable to put her foot to the ground. Jennie recollected that they had delayed their departure day by day, never believing that the Prussians would reach Paris. Leonard grew increasingly frantic, sending wires from New York urging them to leave France. Still they tarried, until one day Clarita's great admirer and a confidant of the Emperor himself, the Duc de Persigny, rushed into the apartment, exclaiming that everything was lost and that the Prussians were at the door. He had managed, he told them, to obtain places for them on the train to the coastal town of Deauville from whence they could flee the country. They would have to pack their belongings and leave within the hour.

As there were no cabs, he found a cart to transport Mrs Jerome to the station. Their maid, Marie, who helped carry their effects to the train, was given instructions to pack the trunks and to bring them with her on the train to Deauville the following day. Clarita left a note for her current flame, the Marquis de Tamisier. They left in tears, distraught at leaving their home, unaware that their train would be the last to leave the city. Marie never arrived the next day, but instead spent the siege alone in the Jeromes' house in Paris, where they found her when they returned two years later. At Deauville, Clara and her daughters were still waiting for a passage across the Channel when the Empress dramatically escaped from Paris incognito, with the help of her American dentist, Dr Evans. He had then contrived to secure her a place on Sir John Burgoyne's yacht to cross the Channel to England.

Mama and the girls finally reached the safety of English shores. Although they did not know it, the days of dining off Louis Napoleon's magnificent initialled gold dinnerware in his sumptuous residences were over. Their aristocratic friends were far away, and their beloved city was under siege. They felt like refugees when they arrived in Brighton. It was the first time that the girls had been to England; it was out of season and the weather was dismal. They had little clothing and no servants. Jennie recollected years later in her memoirs how depressed they had all felt: 'Our friends scattered, fighting, or killed at the front; debarred as we were from our bright little house and our household goods, it was indeed a sad time.'[11] In their misery, they all complained bitterly to Papa, who was merely relieved that they had escaped Paris unharmed.

He sailed immediately to England and took his family to London, installing them in a suite of rooms at Brown's Hotel in Piccadilly. He bought them clothes, hired governesses, and recommenced their intensive music lessons. Mrs Jerome felt wretched and refused to return to New York, as she could not contemplate 'abandoning' her French friends. Within days the Duke de Persigny came to call. Although Clara Jerome was impressed by his title, the truth was that the duke, Jean Gilbert Victor Fialin, was the son of a tax collector. Having been dismissed from the army for insubordination, he had turned to journalism, writing for *Le Temps* in Paris. At this time he assumed the title Vicomte de Persigny, claiming descent from an old Brittany family. Fialin, who had met Louis Napoleon in 1833, became his chief planning officer. The two men, of the same age, shared dreams of a Second Empire, and as Louis Napoleon assumed more and more power, his loyal friend and fellow schemer Persigny rose with him. By the time Louis Napoleon became Emperor, Persigny had transformed himself from a man of humble origins into someone of great pretension.

Clara and the girls were distressed to see him in London, reduced to selling his plate and other possessions. Leonard stepped in and offered to pay his bills at Brown's Hotel. De Persigny spoke of a restoration – Bourbon if not Bonaparte – which cheered Clara, who felt that anything was better than a Prussian cad. Clarita wanted the Emperor to resume the throne and life to become once more the enchanting party it had previously been. Jennie was equally resentful. Her dreams had been snatched away. Instead of dancing in bewitching frocks and making eyes at dashing men in the glorious imperial court, she was marched across Hyde Park every day with her Austrian governess, practising her German conversation. Papa hired a room at the hotel with two pianos so that Clarita and Jennie could rehearse their duets. It was an industrious if dull life, in which Clarita moped incessantly for the marquis and her other admirers.

Leonard himself made a visit to the French capital during the

Prussian siege, as a representative of the United States government, together with the civil war generals Sheridan and Burnside. He found the inhabitants in a state of famine. Some 65,000 Parisians had died of starvation – more than from battle wounds. People were eating rats, cats, and dogs. Leonard met Bismarck in a villa in Versailles, but his entreaties to lift the siege were to no avail. It mattered little, however. Leonard and the generals were led, blindfolded, out of Paris and not long after, on 28 January 1871, the exhausted city surrendered. Defeat was bitter. Prussian troops marched en masse down the Champs Elysées, to the humiliation of the proud Parisians who had lived amid horror for four agonizing months, and who now shuttered their windows and emptied the streets. The soldiers with their spiked helmets filed triumphantly past the Arc de Triomphe, singing 'Die Wacht am Rhein', after which they waltzed with one another on the Place de la Concorde.

There was more bloodshed to come. The conquering Prussian troops were unable to prevent civil war breaking out. French extremists in Paris, backed by the National Guard (which had defended Paris during the siege), were unhappy at the concessions made by the national government to the Prussians as part of the peace negotiations. In particular they were incensed at the proposed new taxes to be levied in order to pay the first instalment of the war indemnities demanded by Prussia. Prussian troops continued to occupy northern France until this first payment took place. Government troops, instructed by Adolphe Thiers (who had replaced General Trochu as the head of the new national government), advanced into Paris to forcibly disarm the National Guard, but were met with popular resistance, and they refused to fire at the crowds. Thiers and his government had no choice but to abandon Paris and withdrew to Versailles with those troops loyal to them. The National Guard took over and, eight days later, elections were held in which a left-wing, socialist government was elected. This new revolutionary government wanted France to be divided into a number of self-governing Communes.

On 21 May, government troops again began to force their way into

Paris, to defeat the followers of the Commune. For four days fierce fighting raged, and the opponents of the Versailles government (a politically heterogeneous group that included many points of view, not just extremists) shot a number of hostages, including the Archbishop of Paris. When the Communards realized that they would certainly be defeated, they set fire to the principal buildings – both the Tuileries and the Hôtel de Ville were destroyed. In retaliation, as they entered the blackened city the government troops shot any supporter of the Commune that they could find. Between 20,000 and 30,000 Parisians died during this civil conflict, in which the damage done to the capital was greater than anything inflicted by the Prussians, who turned a blind eye to the fighting. The Prussian interest was not in running France, but in a stable French government and economy, so that war reparations could be paid.

Leonard had found most of the family's belongings intact during his visit to Paris. Both he and his wife returned to the city in May in order to secure their Italian paintings, which they managed to pack up and ship just before the riots of 'Bloody Week' began. Clara found Napoleon's gold-initialled plates for auction outside the burning Tuileries. With great presence of mind, she bought them all and hired a cart to take them back to the house. Many years later, her granddaughter, Clare Sheridan, sold them to her first cousin, Winston Churchill, who loved using them and telling the story of their acquisition. The plates are still at his home at Chartwell in Kent.

That summer, Leonard organized a family visit to Cowes in the Isle of Wight, where the days were spent *en famille*, sailing and driving. Clara, who preferred France to England, returned with her daughters to Paris in the winter of 1871. Nothing, however, was as before. The ruined buildings were depressing, and the old social life had disappeared for ever. As Jennie explained in her reminiscences, most of their friends were gone; others were devastated and miserable, and could not be comforted. The statues on the Place de la Concorde were draped in black crêpe as a poignant reminder of the sadness of France. Only a few of the embassies, and the Americans, did any entertaining at all. The

French court was reluctant to emerge from the shadows, and the old nobility, which had for so long scorned the pretensions of the Second Empire, were now completely adrift, with no one to look up to, or down on, since all social structures had disintegrated. Jennie was disappointed, as there was no longer any society to aspire to. 'Ruins everywhere!' she wrote. 'The sight of the Tuileries and the Hôtel de Ville made me cry ... And if material Paris was damaged, the social fabric was even more so. In vain we tried to pick up the threads.'[12] Clarita was no help; she spent her time moping over the Marquis de Tamisier and the Duc de Lescara, both of whom her mother found unacceptable. Leonie, then aged thirteen, was sent to boarding school in Wiesbaden in Germany the following year.

Clara lived quietly in Paris with Clarita, who still pined over her suitors, and Jennie, who was bored to distraction. Young Leonie wrote cheerfully from Germany; she looked forward to finishing her schooling in Wiesbaden, then to living for a while in France in order to perfect her French, and after that hoped for some time in England. Life in Paris was so quiet that, in 1872 and again the following year, Clara agreed to spend the summer in Cowes, at the rented Villa Rosetta. In 1873, they went without Leonard, who had to deal with pressing financial problems in New York, after the stock exchange losses that year. Mrs Jerome had finally accepted, with the death of Louis Napoleon in January 1873, that the Second Empire, with all of its illusory magic, was over. With her usual pragmatism where social advancement was concerned, she accordingly looked to England as the most fertile soil from which to reap marital prospects for her daughters. Cowes was the perfect launching ground. It was the undisputed yacht-racing capital of the world. Led by the Prince of Wales, all fashionable London society made their way to this charming seaside town, to relax after the formal London season.

It was an exciting summer, as Jennie was to make her debut. She was now nineteen and a beauty, with raven hair and grey-blue eyes. Her skin was clear and naturally flushed by the vigorous Jerome circulation. She would, of course, wear a white dress; her small, corseted waist showed off the hourglass figure then popular. There was in addition a yard-long trailing skirt. Jennie was an immediate success, as evidenced by the number of invitations she received after coming out. Both she and Clarita were in great demand all summer season. They often played piano duets at dinner parties, delighting audiences with their virtuosity, unusual in British aristocratic circles, where the musical talents of debutantes were usually much more mundane.

Jennie and Clarita were such a success that they seem that summer to have neglected letters both to their father and to Leonie. Papa wrote reproachfully in August that it had been nearly two weeks since he had heard from them, reminding them not to forget 'while sitting under your own vine and eating up your own fig tree that I am awfully disappointed if I don't get my weekly letters.'[13] But the girls were completely absorbed by their own affairs. One invitation to Mrs and the Misses Jerome was particularly appealing: a deckle-edged invitation from the officers of the guardship *Ariadne* to a ball on board on 12 August 1873, in honour of the Grand Duke Tsarevich and the Grand Duchess Tsarevna (the future Tsar Nicholas II and his wife), in the presence of Their Royal Highnesses, the Prince and Princess of Wales. The Tsar's sister, Marie, had just become engaged to the Prince of Wales' brother, the Duke of Edinburgh, and the ball was the most important social event of the Cowes regatta week.

After arriving on board by specially organized launches, both girls were immediately surrounded by admirers. The ship's deck was canopied with lanterns, and a Royal Marine band played as the guests boarded. The *Ariadne's* deck was draped with the national colours of Britain and imperial Russia. Jennie and Clarita were bare-shouldered and must have looked gorgeous. They were soon part of an animated group, and Jennie was whisked off for a first waltz. It was here that Lord Randolph Churchill, the second son of the Duke of Marlborough, first saw Jennie. She made a strong impression, and he asked to be introduced. It was the beginning of a great love affair.

CHAPTER 3

'To Meet: Randolph'

Nineteen-year-old Jennie's effect on Randolph was powerful and immediate. She returned his admiring gaze with a smile, and an introduction was effected by a mutual friend, Frank Bertie. Randolph Churchill was twenty-four and attractive, although not conventionally handsome. He was slim but not tall and sported a walrus moustache, which Clarita found most unbecoming. He was a fine dresser and, as an aristocratic young man who had held his courtesy title from the age of eight, he enjoyed the vain, sybaritic life of those who were friends of the Prince of Wales (later known as the Marlborough House Set). His manners were those of an aristocrat, secure in his superiority, and he had no particular ambitions. What he could do, however, was speak exceptionally well and with conviction. He talked rapidly, with an unusual intensity, and Jennie was captivated.

Randolph invited Jennie to dance a formal quadrille. He was, nevertheless, at a disadvantage; not being a man of music, he was not graceful on the floor. To his relief, Jennie agreed to sit out the next dance; in conversation Randolph was in his element. They had sat together for so long that Mrs Jerome searched them out and admonished her daughter on the impropriety of spending too much time with one man at a ball. Jennie was oblivious. She convinced her mother to extend an invitation to Lord Randolph and their mutual friend, Colonel Edgecombe, to dinner the following evening at their house, Villa Rosetta. Randolph was delighted to accept. Jennie later annotated her invitation to the ball with 'To Meet: Randolph'.

Although Jennie was in high spirits the following day, she also showed signs of nerves. Her grandson and biographer, Peregrine Churchill, claimed that Jennie and Randolph had fallen in love 'at first sight'.[1] She and her sister spent extra time practising their piano duets for the evening's entertainment and she took special care with her appearance. For the first time, their roles were reversed. Clarita's advice was sought on what to wear, and it was Jennie who had an exciting evening in prospect. Many was the time that she had sat and listened to her elder sister's stories of her flirtations and love affairs. Now it was Jennie's turn to take centre stage. She would never leave it.

The dinner was a success. The Jeromes kept a French cook, so the food was excellent. The night was beautiful with an occasional breeze and bright stars in the sky. Jennie recorded many years later that they had 'spent a very pleasant evening, my sister and I playing duets at the piano and chatting merrily'.[2] Randolph and Jennie found that they had much in common. They had travelled to the same countries; they both loved horses; and both had lively and enquiring minds. Although Jennie was bored easily, Randolph did not in the least bore her. After the guests left, she asked Clarita for her opinion of him. Clarita had not liked him overmuch – his appearance was not very dashing and she thought he had tried too hard to be clever. Jennie brushed such criticism aside. She was sure her sister would like him more if she knew him better. Jennie, most seriously, asked Clarita to make this effort, as she had the strangest feeling that he would ask her to marry him – and she would say yes. Clarita just laughed, but Jennie was right. After they left, Randolph confided to Colonel Edgecombe that he would like to make 'the dark one' his wife.[3]

The next day Jennie was so uncharacteristically quiet and withdrawn that Mama asked Clarita whether something was wrong. When Clarita told her of Jennie's infatuation, Mrs Jerome was not at all pleased. She believed that a second son was not much of a catch and felt that her daughter could do much better. After Jennie and Randolph met later that day 'by accident' (she had in fact told him of where and when she took her daily walk), Mrs Jerome refused to allow Jennie to invite him to dinner. Jennie implored, however, and as it was Randolph's last night in Cowes Mama relented. Randolph received a calling card from Mrs Jerome and the Misses Jerome, with Mrs Jerome's handwritten invitation on the back: 'I shall be most happy to see you at dinner this evening, truly yours, C.H. Jerome.'⁴

It was once again a bewitching evening at Villa Rosetta. Jennie later described Randolph's proposal to her at this, their third meeting, in a short memorandum to herself. She wrote that she and Randolph had walked in the garden, 'when, finding ourselves alone for a moment, he asked me to marry him and I said yes. We agreed not to say anything to my mother, as she would not understand the suddenness of it.'⁵ What is clear is that the young couple were smitten and eager to make a commitment to one another, even after so short an acquaintance. Randolph was meant to leave the following morning, but postponed his trip, sending Jennie this note:

Dear Miss Jeanette
I missed my boat & have not been able to go; so shall not start till early Monday morning. Thank you so very much for the photograph which is much better than the others; shall hope to see you after church tomorrow. You see I keep turning up like a bad shilling.⁶

Randolph kept his invitation card for that dinner in a black metal box among his most treasured personal possessions for the rest of his life.

Although the couple were in love, they agreed that for the time being it must remain a secret. Randolph postponed his departure for another four days. Before he finally left, Jennie told her mother about the engagement. Mrs Jerome told her that she could never agree to anything so precipitous, as Jennie wrote to Randolph that same evening: 'I cannot bear to have you leave Cowes – dearest without a last goodbye – I have told Mama who although she likes you <u>very</u> much won't hear of it. But I am sure we shall easily get her on our side later on – when we see you in London or perhaps here – God bless you darling'.[7] Randolph was equally optimistic and wrote the next morning to Jennie, telling her how her note, which he had received just as he was leaving Cowes, had cheered him up 'wonderfully'. 'I cannot think,' he continued, 'your mother will really not hear of our engagement only I am sure she thinks we have known each other for too short a time. You and I do not think so, but it is natural your mother shld.' He would miss her, he added, and would 'certainly' visit her in London. He thanked her for the photographs, as well as her 'dear little pin', which he would have to 'look at'. He would think of her, and urged her to have 'confidence & patience'.[8]

There was further consternation when Randolph broke the news to his mother at Blenheim Palace. The Duchess of Marlborough, formerly Lady Frances Anne Emily Vane, third daughter of the 3rd Marquess of Londonderry, was a commanding woman, with great character but not, perhaps, much judiciousness or tact. She was most displeased that Randolph, her second and favourite son, should have done anything so contrary to her own (extremely high) ambitions for him. The very idea of marrying an American was in and of itself immensely displeasing, and for him to contemplate doing such a thing after such a short acquaintance was folly. The duke and duchess had been hoping for splendid things for Randolph. His elder brother, the Marquess of Blandford, had turned out to be quite a disappointment. Although highly intelligent and greatly interested in scientific inventions, he lacked discipline, and was rebellious and unhappy. Married to a beautiful but dull woman whom he had ceased to love, he was flagrantly unfaithful to his wife – conducting countless, indiscreet affairs.

Despite his mother's displeasure, Randolph was deeply committed to his intended bride. Mrs Jerome had forbidden Jennie to correspond with him, but Randolph wrote passionately from Blenheim. By the second day of separation, he was miserable and missing her:

My own darling Jeanette

I cannot let another day pass without writing to you. I do not think

I ever had such a day as yesterday; such a melancholy journey away from you & then to have to listen to the twaddle & gossip of my mother & sisters when my heart & thoughts were elsewhere. It is so curious that my rooms & my things & my occupations here which I used to take interest in are quite hateful to me now, all I can do is to keep reading your letter & looking at your photographs & thinking thinking [sic] till I get quite stupid. I do not think dearest you have any idea of how much I love you, or what sacrifices I wld not make to call you my own. My whole life & energies shld be devoted to making you happy & protecting you from harm or wrong, Life shld be to you like one long summer day.

Although he had strong feelings for Jennie, he was realistic about their prospects. His mother, he told Jennie in this letter, had been 'vy much surprised & cld not understand anything taking place so rapidly', but he was preparing to write to his father, who was away hunting with Randolph's brother in Scotland. He also planned to write to Mrs Jerome upon receiving his father's reply, in order to 'tell her exactly what my position & prospects & means are'. He felt that although the former two were acceptable, the latter were 'by no means grand'.[9]

Randolph's letter to his father was both passionate and carefully worded. He had affection and respect for the duke, yet at the same time was all too aware that his father represented his only source of income. Until he had met Jennie, Randolph had shown little purpose or direction. Nevertheless, he explained to his father, he now knew exactly what he wanted in life, which was to spend it with her: 'I do not think that if I were to write pages I could give you any idea of the strength of my feelings and affections and love for her; all I can say is that I love her better than life itself, and that my one hope and dream now is that matters may be so arranged that soon I may be united to her by ties that nothing but death itself could have the power to sever.' He understood that his father might be 'very much surprised', but added that despite the rapidity of his decision, it was one in which he believed absolutely. He continued:

I now write to tell you of it all and to ask whether you will be able to increase my allowance to some extent to put me in the position to ask Mrs. Jerome to let me become her daughter's future husband. I enclose you her photograph, and will only say about her that she is as nice, as lovable, and amiable and charming in every way as she is beautiful, and that by education and bringing-up she is in every way qualified to fill any position.

Randolph declared furthermore that in marrying Jennie he would be improving his future:

In the last year or so I feel I have lost a great deal of what energy and ambition I possessed, and an idle and comparatively useless life has at times appeared to me to be the pleasantest; but if I were married to her whom I told you about, if I had a companion, such as she would be, I feel sure, to take an interest in one's prospects and career, and to encourage me to exertions and to doing something towards making a name for myself, I think I might become, with the help of Providence, all and perhaps more than you had ever wished or hoped for me. On the other hand, if anything should occur to prevent my fondest hopes and wishes being realized (a possibility which I dare not and cannot bring myself to think of), how dreary and uninteresting would life become to me![10]

Randolph believed that this approach would appeal to his parents' desire for him to engage fully in a worthwhile career. They hoped that he would stand as a Member of Parliament for the constituency of Woodstock, near Oxford, at the next election, and Randolph was hinting that he might not have the heart to do this without the woman he loved by his side.

His father, however, was unimpressed. For their son to marry an unknown, whose family origins and social background were a mystery, was an extremely disagreeable prospect. The Marlboroughs were one of the premier families of England. The first Marlborough had been John Churchill, who was rewarded for his battles against the French on behalf of Queen Anne with the royal manor of Woodstock, along with an additional £250,000 granted for restoration and building costs by a Parliament grateful for his magnificent victory at the Battle of Blenheim in 1704. The palace was set in 2,700 acres and had 320 rooms, each filled with superlative treasures. King George III observed that the royal family had nothing to equal it. Blenheim was a monument and a national memorial – and the Marlboroughs were a proud family indeed. The family fortunes, however, had gone steadily downhill since the 1st Duke's successes. The 5th and 6th Dukes were notorious for their extravagance, which necessitated the selling of some of the famous art treasures, although the 7th Duke, Randolph's father, had somewhat improved the family reputation by leading a useful life in public service, as Conservative Member for Woodstock and later as Lord President of the Council.

Randolph hoped that his insistence that Jennie's father was very well off, and that his daughters had good fortunes, would help convince his father to approve the match. In fact, Jennie was lucky in falling in love when she did, for her father was barely at the top of the smaller wave of success he had known since his spectacular moneymaking days. Although Leonard was no longer earning the same kind of fortunes overnight, he was still rich because of the property he owned on Madison Avenue, and Jennie knew that she could expect a handsome settlement from him. That settlement was to be an important factor in the negotiations that followed.

The Duke of Marlborough, unconvinced by his son's letter, delayed his reply to Randolph for ten days, during which time he made enquiries about Leonard. The responses had done nothing to reassure him. One American friend had commented, 'Jerome is a well-known man with a fast reputation, has been a large stock speculator and was a few years ago supposed to be well cleaned out and managed to hold onto some purchases of real estate heavily mortgaged.'[11] Most of the correspondents referred to Leonard Jerome's famous lavish spending habits, with one noting, 'the worst inference being that he spends as much as he makes'.[12] The reports, although not conclusively negative, were sufficiently so for the Duke to take a decisive stand against the proposed match, writing to his son:

It is not likely that at present you can look at anything but from your own point of view but persons from the outside cannot but be struck with the unwisdom of your proceedings, and the uncontrolled state of your feelings, which completely paralyses your judgement; never was there such an illustration of [the] adage 'love is blind' for you seem blind to all consequences in order that you may pursue your passion.[13]

Randolph's father added that he had heard that Jerome seemed to be a 'sporting, and I should think vulgar kind of man. I hear he drives about six and eight horses in New York (one may take this as a kind of indication of what the man is.)' In conclusion, Randolph's affections for the daughter, together with all her attractions, could not offset a connection which, it would appear, 'no man in his senses could think respectable'. He ended his letter, stating: 'I am deeply sorry that your feelings are so much engaged; and only for your own sake wish most heartily that you had checked the current before it became so overpowering.'[14]

Not obtaining consent from his parents presented a real problem for Randolph, as he knew that Jennie's parents would withhold their own consent if they sensed any objection from the Marlborough side. The pair were also awaiting Leonard's response. It did not help to receive Randolph's brother Blandford's poem, a sarcastic 'Elegy to a Marriage', which poked fun at a match made in haste and repented at leisure. But Randolph continued to write to Jennie, swearing his undying love and imploring her to persuade her mother to allow her to write. He explained to Jennie that he would not be able to return to Cowes to see her, as his father did not wish it, and he did not feel it right to cross him 'just now when there is no necessity for it'. He felt that it would be very hard on both of them, but they must look forward. However, he betrayed some of his fear of losing Jennie: 'God knows I do not want to pain you by expressing the least distrust of you, but by love I do not mean the cold ordinary attachment that the world is accustomed to call by that name, but something far higher far deeper far more enduring which we often read about, & which does sometimes exist, tho very rarely.'[15] He wrote three days later to say that a one-sided correspondence was very disheartening.[16] Jennie was still not allowed to write.

She worked hard, however, at softening Mama's resistance. Mrs Jerome was not at all in favour of the match. Indeed, she had written immediately to her husband, using words such as 'hasty', 'impulsive', and 'unconsidered', and to Leonard himself the peremptory: 'You must return to England by the next boat.'[17] Mama did not believe that a mere second son, who would inherit neither the dukedom nor the family estate, was good enough for her daughter. She still hoped for an alliance with an illustrious French family. However, Jennie was supported by her sister Clarita, who encouraged the romance. Faced with constant arguments and tears from both girls, Mrs Jerome eventually gave way, although she refused to countenance talk of an engagement before formal consent had been obtained from the two fathers. She wrote to Leonard, stating that she had changed her mind, and also to Randolph, who had written her a pleading letter, saying that she had been impressed by his 'frank and honourable manner'.[18]

Jennie now wrote to her father, mentioning no names, in New York. His reply was cautious:

My dear Jennie

You quite startle me. I shall feel very anxious about you until I hear more. If it has come to that – that <u>he</u> only 'waits to consult his family', you are pretty far gone. You must like him well enough to accept for yourself which for you is a great deal. I fear if anything goes wrong you will make a dreadful shipwreck of your affections. I always thought if you ever did fall in love it would be a very dangerous affair. You were never born to love lightly. It must be <u>way down</u> or nothing. Something like your mother. Not so Clara [Clarita] – happily not so. Such natures if they happen to secure the right one are very happy but if disappointed they suffer untold misery.[19]

There was much truth to this. Leonard knew his daughter and understood her passionate nature well. Jennie was much driven by her strong emotions. In a man, this great energy could have been directed and channelled into a career, but for a woman living at this time in these circles the only outlet for such great feeling was to love and be loved. And Jennie had made up her mind. She loved Randolph, he loved her, and marriage was the only possible outcome. Aided by Clarita, she would wage a forceful campaign to win over her parents and marry the man for whom she had fallen. Randolph kept her spirits up with his frequent letters. At first, Jennie could not reply, as it had been forbidden by Mama, so Randolph had to send his missives with no reassurance in return. He had much to concern him: his father had not given his consent, and to make matters worse Mrs Jerome had urged him to 'listen to your father's advice, whatever it is. He can only have your happiness at heart. As a good son, your first duty is to him.'[20]

Whilst Randolph had been at Cowes, he had presented Jennie to the Prince of Wales, telling him that she was the girl he wished to marry. The Prince liked Jennie at once and was encouraging to the young couple. Now Randolph wrote to the Prince, enclosing his brother Blandford's upsetting poem. The Prince was sympathetic, but advised Randolph that Blandford had no doubt meant well. Francis Knollys, the Prince's private secretary – and a great friend of Randolph's, was also shown the offending letter, and he had much the same advice. Nevertheless, the future king's support was heartening.

Jennie and Randolph were able to meet briefly in mid-September in London, as the Jeromes travelled from Cowes back to Paris. Fortunately, Leonard's response to the proposed marriage proved positive and warm: 'I cannot imagine any engagement that would please me more,' he wrote.

> I am as confident that all you say of him is true as though I knew him. Young, ambitious, uncorrupted. And best of all you think and I believe he loves you. He must. You are no heiress and it must have taken heaps of love to overcome an Englishman's prejudice against 'those horrid Americans'. I like it in every way. He is English. You will live in England. I shall see much of him and you. And my dear Jennie the very best of it is – a <u>love</u> match. Like your mother & me.[21]

So it was that at the end of September Mrs Jerome wrote to Randolph that her husband, knowing nothing about Lord Randolph except for what she had herself written to him and 'listening to his daughter's earnest appeal who thinks all happiness depends on her marrying you', had given his formal consent.[22] Leonard had also outlined to his wife the parameters of a dowry, mentioning a possible marriage settlement of £2,000 a year (about £140,000 in today's values). Clara also related this to Randolph.

The financial terms were to become a key element in the negotiations. Randolph could not afford to marry without his parents' consent, as it was true indeed that his chosen bride was no heiress. The ambitious young couple certainly could not live on Leonard's proposed £2,000 per year and the promise of one third of his estate. It did not occur to Leonard, who was proud of his daughter, that she was marrying above her station. When Mrs Jerome learned of the duke's disapproval, she immediately informed her husband, who sent a curt telegram: 'Consent Withdrawn.' The Jeromes were unhappy that the Marlboroughs did not consider their daughter to be an acceptable bride. Mrs Jerome was herself disappointed that Randolph was a second son. Leonard was happier with his daughter's choice, but rejected any ambiguity concerning her suitability. In spite of Randolph's best efforts to hide his parents' reluctance and their unwillingness to agree to the match, the Jeromes gradually became aware of the problem. Clara Jerome demanded that the duke should write or in some way make his intentions clear before she would allow Randolph to travel to Paris to see her daughter.

Jennie was, however, allowed to write to Randolph, and the couple corresponded almost daily from mid-September, while awaiting parental consent to the marriage. Nevertheless Jennie's first letter, written on 16 September, 1873, was one of reproach. Randolph had evidently made some negative remark about her father. 'I have persuaded Mama to allow me to write these few lines,' she began, 'as they will probably be the last.' She felt that he had changed and no longer loved her:

Do not be angry dear – but I have not been able to sleep all night – thinking of all you said – & the more I think the more convinced I am that you are changed – since Cowes. Sometimes I almost wish I had listened a little more to Mama's advice – from the beginning she asked me not to think of it – & begged me to forget you – as it would only worry & trouble me in the end ... I cannot tell you how deeply hurt I felt at the insinuation you gave me – as to yr having heard something against my father – I was unable to answer you or defend him – as you did not choose to confide in me – All I can say is that I love, admire, & respect my father more than any man living ... Dearest I have no doubt this letter will pain you – & make me appear in quite a new light – & perhaps not a very flattering one – but I cannot help it – *Je suis ainsi faite!* [That is how I am made] – & if I have a bad nature it is difficult to change. My pride always did get the better of me & it certainly has on this occasion ... Forgive me – I really <u>cannot</u> break quite yet – for I feel that I love you more than anything or person on earth – & that I am ready to do or say anything you like as long as you leave my family alone and not abuse it –

    Ever yrs

      Jeanette Jerome

If you write please send me those papers with yr speeches. I still take a slight interest in yr affairs! – 6 Rue Presbourg[23]

Randolph responded immediately, writing from Blenheim on 18 September of his anguish and his anger, but there was no doubt too of his love:

I am more pained & hurt than you can imagine, & if that was your object in writing you may congratulate yourself on having fully attained it. You are the only person on Earth that has the power to say or do anything to wound my feelings & to vex & worry me for long & you certainly know how to use your power ... How can you be so cruel so heartless I really may almost say so wicked as to write to me that your impression is that I am heartily sick of the whole affair & only wish myself well out of it. These are your very words & I can hardly bring myself to rewrite them. And then in the end of your letter to tell me that you loved me still, why it is the heighth [sic] of mockery & nonsense to write in so contradictory a manner. No woman cld ever write so to a man she really loved. … How can you say that I have abused your family, when you know that I am incapable of doing such a thing? … Oh my darling Jeanette pardon me if I have written crossly, but your letter quite took my breath away, & has left me perfectly distracted with grief & worry…

  Yr as ever devoted but despairing
   Randolph S. Churchill[24]

It was their first argument. Jennie, remorseful yet relieved, immediately replied to his letter (which she received on the day it was written), saying that this 'must be – & shall be the last misunderstanding between us', adding: 'Darling I love yr angry cross letter – it has done me more good than twenty tender ones … I could leave Father Mother – & the whole world for you – if it were necessary.'[25]

In response to Randolph's entreaties, and perhaps surprised by his hitherto unknown tenacity, his father reluctantly conceded that permission might be granted for him to marry if the couple were prepared to wait. The duke provisionally agreed to the wedding on that basis:

> What I have now to say is that if I am to believe that your future is really bound up in your marriage with Miss Jerome, you must show me proof of it by bringing it to the test of time. I will say no more to you on the subject for the present, but if this time next year you come and tell me you are both of the same mind, we will receive Miss Jerome as a daughter, and, I need not say, with the affection you could desire for your wife.[26]

This concession – as well as the attached condition – was unacceptable to Randolph, whose feelings were so strong that he found it hard to concentrate on anything but Jennie. He vacillated between euphoria and despair, and wrote her letters of longing, telling her that he read Gibbon to calm himself and to feel at peace with the world.[27] Although he declared that he would wait even longer than the required year if necessary, he felt that no such necessity existed and argued with his father, hoping that the duke would relent. His parents finally agreed that if he stood for election to Parliament, he and Jennie could marry afterwards.

Randolph was delighted. Now all he and Jennie had to do was wait for a general election to be called, when he could fight for the seat at Woodstock. Jennie wrote to Randolph of her happiness at this turn of events. Indeed, she had been pining away since returning home, remarking that she had grown 'quite thin' and was 'afraid you will think me so ugly when you come'. She explained to him that his father's reaction was perfectly understandable, if tiresome, and that she had expected such a response, if not from him then from her own mother, 'who does nothing but sermonize me on the subject'. Jennie pointed out to Randolph, however, that he could not come to visit her until the duke wrote, as she had had another long conversation with Mama: 'She says she cannot have you come here & be seen with us until things are entirely settled & the engagement an understood thing in both our families & by everyone – darling I hope you are not angry at my telling you this – you know how difficult it is to manage parents indeed I am tired of trying to do it.'[28]

Randolph, however, was very angry and wrote at once to Mrs Jerome to tell her so, also announcing his imminent arrival in Paris. Jennie was appalled at his letter and remonstrated with him:

How could you write such a letter to Mama my darling <u>stupid</u> Randolph? Did you not see that when I wrote that wretched letter – neither Mama or I had received either of yours – & I wrote mine on the spur of the moment ('a thing one ought never to do') after a discussion with her which made me feel very cross – altho' she did not say half what I wrote – but in my stupid anger I wrote whatever came in my head – that she did not <u>believe</u> you – words she <u>never did say</u> – I did not know I had written them myself – I shall explain it all to you when you come – & darling for Heaven sake don't spoil this meeting by misunderstandings & quarrels – I have been so longing for it – & looking forward to it – I cld not be so cruelly disappointed – You wld have a perfect right to be furious & feel very much injured if things

were as you thought them – but they <u>are not</u> – Pray believe what I say
that it is all my fault & I beg you to forgive me if you love me & not
be angry & come to me as soon as you arrive … oh my darling don't
ever write such a letter again – when shall we have finished with all
these misunderstandings & distrusts? … DO COME[29]

And he did, taking rooms at the Hôtel France et de Bath in the Rue St
Honoré in the last week of October. Leonard wrote from New York,
saying that he was 'delighted more than I can tell. It is magnificent. The
greatest match any American has made since the Dutchess [sic] of
Leeds.'[30] He was referring to Mary Caton, daughter of a wealthy landowning family from Maryland and granddaughter of Charles Carroll, a
signatory to the Declaration of Independence (of which he was the
only Roman Catholic), who had married the 7th Duke of Leeds in
1828. Leonard believed that Jennie had accomplished something quite
wonderful. He was enormously proud and informed all of his friends.
Meanwhile, the couple enjoyed each other's company in Paris while
also preparing for separation when Randolph would return to England
to fight the next election.

More confident of each other and deeply in love, Jennie and
Randolph continued to correspond, trying to keep their spirits high
while they waited. Jennie told Randolph of the intrigue and rumours
in Paris, of royalists and Bonapartists hatching plots to regain power. In
turn, Randolph urged her to learn about British politics. Jennie did so
with dedication, determined to prove a suitable and able politician's
wife. She read political speeches and, on her fiancé's recommendation,
Gibbon and Horace. She encouraged Randolph to work hard, writing
on 26 September, 'I should like you to be as ambitious as you are clever,
and I am sure you could accomplish great things.'[31] At the very end of
December, Randolph was given permission by his parents to make
another trip to Paris, but was unable to go. His favourite aunt, Lady
Portarlington, who lived in Ireland, had fallen dangerously ill, and he
was summoned to her bedside. Before he left London, however, in early
January, he was able to meet his future father-in-law, who had travelled

over from New York. Randolph spent the day with Leonard and wrote in his daily letter to Jennie: 'I really like him so much, the more I see of him. I am sure we will always be the best of friends.'[32] He ended by urging her to write more often, so he would know she was thinking of him.

Randolph's aunt lingered for a month and he became increasingly miserable at being away from Jennie. He fretted that she did not care for him as she once had; he was concerned by how much she had written of a certain Austrian gentleman named Kevenhuller; he wished she would not have so many late nights; he missed her desperately. Jennie missed him too. 'I wish I was more like other women,' she wrote. 'I regret not being able to care for you wisely & moderately,' adding, 'I shd be much happier myself taking everything quietly as I did when first I knew you.'[33] When at last it seemed he could go to Paris to be with Jennie on 9 January, her birthday, his aunt had a sudden relapse and the trip had to be postponed. His mother telegraphed Jennie and later wrote how sorry she was that the journey had had to be cancelled. It was quite clear that the duchess considered Randolph's first duty to be to his family. Randolph stayed until his aunt died, a month after he had arrived in Ireland. Finally on his way to France in January 1874, he received news that Parliament had been dissolved by Prime Minister Gladstone, and there was to be a general election. He therefore went straight to Woodstock instead, preparing to stand for election as the Conservative candidate. He had not seen Jennie for four months.

Randolph threw himself into action, knowing that victory would bring about his longed-for marriage. He was inexperienced – he hid his speech notes in his hat, to the amusement of his audience – but fought the campaign with great enthusiasm, winning with 569 votes to his Liberal opponent's 404. He went immediately to Paris, followed soon afterwards by the duke and duchess, who wished to meet their future daughter-in-law. Jennie charmed them both, and they were particularly taken with her astounding piano playing. Her good looks exceeded expectation, as the photographs had not conveyed her beautiful colouring: deep grey-blue eyes, naturally flushed cheeks, and red lips. The Marlboroughs were somewhat reassured if not wholly convinced, while Mrs Jerome found the duke 'a perfect dear'.[34] Randolph decided to stay on in Paris while the marriage settlement was discussed.

Such settlements were a standard part of the marriage contract, especially in the great families of England, where they would typically be enormously detailed, with clauses to anticipate all eventualities. This legal document served to cement an economic as well as a social union between the two parties. Lord Randolph had never taken notice of money matters in his life, a trait that was not at all unusual in his circles, and he referred to his father for negotiation of the contract. The duke was prepared to pay off Randolph's considerable debts as part of his settlement on his younger son, as well as bearing the cost of the lease on a townhouse where Randolph and Jennie would live. In fact the duke was being quite generous. He had an annual income of about £40,000 (around £2.7 million today) from his Oxfordshire estates, which carried high maintenance expenses, and his financial commitments included allowances for his daughters and two sons. Money was so scarce that in 1874 he sold his estates of Winchendon and Waddesdon to Baron Ferdinand de Rothschild. He also decided that year to sell the Marlborough gems. This collection of jewels and cameos was sold in a single lot, in 1875, by Christie's auction house in London, for £10,000. The sales continued when the 7th Duke died and his son inherited. In 1881 the first lots of the Sunderland library went on sale and, when the auctioning was completed the following year, the 18,000 volumes had achieved nearly £60,000. In 1883, the Blenheim enamels were sold for £73,000.[35] The asset-stripping continued for years. The 8th Duke sold canvases by Rubens, Van Dyck, Titian, Rembrandt, and Poussin to staunch the income drain from the family coffers. It was unsurprising, therefore, that the 7th Duke of Marlborough should take such a close interest in the marital financial settlement for his second son. He informed Randolph that he was sending Leonard Jerome's proposed marriage settlement document to the family lawyer for perusal.

Randolph was fulsomely appreciative of his father's generosity, writing that he was relieved to enter the marriage financially unencumbered, as he did not wish Mr Jerome to think he was marrying Jennie in order to have his debts paid. He agreed with his father that he was not particularly good with money and told him: 'I am quite decided that Jennie will have to manage the money, and I am quite sure she will keep everything straight, for she is clever and like all Americans, has a sacred, and I should almost say, insane horror of buying anything she cannot pay for immediately.'[36] In this assessment Randolph was quite wrong; Jennie had no regard for money whatever. What she wanted, she had to have – and had simply been in the fortunate situation until now of being able to have all she desired.

The final negotiations between the Marlboroughs and the Jeromes concerned the amount of the annuity and how it would be apportioned. This proved to be a thorny and awkward issue, for two reasons. First, Leonard was not altogether comfortable with the English custom of a husband having control of his wife's money (especially if the money had been provided not by him but by her father). He therefore wished for part of the annual income that was settled on the couple to be paid to Jennie as a separate allowance. Leonard was also concerned about the amount involved, because the New York financier was not as financially secure as he had once been. His recent losses on the stock market had been very heavy, and he was finding it increasingly difficult to recover. Although still a wealthy man, he was not so well off that the commitment to a financial settlement on the couple, for life, was to be undertaken lightly. Matters became complicated and unpleasant. Leonard was unhappy too that Randolph would continue to receive the full annuity even if Jennie died.

Randolph believed that Mrs Jerome was behind many of the difficulties and that she, more than her husband, was a forceful negotiator who could twist Leonard 'round her little finger'.[37] He wrote to his father almost daily, seeking advice. He declared that 'Affairs are come to a most unpleasant pass' and that 'Mr and Mrs Jerome and myself are barely on speaking terms and I don't quite see what is to be the end of it … I think that his conduct and Mrs J's is perfectly disgraceful ... and I am bound to say that Jennie agrees with me entirely.'[38] The negotiations continued nevertheless.

Leonard travelled to Paris to conclude the details, and it was agreed that if there were children and Jennie died before Randolph, the annuity would be apportioned among them; if in such a circumstance there were no children, Randolph would get half and the Jerome family the other half. At this point, the lawyers took over and the discussions became even more acrimonious. There were unseemly squabbles over costs, including such trifles as telegrams and postage stamps, in addition to more serious issues, such as the matter of an allowance for Jennie, which was still undecided. On this subject Leonard would not budge. Although he conceded most points in response to especially cordial letters from the duke, he would not leave his daughter without means of her own:

> In regard to the settlement ... I beg to assure you that I have been governed purely by what I conceived to be the best interests of both parties. It is quite wrong to suppose I entertain any distrust of Randolph. On the contrary, I hope there is no young man in the world safer. Still, I can but think your English custom of making the wife so entirely dependent on the husband, is most unwise. In the settlement, as it is finally arranged, I have ignored American customs and waived all my American prejudices, and have conceded to your views and English customs on every point, save one. That is a somewhat unusual allowance of money to the wife. Probably the principle may be wrong, but you may be very certain my action upon it in this instance by no means arises from any distrust of Randolph.[39]

Randolph's family had to be content with this decision, and all were very relieved when the lawyers at last reached full agreement. Leonard Jerome consented to settle a sum of £50,000 (about £3.4 million today) on the couple, which would produce an annual income of £2,000 (£140,000). Together with Randolph's promised income of £1,100 (£75,000) a year for life, the pair would have total revenues of £3,100 per year (just over £210,000 today).

The wedding date was set for 15 April, 1874, the same day as Clarita's birthday. It was also the duchess's birthday. Neither the duchess nor the duke was, however, present at the wedding, which took place at the chapel of the British Embassy in Paris. This was a slight – a recognition that, although Jennie was accepted by the Marlborough family, this was not a splendid marriage to be celebrated in pomp, merely one that had to be accommodated. As the duke wrote to his son, in a letter he sent to be opened on the day of his wedding, he hoped for his future happiness, although his bride was 'one whom you have chosen with rather less than usual deliberation'. He conceded, however, that Randolph had 'adhered to your love with unwavering constancy', and he hoped 'that, as time goes on, your two natures will prove to have been brought not accidentally together'.[40] It was hardly an overwhelming endorsement, but it was as far as the duke was prepared to go. Leonard Jerome was disappointed that Randolph's parents would not be attending the ceremony. He wrote to the duke of his regret, his confidence in Randolph, and the reassurance he felt that Jennie would be met at once with 'new affectionate friends and relatives'.[41]

Although this was to be a small celebration, instead of the grand society wedding dreamed of by Mama, Jennie and her sisters were very happy. Jennie could not wait to be married to Randolph, who was as eager as she to walk down the aisle. She wrote to herself the night before her wedding, 'This is the last time I shall wind this clock … this is the last time I shall look in the old mirror. Soon nothing will be the same for me anymore: Miss Jennie Jerome will be gone forever.'[42] Her trousseau was ready: twenty-three French-made dresses, seven Paris bonnets, and beautifully embroidered underlinen. Young Leonie – who had only found out about the engagement by reading about it in a paper while away at school in Wiesbaden – made detailed lists of the hundreds of wedding presents, which included a gold Russian coffret, and a locket of pearls and turquoises from the Prince and Princess of Wales, as well as many other gifts from both sides of the Atlantic.

Clarita and Leonie, the bridesmaids, wore dresses of pale blue silk with white embroidery. Around their necks were their bridesmaids' gifts of crystal lockets on which the intertwined initials R and J were traced in sapphires and rubies. Mama wept whilst Jennie was laced by the maids into a gown of white satin, with a long train and folds of Alençon lace. Papa placed a necklace of pearls around her neck and a long tulle veil covered her entirely. Jennie carried in her hand his gift, a beautiful parasol of white Alençon lace with a gold and tortoiseshell handle, as she and her father travelled by carriage to the British Embassy. Mrs Jerome, in a grey silk dress, and her daughters followed in another carriage.

Randolph's brother Blandford attended the wedding, as did three of his sisters and his aunt, Lady Camden. His great friend Francis Knollys was best man. Leonard Jerome had entertained all of them at a magnificent family dinner the night before the wedding. The guests enjoyed a sumptuous wedding breakfast after the ceremony while, according to custom, the bride and groom dined alone together in a private drawing room. Afterwards, Jennie changed into a pretty white and blue dress for travelling, with a white hat and feather, and the happy couple climbed into a beautiful coach drawn by handsome grey horses. Jennie again carried her parasol from Papa, and gave her weeping mother a final comforting hand: 'Why, Mama, don't cry, life is going to be perfect … always.'[43] And they rode away to their secret honeymoon destination in the French countryside.

CHAPTER FOUR

The Prince of Wales and the Marlborough House Set

Jennie's social success had one important consequence for her family. The Jerome sisters' matrimonial hunting ground shifted from France to England. Because Jennie had managed to marry into the English aristocracy of the Edwardian era, she immediately became a member of a small, elite social set. It was natural that her sisters would come and visit. The entrée to select society provided by Randolph – who was especially fond of Clarita, after she had supported his suit through those difficult months – was immensely appealing. Clarita in turn was delighted to spend time with the young Churchills, enjoying the sparkling life of parties and entertainments of London in the 1870s. Its undisputed social leader was Queen Victoria's son, Albert Edward, Prince of Wales.

Queen Victoria had acceded to the throne in 1837 and in 1840 married Prince Albert. This relationship was the driving force of her life. She cared little for her many children, and her eldest son, Albert Edward, known as Bertie, born in 1841, was unappreciated by both his forbidding parents, who found him unattractive and difficult to manage. His life was a disappointment to them, and his mother later blamed him for the death of his father from typhoid in 1861. Prince Albert had been very distressed about a liaison between Bertie and an actress, and the Queen believed that the sleepless nights and illness (exacerbated by a visit to his son at Cambridge University during which they walked at length in the rain on a cold day) that followed were a causal factor in Albert's premature demise. She threw herself into ostentatious mourning, having every part of his room photographed so that it could be preserved exactly as it had been in his lifetime. She required that servants lay his dressing gown and fresh clothes by his bed each evening, together with a jug of hot water on his washstand. A marble bust of Albert was placed between the two beds of his room, where his portrait also hung, wreathed in evergreens. Fresh flowers were strewn nearly every day on his bed, and the glass from which he had taken his last dose of medicine was kept on his table, remaining there for more than forty years. Numerous monuments were erected to his memory. In the meantime the grief-stricken Victoria found it impossible to deal with daily matters of family and governance.

Albert Edward did not believe that he was really responsible for his father's death, but his mother told her daughter, the Crown Princess of Prussia, that she could hardly bear to be in the same room with him. He tried to mend the breach, with little success. Although many of her advisers tried in vain to persuade her otherwise, she refused to allow her son access to state papers, or to take on any responsibility. Bertie gave up and devoted himself to social distractions instead. Some 600 families formed London society, and among these a hand-picked group were the Prince's special friends. They were, like him, attracted to an insouciant and pleasure-seeking lifestyle. Without a proper job, the Prince of Wales had far too much time on his hands, and he was serially unfaithful to his wife, Princess Alexandra. His affairs became a way of life, and a strict code of conduct was maintained by these friends, who later became known as the Marlborough House Set, after his residence. Young unmarried women were not considered fair game. The Prince's affairs amused and passed the time in a more exciting and interesting way than the formal rituals of public life. Falling in love and creating family difficulties was frowned upon, however, as was any flagrant indiscretion. Those who broke the code were ostracized from the Prince's set. While Queen Victoria maintained perpetual mourning, the Prince of Wales and his friends were enjoying dinners, theatre, parties, and fancy-dress balls, as well as country house visiting, hunting, and travelling.

Before settling down to the delights of the Prince of Wales' set in London, Jennie and Randolph paid a visit to his parents at Blenheim after their honeymoon, in early May. They were met at Woodstock station by the townspeople, who unhitched the horses from the Churchill carriage in order to pull the couple themselves through the streets. People waved and cheered at the young pair. They were conveyed through the town, then under Blenheim's tremendous stone archway, after which the magnificent view of the palace lay before them. Blenheim had been created by the architect John Vanbrugh, a comrade-in-arms of the first Duke of Marlborough, who had asked him to design an English Versailles in commemoration of his military victories. The gardens were later designed by Capability Brown. Vanbrugh planned a palace within a dramatic landscape setting where the visitor was greeted by the panorama of the lake in the valley, a monumental bridge spanning it, set in miles and miles of magnificent park. The house was partially hidden by woodland, with its unforgettable roofline etched against the sky. It was an extraordinary sight. Jennie was overwhelmed, although she refused to say so. Instead, when Randolph cried, 'This is the finest view in England,' she replied by quoting Pope's unfavourable lines on the lack of comfort at Blenheim, which concluded: 'That 'tis a house but not a dwelling.' In fact, Jennie later recorded in her memoirs that she had been in awe of Blenheim, but her 'American pride' forbade such an admission.[1]

Life at Blenheim was regimented. 'How strange life in a big country-house seemed to me,' Jennie wrote. 'The Duke and Duchess lived in a most dignified, and indeed, somewhat formal style.' They welcomed their new daughter-in-law, but Jennie was expected to conform to their ways, as she later described in her memoirs:

> Everything was conducted in what would now be considered a very old-fashioned manner. Guests used to sit solemnly through an elaborate tea, exchanging empty civilities for an hour or more until the hostess (who wore a lace cap if 'middle-aged' – then about forty) gave the signal to rise, uttering the invariable formula, 'I am sure you must need a little rest.' The guests, once immured within their rooms were

not to reappear until the dining-hour. However little they wanted rest, however bored by their own society or disturbed by the unpacking maid, there they were supposed to remain.

Meals were equally stiff. Jennie described how at each luncheon, 'rows of entrée dishes adorned the table, joints beneath massive silver covers being placed before the Duke and Duchess, who each carved for the whole company,' and commented that if there was a shooting party 'even breakfast was made a ceremonious meal'.[2] The duchess dictated everything, and Jennie felt under observation, which she no doubt was. She escaped the stifling atmosphere by practising on the piano – she was far more accomplished a musician than any of Randolph's sisters – and writing letters to Mama and her siblings, describing what she saw as her in-laws' ridiculous and often frumpy habits. She laughed at their unfashionable clothes and the shape of their shoes. She mocked their table-mats, the water jugs at the dinner table, and the thick ordinary tumblers – 'the kind we use in bedrooms'.[3] Jennie felt that life there was really rather dull, as can be seen from her description of a typical day:

When the family were alone at Blenheim everything went on with the regularity of clockwork. So assiduously did I practise my piano, read, or paint, that I began to imagine myself back in the schoolroom. In the morning an hour or more was devoted to the reading of newspapers, which was a necessity if one wanted to show an intelligent interest in the questions of the day, for at dinner conversation invariably turned on politics. In the afternoon a drive to pay a visit to some neighbour or a walk in the gardens would help to while away some part of the day. After dinner, which was a rather solemn full-dress affair, we all repaired to what was called the Vandyke room. There one might read one's book or play for love a mild game of whist. Many a glance would be cast at the clock, which sometimes would be surreptitiously advanced a quarter of an hour by a sleepy member of the family. No one dared suggest bed until the sacred hour of eleven had struck. Then we would all troop out into a small anteroom, and, lighting our candles, each in turn would kiss the Duke and Duchess and depart to our own rooms.[4]

In this unfamiliar atmosphere, Jennie was not intimidated. She had the love and devotion of Randolph, which made her feel secure. She was also prettier, better dressed, and far more accomplished than Randolph's five sisters, and she knew it. She had been a spoiled girl and had a high opinion of her own worth. Although she was impressed by Blenheim and especially with its magnificent works of art, she was less in awe of its inhabitants, with whom she forged courteous, if not exactly warm, relationships. Nonetheless she took to the life extremely well. Jennie and her sisters had been brought up by Mama to believe that they were among the elite and would marry into the very best families; they had been taught by Papa to expect and demand only the very best of everything.

At the end of May 1874, Jennie and Randolph moved into a rented house on London's Curzon Street, while waiting for the townhouse at 48 Charles Street to become available. They were ready to enjoy Jennie's first London season. After the restrictions of Blenheim, they threw themselves wholeheartedly into the pleasures of dinner parties and balls attended by diplomats, politicians, and aristocratic land-owners. Randolph made his maiden speech in Parliament, but was otherwise not much concerned with work. His interest in politics was superficial, although he enjoyed the thrill of speaking in the House. Neither of them gave a thought to bills or cash flow.

In June 1874, Jennie's sister Clarita, who now called herself Clara, came to stay for a few months for the London season. This was something of great importance – Jennie recalled that it was 'looked upon as a very serious matter which no self-respecting persons who considered themselves "in society" would forego, nor of which a votary of fashion would willingly miss a week or a day.'[5] Clara revelled in London life and was a companion to Jennie. Clara's letters to her mother during these few months were frivolous, reflecting the shallow concerns of a young woman, who although now aged twenty-three had never really grown up. Unlike Jennie, she took no interest in politics. The dinner parties at Curzon and, later, Charles Street were described to Mama exclusively in terms of the clothes people wore. Mrs Jerome received accounts of all the parties, including the quadrilles for the Prince of Wales' 'Pack of Cards' fancy-dress dance. Clara reported to her mother that Randolph had complained about the £15 (over £1,000 today) spent on the costumes.[6]

The London season was immensely gay. Jennie recollected that after the 'comparatively quiet life of Paris, we seemed to live in a whirl of gaieties and excitement. Many were the delightful balls I went to, which, unlike those of the present day invariably lasted to five o'clock in the morning. Masked balls were much the vogue.'[7] Jennie had a close friendship with the Prince of Wales, which meant that the sisters were invited, and welcomed, everywhere. The Prince particularly sought out the company of American women, stating that they were 'livelier, better educated and less hampered by etiquette … they are not as squeamish as their English sisters and they are better able to take care of themselves'.[8] Clara wrote to her mother: 'I don't know why, but people always seem to ask us [to parties] whenever H.R.H. [His Royal Highness] goes to them. I suppose it is because Jennie is so pretty.'[9] Jennie's beauty, vivacity, and evident success with the Prince of Wales made her much in demand socially. The duchess also helped to launch her daughter-in-law by introducing her to the important social leaders in London society. Jennie described to her mother how 'The Duchess came for me at two and we went off in grand style in the family coach. The Duchess was very kind, and lent me some rubies and diamonds, which I wore in my hair, and my pearls on my neck. I also had a bouquet of gardenias that she sent me.'[10]

During the twenty years following Jennie's marriage to Lord Randolph, there was a steady increase in other Anglo-American weddings. Theirs was the precursor to the era of the transatlantic marriage and of titled Americans. By the 1880s, daughters of (almost always) wealthy American businessmen married into the English aristocracy in a transaction that some at the time were apt to characterize as 'cash for titles'. The best-known of these alliances was that of the eighteen-year-old railway heiress Consuelo Vanderbilt to Randolph's nephew, the 9th Duke of Marlborough, in 1895. This was an unhappy alliance that ended in divorce after the birth of two sons – Consuelo is credited with the quip of having claimed to provide the Marlboroughs with 'an heir and a spare'.[11] The British system of primogeniture meant that a hereditary peerage was passed only to the eldest son in each family, who would inherit the family estate. This estate was often entailed, meaning that he did not have the discretion to sell land or other valuables, such as family jewels and paintings. Thus such peers often needed an influx of money, and in turn many Americans were attracted to a title.

Jennie wrote in her memoirs that in the 1880s there had been an increase in the number of such transatlantic marriages, hitherto quite rare, and that American women were not always warmly welcomed. She knew three of them well: Miss Consuelo Yznaga, a close family friend who later became the Duchess of Manchester; Miss Minnie Stevens, who became Lady Paget; and Mrs William (afterwards Lady) Carrington. In England and on the continent at this time, Jennie wrote, the American woman

> was looked upon as a strange and abnormal creature, with habits and manners something between a Red Indian and a Gaiety Girl. Anything of an outlandish nature might be expected of her. If she talked, dressed, and conducted herself as any well-bred woman would, much astonishment was invariably evinced, and she was usually saluted with the tactful remark, 'I should never have thought *you* were an American' – which was intended as a compliment. As a rule, people looked upon her as a disagreeable and even dangerous person, to be viewed with suspicion, if not avoided altogether. Her dollars were her only recommendation, and each was credited with the possession of them, otherwise what was her *raison d'être*? No distinction was ever made among Americans; they were all supposed to be of one uniform type. The wife and daughters of the newly-enriched Californian miner, swathed in silks and satins, and blazing with diamonds on the smallest provocation; the cultured, refined, and retiring Bostonian; the aristocratic Virginian, as full of tradition and family pride as a Percy of Northumberland or a La Rochefoucauld;

the cosmopolitan and up-to-date New Yorker – all were grouped in the same category, all were considered tarred with the same brush.[12]

Lord Palmerston remarked astutely that by the end of the century, these 'clever and pretty' women would be pulling the strings in half the chancelleries in Europe.[13]

As more transatlantic marriages took place, Jennie befriended many of the American women in London and became a leader of the smart Anglo-American set. By the turn of the century the American woman had become far more accepted. Jennie commented that, some thirty years later, the 'steady progress of American women in Europe can be gauged by studying their present position. It is not to be denied that they are sharing many of the "seats of the mighty" and the most jealous and carping critics cannot find fault with the way they fill them … the American woman is now generally approved of.'[14] Jennie knew all of the American beauties who married into English high society, and so often was she in the company of two of them, the beautiful Americans Mrs Standish and Mrs Sandys, that the trio were dubbed by the press 'The Pink, the White and the Black Pearls'. Dark-haired Jennie was of course the 'Black Pearl' and was usually considered the most attractive of the three.

Not only was Jennie physically beautiful, but she also had the more important gift of badinage – light, clever conversation that sparkled in company and made others feel amusing and amused. The ability to flirt alluringly yet not suggestively was an important accomplishment and one that Jennie possessed. Clara, too, loved to flirt, but did not like to make conversation about weightier topics. She relied on her blonde prettiness and light, girlish conversation to make men feel special in her presence. Jennie was more of a stimulant, like a vintage champagne. Men and women alike enjoyed her company and sought her out. They liked the fact that she was an individual, wearing, for example, a very low décolletage, or a pale blue dress to the theatre, even though traditionally women wore only black. Jennie rapidly became a style-setter and a social pacemaker. By the end of her first season, in 1874, she and

Randolph had become a golden couple, with all social doors open to them. There were garden parties, races at Ascot and Goodwood, the regatta at Henley, the pigeon-shoots at Hurlingham, and naturally the balls, concerts, operas, plays, ballets, and all the other pleasures – a never-ending round of entertainments.

Clara enjoyed being part of this exciting new life. Instead of the court of the Second Empire, which even she wistfully acknowledged would be no more, here was a new canvas upon which to create memories. The aristocracy of England was dashing, the men handsome, the parties delightful. She wrote to Mama in Paris: 'You must not think we are at all fast.'[15] But of course they were fast, they were in a fast set. In Jennie's words, they 'lived in a whirl of gaieties and excitement'.[16]

By the end of the summer, Jennie was pregnant. 'We are very humdrum and stay a great deal at home,'[17] Clara now wrote to Mama. They were at last installed in the house on Charles Street, the gift from the duke. Just three doors along from the chic Berkeley Square, it was staffed by a butler, a footman, and a housemaid. Jennie was very pleased with her household and wrote to her mother:

> We only mean to furnish at the present, two bedrooms and the sitting room downstairs, which we shall use also as a dining room … There is one good thing, we have our *batterie de cuisine* and china, glass and plate and linen, all things which are very expensive … I am so delighted to have a fixed abode at last, and it is such a nice house … Randolph had no settlement made on him when he married, and this of course, makes a settlement. If anything was to happen to him, this house comes to me.[18]

She and Clara also made frequent visits to Blenheim Palace to stay with Randolph's family. These occasions were not always a great success, since Clara found it as difficult as Jennie to disguise her boredom with life there. She also provoked Randolph's mother with her obvious good looks and beautiful dresses, as well as by speaking longingly of the Château de Compiègne instead of admiring Blenheim. Jennie wrote to her mother on 21 October 1874 that on returning to Blenheim she had found the drawing room 'full of lots of people having tea. I escaped as soon as I could,' adding, 'You cannot imagine how stiff & uncomfortable the first hour of their arrivals are. No one knows each other & content themselves with staring.'[19] She and Randolph were preparing for the baby's birth. They were not quite ready, however, for Winston Leonard Spencer Churchill's arrival on 30 November, six weeks earlier than expected. Randolph reported fully on the event for Mrs Jerome:

> I have just time to write a line, to send by the London Dr to tell you that all has up to now thank God gone off very well with my darling Jennie. She had a fall on Tuesday walking with the shooters, & a rather imprudent & rough drive in a pony carriage brought on the pains on Saturday night … & the baby was safely born at 1.30 this morning after about 8 hrs labour. She suffered a great deal poor darling, but was vy plucky & had no chloroform. The boy is wonderfully pretty so everybody says dark eyes & hair & vy healthy considering its prematureness … I telegraphed to Mr Jerome; I thought he wld like to hear. I am sure you will be delighted at this news and dear Clara also. I will write again tonight. Love to Clara.

He added as a postscript: 'I hope the baby things will come with all speed. We have to borrow some from the Woodstock Solicitor's wife.'[20]

Despite Winston's premature birth, he was a strong, healthy baby, and there has been subsequent speculation among historians that he was conceived before Jennie and Randolph's marriage. It is certainly a possibility – the wedding was arranged remarkably quickly once Mrs Jerome rather rapidly and somewhat unexpectedly dropped all of her reservations. On the other hand, it would have been an extraordinary risk for Jennie to take. Had she been pregnant, it would always have been possible for Randolph to refuse or be unable to marry her. She would in such circumstances have become a social pariah and would have been ruined for life. Because of this risk, young women of her class were very closely supervised, and Mama had been an especially ferocious chaperone. Jennie's second son, Jack, born six years later, was also premature. Given the risks and the lack of opportunity for premarital sexual activity for the couple during their engagement, it is most likely that Winston was indeed a premature baby, conceived immediately after their marriage.

The arrival of their first son did not curb Lord and Lady Randolph Churchill's exuberant lifestyle. As was the custom of the period, the baby was confided to a wet-nurse, followed by a nanny, and was raised in the nursery, where a separate regime was instituted: set routines, different meals, separate staff. Parents merely looked in from time to time to ensure all was well. Within six weeks of Winston's birth, Randolph had engaged a nanny, Mrs Elizabeth Everest, who remained with the family for nearly twenty years. It was with Mrs Everest that Winston had his warmest and most affectionate relationship.

Randolph and Jennie were unexceptional in their distant relationship with the new baby, and their attitude was typical of their class. It is worth recognizing, however, that even by the standards of the time, Randolph and Jennie were extremely self-absorbed individuals. Winston wrote that Mrs Everest, who died when he was twenty, 'had been my dearest and most intimate friend during the whole of the twenty years I had lived'.[21] Randolph in particular had difficulty establishing warm relationships with his sons, and neither Winston nor his brother Jack was ever close to him. He never visited Winston at his boarding school, to which the boy was sent shortly before his eighth birthday, and such was the remoteness of their relationship that Winston asked his father just before he went to Harrow School, at the age of thirteen, whether Randolph himself had been to Harrow or Eton.[22] Winston later recalled that in August 1892, when he was almost eighteen (and three years before Randolph died), he had had a discussion with his father, 'one of the three or four long intimate conversations with him which are all I can boast'.[23] Jennie, however, was simply neglectful. When her babies were small, they were uninteresting, and she had better things with which to occupy her time. When they became older, however, she became a much stronger and more positive force in their lives, helping them in their careers, and taking a protective and loving interest in them. 'My mother always seemed to me a fairy princess,' Winston wrote, 'a radiant being possessed of limitless riches and power.'[24]

Jennie's parents came to visit their first grandchild shortly after the birth, Leonard travelling from New York and Mama from Paris. Mrs Jerome, however, did not stay long, wishing to return to her salon in Paris where she entertained a fringe of social aspirants, minor nobility, unsuccessful artists and poets, and other pretentious but essentially unaccomplished dilettantes. Leonard, on the other hand, was in no hurry to return to America. His old love, Fanny Ronalds, who had become firm friends with Jennie, had left the court of the Bey of Algiers and set up her own salon in Cadogan Place in London, where she received the Prince of Wales and the Duke of Edinburgh, among others, for musical evenings. She was always happy to see her old flame from New York. Leonard also met Randolph's parents, the Duke and Duchess of Marlborough, for the first time. He took pleasure in his visit and urged Jennie and Randolph to plan a trip to America soon.

The idyllic existence that the young couple seemed to enjoy was, however, not as perfect as it appeared. Churchill family members quarrelled among themselves in a way that was unfamiliar and most unpleasant to Jennie, who had warm relationships with her sisters and parents. When there were arguments and tempers flared, the Jeromes made up with an embrace, with expressions of heartfelt contrition and tears. But when Randolph and his brother Blandford had an argument with their parents over a ring that Blandford had given Jennie, the resulting quarrel caused great bitterness between the brothers and the duke and duchess. Angry letters were exchanged, and the rift was left unhealed for months. When Randolph had another argument with one of his sisters while staying in Paris in January 1876, Jennie wrote of her distress at the new quarrel: 'Really darling forgive me for saying it – but if you want to *éviter* [avoid] discussions & quarrels on <u>that</u> disagreeable subject why don't you drop it – Why talk or occupy yourself with it?'[25]

Another problem was their chronic shortage of funds. Jennie and Randolph lived extravagantly as befitted members of the Prince of

Wales' set. Leonard Jerome's generous contribution of the income of £2,000 from the capital settlement of £50,000, combined with Randolph's £1,000 allowance from his father, was not enough to cover their outgoings, so, like many others in their class and position, they borrowed. Credit was readily available to members of the aristocracy because they usually had assets or family funds to fall back on. Jennie and Randolph spent money on whatever they wanted and as a consequence were always in debt. It was an expensive lifestyle and looking well was essential. Although Jennie felt a lifelong insecurity about their financial position, she never allowed it to interfere with her dress-making expenditure. The purchase of the latest Worth models was not at any point in question. These gowns were handmade in the couturier's workshop on the Rue de la Paix in Paris, with yards of expensive, luxurious fabrics, and were laboriously hand-stitched with exquisite trims of pearls and jewels. Each gown was unique and could cost as much as £100 (or £7,000 today).[26] An entire season's wardrobe and the requisite accessories from Worth could amount to $20,000 (over £250,000 today),[27] which explains why he was the dressmaker of choice for wealthy Americans rather than more impecunious British aristocrats, who 'made do' with more modest gowns. During her first summer season in London, Jennie wrote to her mother, 'I do so hope Papa will be able to give me the £2000 he promised.'[28]

Finance, however, was of minor concern and the following year, in 1875, Jennie invited Clara once again to come and stay with her in London. Clara wrote many letters to her mother, describing the parties and especially the clothes. After every event she attended, she wrote long descriptions of the outfits, with details of the tulle, bonnets, and trimmings. In one letter she referred to some bonnets that Mama had sent her, pointing out, 'Jennie thinks I ought to wear the white crêpe with sequins as it will be my very first appearance, and it is everything to look well.'[29] In another letter, dated 16 June 1875, she described her evening: 'We had a most charming dinner last night. I wore the blue chosen by Leonie and Jennie her black gauze and Mrs. Standish her black.'[30] At the Ascot races, she had worn 'Leonie's blue silk which was thought very pretty' and for dinner that evening, 'I wore my white muslin and pink roses and Jennie her dark blue low dress.' The following day she wore 'her pink foulard and Jennie her dark blue' and at dinner, Clara reported, 'Jennie wore her pale blue tulle with silver and I my white tulle with jet.'[31] Mama was closely involved with her daughter's wardrobe and even purchased all Clara's clothes from Parisian dressmakers. She was happy to hear that Clara was so well turned out, since both she and her eldest daughter were equally obsessed by the small details of life. Mama and Clara still lived as they had in the days of the imperial court: for the theatre of the moment. Instead of attempting to shape the events around them, they lived for the hushed whispers, the watercoloured memories, the romantic pictures, not the reality of everyday existence.

That year, Clara and Jennie were joined in London by their younger sister, Leonie, who had finally been released from boarding school. She was, however, unable to attend parties as she was still too young at sixteen to make her debut. Although less beautiful than either Jennie or Clara, Leonie had a quiet charm and a sympathetic face. She also had an excellent figure and like her sisters was as accomplished on a horse as she was at the piano. The letters of this time describe party upon party, but make little mention of Randolph. Clara's letters to her mother revealed that he was frequently absent. At the Ascot races, 'Lord Hartington took me to lunch in a private room with the royalties, the Prince himself giving his arm to Jennie'; at another event, 'Jennie took her Sir William Cumming all to herself, he being the swell of the party and does not let anyone else talk to him.' And at a dance after the races Jennie had worn her dark blue dress 'and the men were all *very* nice to us'.[32] Jennie was a great success with men.

One explanation for Randolph's frequent absences is that around this time he had become aware that he had contracted syphilis, a sexually transmitted disease that is highly contagious. A number of stories speculate how he may have done so, but the most creditable of these theories − supported by many historians as well as Randolph's own nephew, and godson, Shane Leslie − is that he was infected by a housemaid at Blenheim around the time of Winston's birth. Shane's son (Leonie's grandson) Jack Leslie believes, however, that Randolph contracted the disease in the red-light district of Paris, saying that his grandmother Leonie told him Randolph frequented prostitutes there, 'the commoner the better'.[33] Randolph often travelled to the continent, from the earliest days of his marriage.

A dreaded malady, syphilis was first discovered in the late fifteenth century when it caused a series of cataclysmic pandemics in continental Europe and in the British Isles, where it was often known as the 'French pox'. The fear and social stigma attached to it had abated little by the nineteenth century, and it was associated with prostitutes and immoral sexual behaviour. Yet venereal disease was a fact of life. Famous sufferers are believed to include Pope Alexander VI, Ivan the Terrible, Henry VIII, Charles Baudelaire, Friedrich Nietzsche, and Henri de Toulouse-Lautrec, while members of the aristocracy often frequented prostitutes and dallied with housemaids. It would not have been especially shocking in society for Randolph to engage in such sexual activity as long he did so discreetly, although the realization that he carried syphilis would have been a terrible blow, not least because he knew he might suffer a painful death, preceded by paralysis and insanity. Treatment of the disease with mercury was only sometimes successful, and never once it had reached its late phases.

Syphilis is manifested by various stages: primary, secondary, and tertiary. All sufferers go through the first two, but some are spared the third and most unpleasant. Physical symptoms in the primary stage take two to four weeks to appear, in the form of one or more sores at the site of infection. These sores, or chancres, disappear within three to eight weeks if left untreated, and the disease inevitably progresses to its secondary stage, some six to eight weeks after the initial sores have disappeared. This stage is characterized by a rash, headaches, tiredness, swollen lymph nodes, and a sore throat. The disease then moves into its latent phase, which can last ten to twenty years. In some patients – about 50 to 70 per cent – the third or tertiary phase never arrives. Symptoms of tertiary-stage syphilis include lesions that develop on the skin, bone, and vital organs. Some patients also develop cardiovascular syphilis, where the bacteria concentrate on the aorta, causing the heart valves to disintegrate. Other sufferers develop neurosyphilis in which the brain is affected, causing dramatic personality changes and leading to insanity.

Certainly Randolph, or his doctor, would have known of both its severity and its contagious nature. Given its physical symptoms, Randolph could not have been unaware of his affliction, particularly as he suffered from poor health generally and was frequently seen by physicians. If one examines the couple's behaviour throughout 1875 and 1876, it becomes clear that something was amiss in the relationship. Randolph and Jennie were often apart, although they professed to miss one another when not together. In April 1875, while Jennie was at Blenheim or in London, he was at the Newmarket races. He sent telegrams to his wife throughout the spring of 1875 from Dorking, Oakdene and Meldon.[34] Throughout 1875 and 1876, while she was in Blenheim, he was often in London; wherever she was, he was elsewhere. 'I don't like this house without you it is awfully dull,'[35] he wrote in July 1876 from London to Jennie who was visiting her mother and sisters in Paris. They were apart for much of that whole year, during which he was away on the continent with his brother Blandford, including Jennie's twenty-second birthday in January. At that time he was recovering from a sore throat, reassuring Jennie in a letter that his companion, Oliver Montagu, had been exaggerating in saying that Randolph had been dangerously ill.[36] He did, however, write that his doctor, Oscar Clayton, had asked to see him two or three more times, 'to put me quite right'.[37] In April 1876 he was recovering from further illness, writing to Jennie that he had a 'shocking bad cold to the head'.[38] Jennie's great-niece and biographer, Anita Leslie, wrote that a 'sheaf of undated letters' written by Jennie to Randolph on one of her 'numerous' visits to Paris at this time express anxiety about his health, exhorting him to restrict himself, 'remember only 6 cigarettes', and to take care of himself.[39] Further, Jennie's biographer Ralph Martin believed that something was wrong with the marriage at this time, describing an 'element of frenzy' to Jennie's busy social life during 1875.[40]

Jennie was only twenty-one, Randolph was twenty-six and in 1875 they had been married for less than a year after a passionate courtship. It is almost certain that, if he were ill, he told her of his illness at this time and that they were never physically intimate again – which would explain why Jennie was never infected with the disease. Syphilis is highly infectious for the first two years, and then progressively less so for the following five. If such were the circumstances of Randolph's contraction of the disease, the surmises of many previous biographers of both Jennie and Randolph – that Jennie was shallow and unfaithful – are inaccurate. On the contrary she remained loyal to her husband. His illness, and her subsequent complicit support and discretion, would explain why they started to live separate lives so soon after their romantic courtship, yet remained close and committed to the marriage. They did not show outward signs of their problems in public.

Instead, Jennie continued her feverish social ascent, revelling in the Prince's heady entourage, while Randolph enjoyed travelling, the races, his own friends, and social amusements, only occasionally attending Parliament. Whether or not he had contracted syphilis at this time, the marriage certainly exhibited widening cracks. By 1877, just three years after their wedding, Jennie wrote sadly to Randolph that she had spent the previous evening reading his old letters to her: 'I had forgotten how nice they were – so full of love & endearing terms! Alas! *Tout cela c'est de l'histoire ancienne* [all that is history].'[41]

Jennie's social distractions came to an abrupt end when, in 1876, Randolph imprudently became involved in a huge row between his brother Blandford and the Prince of Wales. The Prince of Wales was involved in any number of small scandals – usually concerning married women – but they were always hushed up. The Prince's patronage was too important to jeopardize, and husbands made sure to look the other way when such affairs took place. Keeping the Prince busy and out of trouble, however, was a problem for the royal family. His reputation had so deteriorated that his mother, Queen Victoria, supported by Prime

Minister Benjamin Disraeli – who felt that Albert Edward was nothing more than a spoiled child – refused to give him even some token diplomatic responsibility. The Prince decided that he would go on a trip to India and selected a group rather more social than political to accompany him, in spite of the fact that it was official, with a parliamentary allotment for expenses (to which the Prince objected as insufficient). Jennie and Randolph did not join the group, perhaps for financial reasons, or perhaps because Randolph was uncomfortable with the Prince's increasingly obvious desire for Jennie's company. Or it may be that it was just too painful for them to contemplate travelling with the royal entourage as a supposedly perfectly happy couple.

It was on 20 February, while the Prince and his friends were in India, camping at the border of Nepal, that the trouble began.[42] The group included the Prince's great friend and companion, the Earl of Aylesford, a champion polo player and hunter known as 'Sporting Joe', whose wife, Lady Aylesford, was having an affair with Blandford, Randolph's brother. Shortly after Lord Aylesford had left for India, Blandford had moved himself and his horses to an inn conveniently near Packington Hall, the Aylesford residence, to which he had his own key. The affair was serious, and in February 1876, Edith Aylesford wrote to her husband, telling him that she and Blandford planned to elope. Such behaviour could bring deep disgrace and contravened the code of the Marlborough House Set. The Prince was furious and possibly jealous as well, for Lady Aylesford had previously been his mistress. A public scandal would ensue if the Aylesfords divorced.

From Nepal the Prince denounced Blandford as a blackguard, and Lord Aylesford immediately set off for England. In London both families took legal counsel. Edith's brother, Hwfa Williams, wanted to challenge Blandford to a duel. Randolph tried to persuade his brother to drop his plans to elope for the time being, to which Blandford reluctantly agreed. Randolph then surprisingly entered the fray on behalf of his brother by threatening to publish some love letters written by the Prince to Lady Aylesford unless the Prince agreed to withdraw his support for the cuckolded husband. Randolph next went to the Prince of Wales' wife, Princess Alexandra, and told her that if Aylesford sued for divorce, Randolph would produce the Prince's letters as evidence in the divorce court. Should this occur, he told her that the attorney general believed the Prince would never accede to the throne. The attempted blackmail went badly wrong. Prime Minister Disraeli was informed, and Queen Victoria was furious with Randolph. She and the Prince demanded an apology for his treatment of Princess Alexandra whom they felt should never have been involved.

Blandford retreated to Holland, to avoid Aylesford upon his return to England, and Randolph went there to join him in April 1876. Blandford and Randolph's father, the Duke of Marlborough, were keen to avoid being implicated in the bad business, an attitude to which Jennie took exception, writing to Randolph:

> You ask me what I think of your father's 2d epistle. I think it very bad – He is quite willing that you shld do all in your power to prevent Blandford from disgracing himself & his family – but is not at all willing to take upon himself any of the responsibility – or share any of the *désagrément* [unpleasantness] which must arise from being at open war with H.R.H. But my dearest there are few as generous as you & not many brothers wld risk what you are risking for one so worthless as B. tho he be yr only brother.[43]

Jennie's loyalty to Randolph was absolute. She wrote: 'if we are to have all these *ennuis* [troubles] – do for Heaven sake lets [*sic*] go through them together – As long as I have you I dont [*sic*] care what happens,' adding that it was not because she would miss the 'Marlboro [*sic*]' House balls and their social set. 'No darling I assure you it is not so,' she declared; 'how can I help feeling sick at heart when you are away from me – in difficulties *et pardessus le marché, avec un "rhume accablant"* [and into the bargain, with a "dreadful cold"] of which I'm sure you take no care – Shall you return Sunday? I hope so *cher mari de mon coeur – de ce pauvre coeur qui est si gros ce soir* [dear husband of my heart – of my heart that is so heavy tonight]'.[44]

The affair was finally resolved with a minimum of scandal, but at some cost. Lord Aylesford, the innocent party, let it be known on 12 May 1876 that 'in order to avoid great public mischief'[45] he would not seek a divorce and retreated to Texas. His wife Edith, Lady Aylesford, went to live on the continent with Blandford for some years (and bore him a son). Later, Blandford's wife, Bertha, divorced him, but by then the affair had been almost forgotten, except by Randolph and Jennie, who had become social pariahs. The Prince was so incensed by Randolph's intervention that he made it clear he would attend no social function if they were present. By the summer of 1876 their lives in the limelight seemed at an end.

The rift was absolute. When Randolph and Jennie were guests at a ball given by Lord Fitzwilliam, they had to be rushed out through the servants' quarters, down the back stairs, in order to avoid the Prince, who had just arrived unexpectedly. The Prince reprimanded his friend John Delacour when he heard that he was still seeing the Churchills, while Jennie's great American friend the Duchess of Manchester, formerly Consuelo Yznaga, told him that she could not possibly neglect Jennie as they had been at school together. But these were courageous exceptions, and the fashionable world as a whole now frowned on the pair. Although the Prince of Wales had no political authority, he had complete control of high society. His honour had been impugned, and he would not let Randolph forget it.

Jennie hoped for a reconciliation, possibly effected by Randolph's father. 'You must write me all about the interview between your Fr & H.R.H.,' she wrote to Randolph from Paris in June 1876, 'of course I shall feel the greatest interest to know *ce qui s'est passé* [what happened] mind you let me know.'[46] Her support for her husband never wavered. It soon became apparent that a reconciliation was not possible. Randolph wrote to Jennie on 30 June to tell her that the interview between the duke and the Prince had 'led to no satisfactory result', and that the Prince 'seems to have expressed the greatest animosity agst [against] me'.[47] Jennie then decided that it might be a good time to take that visit to America that she and Randolph had promised to her father.

The Marlboroughs agreed, having found the whole affair distressing and most distasteful. When Queen Victoria invited the duke and duchess to spend a night at Windsor Castle, on the 'strict understanding' that there would be no reference to the 'domestic circumstances' that had caused her 'anxiety and deep regret', the Queen was 'much grieved to see the alteration in both of them since she last saw them at Osborne a year & 4 months ago. They looked so <u>distressed</u>, <u>wretched</u> & the poor Dss especially, who cd scarcely restrain her tears.'[48] The duke and duchess had learned to expect such behaviour from Blandford, but Randolph's actions had been an unwelcome shock with unfortunate consequences for the whole family. Blandford was now abroad, living with a married woman, and Randolph and Jennie were social outcasts, all of which was upsetting for a proud family such as the Marlboroughs. By the summer of 1876, Randolph too welcomed the distraction of a trip to Jennie's homeland. Leonard had extended a warm invitation to come to America 'to sail and drive and see what I have left in the way of horses'.[49]

Joined by Mr Trafford and Lord Ilchester, Jennie and Randolph travelled to Canada where they encountered an extraordinary heatwave and, according to Jennie's memoirs, 'seemed to spend most of the time eating melons and having cold baths'.[50] The party journeyed to Niagara Falls and then to Newport. They were fascinated by the seaside town and Jennie remembered that the 'hospitality and kindness shown us by the friends of my family were most gratifying'.[51] It was a balm to their troubled spirits. Few in America knew of or understood the personal crisis that they had been through, and they were able to forget their difficulties back in England and enjoy the sheer exuberance of life in America. Jennie, who had been away for nine years, was delighted to rediscover her childhood haunts and old friends. They spent time in New York with Papa, who also took them to Saratoga Springs to see the races. Jennie noted that the beauty of the ladies and 'gorgeousness' of their dresses astonished the men in their party. It was, however, a very expensive trip, and when Jennie asked her father to remonstrate with their hotel proprietor about the cost, his reply to Leonard was simply:

'The Lord and his wife <u>would</u> have two rooms, hence the expense.'[52] This was the custom for many English aristocrats, but it could lend further evidence to the theory about Randolph's condition and the implications for his marriage. It was also sufficiently remarkable for the hotel owner to have commented upon it.

It was here at Saratoga that Randolph received the draft of a formal apology to the Prince that he was expected to sign, in order to finish the affair. Randolph reluctantly signed the apology, negotiated by the Lord Chancellor, but could not resist adding his own handwritten postscript: 'Lord R. Churchill having already tendered an Apology to H.R.H. the Pr. of W. for the part taken by him in recent events, feels that, as a Gentleman, he is bound to accept the words of the Lord Chancellor for that Apology. Randolph S. Churchill.'[53] His stinging words infuriated the Prince, and it was years before he received Randolph again.

Leonard had the advantage of distance, and his view was to take these things far less seriously. He asked his brother and partner Lawrence Jerome – Jennie's 'Uncle Larry' – to take the Churchills to the Centennial Fair in Philadelphia. Uncle Larry was a wit and great raconteur and, under Leonard's strict instructions, he kept them all amused and gay. Jennie and her husband had a marvellous time, returning to England 'invigorated and refreshed'.[54]

Upon their arrival, they found that the duke had accepted an appointment of Viceroy to Ireland, a position he had previously refused. Now, given the changed circumstances of his sons' disgrace and an inevitable awkwardness in his previously warm relations with the Queen, he was happy to accept the post. It involved a huge expense that he could ill afford. Carrying out the duties correctly would cost him £40,000 (£2.8 million in today's money) per year on a salary of only £20,000 (£1.4 million) and he had to sell more art treasures to pay for his years as viceroy. But the duke believed that he should take this opportunity in order to save his family from further embarrassment. Blenheim Palace was closed except to caretakers, and the entire household moved to Dublin. 'Not being in favour with the Court, from which London society took its lead,' Jennie later recorded, 'we were nothing loath to go.'[55]

Randolph was to act as unpaid private secretary to his father, a role that did not conflict with his parliamentary responsibilities. Before moving, Jennie took a trip to Paris to see her family. From there she wrote nightly to Randolph, describing how she looked after 'Baby' (Winston, now aged eighteen months), went to church, and was reading *Macbeth*. She missed him, she complained, she was lonely without him, and she worried about his health. She wrote reproachfully: 'Darling, I shall never forgive you if this is true – ill & never let me know anything about it & me amusing myself all this time – instead of being with you.'[56]

Later that year, in December 1876, the family made a splendid entrance to Dublin – Randolph and Jennie riding in a carriage with Baby Winston between them. This state entry took place with full military display and viceregal etiquette. The duke in uniform rode surrounded by a glittering staff, and the rest of the family followed in carriages with postillions and outriders. Following this pomp and ceremony, the young Churchills moved into The Little Lodge, set in the magnificent 1,700-acre Phoenix Park, only a few minutes' walk from Viceregal Lodge, the home of the Viceroy. They quickly settled into a life of constant entertaining with the duke and duchess and, for amusement, hunting. Jennie still loved to ride and was very fond of hunting.

She found she liked Ireland, but Randolph spent little time there. The couple's frequent and lengthy separations took their toll on the marriage. Jennie kept herself occupied; she went sailing on the lakes of Killarney and on the loughs; she enjoyed trout fishing in the west of the country, in Galway and in remote Connemara, famed for its rugged beauty. She went snipe shooting at Lord Sligo's residence in Westport and spent weekends at Lord Portarlington's home near Emo. The riding terrain was superb – wild woods, open fields, green meadows – and the many men who accompanied her were handsome and witty. Jennie wrote later that she could not 'remember meeting one really dull man'.[57] Randolph spent increasingly large amounts of time in London, becoming more actively involved in politics, although his record of speaking in Parliament was still very poor. In his almost constant absences Jennie was never short of company. She was twenty-three and looked fabulous. The handsome Lord D'Abernon, an international and very successful banker in Turkey and later ambassador to Berlin, was immediately struck by her radiance:

> I have the clearest recollection of seeing her for the first time. It was at the Viceregal Lodge at Dublin. She stood on one side, to the left of the entrance. The Viceroy was on a dais at the farther end of the room surrounded by a brilliant staff, but eyes were not turned on him or his consort, but on a dark, lithe figure, standing somewhat apart and appearing to be of another texture to those around her, radiant, trans-lucent, intense. A diamond star in her hair, her favourite ornament – its lustre dimmed by the flashing glory of her eyes. More of the panther than of the woman in her look, but with a cultivated intelligence unknown to the jungle … Her desire to please, her delight in life and the genuine wish that all should share her joyous faith in it, made her the centre of a devoted circle.[58]

Many years later, when her son Winston wrote his memoirs, he added to this quotation: 'My mother made the same brilliant impression upon my childhood's eye. She shone for me like the Evening Star. I loved her dearly – but at a distance.'[59]

Lord D'Abernon became an intimate friend, and Jennie, who sparkled with vivacity and good humour, had many such close friend-ships with attractive men. During her three years in Ireland she was frequently left to her own devices. If Randolph had in fact contracted syphilis early on in their marriage, it would explain his complaisant attitude toward her male friendships during this period. Jennie was careful. She wrote to Randolph, apologizing when the young and handsome Lord Rossmore indiscreetly called upon her at home:

> I hope you wont [sic] be angry to hear that Rossmore called here today
> – & that I saw him quite by mistake – I was annoyed because it was

luncheon time & I had ordered next to nothing – besides being in the
midst of my accounts – He did not stay long as I had ordered the
carriage at 3 – I told him he must not call here any more as living alone
I cd not receive any gentlemen & cld not make an exception for him.[60]

In August 1881, Randolph wrote to reproach Jennie for a lack of
discretion; he had opened a letter from the French aristocrat the
Marquis de Castellane, a friend of Jennie's, which he had found offen-
sive. He wrote to her, telling her that he had sent Castellane, 'a little
blackguard', a reply, adding: 'But I really do think my darling you ought
to be more careful in yr manner to men, who are always too ready to
take a liberty. I have such confidence in you that I never bother you, but
these kind of things are very annoying & vexatious.'[61] It is likely, as many
historians believe, that Jennie was having liaisons with these men in
Randolph's absence. Randolph wrote frequently from London, but his
letters were mostly about politics. His letters to the duchess were more
affectionate; the increasingly distant relationship between husband and
wife strengthened his emotional tie to his mother, who was pleased to
see the previous order of things restored. As a result, Jennie's relationship with Randolph's mother improved, which was also partly due to
Jennie's assistance with the Famine Fund, established by the duchess to
alleviate some of the terrible suffering caused by the failure of the
potato crop in 1877. As part of the effort, both Jennie and Randolph
toured almost every county in Ireland. They were appalled at the
misery, the starvation of peasants 'who lived in their wretched mud-
hovels more like animals than human beings'.[62]

Randolph was deeply moved by this experience and became a
champion for improved British understanding of the Irish question.
Without the support of his father, who strongly disapproved, he
espoused the idea of increased independence for Ireland. In fact,
Randolph became one of the very few Members of Parliament who
learned first hand about the problems of Irish conditions. Although it is
hard to believe, Prime Minister Disraeli never visited the island at all,
and former Prime Minister William Gladstone did so only once. This

lack of understanding at senior political levels in Westminster could explain to some degree how Ireland came to play an increasingly troubled and troublesome role in the British Empire.

Jennie and Randolph agreed on the Irish question, but otherwise grew farther apart. Randolph spent more time away, and his visits to London were of longer duration. Even when he travelled to Ireland, he frequently left Jennie in Dublin while he visited friends for shooting breaks and made trips to Mallow for fishing. He wrote to her from Portarlington in January 1879, telling her of a big house party there.[63] Jennie found companionship elsewhere. Her second son was born on 4 February 1880 and was christened John Strange Spencer-Churchill. A close friend, Lieutenant-Colonel John Strange Jocelyn, the third son of the 3rd Earl of Roden, was asked to be godfather. Most historians believe that this second child (known as Jack) was not in fact Randolph's son,[64] and that the Dublin-based Colonel Jocelyn, although thirty years Jennie's senior, was the most likely father, although this has never been confirmed. Randolph does not seem to have taken particular notice of John, but there is no evidence that he treated him any differently to Winston, with whom he was equally distant.[65] The two boys were, however, exceptionally close and enjoyed a warm and happy relationship throughout their lives. Both absolutely adored their mother.

If Jennie was separated from Randolph, she could rely on having her sisters' company. Clara, still unmarried and delighting in the pleasures of being proposed to, made frequent visits to Dublin to be with her glamorous sister. Mrs Jerome still hoped for a wealthy suitor for her eldest daughter. Jennie wrote to Randolph during one of her visits to Paris that the Prince de Clermont-Tonnerre was pursuing Clara, 'but Mama told me it cld never come to anything *car il n'a pas de sous!* [he has no money] – which is a bad *défaut* [fault] – I am sorry – as really it would be such a good thing if she cld get married.'[66] Clara thoroughly enjoyed the parties, the riding, and the outings, although she was disappointed at missing the delights of the London social set. Leonie also paid a visit for the season in 1878, after a year of intensive piano training in Paris and before she returned to New York. She was now nineteen and old enough to attend formal balls. It was at a glittering party in Dublin Castle that she first met the young Anglo-Irish officer, Jack Leslie, of Glaslough in County Monaghan. According to Leonie and Jack's granddaughter Anita Leslie, the blue-eyed guardsman, son of the baronet Sir John Leslie, was much taken with quietly charming Leonie and told her he would like to make her his bride. The proposal was dismissed out of hand by the young lady, who had only just come out and was preparing to enjoy her long-awaited first season.

In 1880, Disraeli was defeated at a general election, and Gladstone became prime minister for the second time. The duke was called to give up the viceroyalty, and the entire family returned home. Randolph was pleased to be in Opposition – attacking the party in power was far more suited to his instinctively pugnacious approach. He had become increasingly interested in the cut and thrust of his political life and threw himself wholeheartedly into a career that had begun merely as a job in order to please his parents so that he could marry. He and Jennie, with the two children and the indispensable Mrs Everest, cook, and servants moved into a fine London house in fashionable St James's Place. Randolph busied himself in Parliament, meeting his political colleagues, whilst Jennie tried to reintegrate into London society after a three-year absence. Although Mrs Everest was still in charge of the nursery, Jennie was finding six-year-old Winston 'a most difficult child to manage'.[67] On the very rare occasion that she did take over, when, for example, Mrs Everest had a much-needed and very occasional holiday, minding the boy was a real chore. On one such night, he could not sleep and insisted that his mother stay up all night, playing 'Pirates and Indians' with him. Young Winston was already developing a reputation within his family as a very high-spirited and rather difficult child.

Jennie's main concerns, however, were social. She was alone in London, without the company of her sisters. Both Clara and Leonie had left for America, where they joined Papa in New York. Mama had moved there, too, so the family were once again together. Although

Clara especially was unhappy living in America, funds were low and Leonard could not afford the upkeep of so many establishments. He was no longer a millionaire, although he would not refute this description, and he continued to hope his luck would turn, when he could once again make another fortune. His investments had never fully recovered from the New York Stock Exchange crash of 1873. However, Leonard no longer wished to take the big risks of yesteryear and now made more prudent investments. It was time for the family to retrench, so the two girls and their parents made the best of things in New York, where Papa could still afford their house, with its expansive stables and private theatre. He had also reserved a private fortune for his wife, which gave her independent means throughout her life. The Jeromes continued to live in a grand style, and Leonie was able to make her debut (albeit in New York), but Clara, who was nine years older, was disappointed by the turn of events. Allen Andrews, biographer of her future husband Moreton Frewen, claimed that Clara 'hated the change'.[68] Although she longed for the day when she could return to England, Papa was delighted to have his remaining family around him. He was hopeful that at least one of his daughters would marry an American and settle in their native country.

Mrs Jerome still dreamed of marrying Clara to a duke. She discouraged her eldest daughter from accepting any of the suitors who flocked at this beautiful girl's feet. Clara spent so long turning men down that it seemed to her the courting would go on for ever. She was dejected at the change in Jennie's fortunes, as she had once revelled in England's high society. She had thoroughly enjoyed her season in London, where she had had many admirers, including Randolph's friend, Oliver Montagu (who famously, and chastely, admired Princess Alexandra). 'Oliver felt [*sic*] so fine with his uniform on,' she had written to Mama in Paris in 1875. 'He has been so kind and nice to me and I hear he goes about telling everyone how nice I am!'[69] At a ball given by the Prince of Wales, Clara had reported that Lord Carrington and the Comte de Vogüé 'were my two particular cavaliers and I never enjoyed a dance so much'.[70] There had been races, and an invitation from the Russian Ambassador to join him at a dinner with the Prince and Princess of Wales. At a ball given by the Duchess of Westminster, Clara had written to her mother that the 'Prince was very good to me and asked me for a dance and I think it was because I looked well, as everyone told me my dress was so pretty'.[71] There were other admirers such as Carrington, Montagu, Vogüé, and Boni de Castellane. Clara had become quite accustomed to all the admiration, which had made her somewhat blasé, as this letter to her mother regarding Sir William Gordon-Cumming's attentions illustrates:

> Jennie wants me so much to be nice to Sir William Gordon-Cumming and wants him to make up to me. I think *entre nous* [between us] that it would take very little to make him devoted to me, although he is a young man who never speaks to a young girl and only flirts with married ladies. He began very *sérieusement à faire la cour* [seriously flirt] to Jennie but last night he would not leave me at the Ball, but I could not think of him at all as he is very very poor and awfully conceited and not *sympathique* [appealing]. I don't think I could really like a man like that ... He really bores me.[72]

When Clara had left London after her second season in 1875, there was every reason to expect another round of social triumphs the following summer. But now, instead of being received everywhere and fêted by the Prince of Wales, she had discovered that without Jennie she was no one, and no doors in London were open to her in her own right. With the exception of a short visit to Jennie in 1876, when they went out little, she stayed with Mama in Paris and returned to New York the following year, in 1877. Mrs Jerome had grown tired of waiting for a big European marriage, although she had never considered any of Clara's suitors acceptable. She had also become bored with chaperoning: 'So dull to listen to young people, but even duller to not quite be able to hear.'[73]

In 1879, Clara travelled with Leonie to London, where Jennie joined them on a rare trip from Dublin. Together, they attended Bizet's new opera *Carmen* sung by their father's protégée (and possible daughter)

Minnie Hauk. Minnie had rehearsed the role by singing it to Leonard in New York and wrote to thank him: 'I longed so to thank you with viva voce for your more than friendly interest and advice given to me as from a father to a daughter.'[74] After this short trip, Clara and Leonie returned home to their parents in New York, where Clara, now twenty-eight and a fading hope in the marriage market, continued to wait for a proposal she was prepared to accept.

CHAPTER FIVE

The Wild West

In London, Jennie hoped that after their absence in Ireland the Prince might have rescinded his ban on their company. She wrote to Clara and Leonie that a speech made by Randolph had pleased the Prince: 'I'm told that Tumtum [the Prince of Wales] expresses himself highly pleased and the result is that we have been asked to meet both him and the Princess tomorrow, at a dance Lord Fife is to give.'[1] It was not to be, however. At the party, the Prince had smiled at Jennie, his old favourite, but refused to forgive Randolph. In July 1880, Jennie wrote to her mother that they were still not being invited to the most important balls. That year, Randolph was much occupied by politics; with his friends Arthur Balfour (later to be prime minister), Sir Henry Drummond Wolff, and John Gorst, he founded the 'Fourth Party' – the other three being the Conservatives, the Liberals, and the Irish. The Fourth Party planned to campaign for 'Tory democracy', that is, reform of the Conservative Party and a stronger opposition to Liberal Prime Minister Gladstone's second administration. During evenings at the Churchills' home, the four of them, observed avidly by Jennie, hatched plots and planned schemes to thwart Gladstone's government by obstructing legislation with clever delaying tactics. Within a few months, Randolph went from being a relative unknown in the House to an important political figure.

Jennie was captivated by the intrigue; she and other high society ladies took to crowding into the Ladies' Gallery at the House of Commons. This small gallery, or 'parliamentary cage' as it was called, might be filled with fifty women, crammed into a small dark space to hear the speeches and follow the debates. Not all of the ladies were quite so enthralled by the actual order of business as Jennie. She described how the thread of many an interesting address would be lost by the coming and going of restless spectators, or by the distraction of their idle chatter. Jennie found that she loved politics. It was a source of rapprochement between her and Randolph. Although he was clever and spoke brilliantly, he suffered from nerves, and Jennie was able to steady his more feverish and misguided impulses. Randolph's greatest shortcoming was his unpredictability; he was prone to sudden fits of fury, and his sharp tongue could lash out at an unsuspecting victim. He was unstable, not an advantageous quality for an ambitious politician. Jennie was a balancing influence, steady and self-confident. She wrote to her mother in the spring of 1881: 'You will be glad to hear that R. has been covering himself with glory and I'm told he has made himself a wonderfully good position in the House.'[2]

While Jennie was helping Randolph in his career, Clara was still fending off suitors in New York. She was considering an offer from Lord Essex when, in late 1879, she met the charismatic and dashingly handsome Englishman Moreton Frewen. Twenty-six, two years her junior, he had a deserved reputation as one of the best gentleman riders in England. He was clever, good-looking, a superb sportsman, and tremendous fun. Clara was immediately beguiled by the breezy charmer, and Moreton, nicknamed 'Silvertongue', swept her off her feet. She was not, he declared, to marry anyone but him. He had just spent a year driving cattle in Colorado and told her vivid stories of the Wild West. Moreton had exciting tales to tell and ambitious plans, but like Randolph he was a younger son with no fortune. Clara was attracted but not prepared to accept his attentions. She and her parents knew that Moreton had no money. When he left New York to return to England, he would write often, addressing his letters to 'Clare', one of his pet names for her. He was in love and longed to hear from her.

When she finally wrote back, her replies were not encouraging. He wrote again at the end of 1879, thankful for her news and refusing to be despondent: 'God bless you. I was beginning to think that you would not write to me at all. Dear, there is a twist in life's skein which I cannot unravel. Let me leave it to fate to decide.'[3] When still she would not yield to his entreaties, he pressed further. 'Rather a sad year it seems to me,' he wrote in reply to Clara's New Year wishes in 1880, 'and whether happier or less happy for your greetings I hardly know.' Moreton was well aware that his prospects were not enough for her:

> Do you know that I am but as a child with you; and that if it be necessary you must find strength for both. But don't write and say you <u>have</u> and that you <u>can</u>. I can better hear it from your own lips. It is not that I don't know full well it is ridiculous. I <u>do</u> know it; and I know it is even unmanly to urge upon you this sacrifice. If things were as they might be, you might give your future into my hands and be at rest. But my love is madness and I know you think so.[4]

He continued to ply his suit, declaring that she 'must not think this is a fleeting fancy of mine. I know that my past has been chequered and that you have a right to doubt me; that I have every reason to doubt myself ... only you will believe, won't you?'[5] Clara gave him scant encouragement and wrote little. In March 1880, he sailed for America. Upon his arrival, she gave him the disappointing news that she herself was to sail for England, to join Jennie and Randolph. On his arrival in New York, Moreton had to leave immediately for the West to consolidate his cattle ranching business, which was the only way he could make the fortune required to win Clara's hand.

Mama was opposed to the courtship, although Moreton's family was one of the oldest in England, and he was supremely well connected. His friendship with the Prince of Wales mollified her somewhat, but in the end it was Leonard's championship of his cause that convinced Mrs Jerome. Leonard recognized something of himself in the stylish, swaggering buccaneer with the silver tongue and ambitious plans. His dreamy eldest daughter needed just this – a bold knight to carry her off to his castle. That the castle was in a remote cattle station hundreds of miles from the nearest outpost was a trifling detail. Moreton pursued Clara with a ferocious determination and, for once, Mama's disapproval proved no barrier.

Moreton did not mind that Mrs Jerome did not approve of him; he disliked her, calling her 'Sitting Bull' behind her back because 'she looked like a hatchet-faced squaw, and she never got up during my courting visits'.[6] Jennie, too, disapproved of Clara's choice. In her view, Moreton, with no money of his own, could not offer Clara the security she needed and she let her feelings be known. Clara, however, had suffered as a result of the Churchills' social exclusion and felt that her opportunities for a glorious marriage were fading away. Moreton understood the family's concerns and wrote a shrewdly judged letter to 'Lady Randolph': 'For fear you may think me ungracious enough to bear malice, let me write you a few lines to say how right and reasonable you were to oppose Clara's selection. I should have thought you a careless sister indeed had you done otherwise. Still, I am not inclined to admit that she is doing a foolish thing.'[7]

Moreton was best known for his attentions to beautiful women (the legendary beauty, Lily Langtry, was one of his paramours) and for his hunting prowess. In 1878 two packs of hounds had asked for his services as Master of Foxhounds, a great achievement. In high-society England in the 1880s, hunting was an important social pursuit. Organized fox-hunting had its origins in the seventeenth century, when it took place by moonlight. In the 1750s, Hugo Meynell, son of a Derbyshire squire, established himself at Quorn Hall, Quorndon, in Leicestershire, where he set the precedent for a new type of fox-hunting that was carried out by day. He inaugurated the winter hunting season and became Master of the famous Quorn Hunt. Soon, fashionable high society was hunting with him, and fox-hunting became, along with the Grand Tour, an essential part of an English gentleman's education. By the 1870s it had assumed its place on the calendar of every country house. Serious funds were required to take part: one stable lad was needed for every two horses, in addition to grooms and second horsemen. A hunting yard usually serviced at least ten horses, and at a large stable (such as that of the Duke of Beaufort at Badminton) the number of mounts could run to sixty or seventy. In the 1880s and 1890s many aristocrats had to sell their packs of hounds or, indeed, give up hunting altogether to save the expense.[8]

The Master of Foxhounds had absolute authority in the hunt and was a significant figure in the local community. Melton Mowbray in Leicestershire was the hunting centre of England; the terrain was ideal and it was within hacking distance of three hunts – the Quorn, the Belvoir, and the Cottesmore. From 1800 onwards, Melton became a key hunting location, and enthusiasts spent the hunting season – from November to April – there.

Moreton belonged to an old and distinguished family of the Sussex landed gentry. He was a well-regarded figure at Melton, riding in races as well as hunting. As a younger son, however, he did not have access to the family fortune and, three years after he had finished his studies at Cambridge, funds ran very short indeed. A gambling man, Moreton staked all that was left of his small inheritance on a two-horse race – the Doncaster Cup. If he won, he would spend a year or two as Master of the Kilkenny Hounds, a post that had been offered to him – and that would have been a great honour. If he lost, he would seek his fortune in America. Luck was not with him. Moreton watched the race on 13 September 1878 with feigned unconcern (showing his consternation would have been considered very poor form) while mentally preparing to leave for the American West. 'The dear, handsome little horse ran most gamely, but in the last hundred yards tired under the weight and just failed to get home,' he wrote in his memoirs, adding: 'So America was under the lee, and I felt quite excited and bucked up. I went to the weighing room, shook Archer's hand [the jockey], and I looked and indeed felt so happy he never dreamed I was a heavy loser by the pretty race.'[9] He sold his stable of hunters, and gave his park hack, Redskin, as a departing gift to Mrs Langtry, who rode it along London's fashionable Rotten Row with the Prince of Wales. After first borrowing some money, Moreton convinced his older brother, Dick, to join the enterprise and invest his patrimony in a permanent settlement on a cattle range in Wyoming. Four friends also decided to join the pair, to shoot big game.

After a journey through mountainous Indian country, buffeted by severe weather, the brothers settled on a site in the Powder River Valley, 200 miles from the nearest rail point at Rock Creek, north-west of Laramie. Moreton travelled south to Cheyenne to recruit labour to build their home and to let people know that there were cattle deals to be struck with the Frewen brothers. He then set out once again for Cheyenne, from where he was to travel to New York to arrange further finance for the ranching business. He left at the end of February 1879. When his horse went lame after travelling thirty miles through deep snow, he continued on foot. 'I was wonderfully well after five months of such conditioning as I had gone through, lean and hard and tough as pinwire,' he recollected. 'A forty-mile walk to Rock Creek Station! What was forty miles to me?'[10] This twenty-six-hour journey, with no rest, across mountains and through snowdrifts, became local legend. Moreton recounted the tale at the elite Cheyenne Club, the social and political headquarters of the Wyoming stockmen, and was elected a member. These adventures were spun into thrilling yarns with which he charmed and seduced the ethereal Clara.

Moreton was charismatic, talented, full of self-belief – and persuasive. Before leaving New York for London later that year to raise capital for his cattle venture, he wrote breathlessly to Clara:

My dearest

'Goodbye', you say 'don't hope', but I cannot must not believe that what is to me a great shining light can be quite impossible quite forbidden. Darling can it be for nothing that a love has entered into all my life which makes the future so bright, so full of peace. Don't say so, at least let me believe while away from you in these dear possibilities, it will be time enough to undeceive me on my return to you, my own: I <u>will not</u> believe it 'too late', give back to me as you and you only can, all my youth, my energy, & my purpose. Darling may we not take the field together & make of life's battle a very happy campaign. Only whatever the future has prepared for us both, I at least shall never forget the bright and beautiful vista your love has opened to me.'[11]

Clara hesitated nevertheless. She was now nearly twenty-nine and, although still lovely, she was no longer young. As she still wanted a way back to England's high society, Moreton's familiarity with English aristocracy was appealing, even though he had no fortune. Clara, as much of a snob as her mother, had reservations that Moreton's future was not in stylish London, but in the American West. And although his family were well known and well connected, there was no title. Reluctantly Clara decided against the match. She went to the dockside to tell him that it was goodbye as she accompanied the departing Leonie, who was to visit Jennie in England and had booked passage on the same ship as Moreton. On the quay, he begged her to change her mind, stressing his determination to use his time in England to raise cash for the ranching venture. He returned to Wyoming later in 1880, and he and his brother bought their first herd with the funds he had successfully raised, which they ran from their settlement at Powder River. There they built the first two-storey, log-cabin ranch house in the West. Moreton called it Big Horn Ranche and it was renamed Home Ranche by the Frewens a short time later, but to the American cowboys it was always known as Frewen Castle.

Moreton travelled frequently to London, trying to raise capital, and still pined for Clara's love. In December 1880, he visited New York from Wyoming to call on Clara, who had herself just returned from a trip to England. He asked her to marry him. She finally accepted, to the delight of her father, who declared: 'I don't wonder you are in love with him. I am in love with him myself.'[12] On Friday, 3 December, Clara wrote: 'Unspeakable happiness. Moreton came at 11 and stayed with us all day till 5. Came back to dine. Mama and Leonie go off to Opera giving us our first evening to ourselves.' A few days later, on 8 December, Clara recorded: 'Such a darling he is. I'm too happy, too proud.'[13]

Around the time of Clara's wedding, Leonie, aged twenty-two, was experiencing her own difficulties in love.[14] She was known as the '*chic,* graceful, but not particularly pretty younger sister of a famous beauty' who had to 'overcome her own sensitivity to comparison' and was very lively socially.[15] In 1879, while Leonie was visiting Jennie in London, Moreton had introduced her to Charlie Fitzwilliam, a younger son of the British peer, Earl Fitzwilliam of Wentworth Woodhouse. He fell madly in love with her. Leonie spent a good deal of time with him and her letters to Mama were full of Charlie's doings. He gave a dance in her honour: 'Of course this dance has added to the report of my engagement to Fitzwilliam – but I can't help it. I can't deny myself all pleasure for fear of having my name coupled with his.'[16] She and Jennie went together with him to the races, to lunches, and to parties; after dinner, Leonie would sing and play the piano. She wrote to her mother: 'I cannot tell you what a nice man Mr. Fitzwilliam is. He is so full of spirits – we laugh the whole time.'[17] Charlie Fitzwilliam, however, had no money and Leonie was no heiress. His family disapproved of the match, and his father threatened to cut off his allowance unless he ended it. He and Leonie continued to correspond after she returned to New York, but by May 1881, eighteen months later, it was clear that the romance was doomed.

Clara and Moreton were married on 2 June 1881 at Grace Church. The Gothic structure, topped by a wooden steeple, was originally built in 1809 on the corner of Broadway and Rector Street but was later moved two miles farther uptown to Broadway and East 10th Street. From the moment of its consecration in 1846, Grace Church was attended by New York's Episcopalian elite. It effectively remained the church of the wealthy because, like other New York churches, its pews were bought by parishioners. This sale was not only a fund-raiser for the church but also served as a means of keeping a distance between the poor and the rich. Members of New York's wealthiest families considered pews a form of real property, which could be sold or transferred with the approval of the vestry. Old New York families, such as the Schermerhorns, the Roosevelts, the Livingstons, the Van Burens, and the Van Rensselaers were all pew-holders at Grace Church, making it the venue of choice for a society wedding.

It was a grand occasion: Clara wore white lace heavy with orange blossom, and was a quarter of an hour late. Moreton waited for her with his best man, Lord Bagot, who had come down from Canada, where he was serving on the staff of the governor-general in Ottawa. The previous day was Derby Day in England and, that morning at the Union Club in New York, Moreton had met his friend and fellow racing enthusiast Pierre Lorillard, who had sent over his horse, Iroquois, to run in the race. They had ordered champagne as soon as the ticker tape had spelled out Iroquois' victory, and Moreton still made it to the church on time for the ceremony. Clara was radiant in her thirty-diamond necklace, a present from Papa and her only dowry, for Moreton did not ask for a financial settlement from his future father-in-law, whom he considered a true friend. After the ceremony, a reception was held at the Jerome home on Madison Square. Moreton then helped Clara to pack her many trunks and they set off for their new life out west. With them went a French maid, Marie. Clara might be going to live in wild, untamed country but she had to have a maid with her – to button up her boots.

Throughout 1881, Charlie continued to hope that Leonie would agree to marry him. In October 1881, he wrote of his continuing love: 'Darling Kismet – one line just as you start to wish you till we meet again every happiness & every comfort it is possible to have. I do feel so very deeply for you.'[18] By January 1882, he despaired at their situation. At the same time, Leonie was being pursued by Freddie Gebhard, the son of one of Leonard's wealthy friends. Leonard approved of Freddie, who was an amusing playboy, but Leonie found his continual high spirits trying. One day she told her parents: 'If I hear Freddie crow like a rooster again, I shall go mad'.[19] Leonard soon gave up trying to persuade her to accept him. The difficulty was that Leonie could not marry Charlie either – he had no money, and his family were set against the match. There seemed no future for them, but Charlie, consumed by his hopeless love for her, wrote desperately:

do but let me come to you, and prove by my devotion and love that I

have nothing but the tenderest possible regard and affection for you ...
I know well what you have had to contend against you have wanted to
please your Father your Mother yourself and me all at the same time.
I do wish most sincerely I had come out, for you say that if we had
married you would have been happier than you now are ... Why
should we both be miserable ... oh my darling <u>do do</u> let us be happy
together be my kismet again who I love with my whole heart and
soul.[20]

She refused, however, and by May of that year he was resigned to the
inevitable. Heartbroken and without funds, he agreed to his father's
wishes and made preparations to leave for India where he might start a
new life. Leonie must have known there was no Jerome fortune left for
her. A man who offered her marriage would have to do so for love
alone and might have to make sacrifices. Charlie was willing to take the
risk, but she could not face his family's disapproval, and he understood,
writing in farewell: 'should you at any time regret what has passed
between us, you must on no account be influenced by any promise you
may now consider you have made to me.' Having released her from any
commitment she might have made, he went on to tell her that his
opinion of her would always be high. He concluded: 'How I regret
having brought trouble upon you and your's, no words can express.' His
departure for India was not a 'very cheery prospect'; however, he saw
no other chance of 'inducing my Father to look at things in the same
light as I do and my most earnest wish is to do that which is
straightforward and honourable by you'.[21]

Leonie wrote poignantly of her difficulties and their resolution, and
of her subsequent trust in Divine Providence:

But happiness is not possible here, <u>it cannot last</u>. Even my short
experience has taught it to me. We are put on this earth to perfect
ourselves – & surely trouble does good to many. Mine have hardly
begun. This last year is the first I have been old enough to realize <u>life</u>
its meaning, its import. This last year is the first I have had trouble, and
still if I could live the year over – & have power to change

circumstances – could I do so for better? Had I found as I grew old enough to understand the world, society as pleasant as I had fancied, had all my dreams been realized would I not have soon found my heart too much attached to the things of this world. Would I ever have been willing to part with it? Oh no! Things are better as they are. The mortifications I went through humbled my pride … I am a better girl than I was. The Almighty saved me from being a vain frivolous pleasure seeking woman.[22]

After Clara's marriage, Leonie remained at home in New York with her parents, although she travelled each year to visit Jennie in London.

Her sister had thrown herself into politics and love affairs. Randolph was often unwell, and his unpredictable fits of temper had alienated many of his political colleagues and friends. As his illness became more debilitating, he was increasingly subject to intense nervous strain. This in turn brought on headaches and bad temper. He insisted on spending more time at Blenheim, the home of his youth, much to his mother's delight and to Jennie's chagrin. She wrote to her mother during a miserable winter spent at Blenheim Palace in 1881:

I quite forget what it is like to be with people who love me. I do so long sometimes to have someone to whom I could go and talk. Of course, Randolph is awfully good to me and always takes my part in everything, but how can I always be abusing his mother to him, when she is devoted to him and would do anything for him – The fact is I loathe living here. It's not on account of its dullness, that I don't mind, but it is gall and wormwood to me to accept anything or to be living on anyone I hate. It is no use disguising it, the Duchess hates me simply for what I am – perhaps a little prettier and more attractive than her daughters. Everything I do or say or wear is found fault with. We are always scrupulously polite to each other, but it is rather like a volcano, ready to burst out at any moment.[23]

In 1883, they moved into a larger house at 2 Connaught Place, and Randolph's political career was on the rise again. Jennie was occupied with furnishing their new home. She enjoyed decorating and wrote in

1908 of how she took pleasure in 'disposing in the new house what my brother-in-law Blandford used to call my "stage properties"'.

> In a former house which we had bought shortly after our marriage I had, in my ignorance of the climate, covered the walls with silks and stuffs, and nearly cried with dismay when I saw the havoc wrought upon them by the fogs and smuts of the dirtiest of towns [London]. My dearly bought experience stood me in good stead when furnishing again. The panelling and clean white paint, which is so popular today, formed the principal decoration of our next dwelling, which, by the way, was the first private house in London to have electric lights. We had a small dynamo placed in a cellar underneath the street, and the noise of it greatly excited all the horses as they approached our door. The light was such an innovation that much curiosity and interest were evinced to see it, and people used to ask for permission to come to the house.

The electric light was not, however, without problems. 'I remember the fiasco of a first dinner-party we gave to show it off,' Jennie continued; 'when the light went out in the middle of the feast, just as we were expatiating on its beauties, our guest having to remain in utter darkness until the lamps and candles, which had been relegated to the lower regions, were unearthed.' There was a further drawback, as Jennie explained: 'Randolph, having spoken enthusiastically in the House of Commons in favour of an Electric Lighting Bill, felt he could no longer accept the gift of the installation which by way of an advertisement a company had offered to put into our home free of cost. Unfortunately, there being no contract, we were charged double or treble the price.'[24]

Over the next few years, Randolph and Jennie gradually re-established themselves on the social circuit, with the result that, on 18 March 1884, the Prince and his wife agreed to attend a dinner party at which the Churchills would be present. The Prince had indicated to Sir Henry James, Attorney General, that he would be willing to dine in their company with Mr and Mrs Gladstone as fellow guests. The dinner was a success, and the Prince soon after dined with the Churchills again, in Paris at the Café Anglais, on 2 June. Although the Prince did not enter the Churchills' home until nearly two years later, the reconciliation had taken place. Jennie became a frequent guest at the Prince's country home in Sandringham, often unaccompanied by Randolph. She enjoyed these visits, writing: 'One felt at home at once; indeed, the life was the same as at any pleasant country house … The sport was exceedingly good and well-managed owing to the Prince of Wales, who, an excellent shot himself, took a personal interest in the arrangements instead of leaving them all to the keepers.'[25]

Being part of the Prince's elite group meant following his trends and tastes. When the Prince showed a distinct preference for shorter dinners, they became the norm, and when he allowed cigarettes after dinner rather than the usual cigar, the traditional after-dinner serving of port was replaced by that of brandy, which better complemented the taste of cigarettes. Everything revolved around the Prince, who hated to be alone. If he wanted to go shooting, one of his favourites – Jennie, or the American Consuelo Mandeville (née Yznaga), now Duchess of Manchester, or yet another American favourite, Minnie Paget – would accompany him. Minnie, for instance, always took a house at Cowes during Regatta Week so that he would be sure of a hostess at his disposal. Pleasing royalty was an important part of being a social success. In addition to the Prince of Wales, Jennie was also at this time intimate with Count Charles Kinsky, an Austrian aristocrat. Her affair with him would be one of many, while she continued to see many other men friends as well.

Following her marriage to Moreton, Clara lived a very different kind of life at Frewen Castle in Wyoming, entertaining the many aristocratic visitors who came to enjoy the Wild West. The men would hunt big game with Buffalo Bill, whom Moreton had befriended. Clara had settled into life there and found it agreeable to be the wife of the owner of the largest holding. The house was snug and well furnished, and there were always plenty of guests, including Lord Granville Gordon, Lord Manners, Lord Donoughmore, Lord Mayo, and Sir Samuel and Lady Baker. She was surrounded by respectful men and beautiful open

country. Life was extremely comfortable; they ate well, for there was plenty of fresh meat and fish, as well as game, duck, widgeon, and teal. Tinned soup, fruit, and fresh vegetables were imported at great expense. The small ranchers who had settled around Powder River near the Frewens helped with odd jobs around the house in addition to herding; in return the Frewens provided them with flour, sugar, groceries, and other supplies from the general store. In August, two months after she was married, Clara wrote an ecstatic letter to Leonie:

> This is our _real_ honeymoon! Moreton is the greatest darling *sur terre* [on earth]. But there I won't gush anymore, *c'est si bête* [it's so silly]. You'd love it out here if you were married; for a girl it is too much out of the world, but the air is perfectly delicious and the scenery so beautiful with the snowcapped Big Horn Mountains in the near distance and troops of antelope come by our house going down to the river to drink. Moreton and Dick are going to give me a little 4 wheeled cart to drive a pair of elk they are taming for me. They are nearly as large as good sized ponies which will be great fun for me![26]

The rural idyll seemed complete with news of Clara's pregnancy. At first all went well and she wrote to to Mama in Marienbad, 'Moreton has been having a correspondence with a capital doctor in Cheyenne who says there can no longer be any doubt that I have "des espérances" so I write to you immediately as I know you would be glad to hear.' Clara was not worried about her health, assuring her mother that after the heat of the summer she was 'quite well again' and asking her to purchase 'a few nice little baby clothes', including 'some pretty long dresses and one or two little cashmere shawls ... perhaps at the Bon Marché you would find some very pretty little things'. Even in the wilds of Wyoming, Clara wanted to be nicely dressed. 'I would like you to bring home a pale blue dressing gown to wear while I'm getting well,' she added. 'We all need a pretty new model so Duperries might make it of pure silk or surah trimmed with creamish lace – very simple and palest sky blue.'[27]

Clara became ill, however, three months later, while on a camping trip, and had to hurry back to Home Ranche on horseback. From there Moreton rushed her by coach to Cheyenne for urgent medical care, but along the hard and rocky road Clara lost her baby girl, who was born prematurely. The infant was christened Jasmine and was buried at Frewen Castle. Clara returned to New York to recover at her parents' house. She never returned to Wyoming. Her days as a plucky pioneer with her cattle baron husband were over.

Moreton could not join his wife for some weeks, however, as the winter season had begun and he could not leave his cattle to survive the snows untended. As well as being separated from Clara, he was quarrelling with his brother Dick, who wanted to dissolve the Frewen brothers partnership. That would mean buying him out, which the cash-strapped Moreton was in no position to do. It was to become a depressingly familiar dilemma in Moreton's career: to liquidate and sacrifice potential profits, or to incur fresh debts. He hated being in debt, which depressed him. When the break with Dick came, it developed into a bitter family row that dragged in their other two brothers, Edward and Stephen. Eventually, both lent Moreton money, and Dick accepted a complicated arrangement with Moreton in which repayment was promised immediately and in the future.

Moreton decided that the only way forward was to establish the ranch as a public company to share responsibilities for finance and support. He would run the cattle operation as its manager rather than its owner. Unfortunately, he made this decision before the oncoming boom, with the consequence that although some £10 million (£690 million in today's values) of British capital was invested in Western cattle, Moreton was able to secure only £300,000 (£2 million) in public investment in his Powder River Cattle Company. He went to New York in order to promote the newly formed company to the city's financiers, joining his wife at Leonard Jerome's home in Madison Square. He also planned to travel to London, to raise funds for the company. Although Clara wished to accompany him, he could not afford to take her with him; as a single man, he could stay with other people as a bachelor guest (a money-saving device that Moreton refined over his life into an art form).With Clara, he would be expected to maintain an establishment that he could ill afford. Accepting her exile from London's parties, she asked Jennie and Randolph to receive her husband as their guest in London, so in June 1882, Moreton sailed alone for England. Jennie welcomed him to London society, while Randolph introduced him to his political friends. Moreton worked hard at getting contacts and funding for his Western venture, but he missed Clara. 'Kali sweet, do you love me really?' he wrote in 1882. 'Would you again agree to walk with me through all these rough paths of life's struggle? Would you, darling?'[28]

Clara was enchanted by Moreton's expressions of love for her. He wrote her many letters, declaring his adoration:

> My sweet one
>
> The nights are long and dreary ... But sometimes a dear dream of love and happiness comes to me, and once again I hold you in my arms, and press long lingering kisses on your lips, your neck, your glowing bosom ... There is nothing on earth like the sweet happiness of marriage with Kali, there is no happiness except that.[29]

Notwithstanding his affection, as an exceedingly handsome man he was frequently tempted while away from his Kali. He told her of how he tried to avoid such snares: 'For such love as ours for one another we can never hope to find again, and all mere passion is a wrong against our nature and our religion. I worship my little one. My own dear wife, how I love you.'[30] This stream of devotion kept Clara reasonably content in New York, while in London Moreton managed to assemble an impressive board of directors, led by the Duke of Manchester. The company was well funded, although Moreton was very short of cash and could not therefore pay his personal creditors. He agreed to give his friend, Hugh Lowther (and the future Lord Lonsdale), Powder River shares in return for the £40,000 (£2.8 million in today's money) he had invested with Moreton. This was the first time that Moreton was to use this tactic for 'repaying' debt, and it was one to which he would turn more and more enthusiastically throughout his life. Trading future shares and profits for current liabilities is a short-term solution that can only work successfully if followed by substantial profit-taking later on with remaining shares. Liquidating large amounts of low-priced shares, while a newly formed company is still in its investment phase, was evidence of Moreton's financial desperation, as well as of his poor business judgement, both of which led ultimately to financial disaster.

In this period, Moreton and many of his contemporaries, raised by families who for generations had relied on guaranteed revenue to support their expensive lifestyles, suddenly found that they needed to earn money in ways that required commercial experience. Some members of high society simply married into American wealth, but others turned to the City and joined company boards as figureheads, where their names gave patrician distinction to the firm in exchange for payment or shares. Still others, such as Moreton, looked to opportunities abroad in America, as well as in Australia where profits from mining and land settlement beckoned. In the 1880s a number of companies were formed to colonize western Canada, for example, and had as their board members such figures as the Duke of Manchester, Lord Castletown, and Sir John Lister-Kaye.[31] For some, such as Moreton's friend Lord Lonsdale, these ventures investing in Australia, Canada, and North America were very profitable. Other people were not so fortunate.

Although Moreton thought of himself as a rich man in the making, he faced a number of obstacles. The downturn that swiftly followed the cattle ranching boom affected his business by reducing revenues. In addition, he had obtained the land in Wyoming by 'pioneer's right' at a time when American farmers were beginning to protest against foreign speculators who took American land from American farmers and ranchers in order to make profits that would be exported abroad. Individual homesteaders, supported by political leaders in Congress, began to move onto Moreton's land, building small homesteads. To add to the problem, all over the West small ranchers started quietly branding for themselves the young unbranded yearlings (known as 'mavericks') that were loose on the land, before their rightful owners, the big homesteaders, could get to them all to brand them themselves. Moreton considered this theft and appealed in 1884 to the Wyoming Stock Growers' Association to take action. The Association did so, by passing a law that year that made it illegal to brand unmarked calves. Under this legislation, a budding rancher could be arrested and convicted for engaging in what had been until then an accepted practice. Moreton, as the director of one of the largest cattle companies in Wyoming, was a natural target for those homesteaders who began to unite in opposition to the large cattle concerns. They were supported in this by the Populist Party, which was against foreign ownership of American land.

In support of his commercial interests, Moreton took a firm political stance in the clashes that followed between the large companies and the small homesteaders. He had investments in Wyoming in addition to the Powder River Cattle Company. He owned a number of houses in Cheyenne, where he was considered a property owner of some consequence. He entertained frequently in a self-appointed, quasi-diplomatic capacity and became known in Wyoming as 'Sir Moreton', or 'Lord Frewen'.

When things began to go badly, with harsh winters and difficult political conditions, Moreton fought to save the business. He tried to save money and increase profits by cutting out the middlemen: the fattening farmer and the shipper who exported livestock to Britain. He lobbied to change the law that prohibited the import of live cattle into Britain. He also threatened the monopoly of the Chicago meat packers by attempting to transport his cattle as far north as Duluth, Minnesota, where he could fatten them himself and then transport them east, without having the animals butchered before shipping them to England. As part of his strategy to convince his backers to have confidence in him and supply more money, he took Clara on her long-awaited trip to England in the winter of 1882. It was her first return visit to Europe since she had married, and naturally she stayed with Jennie and Randolph.

The Churchills at this stage were practically living apart (Randolph was in the South of France early in the year), although their relationship was still warm and they relied upon each other for stability and comfort, if not romantic love. Their financial problems, however, had not improved. Jennie wrote to Randolph in January 1883 after she had been ill, explaining that she could not afford to stay with him in Monte Carlo: 'I can't help thinking of the expense & indeed I am more worried than I can say when I think of our money difficulties.' Although she tried not to agonize too much 'for fear of putting myself back',[32] she fretted over their expenses on the London house. Randolph, unmoved, continued travelling with his brother Blandford in the Swiss Alps. Jennie had other worries about the children; she wrote of these, telling Randolph how glad she would be when Winston, then aged nine, returned to his boarding school (where he was absolutely miserable). 'He is so idle,' she complained, '& of course that is conducive to naughtiness & à la longue one can't manage him.' To add to her woes, Mama had asked her to give up her favourite piece of jewellery, the distinctive diamond star:

> I have got something very sad to tell you as far as I am concerned – & that is that Mama has taken away the Diamond Star & how poor I am – have got <u>nothing</u> – of course I cd not refuse to let it go – & she wants to sell it to put the money in Moreton's ranch as she says if anything were to happen to Papa she might have very little to live on. Luckily for me my heart is not set on jewels – but I do feel sorry to have let it go as it was so becoming & the only thing I ever wore.[33]

Mrs Jerome, who was committed to helping Clara, remained close to all her daughters after their marriages and wanted to help them succeed. She wanted Moreton's cattle business to do well too and was prepared to invest in its future.

Meanwhile, Clara and Moreton were confident of *their* prosperous future and were enjoying London. Jennie reported to Mama that the Frewens hosted dinner and luncheon parties every day. Leonie told Jennie that Moreton had paid himself £20,000 (worth £1.4 million today) from the ranch that year. The Frewens were certainly spending money; Clara was once again pregnant, and Moreton set her up in a luxurious house on Chapel Street, just off Park Lane. He hired a brougham and stables, and paid out £1,000 (nearly £70,000 in modern terms) on decorating their new home. Their first child, Hugh Moreton Frewen, was born on 9 October 1883. Moreton was away when the baby arrived; he had gone back to America and was not due to return to London until a few weeks later. Mama had stayed on in London until the end of the summer, and left Jennie with strict instructions to help her sister with the baby. Leonard was unwell and Mrs Jerome wanted to be at his side: 'I think Papa needs me more than anyone, and that I ought to go home for him.'[34]

By this point, Leonie had left New York and gone to stay with Clara at Chapel Street in London, while Jennie was reluctantly obeying Randolph's wish that they spend more time at Blenheim with the duchess. Leonie was happy to be in England with her sisters, the new baby, and Jennie's children. Mrs Jerome, Clara, and Leonie were all very fond of Winston – known irreverently to the household servants as 'Carrot Top' – and as the first-born he was completely indulged. The doting aunts even allowed him to hammer away on their precious pianos.

Leonie was soon drawn into another romance, this time with a shy, good-looking Grenadier guardsman she had met years before in Dublin. In 1883, Jack Leslie, now twenty-six, fell in love all over again with Leonie, now twenty-four. She was not a radiant beauty like her two glamorous sisters but, according to her granddaughter Anita Leslie, she had great charm and impeccable manners. Her conversation was witty yet thoughtful, and her insights delicate and perceptive. Like all the Jerome sisters, she was always superbly attired and, like her sisters, she was an accomplished musician and linguist, who spoke French and German fluently.

Jack Leslie was the only son of an aristocratic Anglo-Irish family with four daughters, but he had no money of his own. A talented artist (like his father before him who had exhibited a painting at the Royal Academy), Jack wanted to pursue an artistic career and, encouraged by Leonie who loved art and music, went to study painting in Paris at the

Académie Julien. There was no question of Leonard Jerome's providing his youngest daughter with a large dowry. He was ill and tired, and he had no fortune left. Mama wrote to Jennie in November 1883 of their 'good luck' in letting the Club House to the University Club, which would take it for ten years. She told Jennie how 'happy and relieved' she and Papa felt, as it would help with the mortgage and the property would then have the same value as when her marriage settlement was made.[35] Jennie's settlement was a financial constraint on the Jeromes, but neither Mama nor Papa begrudged her the money. Leonard and his wife were proud of their daughter and her social success. As Lady Randolph, she was written about in the society magazines, and her movements were reported in the court circular of the London *Times*. Leonard carried her photograph in his pocket and showed it proudly to all his New York acquaintances. Jennie was the star of her family, and the financial settlement that guaranteed her income at £2,000 per annum was a legal requirement, part of a binding contract hammered out by solicitors in 1874. Even when her father's health was at its lowest, Jennie never offered to forgo her income from him. For all her charm and vitality, she was often oblivious to the needs of others.

There was simply not enough money, and Papa could not produce more. Mama was adamant, therefore, that Leonie should marry a rich man. Since Jack Leslie was not wealthy in his own right, she did not wish him to court Leonie. She sternly reminded Jennie that the young man was not to be encouraged to visit Chapel Street. He was 'only a detriment', she wrote, and Jennie must give her sister 'good advice'.[36] Jack and Leonie, however, were in love and determined to marry. Leonie wrote supportive letters to the struggling artist in Paris, towards whom she felt protective:

> Dear You
>
> Another nice letter from you this morning. You seem indeed to be working hard, and I am only afraid you will over do it, and tire yourself too much. I am sure the close air of the atelier is bad for you – do you stay there from 8 o'c till 12? That is such a long time, I should think you would take a walk at 10, just to get a whiff of fresh air. And you naughty

boy, you never told me <u>where</u> the Rue d'Amminale was, or if you walked every morning to the atelier. You <u>must</u> answer my questions as I like to know <u>just exactly</u> what you do. How I wish I could be with you, when you come home tired from work. That is just the time you need me, I am sure, and I would make you so comfortable and let you rest peacefully – dear dear Jack, I really think of you all day long. Do you know that 'some one' told me that your mother is in a dreadful state, and says she will never allow It – and your Father would rather leave the property to <u>anyone</u> else, if you married me! So you must work hard and become a great artist so that we can do as we like – and then we will be so happy we won't care <u>who</u> objects will we? You dear.[37]

Not only did the Leslies vehemently disapprove of their only son and heir's romance with an unknown American, but he also showed no ability to manage his finances and had constant money troubles. This was an area in which Leonie was sure she could contribute. Although she would bring no dowry, she could help him in such matters: 'What an improvident boy you are. And how you do need a practical person to look after you! (the practical person being of course ME).' She could also mother her beloved, fussing over his eyes and his work habits, exhorting him to be careful. And she believed absolutely in his artistic gifts, constantly urging him to apply his 'great talent'. It was, however, a stressful time. 'Suppose you get sick of the whole business,' she wrote anxiously, 'and think after all that an heiress, with a lot of nice horses and a luxurious house, is better than … a tiresome "Merican" who has nothing to offer but her love.'[38]

She sometimes accused Jack, or 'Poupon' as she called him, of being fickle, but he stayed the course and pressed his parents for permission to marry Leonie. She was terrified that hers would discover that she was not welcome in his family and begged him to hide the truth from them. Once again, a Jerome daughter had fallen in love with a man of whom her parents disapproved, and whose own parents did not wish for the match. Like Jennie, Leonie had to exert her energies in order to bring things her way. But unlike Jennie, who stormed and pleaded, Leonie plotted and planned. When she returned home in

August, she reported back to Jack on her parents' reaction to her news:

> Papa did not say much, except that he had hoped I were coming home free & would have settled here. Of course Mamma thinks that when you <u>do</u> come it will be with yr Father's consent, as she said it was a safe match, if I cared for you, though hardly as brilliant a one, as she had expected me to make considering how nice I was! Isn't it nice to be thought as much by one's family? <u>But</u> – of course there is a but – she thought the idea of yr coming out immediately rather sudden. I told them you would perhaps wait till 10th September – but I would rather you would come the 1st. Mamma begged me not to tell anyone – for she said that if there was any difficulty, which yr Father might make at the last moment, we could drop the whole thing, as of course we would have to. So you see I am rather in a dilemma for if I tell them there is the least chance of his <u>not</u> consenting, they will make it very disagreeable for me. We had better leave them under the present impression, & then you must make a <u>desperate</u> struggle to get a consent however ungracious when you come out.

She was nevertheless his, she declared, with or without consent, if he came to get her in September. And Leonie had practical suggestions to overcome the financial challenges they would face. They could stay with Papa and Mama for three weeks after the wedding, she said, as Mama had proposed, in order to get to know the Jeromes and their friends (so economical, Leonie pointed out). In addition, her mother had promised to find £300 or £400 a year for them (£21,000 or £28,000 today) and had also suggested that Leonie and Jack stay a great deal with his family, to save money: 'I did not contradict her, it is <u>our</u> own affair if we choose to marry on nothing – but can you imagine yr mother & me under <u>one</u> roof!'[39] Sadly for Leonie, that is exactly what came to pass, for Jack could not afford a separate household for his bride. But during the summer of 1884, the young lovers still dreamed of a romantic garret in Paris, until Jack's great talent would bring them success.

Mrs Jerome finally accepted Leonie's choice; she wrote to Jennie in

August 1884 to say how happy she was to have both Clara and Leonie 'home' again. She was disappointed that Jennie had not come to New York with them and plaintively pointed out: 'Papa & I see so little of you my dear Jennie that I sometimes fear you will quite forget us.' She hoped that if Leonie settled in England near her sisters, 'I trust it will bring us closer together and that we shall see more of each other than we have in the past.'[40] Of all the girls, Jennie had in every sense moved farthest away from her parents. She was too preoccupied with her own interests to pay much attention to her mother and father, and her life had become so firmly entrenched in upper-class English society that she was in many ways lost to them.

Throughout, however, she never forgot her sisters. She was supportive of Leonie, as was Clara, when they realized how deeply their youngest sister had fallen in love. The older women rallied round, offering every encouragement to the young couple. Although Clara had followed Mama's directive to keep Jack away from Leonie, the young pair had managed to see each other secretly and to write. But once Leonie had declared herself to Jennie and Clara, they agreed to help. As he set off for America without having his father's consent to the marriage, Jack wrote to Jennie, thanking her for her kind letter:

> I start tomorrow full of confidence and obstinacy: for I regret to say my stern parent has said '<u>No</u>' in the most determined manner and further threatens to acquaint Mr. Gerome (as he spells it) that the marriage has neither his approval nor consent. He still thinks it doubtful if I go. I am writing another line to him to assure him I go and show him he is absurdly mistaken in his opinion and finally to implore him that if he must write to your father to spell his venerable name with a J instead of a G! My mama has evidently lost no time to announce her woes as I found the hall table sprinkled profusely with letters to me from Aunts & Uncles fussy & interfering to implore me not to take a step I shall repent of ... In fact it would drive me mad to stay a moment longer. Pa's only argument is that I am to be unhappy with your sister – he is so obstinate. If you could write conciliatory letter to New York I should be so obliged.[41]

He was right to be concerned. Mr and Mrs Jerome assumed that Jack's father, Sir John, *had* given his consent. Indeed, Mama wrote to Jennie that, once Leonie was married, she was sure Jack's family would like her as she was such a 'nice clever kind hearted girl'[42] who would do all she could to make her husband happy. And, as a further sign of her approval, Mama asked Jennie for a diamond star, which she had lent her the previous year, as she had promised it as a wedding gift to Leonie. It was to be her only present to her youngest daughter, and she wanted Leonie to wear it on her wedding day.

The Leslie family were, however, intent on preventing what they viewed as a *mésalliance*. Jack's sister, Olive Guthrie, wrote years later that her parents had been appalled at the match, primarily because they knew so little of Americans. Another problem was that they were dismayed by what they knew of Leonie's elder sister, Jennie (who was only the second American to marry into British society; the first was Lady Ormonde). Lady Constance Leslie had heard that she was 'very gay socially', implying that Jennie was unbecomingly 'fast'. In addition, Lady Constance had been told that Leonie's mother was three-quarters Indian and that Leonie's father was a bus driver (a 'fact' reported by Lady Hillingdon). This, of course, was the real difficulty. Jack had four sisters, and any stigma attached to a family's name (caused, for example, by an unfortunate marriage), could severely hurt their chances in the marriage market, which for many people mattered very much indeed.

The Leslies owned close to 50,000 acres of land, generating revenues of over £21,000. Although their estates – in Counties Monaghan, Donegal, Meath, Down, Cavan, Tyrone, and Fermanagh – were not as large as those of the greatest landowners in Ireland (such as the Earl of Kenmare, who owned 118,000 acres and had an income of £34,000, or, indeed, the Duke of Leinster, with 68,000 acres bringing in £47,000 annually), the Leslie family was one of the largest landowners in Ireland, in the top 300 in Britain in terms of acres, and well within the top 700 in Britain in terms of income.[43] Typical in terms of wealth and distinction, they were proudly descended from a long line of bishops, writers, and bibliophiles, who had come from Scotland to County

Monaghan in the mid-seventeenth century. Such landlord landowners had in the main acquired their property during the colonization of Ireland, when the plantations and subsequent land confiscations of the sixteenth and seventeenth centuries had handed over land to English and Scots settlers, at the expense of the Gaelic Irish inhabitants. In the 1780s these landowners rose from an estimated 5,000 – when they owned 95 per cent of the productive land – to around 9–10,000 in the mid-nineteenth century. By 1876, fewer than 800 landlords owned half the country. They also monopolized local government as JPs, Poor Law Guardians, and grand jurors.[44]

Some families within this elite group, which was not politically homogenous, were strong supporters of the monarchy and all the British institutions at the time. Many, such as the Leslies, were committed equally to Ireland and to high-society London. Others were more resentful of England and English politicians for not understanding their situation in Ireland. Some members of the Anglo-Irish ascendancy, as they are known, including the Leslies, ruled their Irish estates with a benevolent paternalism, visiting their tenants, bringing them food when they were ill, and distributing gifts at Christmas. In return, their servants and farm tenants treated them with deference, although such deference was certainly on the wane by the 1870s.[45] Servants were employed for life and became members of a large extended family. The poor were given food and alms when they knocked at the (back) door. Life for many in Ireland, however, had been severely disrupted by the terrible famines of the mid-nineteenth century, which gave rise to the migration to Britain and America of tens of thousands of starving Irish men, women, and children.

The famines were caused by a number of factors. The end of the Napoleonic wars in Europe in 1815 had had a significant impact on the Irish economy. The conflict had led to a substantial development in tillage farming in order to supply the armies, resulting in a dependence on the potato as a staple food. At the end of the war, there was a switch from tillage to pasture farming, which caused agrarian unemployment, and the problem was exacerbated by the large growth in population, which had reached 8 million by 1841. Two-thirds of that number – over 5 million people – were dependent on agriculture for survival. When the potato crop failed in 1845 due to blight, and then again in 1846, 1847, and 1848, this, combined with the severe weather, produced a disaster of biblical proportions. Hundreds of thousands starved or died of fever. The Leslies, like many of the landowners who actually lived in Ireland and were committed to the people on their estates, did everything in their power to help their tenants. During the crisis, they ran soup kitchens, employed labourers to build unnecessary walls (there are still four and a half miles of high stone walls around the Leslie estate), and did not collect rents from those who could not afford to pay.

Jack Leslie's parents, the 1st Baronet John Leslie and his wife Lady Constance, were the last of this proud breed of Irish landowners who were loyal to the crown and considered themselves British to the core, yet who lived in and profoundly loved Ireland, its people, its landscape, its way of life. The Leslies had a deep attachment to the land they called their own; they lived part of the year in Ireland and the rest in an elegant townhouse in London. Revenue from the agricultural estates was sufficient to support a very prosperous dual existence: a benevolent *noblesse oblige* lifestyle in Ireland as well as a lavish, sophisticated one in cosmopolitan London. For all their benevolence, however, and despite their love of Ireland, the Leslies and other Anglo-Irish families undeniably contributed to the pernicious consequences of such concentrated land ownership, the most significant of which was that the poor of Ireland were kept impoverished by a lack of land.

By the end of the nineteenth century, the revenues from the Irish estates were diminishing and by the time Jack came to inherit, the grand dual existence had disappeared for all but a few families. Between 1878 and 1883, Jack's father, Sir John Leslie, had sold nearly 6,000 acres of land in Counties Meath, Down, and Cavan, which had previously brought in revenues of over £4,000 per annum (£280,000 in modern terms).[46] The erosion of landlords' power came with the Ballot Act of 1872, which enabled tenants to vote at elections in secret. No longer could Lady Constance boycott the shop owner who had voted against

Fortune's Daughters

her husband, as she had done in the past. Land reform began in 1870, and the Land League, which supported tenants' rights, was founded in 1879. Gladstone's 1881 Land Act established the Land Commission, a body to which a tenant could appeal to have his rent fixed for fifteen years. These changes paved the way for land reform. The Wyndham Act of 1903, although perceived by some leading agrarian agitators such as Michael Davitt and John Dillon as favouring the landlord, led to the break-up of the big estates and contributed to the subsequent end of a way of life for Anglo-Irish landed gentry, previously supported by revenue from these estates. The necessity for these reform bills reflects the fact that most Anglo-Irish were not as enlightened as the Leslies, although even they found the new legislation difficult.

Thus at exactly the time that Jack sought to marry his unknown American, his parents hoped that he would marry into his own class, preferably someone wealthy, so that he would perpetuate both lifestyles: on the Irish estate and in London society. The Leslies' most important properties comprised an estate on a lake in Glaslough, County Monaghan, and land (including a shooting-lodge for grouse hunting) on the north coast, in Pettigo, County Donegal. The Pettigo estate was handed down to Sir John Leslie as the younger son; his elder brother took possession of the large Glaslough estates. Sir John later inherited these when his elder brother died in 1870 without issue. Sir John had married Lady Constance Damer, daughter of the Waterloo veteran, Colonel Damer, and Minnie Seymour, the adopted daughter of Mrs Fitzherbert. Mrs Fitzherbert was the first wife of George IV and it is widely believed that these 'adopted' children, including Minnie Seymour, were in fact the children of Mrs Fitzherbert and the King.

Sir John and Constance were prominent members of an artistic and musical set that included Thackeray, Dickens and other luminaries. When Sir John unexpectedly inherited the family seat at Glaslough, he tore down the dilapidated house and built Castle Leslie, with stunning views of the lake. He filled the house with works of art, mainly collected from Italy during his travels. He was given a baronetcy by Disraeli and for £20,000 bought Stratford House in London, off

Oxford Street, where he and Constance gave lavish parties for 500 or more guests.

When Sir John was told that Leonard Jerome was a speculator, he was horrified. He considered it appalling to make money at what he believed was someone else's expense. With these thoughts in mind, Sir John wrote a stiff letter to Mr Jerome:

Dear Sir,

I believe that my Son has sailed for America with the expressed intention of offering marriage to your daughter. As he is acting entirely in opposition to my desire & without my approval in the course he has taken, I think you ought to know that I am in absolute possession of my estates.[47]

His warning was clear: if his son married against his wishes, he could be disinherited. Sometimes such estates were entailed, meaning that the heir could not be deprived of his inheritance. The Leslie estate was one such, in spite of what Sir John wrote. Leonard's response was a curt: 'Letter received.' He had seen how much Leonie wanted to marry Jack, and once he had met the young man and liked him his support for the union was complete. He was affronted by the idea that Leonie would be anything but a welcome addition to any family, no matter how old or how distinguished. Leonard was determined to give the last of his girls to marry a fine society wedding.

The ceremony took place in Grace Church in the first week of October 1884 and was attended by Clara and Jennie, who had travelled to America with Randolph for a two-month visit. Guests included the Astors, the Lorillards, the Jays, William Travers, Ward McAllister, and Mrs August Belmont. Leonie wore a dress of white brocade draped with lace, cut low in the 'Pompadour' style. She wore a bridal veil of point lace held with pearls, diamonds, and orange blossom. The New York papers reported, somewhat erroneously, that she had married a wealthy man – with an income of over £30,000 per annum.

CHAPTER SIX

Glaslough

Leonie was relieved that it was all over and delighted to be with her Jack at last. She hoped that his family would come to accept her now that the deed was done. She wrote to Clara shortly after the wedding to thank her for her kindness and support, and reported that Jack had written once again to his father, this time receiving an answer that was 'quite nice'. Jack had replied with a '<u>very</u> affectionate letter', she added, and thought that the rift might yet be resolved. She was grateful that Clara had been 'good about it' and had not 'abused the Leslies in any way'. Leonie's hurt feelings and pride were evident, however, as she asserted she did not feel that she should write to the Leslies after their insult to her. Her resolve was to be nice to them and to forget the past, especially as she felt that <u>she</u> had far more to forgive than they did. She concluded by thanking her dear sister and, indeed, Moreton, who had been a '<u>real</u> brother'. Her private postscript added that she was disappointed not be to be already with child – after Jennie and Clara's example, she had hoped she would 'begin immediately!'[1]

But Leonie was not warmly received by the Leslie family. When the young couple arrived in London, they were pointedly ignored by Jack's parents. Two of Jack's maiden aunts, Miss Julia and Miss Emily Leslie, were instructed to meet Leonie and to report back their verdict to the family. Miss Julia complained about the young bride's hair, because she had no fringe, but the music-loving Emily was more complimentary, having discovered Leonie's knowledge of composition. As Leonie and Jack were not welcome at Stratford House in London, they moved in with Jennie and Randolph at Connaught Place. 'What a delightful surprise it must have been to Jack & Leonie, to live with you at Connaught Place instead of going to Clarges Street. I can't get over it, such a nice house, & such a lot of jolly little people living together.' So Mama wrote to Jennie in December 1884, shortly after Leonie and Jack had sailed to England. She was so pleased that they would all stay together; only, she begged, they must 'try to be good, & enjoy yourselves'.[2]

The couple were summoned, however, to spend Christmas at Glaslough and arrived on a rough winter's night. When they entered the main hall, bedecked with antlers and armour, Jack's younger sister Olive rushed down to greet the newlyweds and was struck by her new sister-in-law's charm and grace. 'Leonie was standing there alone looking very slim in a tight-fitting grey dress with a big bunch of violets pinned to the neck,' she wrote years later, adding: 'She looked more elegant than anyone I had ever seen.'[3] Sir John and Lady Constance ran the house along old-fashioned, Victorian lines. A dressing-gong sounded each evening for dinner, as the footmen emptied large brass cans of steaming water into the hip baths set before the bedroom fireplaces. Children would be put to bed, and after an interval the second gong would be rung, summoning the adults to their meal. Everyone dressed for dinner and proceeded arm-in-arm in their finery from the drawing room to the dining room, where they were seated around an enormous table. The etiquette was strict: conversation first with the lady on one's right and, after the fish, on one's left. The ladies would retire after the meal, leaving the gentlemen to their port.

After their Christmas visit, Leonie and Jack returned to London. Lady Constance was still exceedingly unhappy about the match and made her feelings known in a 'vile letter'. It arrived in February 1885 and made Leonie feel 'blue', 'so wretched'.[4] Lady Constance would frequently summon her new daughter-in-law to the daunting Stratford Place residence in London. The house had splendid rooms, but no sanitation. Every year, the Irish servants, who had been healthy when they left Ireland, would come down with unpleasant illnesses. No one suspected (except perhaps the hapless servants) the huge undrained cesspool that terminated under the kitchen floor and the servants' hall. Over time, Leonie's graciousness and also her talent at the piano gradually came to be appreciated and much admired by Sir John and Lady Constance. Soon Leonie and Jack were invited to move from the Churchills' house in Connaught Place into the house at Stratford Place.

Many years later in 1907, Jack's mother, Lady Constance, penned these touching words to Jack and Leonie as she left Glaslough to retire to a house in London. Enclosing one of Jack's letters to his father, which pleaded with him to change his mind and give consent to his marriage, she wrote:

> You will read this when I am gone and I want you to realise what happiness your children and <u>dear kind-hearted</u> Leonie have given me and how grateful I am. This letter of Jack's so charming and it was mischief-makers who persuaded us that Leonie did not care for our only son and so steeled our hearts against this touching appeal. God bless you both dear ones. You and your boys are ever in my heart's prayers and have so helped my old age.[5]

With all three daughters in London, it was a pity that Mrs Jerome needed to be in New York over the winter. Leonie and Jennie must look after Clara, she advised them, as she would be lonely during yet another of Moreton's absences. She was happy 'to think of you being all together & so fond & so devoted to each other', and she hoped that they always would be. She urged them to write to her and Papa, as they led 'a dull quiet life', and her 'greatest pleasure' was getting letters from them to hear 'all about your every day lives, and that you have not forgotten us'.[6]

Their daughters' lives in England were so different that Leonard and Clara Jerome were always in danger of being left behind. Jennie, aged thirty, was in 1884 completely immersed in both Randolph's political career and her own love affairs. She still had a close relationship with the Prince of Wales and was in love with Count Charles Kinsky, an attaché at the Austro-Hungarian Embassy in London. He had been paying regular calls on her since 1882 (a brief diary that she kept during that period mentioned his visits). Kinsky, a dashing sportsman, won the Grand National in 1883, riding his own horse, Zoedone. Leonie, who was staying with Jennie in the spring of 1884, mentioned Kinsky in a letter to Clara.[7] Jennie's relationship with her sons was far less of a preoccupation. Little Jack received next to no attention, and both she and Randolph thought Winston a difficult child. Randolph felt chiefly animosity towards his son, and had no faith in the boy's mind or ability. Winston's school reports were mixed. He was good at English and history but not much else, and his teachers complained that he did not apply himself. His conduct was characterized as troublesome and naughty, and his academic career was described as follows:

> Winston's own failure at public school was also a product of obstinacy. It was not that he was stupid or even lazy. He displayed great energy when anything caught his fancy. He enjoyed the cadet corps, became a champion fencer, recited 1200 lines of Macaulay's *Lays of Ancient Rome* off by heart and learnt how to write an English sentence – 'a noble thing'. But when it came to subjects like Latin and French he refused to invest an iota of his extraordinary powers of concentration. Indeed he wrote English essays for other boys in exchange for their doing his Latin prose.[8]

In a letter to Randolph, Jennie wrote that Winston had made no improvement, but when she criticized the nine-year-old to her father, he leaped to his grandson's defence: 'Let him be. Boys get good at what they find they shine at.'[9] Jennie was a neglectful but not an irresponsible parent. When Mrs Everest indignantly showed her Winston's bruises from beatings at the brutal prep school he attended, she found a smaller, more informal school for him in Brighton. Winston joined his parents on a holiday to the Austrian Alps, where they took mountain walks.

When they returned, Randolph's political career once again absorbed the Churchills' lives. Randolph's friend, Sir Henry Drummond Wolff, had the idea of wearing a primrose, Disraeli's favourite flower, on 19 April, the anniversary of his death. The Primrose League, which developed from this, was founded as an organization through which the Tory Party could recruit Conservative voters, regardless of social class. The members would be encouraged to become politically active by discussing issues, listening to their leaders, and taking part in election campaigns. Although Randolph's critics at first dismissed the League as 'another of Randy's pranks', the League's membership soon grew to nearly 2 million. This transformed the Conservative Party, previously the party of the squire and parson, into one with greater democratic support across the social spectrum, which was particularly critical after the Reform Acts of 1867 and 1884 had widened suffrage to include larger numbers of men from lower socio-economic strata.[10]

Although Jennie did not hold strong political convictions, much like her husband, she threw herself wholeheartedly into campaigning for the League, which, unusually, welcomed women. Randolph's mother was made President of the Ladies Guild Council. Men were Knights, the women officers were known as Dames, and the clubs were called habitations. Jennie became Dame President of many of these habitations and toured the country visiting them, making her own speeches in support of the League.

She also accompanied her husband on his political trips, which brought the couple closer together, although the relationship that mattered most to Randolph was still that with his mother, the duchess. She worshipped her second son and stopped at nothing to further his career. After the death of the duke in 1883, her entire life was centred on Randolph. He visited his mother often, and wrote long and affectionate letters to her when he travelled. Those he wrote to Jennie at this time were shorter and mainly about politics. Although he admired and respected his wife, seeking out her company and her political advice, his heart was no longer hers. Jennie's self-absorbed nature could not be satisfied with second best, hence her pursuit of affection elsewhere.

Clara, meanwhile, was living mostly alone with her servants in her London home near Chesham Place. Moreton – who was almost always absent – failed to make money but not before he had borrowed £25,000 (over £1.6 million in today's money) from the company to fund their lifestyle. He chose not to leave the company, even though it was failing and the panicking directors were selling out. Moreton was forbidden to sell his own shares by contract, so the whole venture was a loss for him. He had long had political ambitions and in September 1885 was proposed for Parliament, as a Liberal candidate at Barrow. He was, however, rejected, by the selection committee. In March 1886, when Moreton resigned from the Powder River company, he found that his ordinary shares were worthless, as, indeed, were those of his many friends and relations who had invested in the business. In addition, he owed £30,000 (over £2 million) in private debts to a number of creditors, including his three brothers.

They were philosophical about their losses. The long-suffering Dick offered the following advice:

> I can't help telling you one thing even at the expense of your displeasure, and that is that if you are ever to get out of your hole not only you but Clare [as she was also known] must reduce your expenditure to the smallest possible amount … Clare ought to live in a country cottage or seaside. And all the servants ought to be discharged. One nurse ought to be all you ought to keep. This raising money at a very heavy price can't go on for long and at best can only put off the evil day … I can't help telling you in my opinion you ought to put it pretty plain to Clare."

Clara was not at this time particularly extravagant (indeed, there was never any cash available to her to spend). A daughter, named Clare, was born in 1885, shortly after which Clara was left at home on her own. Within four days of the birth, Moreton had gone north in his bid for a political seat and, once away from home, decided to travel from friend to friend, as was his habit, writing to his darling Kali that he missed his 'little woman'. She must have found it disconcerting to read his cheerful accounts of jolly house parties, with 'lots of nice people about', and of his pleasure to be in the country. He was thrilled to see 'so many old friends' that he had not seen in years.[12] Moreton was enjoying the shooting at Appelby Castle and wrote: 'I am quite glad to be away because I know that means such quiet for you, sweet darling, that you get well twick [*sic*].' From Castle Menzies he wrote, 'You dear sweet thing, I know you are lonely and bored. I suppose it is good for you.'[13]

Clara was a devoted spouse. She may have been impractical, but she loved and admired her husband. Her extravagance in retaining the household servants derived from ignorance of their situation; Moreton was never really honest about their finances. Eventually she realized that money was a problem. During his travels, Moreton rarely failed to hit his hosts for a loan and was usually successful, for he charmed his friends. He also continued to conduct a public life, writing for journals and composing letters to *The Times*; his relationship with Randolph was his most valuable political contact. His greatest project was his enthusiastic support for bi-metallism, for which he later became famous. He believed that silver should be given equal status with gold as a currency medium, in a fixed ratio, of perhaps fifteen and a half ounces of silver to one ounce of gold. It was, however, a highly complicated proposition, and few people understood it or even cared. Moreton was nonetheless obsessed and lectured all the politicians and other persons of influence he knew.

He would have been better off, and financially secure, if he had turned his energy and intelligence to the systematic pursuit of a lucrative career. Instead, he frequently changed direction. In 1885, he became a salesman, peddling American patent grease for railway loco-motives and cars – for which he was promised a 10 per cent com-mission on sales – and trying to lobby for the building of a new railway line at Port Nelson on Hudson Bay, for which he was promised a hefty payment if successful. He championed a patent icemaker and sum-moned the press to view the instrument in his home, enthusiastically promoting its rather uncertain technology. Leaving Clara behind once again pregnant, he travelled to Canada in 1886 in order to lobby the Secretary of the Interior about the railway at Port Nelson. When he returned to England he found himself faced with bankruptcy. By the time of the birth of his second son, Oswald, in January 1887, Moreton's financial position had so deteriorated that he could not pay the bill from his fishmonger (he promised him regular instalments of £15 – about £1,000 in today's money). He could no longer attend the theatre or the opera unless invited by friends. People began to snub him, afraid to be touched for yet another loan. Moreton's response was to take a typically rash decision: in March 1887 he journeyed to Monte Carlo supposedly to win a fortune at the gaming tables. Within a week he reported to Clara that the 'system' had not worked and that his capital was now so low that he dared do nothing.

Fortunately, Leonard came to the aid of his daughter in distress. Although there is no record of Clara's response to the threat of bankruptcy, her father's actions make clear that the family was very concerned about her. Leonard wrote to Moreton that he had recommended him to Joseph Pulitzer as a journalist; at the end of 1887, Moreton agreed to take the job. He also made some difficult decisions: he decided to sue the Powder River Cattle Company for his lost profits; he negotiated to let his London house for £1,500 (over £100,000 in modern terms); and he entered the furniture in an auction sale. He assured Clara that the situation would improve. 'I am feeling full of courage,' he wrote. 'There may be hard times ahead, but we shall struggle through into open water, I feel sure.'[14] He sent Clara to Ireland to stay (economically) with the Leslies. Jennie also stepped in and bought Clara's own diamond stars for £500 (about £33,000), to save them for when her sister could buy them back again, a touching gesture, as the Churchills were once again, Moreton acknowledged, 'hard up, very hard up'.[15]

Clara was eagerly welcomed in Ireland, where Leonie had won the hearts of the Leslies by producing a healthy son and heir, John Randolph, in 1885. He was followed by another boy, Norman Jerome, the following year. Jack's father wrote jubilantly: 'Well done my dear Leonie, Well done! Another Son & punctual to the moment. I can't say how delighted I feel, & hope to hear of no drawbacks but that you will continue to make progress, until you arrive at a complete recovery.'[16]

The Jeromes were relieved, and even Randolph wrote to Jennie of his pleasure at Leonie 'having got over her troubles. The son and heir is a great thing & must remove all remaining bad feelings in the Leslie bosom.'[17] Leonie settled well in the life of an Irish chatelaine-in-waiting – she rode every day, she wrote letters to her friends and family, and she went hunting regularly. Jack's sisters were 'awfully good about going among the poor tenants and giving them things', she wrote to her cousin Eva Thompson (the daughter of her mother's sister Katherine). 'I am working very hard at my music, as Jennie and I are to play at two concerts in London. Tomorrow night there is a servant's ball here, and about 50 of the farmers & wives come to it. I have never been to one, but they say it is great fun – I have learnt the Irish jig! A policeman who is an excellent hand at it comes once a week and teaches me.' Leonie finished by telling her fashionable cousin that she had not lost her figure, and 'with a struggle' was able to wear all her dresses again after the baby's birth.[18]

She enjoyed 'the season' and the following winter in London, but also grew fond of the country life in Glaslough. They had five saddle horses and four carriage ones, so they did plenty of riding and driving. Jack went shooting nearly every day, bringing back pheasants and snipe. She was living 'a rural life – go & visit the tenants & take them soup! Lead the quire [sic] in church & play the organ while Jack hands the plate!' Leonie also grew interested in farming, and was 'delighted because one of our bulls took a prize at Belfast cattle show'.[19] And she was happy with her two boys; the eldest, John Randolph, known as Jacky, was only two and trotted about everywhere behind his mother.

Randolph Churchill had travelled to India in December 1884, repeatedly stating that it was for his health, which was very poor.[20] He was still in the subcontinent in late March 1885, however, with an ambitious schedule that included visits to Bombay, Lucknow, and Calcutta, as well as Benares and Hyderabad. Although his letters home were full of tigers and elephants, he also devoted himself to getting to know the country, and his trip was well publicized in the press back home. He soon considered himself an expert in Indian affairs. As with

Ireland before, Randolph had become familiar with the country at first hand and was appointed Secretary of State for India in June 1885 when the Liberal government was replaced by a Conservative one. With his advancement to office, Randolph gained a reputation as a serious politician, although he had also acquired many political enemies, who resented his opportunism and manoeuvrings. His political stature rocketed; by 1886 he dominated the House of Commons and was the most popular politician in the country. That year, at the age of only thirty-seven, he was made Leader of the House and Chancellor of the Exchequer in Salisbury's government, which was formed that July. It was not an appointment universally favoured; Salisbury was known to be reluctant, and Queen Victoria recorded in her journal entry for 25 July that the prime minister 'feared Lord Randolph Churchill must be Chancellor of the Exchequer and Leader, which I did not like', adding: 'He is so mad and odd and has also bad health.'[21]

Notwithstanding the reservations, Randolph was now a man of great influence. Jennie, who thrived on the political campaigning, gave dinner parties to help his career. She devoted herself equally to her smart social life and to politics, writing: 'Our house became the rendezvous of all shades of politicians.'[22] As Randolph turned more and more to his mother as confidante, Jennie threw herself into the role of political and social hostess. She was now acknowledged to be one of the most influential women in London. As her position and stature increased, she grew ever more confident in her beauty and ability. She invented the dinner party of deadly enemies, where she invited people who were known not to be on speaking terms with one another as an entertaining social device. A guest at the first such dinner, George W. Smalley, wrote: 'It was thought a hazardous experiment. It proved a complete success … As guests, they were neither friends nor enemies. There were no hostilities. The talk flowed on smoothly.'[23]

In addition, Jennie played at concerts and took pleasure in her social importance. 'Randolph's growing prominence in the political world was attracting considerable attention in the social world,' she would later recall, 'and we were bombarded with invitations of every kind. The fashionable world, which had held aloof, now began to smile on us once more.'[24] After working energetically for Lady Dufferin's Medical Fund for Women, Jennie hoped to be given the Order of the Crown of India, but Randolph refused to request it, feeling that it was inappropriate for him to ask on behalf of his wife. It is likely that her great friend the Prince of Wales discreetly intervened, however, for at the end of November 1885, to Jennie's great delight, she was rewarded with the Insignia of the Order of the Crown of India. It was an honour bestowed by the Queen in her capacity as Empress of India, who ceremoniously pinned the pearl and turquoise cipher, attached to a pale blue ribbon edged with white, onto Jennie's dress. Jennie then commissioned her favourite dressmaker, Worth, to make a gown matched to the exact shade of the pale blue silk.

Shortly thereafter, she and Randolph were invited to dine with the Queen at Windsor Castle and to stay the night. Jennie was conscious of the distinction, but found the occasion dull. Conversation, she recorded, was carried on in whispers, which did not make for a convivial atmosphere. Still, it was another sign that the Churchills were doing well. Even though Randolph's health was poor, he was driving himself very hard. The years 1885 and 1886 represented a complicated period in British politics, as there was not only a struggle between the Liberal and Conservative parties, but also one for leadership within the parties. Ireland was one of the main issues that could unite men and parties that were otherwise divided, and Randolph, with his previous experience there, threw himself wholeheartedly into the debates over the future of England's neighbour. This was the sort of politics he and Jennie loved: scheming, plotting, consolidating and breaking alliances, and making carefully crafted speeches, which played to his strengths as the masterful orator he had become. Although it would be unfair to see Randolph as a mere opportunist, it is true that he was not a politician of conviction and was at his best in Opposition. Although he believed in a more democratic order of government, he switched sides on many issues quite readily. He had, for example, made overtures to Parnell and the Irish Nationalists, sympathizing with their demands, and had then reversed his position, making his now-famous statement on 7 May 1886, in which he declared, 'Ulster will fight; Ulster will be right.'[25]

During Randolph's visit to India in late 1884, he had been entertained by the Nizam of Hyderabad, the Muslim ruler of an important Indian princely state, who governed his state independently, although he recognized Queen Victoria as his empress and was advised on affairs by a British resident. The British government took a very close interest in these princely rulers, and there was some concern at the intrigues within the state of Hyderabad. In addition, the prime minister of the state, Sir Salar Jung, had recently been sacked by the Nizam and was planning a European tour that included a visit to Britain. The British government believed that Sir Salar, as an influential Muslim and a member of one of the most important dynasties in Asia, should be given guidance and delicate handling. His visit to Europe in general and England in particular might be construed by his supporters as foreign approval of his plans to be reinstated as prime minister. What was needed was an unofficial safe pair of hands. Randolph was approached in 1887 by Joseph Rock, the Hyderabad agent, and he suggested that none other than his brother-in-law, Moreton Frewen, would be the ideal person to accompany the young Sir Salar Jung on his visits.

Moreton, now practically penniless, set out straight away in May 1887 to join His Excellency the Nawab Salar Jung, Knight Commander of the Order of the Indian Empire. For an initial payment of £250 (about £17,000 today), a monthly salary of £100 (nearly £7,000 in modern terms) and all expenses paid, he became the Nawab's personal assistant. Once installed in Shepheard's Hotel, in Cairo, he went to meet the Nawab. The two got on very well and Moreton wrote confidently to Clara that Sir Salar believed that he would be back in power in no time. He did not, however, have good news on the financial front:

> I am so sorry, sweet thing, but I find myself obliged to take a hundred pounds of that 250£ and Whitehead [Spencer Whitehead, his solicitor

and accountant] will keep 50£ for the rent so there will only be a hundred for you at the present moment. The 100 [that he was taking] has to go in the shape of interest on a loan, there is no help for it though it goes to my heart to have to take it ... Meanwhile if you are really pressed, perhaps Jennie can lend you a hundred if it is only for a few weeks. What a curse poverty is. It kills all the pleasure in life.[26]

Moreton found that the job involved some unexpected duties. Sir Salar Jung, a young man, decided that he must take a wife. Within a week, Moreton had presented three high-born possibilities, and was negotiating settlements and dowries, but none of them came to anything. In addition, the Nawab had a rather serious alcohol problem, and his noisy entourage lacked social graces. To help him meet the right people and make a favourable impression, Moreton commissioned Clara to take a house for Goodwood race week, which was the climax of society's summer season. He had very explicit instructions about whom to invite and was particularly concerned that the ladies be attractive, insisting, for example, on the presence of his friend Pussie Farnham: 'She will add to our beauty division, it is an insult to appear on such a course as Goodwood with a lot of old cows!!'[27] He knew he could rely on Clara's innate snobbery to get it right, and she did not let him down. As always, her sisters rallied. Jennie came, looking magnificent, accompanied by her lover, Count Charles Kinsky. Her brother-in-law, Blandford (now Duke of Marlborough), arrived with a semi-state coach, and led the daily parade to the racecourse. Other friends included the banker Ernest Beckett and, Sir William Gordon-Cumming, in addition to the band of 'Blue Hungarians', provided by Kinsky, which serenaded guests on the terrace.

To impress his guest further, Moreton arranged the rental of a house at Rutland Gate, where he planned a dinner for twenty-eight, with Clara as hostess. These kinds of occasions played to her strengths. For the first time since their courtship, Moreton was constantly by Clara's side, for he needed her graces and social dexterity to impress the Nawab and his entourage.

Clara expected to accompany Moreton to live in India and planned to follow him out there soon after he had found a house. In their five years of marriage, they had never been together for more than a few weeks at a time. Moreton swung from being optimistic about the future to being depressed about their finances. He left in September 1887 for India, writing encouraging letters to Clara on the way, promising that they would soon be together. 'We shall have such a delightful restful winter in India after all our late torments,' he wrote from Paris. 'I will meet you in Bombay.'[28] From Turin he wrote: 'I am sure we shall have a lovely winter and no duns or worries,' and from Brindisi, 'What a relief it is to have got away from all those cursed worries … I wonder when you sail.'[29] But some weeks later, he sent her a cable saying: 'Do not start until I cable you from Bombay.'[30] While awaiting news of his plans, Clara took the children to meagre lodgings at the seaside in Sussex, living there in some discomfort. There was, once again, no money. Moreton had sent her £10 (just under £700 in today's money) that September with the discouraging view that he had no idea where the next pound would come from.

The political situation in Hyderabad had worsened, and Sir Salar had received a cable from the Nizam, telling him *not* to travel to Bombay. Moreton prevailed on him to continue the journey regardless, but had to put Clara off until the situation became resolved. After exchanges of cables throughout the sea journey, it became clear that Sir Salar and his party would receive a very poor welcome in India. Despondent, Moreton suspected that his plan to get rich by serving the Nawab would come to nought. Sir Salar would either be exiled to Europe, or be forced to get rid of his adviser. He wrote to Clara that he must at the very least attempt to push sales of an American patent grease for railway locomotives, as 'That commission, it seems to me, will shortly be all we have to live on, unless things improve.'[31]

The government forces in Hyderabad decided, however, that Sir Salar could remain in India for a fortnight. Moreton was pleased with this concession, which for him meant a further two weeks of negotiations to sell his patent grease as well as to search for other promotion opportunities. Thus they travelled slowly to Hyderabad. Clara waited in

London, her luggage packed and waiting in a depot. Meanwhile, Moreton met various political leaders and investigated business opportunities (such as building a railway) that might come his way once Sir Salar had regained power. Together with the Nawab, the Frewens planned to set up a sort of alternative court, a 'society centre' that the right people would frequent, instead of going to the residency. These details were intoxicating to Clara, languishing in England. They would be smart, *very* smart, warned Moreton in his letters, and he promised that they would have many servants, a magnificent house, a wonderful a new life. She might even, he suggested casually, bring one or two of the children.

Unlike their sister Leonie, who dressed her two little boys in sailor suits and took them on boating excursions and picnics in the Irish countryside, Clara and Jennie had little time for their children. Winston wrote increasingly wretched letters to both his parents from boarding school, begging them to visit him. The Frewen children also recorded their feelings about being ignored by their glamorous, fey mother, who seemed to live only for her husband. Although it was customary in the society in which they moved for there to be distant relationships between parents and offspring Jennie was, even by the standards of the day, particularly preoccupied with herself, and Clara, while sweet, was ineffectual. Her eldest son, Hugh, later attributed this to the fact that Clara remained a child herself throughout her life. Even with the responsibilities of motherhood, she never outgrew her girlishness. She sought escape from the dunning and the angry creditors by living in a make-believe world of ribbons and lace, fed by memories preciously conserved in scrapbooks and photographs.

Leonie was made of far sterner stuff. When she married her gallant officer, her father wrote words of caution to her that she cherished her entire life:

A word for Leonie which you must whisper to her privately. A wife of a domineering disposition should be careful how she treats a particularly amiable husband. If his opinions and wishes are not treated with due respect apparently he don't mind it but he does. It rankles. It lives with him years when the wife thinks it forgotten in an hour. An amiable gallant gentleman can hardly bring himself to be rude to a lady especially if he loves her. He won't talk back and bully and scold and assert himself – but he <u>can't forget</u>.[32]

Jack's parents had decided that if their son must marry a 'rich American' the couple could live on her money, which left them pathetically short of funds. While Jack continued to receive a small income from his parents, Leonard scrambled to send funds to Leonie. In 1885, he sent $2,000. He also sent Jennie £2,000, which he was happy to do. 'You have no idea how universally Jennie is talked about and how proud Americans are of her,' he wrote to his wife that year.

Jennie received her agreed income, and Leonie her injections of cash, from their father every year until his death in 1891. In 1888, when old and ill, he was still sending what he could. In 1887, he commented to his wife how kind it had been of Leonie to share with Clara some of the money he had sent – he hoped to send them $400 each before long. Moreton never asked his father-in-law for money; he was too proud. He was not too proud, however, to assume that Mrs Jerome would help her eldest daughter – to whom she was closest – and he was often proved right. When Mrs Jerome visited England (which she did frequently), Clara and the three children lived with her, and she paid all their expenses. It was, said Leonard, a good arrangement in many ways. Together with the invaluable nanny, Susan Thynne, known as Nene, Mrs Jerome was a great help in supervising the growing Frewen family, remaining a fixture in their lives until her own death in 1895.

In the summer of 1887, Leonard wrote to his wife in England that he was always happy to hear of his daughters having such a nice time – and declared himself in agreement that Leonie (who had recently given birth to her second son) should 'make hay while the sun shines'. He could not understand, he added, how Moreton could have lost his money.[33] In 1886 Leonie wrote to her mother that Jack was to ask his father for an additional £200 (just under £14,000 in today's money) a

Leonard Jerome, entrepreneur and
quintessential New Yorker

The socially ambitious Clara Jerome was
rumoured to be of Iroquois descent.

The magnificent Jerome mansion on Madison Square in New York City.
Built in 1859, it housed a private theatre and an adjacent three-storey stable.

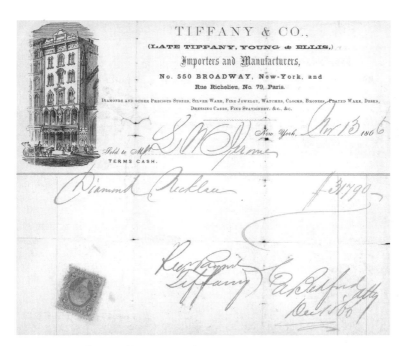

A receipt from Tiffany & Co. for a diamond necklace bought by
Leonard Jerome for $31,790. Jewellery in late nineteenth-century
New York was a fashionable and ostentatious way to display wealth.

Young Leonie Jerome in Paris, c. 1873.

Clara (left) and Jennie Jerome,
dressed in identical gowns.

Lord Randolph Churchill, second son
of the Duke of Marlborough.

Jennie, around the time of her
marriage to Randolph.

Blenheim Palace, the 'English Versailles', where Winston once said he took
two very important decisions: 'to be born and to marry'.

Leonie (left) and Clara, in identical dresses, looking at a picture album *c.* 1875.

Jennie in riding habit in Ireland *c.* 1876. Lord D'Abernon remarked that she had 'more of the panther than of the woman in her look'.

Dreamy Clara.

Moreton Frewen dressed for his cattle ranching business in Wyoming *c.* 1880.

Below left: Leonie wearing a diamond star *c.* 1882.

Jack Leslie, son of the 1st Baronet John Leslie, and descendant of an old Irish landowning family.

The Leslie house on Stratford Place, off Oxford Street in London.
The family carriage stands outside.

The Leslie Estate at Glaslough.

year, bringing his income from his parents up to the full £1,000 (nearly £70,000) that he had been promised. It was so hard, wrote Leonie, to live within their means: 'our expenses are very little now – but with a double nursery – & Jack having to have a servant, one <u>can't</u> manage on 1200.'[34] They were hoping to move to Dublin, to follow Jack's posting, but Leonie worried that they would not be able to afford a house there. Still, she felt that they could count on the Leslies, and fortunately they had no debts, save for a few small bills.

In late 1886, Leonie wrote to Clara: 'I have just received a telegram from Jenny [*sic*] saying she will be in town today for luncheon, so I will go & glean what news I can & add it to this before posting.' Over lunch, Jennie had confided in her sympathetic younger sister her fear that she was losing Randolph's affection. Randolph had stopped marital relations some time before, possibly as early as 1874 after Winston's birth (although some biographers believe it to be later, perhaps around 1882). Jennie now believed that he had even withdrawn his love and was very upset about his close friendship with the beautiful Gladys de Grey. Leonie consoled her sister but privately believed that Jennie was being unrealistic and wrote as much to Clara: 'it seems R. [Randolph] was rather devoted to Gladys … However I do not encourage Jennie's abusing her – as I think it is better not to stir up R. I don't think Gladys is really so much to blame – as I think R. has <u>other</u> loves, only Jennie had better not know this, so don't you or Mamma [*sic*] mention it.'[35] Leonie stressed to Clara how unfair she felt Jennie's attitude was: 'I think she is very silly about R. although I never like to say so to her, as she takes it to heart. But he is not in the <u>least</u> devoted to Gladys – & is <u>just the same</u> to Jenny, as he always was.' The problem, Leonie believed, was that 'as she has no flirtation on hand she suddenly notices his coldness, he has been like that for years … after 13 years married life, both living in London & going *chacun de leur côté* [each their own way], she ought not to expect more.' She had tried reasoning with her, explained Leonie, but it was impossible: '& if Jack & I lived as separately for ten years, & then were on as good terms, I shd be very thankful.'[36]

Jennie had had some real anxieties in the years when Randolph was doing so well. Winston had always been a delicate child, prone to illness, and early in 1886 he contracted pneumonia. His survival was due in large part to the devoted care of Mrs Everest, although he would suffer the after-effects of the disease for the rest of his life. In August of the same year, Jennie became convinced that Randolph no longer loved her, as she had confided to Leonie. She turned to Randolph's family, first his sister, Lady Cornelia Guest, and then his mother, the duchess. The latter, although not particularly sympathetic to Jennie, whom she still thought rather fast, was determined above all that no scandal should hinder Randolph's career. She repeatedly urged discretion upon Jennie, stating that with time and patience the situation would improve. 'I know well how impulsive & excitable you are & it will be very hard for you to keep a watch over your words & thoughts even,' she wrote. 'But do my dearest Jennie make a firm resolve to seal your lips & govern your thoughts & do not let any friend male or female beguile you henceforth into confidence & be calm & gentle with him [Randolph].' She added that she knew 'so well how hard it is for you & pray believe it's no want of sympathy makes me say this but simply that it is the only possible way of getting his Love & respect & of preserving your own Dignity.' She was also not entirely convinced that the fault had been Randolph's – it could equally well have been Jennie's: 'It will bring you a blessing if you accept patiently this trial & look on it as a sort of retribution for indiscretions or errors.'[37]

Their home at Connaught Place was busy, with dinner parties and a constant stream of visitors, but it was not a cheerful place. Leonie wrote to her father that Winston when he was home wandered around aimlessly, that he 'flitted in the background'.[38] Their cook, Rosa Ovenden, recalled that the marriage was unhappy and that Randolph treated his wife badly. In addition, Randolph was gambling heavily and running up debts at a time when finances were low. This was not the image Jennie wished to present to the world, nor, indeed, to her family. Her parents had been so impressed by Randolph's political triumph; Papa wrote from New York in August 1886 of his excitement at Randolph's 'magnificent success', and Mama wrote from Buxton,

England, where she was taking the waters, of how pleased she was that Randolph had got the office he wanted. She had 'done nothing but read the newspapers the past three weeks' and had 'seen everything that has been written about Randolph both in praise & against him'.[39] Like her ambitious daughter Jennie, Clara Jerome hoped to see Randolph elected prime minister. She wrote to Jennie from Leicestershire, where she was staying with Clara, of how she and her eldest daughter lived for Jennie's letters, with their descriptions of glittering occasions and weekends with the Prince of Wales (often without Randolph): 'I am sure you will enjoy Sandringham [home of the Prince of Wales]. I do hope you will write me all about it, I shall be dying to hear. Pickwell is dull as ever. However we are very comfortable & manage to pass the time … My best love to Winston when you write & a kiss for my dear little Jacky with love from Clara.'[40]

Mrs Jerome visited the Leslies at Glaslough for the first time in October 1887. After the splendours of Blenheim, which overwhelmed her, she was not impressed. She found the large house gloomy, although she conceded that every comfort was provided and the landscape was lovely. She approved of the bedrooms furnished in white wood (very modern) and remarked on how beautifully everything was kept, 'so different'[41] from the Leslie mansion on Stratford Place in London. She found Leonie's two children very sweet and particularly admired Norman – the largest baby she had ever seen and much, she thought, the better looking of the two. She also asked Clara for news of Jennie. They were all worried about her.

Jennie was confident of Randolph's political future, but in December 1886, everything changed. Her fashionable, worldly, and successful life was about to be shattered for ever. Randolph had been struggling as Chancellor of the Exchequer, a position that required numerical skills, concentration, diligence, and sound judgement at all times, qualities that he had in short supply. He was also ill, almost certainly with syphilis, and his behaviour became even more erratic and unpredictable than usual. Colleagues were concerned about his deteriorating health. Randolph's good friend Henry Labouchere, the radical editor of *Truth*, wrote to Lord Rosebery: 'R. Churchill is in a very bad way, the action of his heart has given way, and he takes a lot of digitalis.'[42] In August and again in November 1886, Randolph was confined to his bed with illness. He was now under the constant care and supervision of Dr Robson Roose, a fashionable gout specialist and an expert on debilitating neurological disorders. Although it is possible that Roose may have misdiagnosed Randolph, who may have been suffering from a brain tumour or multiple sclerosis, he believed that his patient was suffering from syphilis – which was a far more common affliction of the time. Randolph was also under the care of Thomas Buzzard, a specialist in this area, who prescribed the classic and only known treatment for the disease, potassium iodide and mercury. Typical reactions to this mixture include darkened skin, progressive loss of hearing, vertigo, and hoarseness. All of these were noted by Randolph's friends and colleagues from the mid-1880s.[43] Randolph also suffered from loss of mental astuteness, recurrent headaches, and bouts of extreme irritability – all classic symptoms of meningovascular syphilis. The other manifestations, such as changes in personality, poor judge-ment, speech defects, and numbness in the hands were also noticed by those around him.[44]

Randolph was now very unwell and quarrelled constantly with his colleagues, making ever more critical speeches and even attacking his friends. He was arrogant and belligerent, and his policies were alarmingly inconsistent. More serious still, he argued with Prime Minister Salisbury, especially on foreign policy issues. His sustained use of the tactics of Opposition politics made him a difficult member of government, when cooperation with colleagues and a united front were considered proper form. Randolph took an entrenched position on economies in the War Office, for example, and refused to budge, threatening to resign (not for the first time), despite the opposition of his colleague, W.H. Smith, Secretary of State for War, who had the crucial support of Salisbury.

Randolph and Jennie had grown so far apart, however, that she, his former political confidante, was unaware of the extent of his isolation.

They spent much of 1886 apart, and there were rumours of a separation. According to Randolph's biographer, R.F. Foster, Randolph was at this time estranged from his wife and abused her to his friends.[45] He was alone both personally and politically. In November 1886 he planned his budget, which proposed as its main planks to reduce income tax and reform local-government death duty, which would be restructured into a graduated tax on real estate. House duty and corporate duty were to be increased, and taxes instituted on horses and wine. It was an audacious budget and a populist one, inextricably linked to substantive reform at local government level. As it was also unfavourable to country gentry and business interests, it inevitably met with resistance from Salisbury and other Cabinet members. The Secretary of State for War was especially concerned as Randolph's calculations depended on Smith keeping down Admiralty and War Office costs. Randolph's refusal to listen to Smith increased his isolation in the Cabinet, and the situation grew more tense.

By 18 December, Salisbury and Smith had warned Randolph that they would not back his budget proposals. On 20 December, after weeks of argument, Randolph travelled to Windsor for an audience with the Queen and stayed the night. After dinner, he wrote a letter, on Windsor Castle notepaper, to Salisbury in which he volunteered to resign his office in protest at the opposition to his budget, including the army and navy estimates to which he could not agree. As he had often threatened resignation on a slight pretext, he neither expected nor intended that the prime minister take him at his word. He said nothing to the Queen nor to Jennie. On 22 December, Randolph lunched with Smith, while Jennie shared an intimate meal alone with the Prince of Wales at Connaught Place. That night, a letter from Lord Salisbury reached Randolph at the Carlton Club, where he was dining. His resignation had been accepted. He immediately despatched a messenger to the prime minister, acknowledging receipt of the letter, and then returned home with his dining companion, Sir Henry Drummond Wolff, where they found Jennie waiting for them to accompany her to the theatre. She asked him about a list of guests for a reception she was planning at the Foreign Office. He replied offhandedly that she should not worry about it, as it probably would not take place – a comment to which she paid little attention.

At the interval of the play, *The School for Scandal* by Richard Brinsley Sheridan, Randolph left their box to go, he said, to his club. In fact he went to the *Times* office in order to deliver a copy of his resignation letter, so that it would appear in the morning's first edition. Reading about her husband's careless rejection of his high office was Jennie's breakfast surprise. When she emerged from her room, she found Randolph calm at the breakfast table. 'Quite a shock for you,' he said with a smile. Jennie sought with great difficulty to hide her dismay. Randolph's resignation caused a sensation. The *Times* leader stated: 'Lord Randolph Churchill declared not long ago that the whole basis of the government to which he belonged was to maintain the union of the party ... We may well ask what has become of that conviction concerning the paramount duty of unity, when he himself drives a wedge into the very centre of the party at the most critical moment of its existence.'[46]

The day after the public announcement in *The Times*, Randolph's friend Reginald Blatt visited him at Connaught Place and found him on the sofa, looking 'completely prostrated'. Randolph declared that he had been 'shunned like a pest', and had been visited by almost no one, 'not even those who owe everything to me'.[47] The Queen was outraged that she had not been given the customary courtesy warning of the resignation. She believed, as did many others, that Randolph had treated his prime minister badly. It was hardly surprising that Salisbury did not intend to take him back.

Randolph Churchill's political career seemed to be over. He was only thirty-seven. Jennie tried to put on a brave face, but after all her hard work and help with campaigning, the Primrose League, the dinner parties – life was suddenly empty and without purpose. 'When I looked back at the few preceding months, which seemed so triumphant and full of promise, the *debacle* appeared all the greater,'[48] she wrote. The days seemed so dark, she recollected years later. One of Jennie's most attractive traits, however, was her ability to make the best of any given situation and to recover from adversity. She had many friends, and her admirers sprang to her defence. Naturally, her family stood by her, and there were still many social invitations.[49] Even better, the situation prompted a reconciliation with her husband. The couple exchanged affectionate letters when Randolph went away to the warm Mediterranean to clear his mind of politics, and Jennie stayed in London to enjoy Queen Victoria's Golden Jubilee. As with her father, Jennie's fighting spirit never left her and saved her from bitterness. She wrote to Randolph, now in Tunisia, of her commitment to him:

> It is a blessing to think that you are well & happy. It reconciles me to much that is disagreeable here – where people are as venomous & ill natured about us as possible – But you are good to me & I trust you utterly, & don't care two pence what they say – Enjoy yrself as much as you can & come back well, ready to fight the whole lot – And if you are only glad to see me, & understand how much I think of you & all that you are to me – I shall be quite happy.[50]

Although Jennie hoped that one day Randolph might return to power, she confided her distress to Leonie: 'But Sniffy I feel very sick at heart sometimes. It was such a splendid position he threw away.'[51] There were other unfortunate consequences. The Churchills were already finding it difficult to balance their domestic budget, and now Connaught Place would have to be run without Randolph's annual salary of £5,000 (nearly £350,000 today). He had already borrowed extensively, and credit lines were running dry.

Clara and Moreton had suffered as well. Moreton had taken the position of Sir Salar's adviser because he had had to resign as secretary to George Goschen when Goschen was chosen to replace Randolph as Chancellor of the Exchequer. Moreton, as Randolph's brother-in-law, could not then in honour retain the post. Now, the Frewens had less money than ever, and the three sisters, who lived within a few streets of one another in London, all had to make economies. Leonie solved her problems by spending more time in Ireland, to avoid the expense of maintaining a metropolitan establishment and lifestyle. Clara, the most impoverished, pinched pennies in Chapel Street and relied on her sisters to help her. Jennie lent her money to pay the Frewens' most pressing creditors, and Leonie did her small kindnesses, such as sending her library books on her own subscription.

Leonie, who was always short of ready cash, had to make choices that fitted in with the wishes of her in-laws, who had the money. Provided she did not overspend, she did not have to worry about paying for the basic infrastructure of her life. She and Jack might not have an elegant separate establishment of their own, decorated to their personal taste, but they had the use of the mansion at Stratford Place, and they had a wonderful home at Glaslough. Leonie might not have financial independence but neither did she suffer from want. Jennie lived with great extravagance and never denied herself anything. She and Randolph had sufficient income to live the lives of the very rich, even if they went into debt, and family resources were there, if not readily available. Jennie had her guaranteed income from Leonard and from the Marlborough estate. Clara had none of these benefits. Although she and Moreton lived as though they had money, they were profoundly insecure. Moreton fretted constantly about the possibility of becoming bankrupt – a prospect that he vowed would kill him. His daughter, Clare, recollected that the family for years 'had struggled on, smiling in the face of misfortune in order to dissemble the truth to the world'. She wrote that 'bankruptcy loomed so close that there was a hush, almost of death, upon our house. My father told my mother that if it happened he would shoot himself.'[52]

Moreton was constantly planning new financial schemes. 'There is no duty so paramount, dear Kali, as to keep the name I bear clear of bankruptcy,'[53] he wrote to Clara after his four-year attempt to make a fortune in Hyderabad. He was lucky that there was little stigma attached to his known attempts to make money for himself on the side. He wrote a book on currency, *The Economic Crisis* (his daughter later said it was a 'perfect description of our family's chronic condition'[54]); he gave away 200 copies to influential people and 43 to the press, selling only 249. His profits were £17 19s 4d (about £1,200). He still hoped to promote a railway in Canada and instructed Clara to follow up his sales work by giving dinner parties to potential investors. Moreton also investigated the possibility of coal-mining in Wyoming, before he decided to use his expertise in currency matters to make a large personal profit by attempting to corner the silver market. This was a strong indication to Leonard that the 'dear man' he loved so much was not a sound partner for his daughter. He thought the attempt to monopolize silver was extremely unwise, especially given the powerful syndicate of the Rothschilds and Barings, etc., and instructed his lawyer to draft a new will for his wife to leave property to Clara and her children that could not be touched by Moreton. 'I fear he is hopelessly visionary,' Leonard said of Moreton. 'Even if he makes a strike, it leads him to a dozen more visionary schemes.'[55] That year, in 1888, he settled £400 (£27,000) a year on Clara, to be paid quarterly.

Undeterred by Leonard's scepticism in the silver market – he had apparently said 'Any attempt to corner silver I believe to be utterly wild'[56] – Moreton sought investors. He wanted millions of pounds, not thousands. He urged Clara to cultivate the wealthy Baron von Hirsch, who was more a friend of Randolph's. Clara duly went to stay with him and his wife in Paris. But instead of investing, von Hirsch invited Clara and Moreton, to her great pleasure, to stay with him in Austria. She wrote to Moreton, delighted at the idea that they might at last enjoy a holiday together, at someone else's expense. Moreton was dismayed, however, that von Hirsch was not providing the investment cash, but nevertheless he accompanied Clara to Austria. They had no money at all, and when Moreton returned alone to London to the sanctuary of his clubs (the bills for which were always paid, as failure to do so resulted in being asked to resign), he left Clara with no money to tip the von Hirsch servants. From White's, he plotted a killing on the stock exchange by forming a syndicate to purchase shares in De Beers Consolidated Mines, Ltd., the South African diamond monopoly that Cecil Rhodes had just founded. Moreton had no cash to invest, but he convinced his friends, and his brother Stephen, a promising cavalry officer, to invest heavily.

Clara drifted from friend to friend, spending long intervals with the von Hirschs, then moving on to stay with her great friend Helen Hatzfeldt (the American-born wife of the German Ambassador to Great Britain), and Jennie. The children were sent away to their grandmother, while Moreton stayed with his friends or at his club. The family had no home, for the Aldford Street house had been let and the rental income spent. Then in October 1889 the market plunged, and Moreton's shares in De Beers, which had been doing well, fell sharply. He lost his chance of the future profits on which he had counted; his brother Stephen, however, lost everything and had to resign his commission. It was Stephen's regiment, the 16th Lancers, who gave Moreton Frewen his unforgettable nickname: 'Mortal Ruin'.

CHAPTER SEVEN

The Churchills in America

To salve their sorrows, Jennie and Randolph decided to leave London in the winter of 1887 for a seven-week visit to Russia. Although their trip was to be unofficial (the Queen was very much against the idea of their going at all), the Prince convinced his wife, Princess Alexandra, to give Jennie a letter of introduction to her sister, the Tsarina. With this in hand, every door was opened to the Churchills and they were received as if they were themselves royalty. Jennie loved the pomp, the parties, the jewellery, and the horses. In long letters to her sisters, she described all their engagements, and this correspondence became the basis of a magazine article she later wrote. 'Everything was new and attractive to us,' she recorded, 'The people were charming and hospitable, and seemed full of *bonhomie*, and we saw no signs of that grinding despotism and tyranny which is supposed to be synonymous with Russian life.' Jennie delighted in particular in winter sports: 'I thoroughly enjoyed the outdoor life of sleighing and skating. Comfortably seated in a sleigh, behind a good fat coachman to keep the wind off, I never wearied of driving about.'[1]

Leonie also had a treat. In February 1888 she and Jack travelled to Italy. Leonard had sent her £100 that summer and was still busy, aged seventy, trying to make another fortune on the stock market. He wrote to Leonie: 'I think you must give up your Newport excursion. It would be very charming, but unavoidably expensive. It's the first time I refused any of you girls anything on the ground of expense. I must really know how some things are going to turn out before spending any more than we can reasonably help.'[2] Times were hard; earlier that spring, he had written to his wife that he expected some difficulty in providing the next instalment for Jennie and was very relieved at receiving another payment from the Union Club. He was worried about providing for Clara, too, although Moreton insisted that their fortune was just around the corner. He sailed constantly back and forth to America, almost always alone. Clara was especially jealous of the fact that on one trip he travelled to the United States on the same ship as his former love, Lily Langtry, and was seen out with her in New York. She put her feelings in a letter to her husband, who replied unsympathetically: 'Oh Lord what a creature you are – I don't see any nice women out here – and I fear I am getting … a little beyond that game! But if it were otherwise, and some nice creature took care of me while I am 5,000 miles away – you ought to be rather pleased than otherwise. On the other hand, if someone looks after you while I am that distance off, well … that is quite another pair of shoes.'[3]

It is likely that Moreton's travels led the handsome gallant into many beds. Clara had been groomed by Mama to expect this of a husband and did her best not to complain. She was still fascinated by Moreton – and in love with him – and she believed that one day they would have a wonderful life together, with every extravagance. On his behalf, she cultivated friendships with the wealthy and never missed an opportunity to promote her husband's case. Baron von Hirsch and his wife were a perfect example of this; they harboured social ambitions and were impressed by Clara's sister, in particular her proximity to the Prince of Wales. Knowing of Clara's precarious finances, they inundated her with invitations to stay with them in Paris and in Austria. Jennie, as loyal and helpful to her sister as ever, duly invited the von Hirschs, to their great delight, to one of her 'mixed parties' for the Prince of Wales at which guests included the Roseberys and the Russian Ambassador.

Clara's heart remained in Paris. In 1889, while Moreton came and went in his usual fashion, Mama held the fort back in London, supervising the household so that Clara could visit her beloved city. Clara, now aged thirty-eight, certainly made the most of her trip. She did not miss her children overmuch because she was so accustomed to not seeing them. Like her sister Jennie, she had left them to the care of nannies. Clara relaxed and went about her beloved French capital in friends' carriages, fêted by one and all. Surrounded by memories of her charmed youth, she blossomed once more, speaking French and using all of her flirtatious techniques to great success. She was alluring and had a very individual charm: a curious deep voice and an unusual elegance. It was said that even in her second-hand gowns (usually Jennie's cast-offs), she looked exquisite. Monsieur Eiffel, among many others, admired her greatly and he entertained her little salon with speeches about engineering. In August 1889, she was the first woman to go to the top of the Eiffel Tower, which she considered a great honour. Clara loved her children and her husband but they exhausted her. Living with a chronic shortage of funds was confusing and most unwelcome to someone as inept as she. But in Paris she laughed and danced all night, her troubles forgotten.

The support of her family helped, too. The sisters had an unbreakable bond. Leonie and Jennie were great friends; as time passed their social lives became more similar, and their closeness increased. Jack Leslie was very fond of Jennie, and the two families liked being together. In September 1889, Leonie wrote to her mother-in-law that Jack had gone with Jennie and her two boys to the London Aquarium. Jennie also flitted back and forth to Paris that year, visiting Clara, seeing friends, and spending time with Count Charles Kinsky. She also had a new lover, the Frenchman Paul Bourget, a popular literary figure of the day. Jennie was just turning thirty-six and still a great beauty. She no longer made any pretence of being faithful to her husband, although they were on amiable terms.

Around this time, in 1890, Jennie joined 'The Souls', an aristocratic literary cult of high-minded men and women — some of whom were considered the most beautiful in London. Poetry was read and admired, but the group's activities centred rather more on bedroom pursuits than literary ones. Jennie developed quite a reputation and the gossip magazine *Town Topics* wrote: 'Society has invented a new name for Lady R. Her fondness for the exciting sport of husband–hunting and fiancé–fishing has earned her the title "Lady Jane Snatcher".'[4] Jennie's appetite for younger men grew as she matured, given that all her energies were now absorbed by the pursuit of romantic and sexual excitement. By the end of her life, her lovers – apart from Count Kinsky and Paul Bourget – were known to have included Henri Breteuil, Thomas Trafford, Baron von Hirsch, Sir Edgar Vincent (later Viscount D'Abernon), Lord Dunraven, Herbert von Bismarck, Norman Forbes Robertson, Hugh Warrender (of the Grenadier Guards), the American orator Bourke Cockran, the American millionaire William Waldorf Astor, Harry Cust, and probably the Prince of Wales (later Edward VII). She became a confidante of the latter and was one of the very few who could enjoy a relatively unsycophantic relationship with him. He granted her the rare favour of using Buckingham Palace's private garden entrance and relied on her to organize parties for him, as she knew his particular friends, as well as his favourite foods and music. She understood how to please him and how to manage him; in return he lavished gifts and affection upon her. Such was Jennie's tact, however, that she was able to remain on friendly terms with his wife, Princess Alexandra.

Randolph accepted all of this. Although he once became angry enough to physically assault Sir Charles Dilke, who had beseeched Jennie to become his mistress, and also ordered the Prince of Wales out of his Mayfair house because of his attentions to his wife, he was resigned to her way of life. He was friends with Jennie's lovers, rode with them, dined with them, and met them at his club. There has been considerable speculation about why Randolph, a proud and even arrogant man, should have accepted his cuckolding quite so publicly. The most likely explanation is his guilt at having contracted syphilis, especially if it was indeed so early in the marriage. Some biographers have suggested that he was homosexual, which might explain his extremely close relationship with his mother, his physical estrangement from his wife, his many trips abroad in the company of male friends, and his almost pathological dislike of his son, Winston. All that is known for certain is that Randolph not only accepted Jennie's extramarital affairs but was on amiable terms with her lovers. He had his own life. In the autumn of 1890, he and his friend Harry Tyrwhitt leased a houseboat in Egypt for several months. 'The days slip by as if they were hours,' he wrote to Jennie; 'life on the Nile is ideal ... good food, hock, champagne, Pilsener beer, Marquis chocolate, ripe bananas, fresh dates and literally hundreds of French novels.'[5]

Jennie's sons also knew of her affairs, although there is no evidence that they acknowledged them. In a schoolboy letter to his brother, Winston spoke of arriving in London for the weekend, where he had found Mama and Count Kinsky breakfasting at the Aldford Street house. On a visit to Paris, Winston was entertained by three of his mother's lovers: Breteuil, von Hirsch, and Trafford. Later on, as Winston grew older, his mother used her many contacts to advance his career. She called in favours and cajoled her former admirers to help her son.

Her application in assisting her sons' ambitions made up, to some degree, for the neglect they had suffered as children. Although Jennie had taken a keen interest in their education and had encouraged her boys to work hard, it was often 'Tante Leonie' who took Winston in hand during his holidays. Leonie loved children and in 1889 gave birth to another son, Seymour. The baby was a disappointment to Jack, who had wished for a daughter. The day after the birth, he wrote: 'Leonie was not ill [in labour] more than 20 minutes; it was brought on by an uncomfortable drive, the horses running into a hansom, also the day before her nerves had been much shaken by the crossing-sweeper mistaking her for Mrs. Cyril Flower! The boy is a fine one, but it *is* a bore not having a girl!'[6] There is no record of Leonie's feelings on the matter.

In 1890, however, she had other worries. Papa was feeling unwell, and Mama had been alarmed by his haggard appearance when she was in New York. The man who had made and lost three fortunes, and who had founded the Jerome Park racetrack and the Coney Island Jockey Club, was reaching his journey's end. Leonard never stopped trying to help his daughters. In 1888, when he was seventy, Leonie's mother-in-law, Lady Constance, wrote to the Duchess of Marlborough that, after a visit to Europe, old Mr Jerome had set out for America 'to make a new fortune for Clara and Leonie'.[7] He had, however, all but abandoned his attempts to do this via the stock market, simply keeping an interest in his racehorses while living frugally and simply in the Brunswick Hotel, where the Coaching Club held their annual meeting and where he could see his sporting friends. He urged his wife not to worry about his health, stressing that he absolutely did not need to be taken care of and was most comfortable in his small room. She should, he insisted, stay in London with her daughters who needed her most.

In December 1890, however, his wife insisted that Leonard visit Europe, travelling first to France and on to England. He was then living at the Lenox Hotel (having moved there from the Brunswick in May 1890), where he made himself comfortable. He denied any need for a servant: 'When one has been in the habit of putting on one's own shoes and stockings for 60 or 70 years it would become rather awkward to have another do it.'[8] This from the man whose eldest daughter travelled to the wilds of Wyoming with a French maid because she had never done up her own boots! Finally, Leonard agreed to leave New York. He settled his hotel bill, packed his trunks, and embarked on the journey, refusing a servant to accompany him. Leonard's nephew, Eugene Jerome, wrote to Clara Frewen, explaining how little help the old gentleman would accept:

> I can understand how much you regret that one of you did not come over to him. But he would <u>not</u> consent to change his surroundings … it was his wish to remain at the Hotel Brunswick [*sic*] and we <u>had</u> to submit … Had Uncle Leonard permitted me to do so I certainly shd have cabled you to come … When he sailed Henry Jerome [a relative] went on board with him, and did all to make him comfortable … None of his family here were inattentive to his true condition. On the contrary he was a constant source of anxiety.[9]

The family were worried. Leonard rested in London at the Frewens' house in Aldford Street, where Clara was once again living with the children. Leonard's nephew Eugene wrote to Moreton, saying: 'It must have been something of a shock to you to see how much he has failed and how helpless he has become.'[10] The three girls stayed by their ailing father. In January 1891, Leonie wrote to her mother-in-law to say that it was 'thawing today and we hope Papa has a good day. Jennie wants to go and meet Randolph at Marseille, but I doubt her getting away.'[11] Leonard had been moved to Brighton, where it was thought the sea air might improve his lungs, but in March 1891, he died, aged seventy-three. His wife and three daughters were with him at the end. Moreton took Leonard's body back to his beloved New York for burial. Leonard left behind some unsecured debts, which his wife Clara quietly determined to pay, as a matter of honour. She never told the girls, and they were left to wonder at her meanness, going without fires in the grate on bitter evenings at the house she had taken in Rochelle Mansions in Tunbridge Wells. She was also determined to leave her grandchildren with an inheritance. Her grandson Hugh Frewen recalled many years later that she had paid off the last of Leonard's debts within a few weeks of her death in the rented house in 1895. In spite of their many differences, she had remained loyal to her husband until the very end.

The three girls were unaware of the financial difficulties Mama faced; there were so many other things to think about. It had been tiresome for Clara, on returning from Paris in 1890, to face the debts at home. Mama wrote that she and Papa had discussed the situation. Clara's financial situation had become a preoccupation with her parents, who frequently offered suggestions on how she could economize. Mrs Jerome strongly urged her eldest daughter to be more frugal and to keep a careful record of what she spent each week. Meanwhile Moreton had a new moneymaking scheme, the 'gold-crusher', a machine that could extract gold from refuse ore in derelict mines. He believed that he would make a personal fortune and simultaneously increase the world's gold supply. If the American government would not listen to him and make silver a currency, he would double the supply of gold currency. Moreton procured a miniature model of the machine, which was displayed on their dining room table; visitors would be brought in to admire it. Clara entertained on an even larger and more lavish scale, in the frantic hunt for investors. The family helped again. Randolph Churchill and Jack Leslie both invested in the new invention, as did Mrs Jerome.

Although Clara was kept busy entertaining at Moreton's behest, he continued his frenzied travel schedule. He was often away for weeks or months at a time. Shortly before her father's death, Clara had fallen in love with one of her first gentleman callers, a previous admirer of Jennie's, King Milan of Serbia. This enormous, dark-haired man had become prince of Serbia at the age of fourteen in 1868 and king in 1882. As a young man he led a war (with the aid of the Russians) against the Ottoman Empire, which won his country's independence. Subsequent heavy taxation, an unpopular pro-Austria foreign policy, and a divorce from his Russian wife, Queen Natalie, prompted bitter opposition to his regime; in 1889 he abdicated in favour of his son Alexander. Milan then moved to Paris, where he met Clara. He followed her to London and began his courtship. Flowers, dinners, visits to the theatre and the opera, and increasingly impassioned daily letters were his tools of seduction. His notes, some of which Clara kept all her life, usually began: 'Chère et charmante amie,' (dear and charming friend) and ended: 'Je vous baise les mains et suis votre devoué Milan' (I kiss your hands and am your devoted Milan).[12]

Clara was intrigued and flattered. In contrast to Moreton's careless words and frequent departures, this was romantic love, as ironically she had once experienced with Moreton. Milan adored and loved her in the way she wanted to be loved – on a pedestal. He begged Clara to marry him. When Milan learned that Clara's favourite flower was the gardenia, he sent her bouquet upon bouquet daily until she begged him to limit the gifts to one a month. At the end of the first month, he presented her with thirty flowers, in varying degrees of freshness because he had set one aside for each day in his own apartment. Such grandiose gestures appealed to Clara. She festooned herself with mauve ribbons, her favourite colour, and surrounded herself with fanciful bibelots and accessories. Milan's embossed letters added to her treasure trove of romantic frivolities; they were carefully read and reread, then tied up with ribbon and preserved in a coffer. Eventually they filled a trunk. As they were written in French, Moreton could not read them. (He abhorred foreigners, particularly the French, and mistrusted foreign languages.)

Because Moreton *was* so arrogant he never imagined that his scatterbrain 'goosey wifino',[13] so trying in her tardiness and fussy ways, might contemplate an alternative life. Their youngest child, Oswald (whom his sister Clare called Peter), was three, and all three Frewen children were still in the nursery. Clara was therefore free to cultivate male friendships, and she stepped out to the theatre, the opera, and to parties, where she danced and flirted. She and Moreton always lived as though they were rich, for Moreton had exhorted that if they behaved as if they were wealthy, wealth would somehow find them. By 1890, however, his efforts to make a fortune had taken on an increasing air of desperation. Clara paid little attention. She had just begun to look outside Moreton's world and, in Milan, she liked what she saw.

Jennie wrote of Milan that he was 'certainly one of the most uncivilized beings I have ever encountered', although she added that this 'thick-set man with inky black hair and moustache, of little or no education save what his natural intelligence helped him to pick up … was, notwithstanding, an agreeable personality'.[14] She made no mention in her memoirs, however, of his devotion to her sister Clara. Apparently Jennie also criticized the ex-king's table manners, which upset Clara, who was hurt by her sister's denigration of the man for whom she told herself she might leave Moreton. Clare recalled in her own memoirs how her 'mother used to regale us in after years with the assurance that she could have been Queen of Servia [Serbia], that Milan had offered, if she would divorce and marry him, to take back his throne'. When asked by the children 'almost in one voice' why she had not, she replied: 'For the sake of my children.'[15] Clara had treasured memories of a dinner he had given in her honour, at which the flowers, 'Cattleys' orchids, had cost £300 (a remarkable £20,000 in today's money). Milan also gave splendid (and costly) gifts to her children. Clare received a ruby heart set in diamonds, and Hugh a huge box of lead soldiers, representing every regiment in the British army. He was especially pleased by this present, because his cousin Winston had a large collection of toy soldiers and was gratifyingly jealous. The older boy soon swopped some of his foreign dragoons and other pieces for some units from Hugh's new collection.

Clare later recalled how Milan had once visited her in the nursery, after she had been ill, and arrived laden with gifts: 'He sat by my cot, smothered it in lilac and mimosa and a multitude of toys'.[16] On the occasions when he called, the children would be summoned from the nursery. Clare would be dressed in her lace dress, as her mother Clara whispered that she must curtsy to the 'King'. Clara still found all monarchy – even royalty in exile – intoxicatingly grand. She could not, however, be persuaded to cast her lot with the man who signed himself 'Mille ans', meaning One Thousand Years.

Milan's proposal forced a decision from Clara. It had been a charming romance, and it was much more pleasant to be the 'Chère et charmante Amie' rather than Moreton's 'Dear Old Thing', but radical change was not her style. Her fragile demeanour camouflaged her resilience. Clara's fey, other-worldly approach to life belied an impressive ability to sum things up, ignore the distasteful, and sail through. She was a fundamentally conventional woman to whom divorce did not appeal. Moreton may have disappointed her expectations, but he was her husband. She did, however, consider Milan's proposal seriously, and the doubts that she expressed about her future with Moreton, who was once again away, produced this response from him:

> Yes, dear, we shall be happy – happier than we ever were, when we get 'home' once more. But I am sorry you get these ideas into that dear head. We don't drift apart one practice [*sic*]. But you have the secret of perpetual youth, and I have not: and I grieve very much that you keep your attention on the changes in me. You are not the only one! The Kid [his brother Stephen] says 'How can you be happy when you never

get on a horse, nor see a hound?' – passions with me once. It is no use. You can not rekindle certain enthusiasms. You must be content – nay, happy – to recognise that my life has now more earnest studies, and I have even lost the physical phantasies of my youth! Best Love – more philosophical than of old, but much more valuable.[17]

When investment for the gold-crusher fell through, Moreton's confidence was shaken. Worse still, Lord Randolph, who had been a keen supporter, decided to withdraw his backing and also cancelled a trip to South Africa that the two had planned together. He wrote to Moreton that they would inevitably disagree on business matters and that a quarrel must be avoided. Although Moreton's feelings were hurt, his pride forbade him from showing it, and he bought back Randolph's shares (with difficulty). He was still struggling with his creditors, who dated from the early days of his marriage, and had had to cash in his holdings in the development of Superior City on Lake Superior, where he had bought land back in 1883. This purchase would have ensured his lifelong prosperity if he had waited for it to be developed commercially. As usual, however, he was unable to profit from his assets and sold the land too soon in order to pay for his newest scheme. In July 1891, he set off with soaring hopes for California to market the crusher:

> God bless you, darling Kali, don't miss me over much, sweet thing. I shall soon be back again to wander no more … What a different joyous thing life looks now, compared with that dead time when I went off to India with Salar Jung. I have got the ball at my feet once more, and this time I'll keep it – you will see. It is a very far-reaching expedition this, is it not? I do hope I shall make the very most of the chance. It will be so ripping to turn the tables on Randolph.[18]

Proving Randolph wrong was a preoccupation. Later in the journey he wrote: 'Everything that transpires shows how right I was to be confident and what a fool Randolph would feel at having thrown away an immense fortune just when he needed it … Yes, the end of our troubles is, I feel, very near indeed.'[19] In high spirits he bought options on gold mines and waited for more crushers to be made at a

Californian ironworks. He anticipated with relish how 'sour' Randolph would be when he learned of the crusher's success.

Their troubles were, however, of near insurmountable proportions. Moreton's biggest problem was how to extract himself from the liabilities generated by the combination of bad luck and poor management that had bedevilled Powder River. Failing to eliminate these debts over the years was a critical factor, hindering his later business schemes just as poor credit facilities and lack of capital crippled his big ideas, holding him back at the very moment that he most needed to hold onto his potential assets.

The hardest task for Clara was to manage a growing family on so little income, while maintaining her husband's obsession with preserving the Frewen name and superior social status. Appearances were everything. Bankruptcy was never an option. Children would be farmed out haphazardly to Mama, other relatives, or friends abroad. Clara, meanwhile, would evade creditors or pay bills by borrowing five-pound notes from her sisters. Moreton was bright; he spoke and wrote with charm and wit, and he had great vision. But he was too arrogant to recognize his limitations and was, as a result, a poor delegator. These flaws would have pernicious consequences.

Leonie and Jack Leslie's partnership was entirely different. As her father had accurately noted, Leonie was much the stronger character, and her level-headed approach to life's trials and pleasures provided the solid foundation on which she and her husband raised their family. Leonie had learned to assess her circumstances and to make the best of them. She cultivated the Leslies, because she had to; they soon loved her, becoming dependent on her good judgement and friendship. She treated her parents-in-law with respect, while also keeping her distance; to the end of her days, Jack's mother was always 'Lady Constance'. If Leonie's future lay in the Irish countryside rather than, as planned, a Parisian art studio, then she would take pleasure in the many pursuits and delights offered there. Leonie made the conditions of her existence work in her interest, neither feeling resentment nor looking elsewhere. Besides, she and Jack had a happy life, despite his lack of ambition. Their trip to Italy had been a great success; Jack had shared his love of Italian art with Leonie and they had both made sketches. They had also revelled in sightseeing and visiting friends.

They still hoped that with Sir John's help they might buy their own house in London. In 1890, Leonie wrote to Clara from Glaslough that she was anxiously awaiting news, as the house they wanted had not been secured. Clara was once again away (this time in Wiesbaden) to save money. Leonie shared with her sister her current worry: although Sir John was 'quite willing' to assist them with their house purchase, there seemed to be difficulty in raising the necessary money. She was very excited about having a home of her own and asked her sister to send her a sample of her green silk curtains. Like the rest of the family, she hoped that Moreton's gold-crusher would prove a great success: 'I hear good accounts through Mama of the G. [gold-crusher] machine but somehow it is no use setting one's heart on it. Things are never as one expects them & it is always *l'imprévu* [the unexpected] that turns up. However it wd be so delightful to have you & M. rich, apart from our own little picking.'[20]

Meanwhile, high-society life in Ireland continued its usual rhythm. House parties were frequent, and the Leslies often entertained house guests. Shooting parties were arranged with the Caledons, who lived on bordering land, and a select group of other large landowning families. Each winter, suites at the Shelbourne Hotel on St Stephen's Green in the centre of the city were booked by aristocratic visitors from England who came for the Dublin season. This, known as the Castle season after Dublin Castle, the magnificent building in Dublin in which the viceroy worked and entertained, ran from January to March, adding much festivity and excitements to the winter. Viceregal hospitality was lavish, and in addition to the elegant regimental balls, there was much private entertaining. Dublin was a city of contrasts, and Ireland a nation of opposites: poverty was rife, but the social set entertained on a grand scale in the capital. The Irish author Elizabeth Bowen[21] described the Shelbourne Hotel thus in the 1880s:

The departure in splendour, from the hotel, of guests bound for a ball or Drawing-room was one of the spectacles of Dublin, a drama played to an audience of old-timers, critical, but well mannered. Nor were the rights of this audience ever denied. Very early, people took up their places – some climbed the Stephen's Green railings, to see better. All eyes, expectant, were fixed on the Shelbourne's door – which, frequently opening, exposed to view the bright-lighted hall, ivory pillars and crimson carpet. The actors in this drama were grouped ideally – tier upon tier up the steps of the noble staircase would be seated the ladies and gentlemen waiting for their carriages. They wore the impersonality of extreme grandeur – ladies' plumes nodded, satins gleamed, jewels shot out rays; the black-and-white of the gentlemen was immaculate. One after another, round rolled the carriages … Each time, a name was called: a couple or a party rose from the stairs, advanced down the carpet, emerged from the porch, drove off … That ceremony, satisfying to all, was repeated night after night for un-numbered winters – being briefly renewed each August, when Horse Show Week brought its own special round of festivities.[22]

In addition to the parties there was hunting and the races. In spite of diminishing land revenues, much of the social elite in Ireland lived well. Leonie's boys, now aged four and five, were at home in Glaslough, where they were minded by a German governess, Fräulein Clara Woelke. Since there was only a year between Jacky (John Randolph) and Norman, they did everything together and had become extremely close. When little Seymour arrived in 1889, his boisterous siblings took pleasure in setting him up against the wall and felling him with well-aimed cushions. He remained good-humoured throughout, his cherubic smiling face surrounded by brown curls. Afternoons were spent agreeably with the gamekeeper, who taught the boys the outdoor skills essential to rural life.

Leonie took her maternal responsibilities very seriously. Her 'sailor boys', as she called Jacky and Norman, followed her about the house, rode ponies, went boating on the lake, played with the dogs, and generally enjoyed a healthy, outdoor lifestyle in a village where they were treated with deference and respect. She wrote of her peaceful existence to her cousin Mamie in America:

> You have no idea how heavenly this place is in this weather. I arrived at 11 o'c – rested & dressed – lunched with Sir John & Olive [Jack's sister] who left by the three train & then Jack & I went out on the lake – had tea – & roamed about till dinner time. It was twilight at <u>10 o'c!</u> & as warm as in America – not scorching, as the nights are damp. Today Jack has gone to Belfast for cattle show – & will not be back till late ... The children beaming. We have been sitting under a big tree in the garden all the morning – Jacky building a 'tour Eiffel' – both of them in the thinnest of pinafores. I can't tell you how delightful the complete change is after the hustle & hurry of Paris & London. Perhaps at any other time I should think it dull, particularly during the season – but as it is I enjoy the calm & peace & shall not feel like losing my temper every other moment![23]

When the 'sailor boys' were tired, they would listen to their mother playing her favourite pieces on the piano in the drawing room. Leonie would go on doing this for hours, finding her music a source of pleasure. When they were not at Glaslough, she and Jack travelled to England, often with the boys. In London they stayed at Stratford House; in Brighton they took lodgings; sometimes they hired a house in Eastbourne or Berkhamsted, where they would winter at the home of Lady Sarah Spencer. Christmas was sometimes spent at Deepdene in Dorking, home of the Beresfords, cousins of the Leslies by marriage. At the seaside, in Brighton or Eastbourne, the Leslie boys holidayed with their Frewen cousins: Hugh, Clare, and Oswald. Hugh was the eldest, followed by Jacky and Clare who were the same age, then Norman, Oswald, and little Seymour.

A serious accident befell Seymour in 1894, when he was five. There are few records describing the incident, save Seymour's own recollections, published in his memoirs. 'The story seems to be,' he wrote, 'that I slipped on our frozen Irish lake, and bovine T.B. being rife, no doubt, in our dairy herd as everywhere in those days, tubercular hip disease set in.' He was taken to a famous London specialist, Sir Tom Smith, who, according to Seymour, pronounced: 'He will never reach the adult stage.'[24]

Jennie wrote to Clara: 'Don't tell Mama but Leonie is very low about Seymour. Vernon's doctor saw him and thought very badly of him.'[25] But Mama apparently *did* know, for Seymour later claimed she wrote: 'poor little Seymour has the doctor every day. I am *so* sorry, he's such a dear, darling, boy — everyone loves him and is devoted to him.'[26] The following year, in 1895, when Seymour was six, Leonie took her sick son to Paris to see more specialists, including the well-known physician, Dr Charcot. Seymour described the horrors that followed:

> Two doctors peeped at me and whispered to Leonie and a third (but English and clean shaven) arrived, while Miss Tree [his governess], very spruce in white, went behind a Japanese screen from whence came sounds of scrubbings, boilings, rinsings. A wad of sickly chloroform was, without explanation, held firmly over my face. I lay in my full-length plaster jacket, into which I had been almost poured before leaving England by being hoisted on a derrick and painted with liquid plaster-of-Paris, to be dried by the side of the fire during a very long night … The plaster casket was now ripped away with a sharp knife, the doctors getting angry at my screams. They then left cheerfully after fitting a pulley and weight to one leg.[27]

Seymour was moved to Eastbourne with Miss Tree for the beneficial sea air. In Eastbourne, Dr (later Sir) Charles Harding operated on Seymour, who was by now suffering from a kind of paralysis. It meant that he had to remain mostly on his back for the next five years. 'Never was I able to run, swim, ride a bicycle, climb a tree, play a game or have any companions of my own age,' he wrote, 'for what indeed would we have in common?'[28] Leonie travelled often to see her son, but he lived mostly away from his family. One Christmas Eve he wrote to his mother that he looked 'forward to your present when I look in my pillow-case'.[29] The stress of being separated from her son was hard on Leonie, and the cost of boarding Seymour and the nurse, as well as the large medical bills, were an added burden to the family finances. Seymour wrote, 'My condition was of course a secret grief to my mother and my separate establishment a severe drain on her slender resources.'[30]

Although Seymour missed having time with his siblings and his extended family, the other Leslie children spent many of their holidays with their Churchill and Frewen cousins. Clare Sheridan described her cousin Winston, the eldest of all the cousins by ten years, in one of her books about her family:

> Winston was a large schoolboy when I was still in the nursery. He had a disconcerting way of looking at me critically and saying nothing. He filled me with awe. His playroom contained from one end to the other a plank table on trestles, upon which were thousands of lead soldiers arranged for battle. He organized wars. The lead battalions were manoeuvred into action, peas and pebbles committed great casualties, forts were stormed, cavalry charged, bridges were destroyed – real water tanks engulfed the advancing foe. Altogether it was a most impressive show, and played with an interest that was no ordinary child game.[31]

Winston made a great impression on his younger cousins. He was the leading spirit and the others followed or marched along behind him, following his many instructions. Jacky, Leonie's eldest son, later recalled that his cousin Winston

> sailed into my life early, as the black sheep of the family. We were eight cousins of Jerome stock and in spite of whisperings and warnings we admired Winston intensely ... We children followed Winston though he had few admirers amongst grown-ups except my mother and his beloved old nurse Mrs. Everest ... Winston already showed signs of a commanding nature. In his army there were only two rules but they were strictly enforced on the cousins: firstly Winston was always General and secondly there was no promotion ... To such an extent I followed my leader that I imitated Winston's famous threat that if he were punished he would go and worship idols![32]

This rambunctious extended family attended the circus and theatre matinées together when in London. Jacky would write fondly of his memories of these outings with friends and cousins: 'When we attended the theatre with our friends and governesses we were always seated half an hour ahead of matinee time and kept up the highest spirits. I remember watching a very ordinary play, but we were in such convulsive hysterics of enjoyment after our long wait that we hailed the most ordinary conversation with peals of laughter much to the surprise of the actors.'[33]

A great treat was being taken to Buffalo Bill's Wild West Show. The cowboy performers recognized 'Uncle Moreton' and whooped with abandon, shouting his cattle brand 'Outfit 76!' to Jacky's delight:

> But of all pageants and shows the most resplendent was Buffalo Bill's Wild West Exhibition at Earl's Court in the early Nineties … The whole scene of hanging a horse thief (his face actually turned green in the process) was taken from an afternoon's work on the Powder River Ranch. To our huge excitement our elders were invited by Buffalo Bill himself to take a drive in the battered old Deadwood Coach. It was an inspiring sight to see Uncle Moreton, Charlie and Bill Beresford and our fond father setting off in that famous vehicle, each wearing top hat and frock-coat but holding a rifle. Cowboys drove them and a sharpshooter lay on the roof. The coach was duly scented and pursued by mounted Indians who received a heavy fire from the well-dressed occupants. The combination of whirling horses and Indian feathers with fashionable gentlemen firing for their lives made one of the most wonderful of afternoons in memory.[34]

Randolph had returned from Egypt in February 1891, shortly before the death of Jennie's father. He had then departed almost at once on a lengthy nine-month trip to South Africa. Jennie was lonely and wrote to Randolph that she felt 'as though I were living in an atmosphere of disease, funerals, graves!' She added that 'the black fog on top of it makes me feel too depressed for words … I am making myself too melancholy.'[35] In another letter she told him that she fought 'against depressions the whole time … I am always saying to myself that life is too short for the blues.'³⁶ It was unlike Jennie to be brought so low.

Randolph had different preoccupations. His purpose in travelling to South Africa was to search for gold. The *Daily Graphic* had agreed to pay him 2,000 guineas (about £150,000 today) for twenty articles of 4,000 words each. His good friend Lord Rothschild had loaned him £5,000 (nearly £350,000) and sent his best mining engineer to accompany him. Randolph was so concerned about his financial situation that he had insisted Moreton return the Churchills' remaining gold-crusher investment of £200 (£14,000) before he left. Jennie was reluctant to press her sister, knowing her circumstances, and had refused to accept the money when the cheque came, but Moreton insisted on repayment, writing to Randolph, 'Jane [Jennie] threatened to return this second cheque to Clara, which was very kind of her, very; but it would hurt my feelings if she did.'³⁷ And Randolph had no qualms about insisting on payment: 'I have had so many accounts to settle and payments to make before leaving that I am rather short and racing has been distinctly adverse … If you will pay the £200, I will be much obliged.'³⁸

The period following her father's death was a difficult one for Jennie. She was thirty-seven, and she and Randolph were once more leading more or less separate lives. After their reconciliation following his resignation, Randolph had again begun to travel without her and was often away. Jennie was still involved with her lover, Count Charles Kinsky, but he did not devote himself to her exclusively. She was worried about sixteen-year-old Winston, writing to Randolph in 1891, 'Honestly he is getting a bit too old for a woman to manage … He really requires to be with a man.'³⁹ Jennie was also concerned about money. 'I have been obliged to pay a few bills, one big one, and of course, the boys' school bill and the tutors will have to be paid,' she wrote to Randolph. Later in the same letter she added, 'I'm afraid you must feel that our future is in a bad way, as regards money … But we must not despair.' She told him that at a recent party where everyone had made a wish, she had 'wished that you might make a lot of money'.[40] She and Randolph still had her annual income, which was a source of bitter resentment to Moreton. 'Cannot your mother help you,' he wrote to the impecunious Clara. 'Your mother seems to think R and Jenny's future is alone of any consequence, that whether we sink or swim is nothing!'[41]

In 1891, the entire Jerome family – minus husbands, who were all elsewhere – spent the summer together in the country at Banstead. Charles Kinsky took a house adjacent to theirs and spent much of the time entertaining Winston and Jack Churchill. A letter from Jennie to Randolph gives evidence of a warm relationship between her children and her lover. 'The boys are very happy,' she wrote. 'Kinsky has gone out with them to put up a target. I am going to try to buy a gun for Winston.'[42]

In spite of the summer idyll, Jennie's future towards the end of 1891 seemed uncertain. Kinsky had left for a shooting trip to Austria. In the autumn, the boys were back at school, Randolph was still away in South Africa, and Jennie moved in with her mother-in-law. She was saving money by letting their Connaught Place house. It was a disagreeable situation for the proud Jennie: 'I know beggars can't be choosers but I feel very old for this sort of thing,'[43] she wrote to her husband. She longed for Randolph to return and, no doubt in response to her unhappiness, he sent her a diamond. She was delighted and had it made into a pin, then a ring.

She also threw herself into music. Jennie was still a concert-standard musician and playing the piano was a tremendous release (as it was for Leonie). In 1891, she attended the Bayreuth opera festival with Leonie, Lady de Grey, Evan Charteris, and one or two other friends. They lived simply, she wrote, as 'it was only frequented by the real lovers of music, who were prepared for the sake of it to be as uncomfortable as German ideas of comfort could make them. We were all billeted on different people, who in some cases could only have one lodger. My sister and I were fortunate enough to secure rooms at a banker's, where we fared sumptuously compared to some.'[44] She wrote later of her profound enjoyment of the music:

My first impression of 'Parsifal' was, as the Teutons say, <u>colossal</u>. The pilgrimage to Bayreuth, the 'low living and high thinking,' combined with the musical atmosphere we were living in, contributed no doubt, to the rapture we felt; but that it existed was undeniable. Our little party had settled to meet between the acts and exchange opinions, but so great were our emotions that we all fled in different directions, avoiding one another until the performance was over, when we should be more calm.[45]

In the 1890s Jennie gave a number of charity recitals back in London. She performed, playing duets with the renowned Polish pianist Ignacy Jan Paderewski, heard Arthur Rubinstein play, and met the composer Franz Liszt at the Russian Embassy in London. In 1891, she played a concert for one of the duchess's favourite charities, the Paddington Recreation Centre, attended by 900 people. In spite of being experienced, she acknowledged in her reminiscences that she 'had never been able to surmount the nervousness one feels in playing before the public, whether in concerted pieces or alone'.[46]

Jennie had also been cheered in the autumn of 1891 by a trip to her friend Baron von Hirsch's hunting lodge at St Johann in Hungary. When she passed through the Gare du Nord train station in Paris on her way home, she witnessed a murder. 'I suddenly heard a shot fired,' she recalled. She was unharmed and later wrote: 'It was proved at the trial that love and money were the motives of the crime.'[47] On returning to London, she was diagnosed with a rectal abscess, writing to Randolph: 'Those pains I used to think were in my "mind" were really the thing beginning. I've got lots of pain.'[48] She was also bitterly disappointed by the news that Randolph's written request, from South Africa, to Prime Minister Robert Salisbury for the ambassadorship to Paris had been refused. Jennie wrote to Randolph that she had been 'horribly low ever since', adding indignantly that she had not 'breathed it to anyone, not even your mother. The idea is too galling that the only thing you ever asked for should be refused!'[49]

Jennie's concerns about managing her eldest son, now seventeen, continued. Winston planned to apply for a place at the military academy Sandhurst, and he needed good examination results. In December 1891, she agreed with his schoolmaster at Harrow, Reverend J.E.C. Welldon, that Winston should spend 'a good part' of his holidays in France to perfect his French. Jennie decided to send him to Paris for the Christmas break. Winston was very unhappy. 'Darling Mummy,' he wrote that December, 'I shall think it will be very unkind and unnatural of you to allow him [Welldon] to do me out of my Christmas … I have firmly made up my mind not to go abroad till after the 27th. If you in spite of my entreaties force me to go I will do as little as I can and the holidays will be one continual battle.'[50] Jennie was not impressed by Winston's response and wrote in reply: 'My dear boy, I feel for you in every way & can quite understand your anxiety & desire to be at home for Xmas, but quite apart from other considerations, the tone of your letter is not calculated to make one lenient. When one wants something in this world, it is not by delivering ultimatums that one is likely to get it.'[51] Winston was duly despatched to Paris, with promises from his mother that her friends would look him up over the holiday. By Christmas Eve, he was desperate. 'Write to Baron Hirsch,' he implored. 'Do! I have not heard a word from all those "friends" you spoke about.'[52] A few days later, he wrote again. 'Not a word from Baron Hirsch – Not a line from M. de Breteuil – Not a sound from Mr. Trafford. I don't know any of their addresses so what can I do?'[53] He begged his mother to write to him. On 29 December, he declared: 'It seems to me that with you "out of sight and out of mind" indeed. Not a line from anybody. You promised to write 3 times a week – I have recd 1 letter.'[54] In January, finally, Jennie's friends Baron von Hirsch and M. Breteuil sent him invitations. But it had been a lonely Christmas for Winston.

Randolph returned to London from South Africa in January 1892, where he had been hunting big game and prospecting for gold. He looked every inch the grizzled hunter, complete with beard. He and 'Pa' Perkins, the engineer representing Rothschild, had in fact struck gold. Rothschild lent Randolph another £5,000 to purchase shares in his Rand Gold-Mining Company before the news broke and the price went up. Unfortunately, Randolph found that while he had been away his reputation as a statesman had diminished and their financial situation had become so dire that he and Jennie were going to be forced to sell their house at Connaught Place. Jack and Winston were at Harrow; Randolph and Jennie moved in with Randolph's mother on Grosvenor Square. The nanny, Mrs Everest, became a housekeeper. Although Randolph continued to write articles for the *Daily Graphic*, they could not live within their income, which comprised Jennie's £2,000 per annum from the marriage settlement and any money Randolph was able to earn through his writing (although ministers were paid, Members of Parliament did not receive regular salaries until 1911). As living with Randolph's mother to save money was not attractive to Jennie, she spent the summer of 1892 in Scotland visiting friends and then travelled to Paris. When she returned in September, she was very ill and was diagnosed with pelvic peritonitis.* Randolph, who was in Newcastle, returned to London hastily as soon as he heard, writing to Winston, who was in his last term at Harrow: 'Your dear mother was extremely ill yesterday and we were rather alarmed. But thank God today there is an improvement and the doctors are very hopeful.'[55]

Randolph himself was frequently ill. He now appeared to be suffering from the tertiary stage of syphilis, with palpitations, numbness of the hands, increasing deafness, and difficulty in articulating. He tried nevertheless to sustain his political career and in the spring of 1893 attended political meetings. However, his behaviour was erratic and his speeches in Parliament, so long his strong point, were faltering. He was still worried about his finances. In October 1893, Randolph wrote to Jennie in Paris that he had no money and that he was putting his South African mining shares on the market. 'Dearest I am vy sorry,' he began, 'but I

---

* Pelvic peritonitis, now more commonly known as pelvic inflammatory disease, is most often caused by sexual transmission from an infected partner. Significant risk factors include multiple partners.

have no money at the present moment & balance overdrawn at the bank.'[56]

In London, the duchess decided that she had no further need for Mrs Everest's services and sacked her. Winston was appalled when he heard the news. Mrs Everest had served the family for nineteen years. He wrote in October 1893 to his mother from Sandhurst, where he had begun his first term: 'My dear Mamma, I have felt very uncomfortable since I got here about Everest,' he began. 'I fear that at the time you told me – I was so occupied with Jack & Harrow that I did not think about it seriously. Now however – I have a very uneasy conscience on the subject.' He was as much upset by the manner in which she had been given notice as by the sacking itself. The duchess had sent her away, ostensibly for a holiday, without paying her wages and had then terminated her employment by letter. 'At her age she is invited to find a new place & practically begin all over again,' wrote Winston indignantly. 'She has for 3 months been boarding herself out of her own money and I have no doubt is not at all well off … Dearest Mamma – I know you are angry with me for writing – I am very sorry but I cannot bear to think of Everest not coming back much less being got rid [of] in such a manner.'[57] Although he pleaded for his mother to at least keep their faithful servant until she had found another place, Jennie did not reply. Randolph sent Mrs Everest a small sum. Other little presents followed sporadically, but she had been discarded by the family she had loved and served for so many years and was only kept from destitution by her sisters. She continued to write to her beloved Winston and Jack, sending them gifts at Christmas and on their birthdays, until her death the following year.

Jennie and Randolph were now permanently living with the duchess at Grosvenor Square, in what had begun as a temporary arrangement. The effects of Randolph's illness were now apparent to everyone. Friends such as the Liberal Lord Rosebery (later prime minister) begged Jennie to stop her husband from attending the Commons and making nonsensical speeches, as he was an embarrassment to himself and the party. It was Rosebery who, in his biography of

Randolph, stated: 'There was no curtain, no retirement, he died by inches in public.'[58] Lord Carnarvon wrote that at a dinner Randolph's conversation was 'as mad a one as I ever listened to from mortal lips'.[59] It was partly to keep him away from such dinners and from Parliament that Jennie agreed in 1894 to accompany Randolph on a trip he wished to take round the world. At first the doctors consented reluctantly but then changed their minds. Doctors Thomas Buzzard and Robson Roose wrote to Jennie in June 1894, expressing their concern about Randolph:

> Our wish was that previous to his attempting a lengthened journey he should go with a Medical man to some place near at hand by way of experiment as to the effect of change upon him. In these circumstances it appears to us advisable to repeat in writing, what we have already expressed by word of mouth, that we cannot help feeling a good deal of anxiety in regard to the future, and would earnestly counsel your Ladyship to insist upon an immediate return to England in case Lord Randolph should shew any fresh symptom pointing possibly to disturbance of the Mental faculties.[60]

It was decided that Dr Thomas Keith, a prominent surgeon who specialized in treating the genital and ovarian areas, would accompany them. Randolph sold more of his gold stocks to settle his bills and provide funds for the trip. He also sold his share in the racehorse Abbess to his friend Lord Dunraven for £8,000 (over £500,000 in today's money).[61] Jennie and Randolph departed on 27 June 1894 from Euston Station. A number of friends as well as their families came to see them off. According to Peregrine Churchill, Jennie's grandson and biographer, in addition to various servants and the doctor, they also took with them a lead-lined coffin.[62] They sailed to America, first visiting New York and then travelling on to Maine by private train car. They liked Bar Harbor; Jennie wrote that it 'seemed a haven of rest, with its fresh sea-breezes, lovely drives and mountain walks'. What she liked less was its formality: 'the life there was very much a second edition of Newport, and consisted in perpetual dressing, dinners, and dances, and that horror of horror the leaving of cards [courtesy calls to friends and acquaintances at which no meeting took place, but a visiting card was left on a silver tray as a formality, indicating that the call had taken place]'.[63]

Bar Harbor was indeed similar to Newport, a summer resort that offered to wealthy Philadelphians and Bostonians an escape from the oppressive heat. Rusticators, as they were known, built huge shingle cottages, furnished with every amenity; together with their luggage and their servants, they travelled by steamship up to the little town for three months of the year. Once there, they continued their usual flurry of social events, which were merely transplanted to a greener and more rural setting.

Bar Harbor was fun for the Churchills; they dined with the millionaire George Vanderbilt in his house facing the sea, admiring his swimming pool open to the sky, through which fresh sea water constantly flowed. Jennie was surprised to see that men and women swam together, 'without shyness, and I must say, without vanity, for it must be owned that women do not look their best under such circum-stances'.[64] They dined with the socialite Mrs Van Rensselaer Jones and met the handsome author Marion Crawford, as well as the young amateur pianist Courtland Palmer. He and Jennie met frequently to play piano together. She wrote to her friend and trusted confidante, Consuelo, Duchess of Manchester, giving a description of Marion Crawford, for whom she had developed a passion (she tried unsuccess-fully to convince him to accompany them to Japan). She was also in love with 'Lord W' (possibly Frederic, Lord Wolverton, a member of the Prince of Wales' inner circle) and declared that Bar Harbor 'must be delightful ... for the people who do not have better things behind them'.[65]

Jennie enjoyed herself in spite of the irksome social formalities. She danced the 'Boston' at the Kebor [now known as Kebo] Valley Club, a dance, she remarked, that 'only Americans know properly'. Jennie continued to think of herself as American and had never lost her American accent. She was happy to meet 'some delightful women, with whom I found myself in that perfect sympathy which can only be felt between compatriots'.[66] It was with regret that she left America as they travelled across Canada to Banff Springs. From there they moved on to Vancouver and then San Francisco. Randolph's health and temper did not improve; indeed, he got worse, and there were scenes. Following one incident a manservant had to be sent home, and there were ugly arguments. It was a repetition of what became a familiar pattern of Randolph abusing his wife when he grew irritable. He was often unwell, because he insisted that they keep on the move. Jennie wrote to Leonie from Banff in August 1894: 'As soon as he gets a little better from having a rest and being quiet he will be put back by this traveling – and <u>nothing</u> will deter him from doing what he likes. He is very kind and considerate when he feels well – but absolutely <u>impossible</u> when he gets excited – and as he gets like that 20 times a day – you may imagine my life is not an easy one ... I try to make the best of it.'[67] Before their departure from London, Clara had witnessed angry clashes between the couple and had described these scenes in detail in letters to her husband. Moreton replied that he was sorry for 'dear Jane' and that he hoped her circumstances would improve, stating that Randolph was an 'impossible man'; a bad-natured man essentially.[68] Jennie wrote to Clara: 'I cannot go into all the details of his illness, but you cannot imagine anything more distracting and desperate than to watch it & to see him as he is & to think of him as he was. You will not be surprised that I haven't the heart to write to you about the places & things we see.'[69]

To make matters worse, when they reached Hong Kong in August 1894, Jennie received a telegram from a friend, announcing that Charles Kinsky was to be married. Family pressure had been exerted on him and he was to marry the eminently suitable Countess Elizabeth Wolff Metternich zur Gracht. Although it is unlikely that he and Jennie were faithful to each other, Jennie undoubtedly cared deeply for him and was shocked by the news. She kept almost all of her correspondence throughout her life, yet there is almost nothing left of Kinsky's letters to her, which suggests that she either returned his letters to him, or destroyed them. Jennie's distress was exacerbated by her low spirits at this point of the journey. For over three months she had accompanied her dying and irascible husband and she was thoroughly discouraged. She missed her sisters, writing to Clara in November from the Bay of Bengal, 'I wd give much to be with you all now.'[70] Jennie also wrote later to Leonie of her pain at hearing of Kinsky's engagement:

> I do not blame him. I only blame myself for having been such a fool & wanted *l'impossible*. These 4 hard miserable months I have thought incessantly of him & somehow it has kept me going. But there! It is best for me not to write about it all – what is the use. The one thing which stands out … is the thought that I have sacrificed to him the one <u>real</u> affection I possessed, & that I shall never dare to turn to – for fear of finding that it has gone … Leonie my darling I am ashamed of myself at my age not to be able to bear a blow with more strength of character. I feel <u>absolutely mad</u> … it hurts me so. I really think if I have, I have been paid out for all my own iniquities. Even now I cannot bring myself to think ill of him in any way. I know you don't like him – but I loved him, I don't think any one half good enough for him. It is only right & fair that he shd have a nice wife – young & without a past – who will give him children & make him happy. I suppose the world will pity me the thought is distracting – they will have forgotten it by the time I return & barring to you & Norah [Randolph's sister] I shall not mention his name. They can all think what they like. From henceforth he is <u>dead to me</u>. I want to know <u>nothing</u>. He has deserted me in my hardest time in my hour of need & I want to forget him tho' I wish him every joy & luck & happiness in this life. Voilà – n'en parlons plus [That is it – let us not speak of it any more].[71]

Her situation was bleak. Randolph was certainly dying, although she was still concealing it from as many people as possible, including sons Winston and Jack. The illness was making him vile. She was nearly forty years old and had insufficient financial resources. Her sons were growing up and would soon leave her. Jennie blamed herself for Kinsky's decision to marry another because she herself had taken up with another man (whom she described in a letter to Leonie as 'F.W.', possibly Frederic, Lord Wolverton, or 'Freddy'). In spite of her determination not to think of Kinsky, in December 1894 she wrote to Leonie:

Oh Leonie darling do you think it is <u>too late</u> to stop it? Nothing is impossible you know. Can't you help me – for Heaven sake write to him. Don't be astonished at my writing this – after my last letter – But I am frightened of the future all alone – & Charles [Kinsky] is the only person on earth that I cd start life afresh with – & if I have lost him – I am indeed paid out for my treatment of him – The only thing I reproach F.W. for, is for telling me to give Charles up – knowing that he himself did not intend to stick to me – Leonie darling use all yr cleverness & all yr strength & urge him to put off his marriage. Anyhow until I have seen him – He cared for me until quite recently – & if I am only given the chance – I will redeem all the past ... Give my love to Mama & Clara – of course I will write – <u>Don't breathe</u> what I have written about Charles to anyone.[72]

Jennie had not often been so thoroughly thwarted. She was courageous and loyal, and those she loved were enchanted by her. Now that she had played and lost, she despaired. She had written with painful honesty to Clara that November: 'I HATE IT. I shall return without a friend in the world and too old to make any more now.'[73] In Rangoon, on the far side of the world, sick at heart and daunted by her future, Jennie prepared in December 1894 for the long journey home to London with Randolph, for what promised to be a grim Christmas.

CHAPTER EIGHT

The Funeral Tour

After six months overseas, during which they had travelled from America to Canada, Japan, Hong Kong, Singapore, Madras, Egypt, and finally back to England, Randolph and Jennie arrived on Christmas Eve at Grosvenor Square. By now, all the family knew that Randolph was dying. His son Winston saw that he was 'as weak and helpless in mind and body as a little child'.[1] There was no hope of improvement. All that was left was to await his death. Jennie was resigned to losing her husband and to having lost Kinsky. She confided to Leonie in January 1895:

> The bitterness if there was any, has absolutely left me. He [Kinsky] and I have parted the best of friends and in a truly *fin de siècle* manner. So darling don't worry about me on that score. I am not <u>quite</u> the meek creature I may seem to you. Pity or mere sympathy from even <u>you</u> is wasted on me. No one can do me <u>any</u> good. He has not behaved particularly well & I can't find much to admire in him but I care for him as some people like opium or drink although they wd like not to. *N'en parlons plus* [Let us no longer speak of it].[2]

Kinsky was married on 9 January. Two weeks later, on 23 January, Randolph slipped into a deep coma and died the next morning. The cause of death was given as 'General Paralysis of the Insane', almost certainly caused by the tertiary stage of syphilis. He had suffered greatly before his death. Clara Frewen, who was in London and was often with Jennie during those final days, wrote to Leonie of how Randolph 'groaned and screamed with pain and instead of the dose of morphia they gave him acting in five minutes it took 20 before he got relief and went into a sleep which lasted 4 hours. Jennie never left him ... she hasn't eaten or slept since she arrived.'[3] He was just forty-five.

Randolph was buried on 28 January in Bladon churchyard, near Blenheim. His death was a release for those who loved and admired him. His friend Lord Rosebery later wrote of his final years that he had been 'the chief mourner at his own protracted funeral, a public pageant of gloomy years'.[4] The funeral service was held at Westminster Abbey, and Randolph's nephew and godson, John Randolph Leslie, recorded that it was an 'immensely solemn' service, attended by 'Parliamentary heroes' such as Arthur Balfour, Michael Hicks Beach, Sir William Harcourt, and Lord Rosebery.[5] Three years later, a bust of Randolph was unveiled in a ceremony at the House of Commons. The Chancellor of the Exchequer, Sir Michael Hicks Beach, spoke before the assembled crowd, comprised of Lady Randolph and a number of members of the House, including Sir William Harcourt, Lord Curzon, and many others. His speech was printed in *The Times* and included the following words of praise: 'We admired Lord Randolph Churchill as a brilliant orator and a great statesman; but, further, we loved him as a friend (cheers), whose very faults made him only the more loveable.'[6]

Randolph had left behind large debts, totalling £75,971[7] (over £5 million in today's money), and his remaining Rand shares were sold to pay them off. Jennie, now forty-one years old, was worried about her future and had written of this to Leonie shortly before Randolph's death:

> Randolph's condition and my precarious future worries me much more ... mentally he is 1000 times worse. Even his mother wishes now that he had died the other day. What is going to happen I cant [*sic*] think or what we are to do if he gets better. Up to now the General Public and even Society does not know the real truth [about his illness] & after <u>all</u> my sacrifices and the misery of these 6 months, it would be

hard if it got out. It would do incalculable harm to his political reputation & is a dreadful thing for all of us.[8]

Although Randolph had been a difficult husband, he had opened up a new world to Jennie. He owed her much for her support and encouragement through the years, but she owed him, too. He had demanded little of her, probably because his illness precluded any expectation of fidelity on her part, but he had nevertheless been remarkably tolerant of her flagrant affairs. Now she was alone.

Her sisters stood by her, although they too were experiencing troubling times. Clara was penniless, and Moreton was almost always away. Having failed to make his coup on diamonds, he had decided that his future lay in selling the gold-crusher mills to Australians. He once again took leave of Clara: 'I did not get to my window fast enough to get a last glimpse of you. However, either I join you or you me early in the New Year. That is a promise, sweet dear brave Kali.'[9] He was travelling via the United States because he did not have enough money for the full fare to Australia and needed to borrow. His friends, Lord Albert Grey and Spencer Whitehead, helped him, two of the very few still prepared to do so. He wrote to Clara from the Knickerbocker Club in New York that he was feeling blue but that he would 'never forget the bad time you have had all alone this year and your courage and sweetness'.[10] To Jennie he wrote: 'Please God good times are near, and I will have a lot of horses for you and we will renew our youth and health also at the dear old game … Clara is so sweet and good and brave – I really am far more in love with her than ever before.'[11] Moreton, bearing three of the mills, arrived in Adelaide just before Christmas 1894. He immediately settled in with the Governor of South Australia, the Earl of Kintore. While Moreton made his speeches on silver and met the 'right people' to take up the gold-crusher, Clara was in London, summoned in haste to be with Jennie at Randolph's deathbed. Even in the midst of her terrible ordeal with Randolph, Jennie had often thought of her sister, wishing she could hear some 'good news'[12] of her and Moreton.

Clara had been in Brighton when Jennie's distress call came at the end of December 1894. She made immediate arrangements for her departure, leaving the 'chickies'[13] there with her mother, who had by now assumed financial responsibility for both mother and children. Moreton sent his long-suffering wife next to nothing, and Mrs Jerome could not bear to see her daughter and grandchildren suffer. Moreton was fulsomely grateful and wrote her to thank her for her goodness during these hard times. After Randolph died, Moreton commented: 'So poor R – has flickered out. Dear sweet little Jane, my mind runs on her very much.' He hoped that her financial situation would improve (always an obsession with Moreton) and that her life would be more comfortable henceforth: 'Oh! To have got rid of that hair shirt – poor fellow – for ever.'[14]

By the end of January 1895, Jennie was indeed ready to cast aside the hair shirt. She had suffered over the past year and was ready for release. She left the grieving duchess, who had now lost both her sons to premature deaths (Blandford had died in 1892) and went with Leonie to Paris. The Leslies had agreed to join her with their two young boys, and they moved into an apartment together on Avenue Kléber, near the Champs Elysées.

Winston now had his first army commission. He had passed, on his third attempt, his entrance exam to Sandhurst in 1893. His marks were not sufficient for an infantry cadetship, so he was assigned to the cavalry, a situation about which his father had been extremely critical, not least because it would cost an additional £200 a year and the upkeep of several horses. In response to an exuberant letter from Winston, he had replied with bitter sarcasm:

The first extremely discreditable feature of your performance was missing the infantry, for in that failure is demonstrated beyond refutation your slovenly happy-go-lucky harum scarum style of work for which you have always been distinguished at your different schools. Never have I received a really good report of your conduct in your work ... With all the advantages you had, with all the abilities which you foolishly think your self to possess ... with all the efforts that have been made to make your life easy and agreeable … this is the grand result.[15]

Randolph also had to face the humiliation of rescinding his previous request to the Duke of Cambridge to hold a place for Winston in his regiment. He wrote to his mother that Winston was a worthless scholar and indolent, and that his son need not expect much help from him. It is perhaps as well that Winston had long since learned not to rely on either of his parents. From his earliest miserable days of bullying at St George's, while at his prep school at Brighton, followed by his time at Harrow, his letters begged for visits from his parents. Although many Victorian parents did not form especially close relationships with their children, Winston's correspondence indicates that he believed his classmates received more visits and attention. Neither Randolph nor Jennie replied to many of his letters, and his attempts at getting their attention were almost always disappointed. When he realized that he could not expect visits while at Harrow, he began instead to request money and food. There is little evidence that these appeals met with a more favourable response. His later years at Harrow were characterized by greater independence and self-reliance, and his bids for parental attention diminished. His two years at Sandhurst coincided with his parents' world tour, and he saw little of either his mother or father in the period just before Randolph died. Both Winston and Jack adored their mother in spite of (or perhaps because of) her neglect. After Randolph's death, Winston took it upon himself to help her, and to assume responsibilities as head of their small family. Jennie in turn became more inclined to assist her sons. Her husband's death meant that she was able to focus more on them, and she turned her attention and drive to aiding them in their careers.

After Randolph's debts were paid, the remaining estate was meagre, with most of it tied up in trusts for his sons. Jennie was allowed a small legacy of £500 (about £34,000 in today's money) plus all of their belongings. She could expect little from Randolph's mother, with whom she did not get along. The dowager duchess was not fond of

Jennie, nor of Winston. Indeed, when her grandson, the 9th Duke of Marlborough, married the American heiress Consuelo Vanderbilt, the dowager duchess made her feelings for Winston plain. According to Consuelo, after a lengthy honeymoon she was received by her mother-in-law in November 1896 to be told: 'Your first duty is to have a child and it must be a son, because it would be intolerable to have that little upstart Winston become Duke. Are you in the family way?'[16] The duchess's feelings towards Jennie were also known to her sisters. Clara wrote to Moreton after Randolph's death, 'she [the dowager duchess] isn't likely to befriend Jennie, whom she doesn't like, or the boys, whom she never liked either.'[17]

Jennie still collected her settlement income from the rental of the house on Madison Square and refused to allow lack of funds to curb her style. She was still an intimate friend of the Prince of Wales, who could not have been more solicitous of her after Randolph's death, writing: 'The sad news reached me this morning that all was over … & I felt that for your and for his sakes it was best so … There was a cloud in our friendship but I am glad to think that it is long forgotten by both of us.'[18] A few days later, he had written to suggest that he might visit 'should you wish to see me'.[19] He wrote often, addressing her as '*Ma chère Amie*' (my dear friend), and made clear to her that his affection had not waned. Jennie was part of a privileged, inner circle dominated by a king-in-waiting, who was now fifty-four years old, portly, and a 'corpulent voluptuary'.[20]

He and Jennie were openly affectionate. Like the Prince of Wales and others in their circle, she sported a tattoo; hers was a snake, coiled around her left wrist. Tattooing had gained royal approval in 1862 when the Prince of Wales had visited the Holy Land and had the Jerusalem Cross tattooed on his arm. Later on, as King Edward VII, he acquired more and when his sons, the Duke of Clarence and the Duke of York (who later became King George V), visited Japan in 1882, he told their tutor to take them to the famous master Hori Chiyo, who tattooed dragons on their arms. By 1890 tattooing had become extremely fashionable among both sexes in Edward's aristocratic set.

Jennie now wanted to help her eldest son in his career. She asked her former lover, Colonel John Palmer Brabazon, who commanded the 4th Hussars (billeted at Aldershot near Sandhurst), to take Winston into his regiment. Randolph had previously refused to make the request, but soon after his death, Winston asked his mother to intervene, which she acceded to within a week of her husband's passing. In what would become a familiar pattern, she did so with success. As Winston later acknowledged, his mother was an infinite resource of advice and contacts. She had the remarkable gift of remaining good friends with her many lovers and never hesitated to ask them for favours. Winston later remembered: 'My mother was always on hand to help and advise … she soon became my ardent ally, furthering my plans and guarding my interests with all her influence and boundless energy. She was still at forty young, beautiful, and fascinating. We worked together on even terms, more like brother and sister than mother and son. At least so it seemed to me.'[21]

Jennie travelled to Paris in April 1895. After the coldness of the duchess and the restraints of formal mourning in London (where for six months she would be expected to wear black and refrain from attending any social events), in Paris she was free. Other American expatriates were there, too, including her close friend, Consuelo (formerly Yznaga), Duchess of Manchester. Leonie arrived with her two sons, and they were joined by little Seymour. Clara stayed behind in Tunbridge Wells, penniless as usual and busy looking after Mama, who was unwell. Moreton was away, as was Jack Leslie, another increasingly absent husband, who these days was often to be found at the racecourse. Paul Bourget and the Marquis de Breteuil, now both married, were very pleased to have Jennie once again in their midst. When she heard that Breteuil had married an American girl, Marcelite Garner, Jennie had broken off their relationship. He wrote back, saying: 'What I miss most is not seeing you anymore.'[22] He now saw her again, as did Bourget and other friends. In March 1895, Jennie met and fell in love with a good friend of Moreton Frewen's, the Irish-born American lawyer and statesman Bourke Cockran, who had recently been widowed.

Jennie and Bourke were charismatic bon viveurs. Bourke had emigrated alone from Ireland at seventeen, been a sales clerk in a New York department store, taught French and Latin, then become principal of a public school and worked as a foreign correspondent. He had obtained his law degree by studying at night, and was now a successful lawyer and a brilliant orator. He and Jennie shared a ready wit and sharp intelligence. They both loved horses, the theatre, and music; both were wonderful conversationalists. They went everywhere together, riding and bicycling (Jennie wearing fashionable black bloomers) or strolling through tree-lined streets. Jennie wrote to her sons that she was 'very busy' and that Paris was 'charming'. She loved ice skating at the Palais de Glace: 'I find I have not forgotten my various figures – Sea Breeze, etc.'[23] When Jennie received an urgent summons to join her ailing mother in Tunbridge Wells and left for England, Bourke set sail several days later.

Mama, now seventy years old, was failing fast. Her last years had been lived in pinched misery. 'Poor darling,' wrote Clara, of all the sisters the closest to her strait-laced mother, 'she has had so little pleasure these last years.'[24] Her goal had been social prominence, which she had hoped to achieve through her beautiful and accomplished daughters, but she had been disappointed by all of their marriages, despite the social cachet they had brought. Randolph was terrifying, Moreton had wasted both his talent and the family's money, and the Leslies had always seemed patronizing.[25] Clara's daughter Clare recollected that 'At the end of her days she became superbly squaw-like and would sit impassively for hours staring into the fire, her head shrouded in a shawl … Because of our grandfather Jerome's vicissitudes of fortune, she had maintained a Spartan way of living, saving and accumulating, in order to leave some fragments of a once great fortune to her grandchildren.'[26] Mrs Jerome wished to pay off her husband's last debts, and she wanted to leave her daughters Clara and Leonie with an inheritance, Jennie having been provided for already. She also wanted to help her grandchildren, as she had tried to do all their lives, being only too aware of their chronic lack of funds. 'My dear Winston,' she had written in 1893 before he went to

Sandhurst, 'I was so pleased to get your letter this morning. You remember the conversation we had about the watch, about how easily one could borrow money on it.' This was obviously something she expected that Winston would do. 'So I was afraid you might have done so. It is all right. "All's well that ends well" ... I will send the cheque to the tailor so that will settle the matter according to your Father's wishes. I am sure in fact he need never know that you borrowed it.'[27]

The three sisters all travelled to Tunbridge Wells to be with their mother. Clara especially was saddened by her impending death. Unlike Jennie and Leonie who had spent little time with Mrs Jerome over the previous few years, she had remained close to her mother. In late March, Clara wrote to her cousin Eva Thompson, who had come to visit them: 'Darling Mama has had a relapse & Jennie & Leonie have come over from Paris ... I am utterly miserable but still hope as the doctors say if her heart can bear the strain of the crisis today & tomorrow all will be well.'[28]

Mama rallied briefly, then died on 2 April 1895. All her daughters were present. With their mother gone, the inheritance became the central question. Leonie immediately cabled Eva's husband, David, who was a trustee of Clara Jerome's estate, with a legal query, explaining in a later letter: 'we <u>had</u> to know a little how we stood on account of Clara.'[29] Mama had tried her best to look after Clara, leaving her two-thirds of her estate and the remaining third to Leonie. This gave Clara an annual income of £1,600 (£110,000 in today's money) and Leonie £800 (£55,000). Clara was touched and emotional: 'What breaks my heart, Moreton,' she wrote to her husband, 'is that she sacrificed so much these last years of her life economizing and saving just to leave me in comfort.'[30] Unfortunately there is no record of Jennie's reaction to her mother's will.

As ever when it came to money, Moreton was far less sentimental than his wife. The outcome of Mrs Jerome's will had another, more direct effect on his finances. Some years earlier, he had sold his reversionary life interest (that is, his right to inherit the estate at Innishannon in Ireland after his brother Dick's death) to his mother-in-law for

£1,000. The act was prompted by one of his cash crises, and Mrs Jerome intended to secure the reversion for his children. He had tried to buy it back before she died, but was unable to finalize the deal, which she would probably have refused. He immediately cabled Clara: 'The reversion (that is my life interest) now belongs to *you* and it is left to you in your mother's will. Ask Dick if he will buy it for 500£ [just over £34,000 in today's money] giving you the right to buy it back inside of two years for a thousand. The matter is urgent.'[31] Moreton wanted to keep the property, but also needed to raise £500 immediately for another new project, the Ashcroft process for the treatment of sulphide ores; this separated zinc from lead, silver, or gold. He was determined to bring the process from Australia to America and was insistent that Clara should raise the capital to fund the venture immediately. While he made the long journey home from Australia, she was to travel to America to get the money. The three sisters had already agreed to travel together to take their mother's body back to the United States for burial in Greenwood Cemetery, Brooklyn, next to Papa. They now decided to postpone their trip until Moreton's return in June. 'I have been waiting day to day to know what steamer we could come on, as our plans have been rather upset by Moreton announcing his arrival for the 30th of June,'[32] wrote Leonie to her cousin Eva.

In the end, only Leonie and Clara made the crossing, as Jennie had decided not to join them. She did not record her reasons, and there are no letters that might illuminate them. There was no estate for her to settle, and the affair with Bourke had ended. She chose to remain in Paris until the middle of July and then planned to travel to Scotland with her younger son Jack. From there she planned to go to the spas at Aix-les-Bains. Bourke had been a good friend of Leonie's, and both he and Jennie had confided in her, particularly about the end of the affair. Bourke had claimed that Jennie was too energetic for him; she in turn had explained to her sister that Bourke was too sociable and that it was exhausting to be with him.[33]

Clara and Leonie were excited about their trip. It would be the first time that Clara had been to the United States without Moreton and it was also her first visit to her native country in twelve years. Leonie had not been to America since she had married there eleven years earlier. They would visit family in New York and then travel up to Newport for a holiday. They could not spend much money, warned Leonie in a letter to Eva, who was booking their hotel in New York; they would be economical and live quietly. Clara received letter upon letter while in America from an increasingly frantic Moreton. 'Do everything you know how to bring back a little money,'[34] he wrote from London. And then, 'I am terribly pressed for money. The value of our sulphide shares has risen to 4000£ [£275,000 in today's money] per share; so that the half I have remaining is worth 2000£, but it would be madness to sell any portion of it if I can hold on by hook or crook.'[35] Unfortunately, he did have to sell half his shares for cash, only to see their price rise within days. Clara returned in August with a half-year's income − £800 − which was immediately absorbed to pay the most pressing debts.

The lease on their house in Aldford Street had expired, so the Frewen family now had nowhere to live. Clara took the three children to stay with her friends, the Hatzfeldts, in Sommerberg. She waited there for two months, increasingly embarrassed that she might be wearing out her welcome, while Moreton, still in London, awaited the verdict of the experts' final test on the Ashcroft process. In October 1895, the news came and it was positive. Jubilant, he cabled Clara a much-needed £100 (just under £7,000). She was thrilled and relieved:

My darling − you can't imagine all my joy − so it is all true!!! Well, well, I feel as though the world was coming to an end, that we should have such happiness. Only oh! how <u>how</u> I wish I could be with you to see your happy face and the radiant boyish look I used to know so well. It is a real sorrow I can't be with you … How I would have enjoyed hearing the 'Well, well, Kali, we're out of the woods at last' and the look on your face. And now by the time I'm home again you'll get used to it, and only look happy and content. I have been longing so for that look of utter joy, like years ago, I shall, all the same, expect to see you ten years younger, and you'll see me quite changed, too! Darling, I <u>am</u> so glad.[36]

It had been close to fifteen years of disappointments bravely borne, during which time Clara had had to shuttle back and forth between family and friends. Although she had lived quite well, her flirtations with Milan and other handsome admirers providing momentary pleasures, it had nevertheless been a volatile existence and her outlook had been darkening. Now, finally, it seemed their dreams were to come true.

Moreton and his partner Otto Stalmann, an extraction engineer, had acquired the exclusive right the previous summer to exploit the Ashcroft process in America, but the licence was valid only until 1 April 1896. There was not much time – a few months only – to buy up all the sulphide ores they could before it became general knowledge that this process would make the ore, previously seen as waste, very valuable. As the agent of the Australian Exploration Company (AEC), Stalmann went to America to make the purchases, in an arrangement made hurriedly when it was not known how valuable might be the rights to the American market that had been conceded to Moreton and Stalmann. When the potential value became more apparent, the AEC decided to take another look at the agreement and declared that it was not in the correct legal form. It was a minor point of detail, but the stakes were high. The AEC repudiated their agreement and disclaimed Stalmann as their official agent. Discarding Frewen and Stalmann's prior exclusive agreement, the AEC re-formed as the Sulphide Corporation, which over the next twenty years, paid out dividends that totalled 2,500 per cent profit per share. Moreton Frewen had lost, once again. He was the pioneer of what became a very profitable extraction industry in America, but it was others who earned the millions. His friend, Lord Kintore, who had made an original large investment of a founder's share, reaped a fortune when those shares later rose in value. Moreton, who had siphoned off his share into other half-formed companies, made nothing. Two years of hard work had resulted in a massive financial loss.

The family were not surprised when the Ashcroft venture went badly for Moreton. Jack Leslie's sister, Olive Guthrie, had written to

Leonie that the AEC was a great success and that, hopefully, Moreton would be a rich man: 'It will begin to pay in about eighteen months, if Moreton does not spend his money in advance. I will make Murray [her husband, a financier] try and get him to tie some up for Clara. He is sure to chuck it away.'[37]

Moreton immediately transferred his energies to the next project, the marketing of a new fluid disinfectant, called Electrozone. This was essentially a fluid obtained by the electrolysis of sea water, efficacious in neutralizing noxious smells. It was extremely useful for treating town sewage, but as always, Moreton had greater plans. He was determined to have Electrozone accepted in high society and sent it to ladies to use in their baths; he poured it on 'high' game at dinner parties, and despatched a sample bottle to every chemist in London. The smell of it was appalling, however, and it proved difficult to sell. Even with the support of Cecil Rhodes, who put in an order of 50,000 bottles to treat the saddleback sores of transport animals in Rhodesia, the financing of the British Electrozone Company was problematic. Moreton turned to the distinctly disreputable services of the promoter, Horatio Bottomley, to help set up and endorse the company. However, he was so impecunious that he was forced to resort to moneylenders, who lent him capital at extortionate rates.[38]

Later in 1897, Moreton's brother Dick drowned while sailing his boat off the Pembrokeshire coast. Under the reversionary life interest, this meant that his Innishannon estate in Ireland was inherited by Clara and would pass to her eldest son Hugh on her death. Moreton and Clara at last had a home of their own – a lovely place in the country, by the river and surrounded by beautiful woodland. There was further good news: the estate was unencumbered and brought in an annual income of £2,000 (nearly £140,000 in today's money).

Before Dick's untimely death, Moreton had also taken a lease on a London house near Chesham Place, to replace Aldford Street. But before Clara saw Innishannon, she had fallen in love with a country house that Moreton's brother Edward had shown her. Brede Place was a manor house on the Frewen family estate in Sussex, dating from 1350 with two wings added in 1570. In the great hall was a double-sided fireplace; the house possessed its own chapel and a priest's room. Brede had been unoccupied, however, for over a hundred years and was falling to pieces. Clara was immensely enthusiastic, writing to Moreton in her inimitable fashion:

> Oh, oh, oh, if I had <u>only</u> seen Brede before. I should never have taken Chesham Place, but got you to make some arrangement with Ted [Edward] to let us have Brede and spend our money there. It is simply <u>divine</u> and <u>so</u> little would have made it beautiful and habitable – indeed it is almost and at a push habitable now. <u>How</u> I regret you couldn't have been with me there – you would have been so interested and delighted. I can imagine lovely terraces down the hill in front and <u>what</u> a lovely view, and the chapel is quite beautiful – and the whole thing so compact and small would make an IDEAL country place for us – and considering the family name attached to it since 1650 – it would be a lovely property to leave behind us – as we might, I am sure, buy it from Ted.[39]

Clara was 'crazed' about the place, wrote Moreton to a friend, and they bought the property from Ted for £1,600 (£110,000 in today's money). The deeds were put in Clara's name to forestall creditors, but it was not long before the Frewens took on a mortgage of £2,500 (£172,000). While awaiting the building work to make the house habitable, they agreed to rent the house to Cora and Stephen Crane. Cora, a former madam from the Hotel de Dream at Jacksonville, Florida, was devoted to her husband, the author of the critically acclaimed civil war novel, *The Red Badge of Courage*, published in 1895.[40] She offered the Frewens a rent of £40 a year (which Moreton never accepted out of kindness) in addition to doing the necessary repairs named in the architect's report that the Frewens had commissioned for the property. The Cranes lived at Brede until Stephen died, on 3 June 1900, leaving behind large debts. Moreton could not have been more helpful, starting a fund to help pay them. Cora wrote to him after her husband's death: 'For all that you and your dear wife have done for us only God can reward you. I never, never could tell you of all the love and gratitude my dear one had in his gentle heart for Moreton Frewen.'[41]

During the same period, Leonie was absorbed in her world of social pleasures. She and Jennie had much enjoyed living together in Paris, with their own salon, frequented by the literary and musical talents of the day, as well as many handsome admirers. As she grew older, and after the births of her first three children, Leonie started to enjoy society more, becoming more worldly in her outlook over the years. Well into their marriage and long past the early flush of romance, Leonie and Jack discreetly went their separate ways and followed their own amusements.

Looking well was essential to social success. Leonie and Clara had the advantage of inheriting Jennie's cast-off gowns: the Prince of Wales liked women to be beautifully turned out and not to be seen twice in the same gown. This meant that Jennie had plenty of gorgeous frocks to hand on to her sisters. For Clara, a few pretty gowns were enough, but for Leonie, who now moved in the same swish circles as Jennie, many outfits were required. In the early morning, women wore skin-tight riding habits of a dark colour, accessorized with gloves, boots, hat, veil, and a posy of flowers in the buttonhole. In the late morning, ladies changed into a plainer dress with long sleeves (to emphasize that one did not do manual chores) for household duties, which included drawing up menus for the cook, interviewing the housekeeper, and writing letters, something that Jennie and Leonie developed into an art.

For luncheon, there were visiting dresses of silk or brocade, with trimmings such as bobbles and chenille, or delicate ruffles. In addition a bonnet or a hat, together with other accoutrements such as a parasol, a reticule, a mantle, and gloves, would be needed for paying calls in the afternoon or strolling through the park. At events such as garden parties, cricket at Lord's, or polo at Ranelagh, lighter and more elaborate fabrics were worn. For yachting only the most strictly tailored dresses were appropriate, with a simple trim of buttons and braid. Evening receptions demanded high-necked, long-sleeved formal dresses in an expensive fabric, sometimes with a train. For the theatre, modest attire was expected, such as a black or navy-blue dress with high neck and long sleeves, in order to differentiate genuine ladies from the gaudy actresses on stage and also to discourage public gawping. If the theatre was followed by a ball, however, another change of clothes was required. For a ball, or an evening at the opera, society women made their most opulent display and wore their most splendid décolleté gowns. These beautiful dresses were made from velvet and brocade, trimmed with pearls, antique lace, gold lace, jewels, and metallic threads. If royalty were present at a ball, married women wore a tiara. Ladies' maids were on duty in the dressing room throughout the evening to reposition headdresses, mend torn hems, and generally ensure that Madam looked perfect all night.[42] If royalty were present at a reception, and only when specified on the invitation by the word 'decorations' printed on the bottom left-hand corner, orders and medals could be worn.

Leonie enjoyed the glamour. Although she espoused a more worldly lifestyle after 1895, she still retained her sympathy and charm. In 1895, Jack Leslie introduced Leonie to his former commanding officer, His Royal Highness Prince Arthur, Duke of Connaught. He was the third son and seventh child of Queen Victoria and Prince Albert, and Victoria's favourite son. He was also one of the few royals permitted to have a career. As with all of Victoria's offspring, however, he was given little attention and still less affection by his busy parents. When he met Leonie for the first time he had just received news of a major professional disappointment. That year he had hoped to succeed the old Duke of Cambridge as commander-in-chief of the British army. To Prince Arthur's dismay, he had been passed over for Lord Wolseley. When he met Leonie, he and his wife, the shy German Princess Margaret (now Duchess of Connaught), were immediately attracted by her kindly nature.

Leonie was the first to reach out socially to the somewhat forbidding Connaughts. The duchess once commented to a younger member of the royal family that the couple never had fun before they met Leonie. Although Leonie possessed neither a big house nor a large fortune, she knew how to throw successful parties and was popular both as a guest and a hostess. The duke and duchess were invited to her house parties at Glaslough, and in her company they shone. As lesser royals could be difficult to entertain, the grandest hostesses tended to ignore them. Leonie was the first to recognize the potential of the duke, who until then had been thought rather ponderous. Her wit, which could make others seem amusing and clever, drew out the best in the couple, and they increasingly spent more time with her. As they became more popular, hostesses included them in their house parties, along with Leonie.

The duke had, in fact, fallen in love with Leonie. In 1900 he was appointed commander-in-chief in Ireland, a disappointing post, as he had hoped for a command in South Africa, during the Boer War. He looked forward, however, to spending more time with his beloved Leonie. Their friendship lasted over forty years, and they exchanged thousands of letters. They had a secret arrangement whereby intimate postscripts were inserted in their letters, to be removed if the main missive might be seen by others. Prince Arthur signed his letters 'Arthur' or 'A', but most often used the nickname 'Pat', which originated as a joke during his days in Ireland.[43]

There is no doubt that the duchess suspected she was not the partner to satisfy her husband. The shy child of estranged parents, Princess Margaret Louise of Prussia had suffered a tormented childhood under a father who terrified her. She was not a beauty and this, coupled with her shyness, made her seem rigid and unapproachable. She suffered from poor health too, and her ailments dominated her life. Constantly in search of cures, she was often engrossed with her woes and obsessed with trivialities. She was a loving wife but not, perhaps, a helpful companion to her sensitive husband. The position of a minor royal was both curious and complex. The duke was the Queen's favourite son and, when she died, the King's only brother. He therefore demanded, and received, the respect he felt entitled to. He was, not, however, in power and he had access to, without exercise of, real decision making. Consequently he felt the slights that he encountered deeply. A man of unstable temperament, subject to depression, he needed a steady and sound partner to whom he could pour out his cares and be advised and soothed in return. This his wife could not do. She had neither the necessary depth of character nor the selflessness to perform this vital function for her husband, much as she loved and needed him.

Leonie stepped into the duke's life with just such gifts. She was a responsive and compassionate listener. She admired the duke and was impressed by his title. Years later, her children would recollect the effort that she put into every royal visit, and how much she fussed over every detail so that their royal highnesses would be received with perfection. But whilst Leonie was awed by the duke, she was a sensible woman who gave sound advice, and she always cautioned moderation. For such a man, alert to every perceived snub and subject to volatile emotions, she was the ideal foil. He became increasingly dependent upon her, and the duchess, witnessing how helpful her friend was, encouraged this. Dark-haired Leonie was now the duke's 'beloved' and he was miserable without her. It was a remarkable achievement for Leonie to sustain a relationship with a man who was in love with her as well as a friendship with his wife who admired her and sought her advice.

It is known that their relationship became so intense that at one point Leonie suggested she must withdraw her friendship. It was the duchess who begged Leonie to remain friends with them both, writing in 1902, after a visit to Glaslough, in praise of her own self-denial. The duke's biographer, Noble Frankland, saw the letter and summarized it as follows:

> The Duchess thought there had been a crisis in his [the duke's] relationship with Leonie. The Duchess knew that Leonie had been near to folding up her tent and the Duke had confided to his wife how miserable he was and she thought this must have been caused by such a moment. The Duchess told Leonie that she was determined that the Duke and herself would continue to be her friends, though she conceded that it was difficult to know how to steer absolutely straight and for the right goal. She was sure Leonie would always help her. With the Duke, she said, she had 'but to touch the chord of honor [*sic*] & all is well & with it I know I still count for something & am not put

aside'. She realized that everyone had difficulties in life, but she said she would rather give up hers than lose the Duke. If anything was to go wrong, she doubted if Leonie would ever see or hear of her again and people would say, poor thing; she was silly and of no account. Feeling that she had now said everything and that it was perhaps easier to write than to speak, she sent Leonie her best love and signed herself 'Ever Yr grateful & aff. L'.[44]

This was a letter written by a woman who understood what she had to gain as well as to lose in the odd triangle in which she found herself and who had made her choice accordingly.

For Leonie, assuming a key role in the lives of the Connaughts was exciting, not least because their social position brought many advantages. In 1897, the Leslies were invited to accompany the duke and duchess to Egypt. Being in such exalted company meant travelling in luxury and style, and they were fêted wherever they went. Leonie wrote to Jennie from HMS *Renown* off the coast of Messina to say that five destroyers had come out to meet them. From Cairo she wrote of the pomp that had accompanied their ten days' travel in Egypt: 'the sightseeing all so interesting & the ceremonies part amusing − I feel I must always find stations decorated − & drive with military escorts.'[45]

Leonie had found it difficult to return to Europe from America, after sailing there in 1895 with Clara after her mother's death, and wrote to her cousin Eva in America of how much she minded leaving her old home country. In another letter, written just before leaving her ship, the *St Louis*, she wrote that she felt that this was truly the end of her American trip: 'On looking back at the three weeks we spent over there, I can't help realizing how much kindness we received from both old friends and new.'[46] On her return to Ireland, she wrote to David Thompson, Eva's husband and a trustee of Mama's estate, of her homesickness. Her letters to Eva and David at this time are wistful; she had taken up music again and was soon to return to Glaslough where a big family party awaited, 'rather trying', she felt. Everything seemed 'rather quiet after the rush of America'. Jennie, she wrote, planned to buy a house in London, and Clara would be going to stay with her children at the Hatzfeldts' – a good plan, Leonie believed, as the children would learn German and it would all be 'economical'.⁴⁷ Jack Leslie, a lieutenant in the Grenadier Guards, was frequently away from home, whether on military training or travelling. He went yachting around the coast of Greece with his sister Mary and made other trips without Leonie. The entrance of the Connaughts into her life was thus ideally timed. She was, perhaps, a little lonely as well.

While the duke and duchess were in Ireland, they naturally saw much of the Leslies. Occasionally the duke visited on his own. In June 1900, Leonie had a fourth son, Lionel. He was fair and blue-eyed, like Jack Leslie and also like the duke. If the duke and Leonie were having an affair, it is possible that Lionel was the duke's son. There is no evidence of this, however, and Jack seems to have treated Lionel in the same pleasant but offhand manner that characterized his relationship with his other boys. It is difficult to imagine that Leonie would have felt comfortable having the child of a close friend's husband, but this depends, of course, on how she perceived her own behaviour – which was always perfectly discreet and perfectly respectful. Certainly Leonie was delighted with 'Baby' and pleased to have another child. There was a great gap in their ages: her eldest, Jacky, was fifteen, Norman fourteen, and Seymour eleven years old. Lionel, however, was a tough child, whose brothers, he claimed, used him as a sort of football.

Leonie and the duke continued their warm and close relationship. In an undated letter, she wrote:

> I am so sorry *mon Bon Ami*, that there was no letter from me to welcome you back to Dublin Tuesday – but your Sunday letter did not reach me till a day late – and I did not like to write, not knowing for certain when you returned – I was glad to hear again from you yesterday – I like to know what you do each day and who you see – what you think – and who you like! Your letter is the event of the day, as I am very quiet here – just alone with the children and my thoughts – I think a great deal and shall never be able to tell you all I think. The Duchess has written me a most kind letter – and I hope I shall always be worthy of her friendship. I can't help writing postscripts. I like to

feel I can speak *à coeur ouvert* [with open heart] – it is like shutting the door and having a quiet talk – instead of trying to make conversation before inquisitive onlookers! I found these lines which I think you will like –

> *Le Bonheur – Etre seul avec toi porte chose,*
> *Bien loin du bruit et des gens ennuyeux*
> *Et rester là – tous deux ensembles, tres joyeux,*
> *Mais graves, dans un calme absolu, qui repose.*
> *Nous écoutons en nous un rhythme qui ressemble*
> *Au double battement d'aile d'un même oiseau –*
> *Etre ensemble – oublier même qu'on est ensemble.* ★

Will you write again *soon*. Best of friends, *Votre Amie*, L.[48]

★ Happiness – To be alone with you brings something
Far away from noise and tiresome crowds
And to stay thus – both together, very joyful
But solemn, in perfect calm, which is peace.
We hear within us the same rhythm which resembles
The twin beat of wings of the same bird –
To be together – to even forget that we are together.

CHAPTER NINE

Lower Jerome Terrace

After her morale-boosting stay in Paris in 1895 and a trip to
Switzerland with fifteen-year old Jack, Jennie had returned to England.
She never missed the Cowes regatta – all three girls inherited their
father's love of yachting. Jennie loved the Royal Yacht Squadron, the
most fashionable in the world, and in Cowes she was soon surrounded
by her friends. With her tiny waist, the current fashion, an hourglass,
full-bosomed, full-bottomed figure, suited her well. She and her sisters
wore white serge sailor suits during the day, with the sailor hats that had
been made all the rage by Princess Alexandra. Their American cousin
Kitty Mott, daughter of Mama's sister Catherine, was a frequent guest;
she and her millionaire husband Jordan arrived on a luxurious three-
masted schooner called the *Utowana*. The three sisters took turns to
spend Cowes week on board, often followed by a cruise. They enjoyed
this, although they found Kitty a dim-witted, if rather amiable, snob.
Her greatest trial was the fact that her wealthy husband's ironworks
firm specialized in lavatories and their name was emblazoned on each
toilet.

Although now forty-one years old, Jennie had many admirers,
including the handsome, twenty-seven-year-old Grenadier guardsman
Hugh Warrender. Even though it was diverting to have devoted lovers,
Jennie agreed with Winston, who had written over the summer while
she was living in a rented apartment in Paris: 'I am longing for the day

when you will be able to have a little house of your own and when I can really feel that there is such a thing as home.'[1] She took a house on Great Cumberland Place, in sight of Marble Arch, a respectable, quiet address. Clara rented a small house directly opposite, and Leonie stayed in a house near by. Such was the power of their reputations that the street became known as 'Lower Jerome Terrace'. Jennie, who was keen to establish a home for herself and her two boys, was surprised in October 1895 by Winston's sudden decision to travel with a friend, a subaltern of his regiment, to America and the West Indies – by way of Havana so that he could observe the Spanish troops collecting there to suppress the Cuban revolt that was simmering. Stung, she wrote sharply in reply:

> You know I am always delighted if you can do anything that interests and amuses you – even if it be a sacrifice to me. I was rather looking forward to our being together & seeing something of you. Remember, I have only you and Jack to love me. You certainly have not the art of writing & putting everything in their best lights but I understand all right – & of course darling it is natural that you shd want to travel & I won't throw cold water on yr little plans – but I'm very much afraid it will cost a good deal more than you think. N.Y. is fearfully expensive.[2]

Jennie added, acerbically, that she would have preferred to have been consulted, as she was providing the funds for the trip. She was incapable, however, of staying angry for any length of time and soon came round to the idea, suggesting old friends (and admirers) whom he might contact for help. These included Sir Henry Drummond Wolff, now Her Majesty's Ambassador to Spain, who could help get Winston into Cuba, and Bourke Cockran. Although their affair had only just ended, Jennie did not hesitate to ask him to help her son. Bourke, who had no son of his own and who liked Winston, was happy to lend a hand. For Winston, he was an attractive father figure, a man of experience, wisdom, and style, with a magnificent Fifth Avenue apartment in New York that could not fail to impress. The two spent long evenings discussing many subjects, including the skill and art of oratory. Avoid cant, Bourke advised him, as well as mannerisms, invective, or egotism. He and Winston analysed their mutual admiration for the great English orator Edmund Burke, and Winston persuaded Bourke to read him some of his speeches. Bourke explained how he prepared to give his own, by studying the subject in detail, storing in his memory material from his wide range of reading, and then trying to simplify complex questions with more familiar illustrations. Winston was learning solid technique from one of the best orators and forgot nothing of what he learned.

This was Winston's first visit to his mother's homeland, while Bourke was hopeful that Jennie would change her mind about their relationship and join him in America. He planned many exciting outings for her son. Winston had a trip on a tugboat and visited the Forts of the Harbour and West Point Academy – the 'American Sandhurst', he wrote to his brother[3] – as well as the Horse Show, and the Fire Department. He experienced at first hand in the mansions he visited the ostentatious vulgarity of New York as well as the growing informality in the streets, evidenced by the men's fashions for soft shirts with detachable cuffs and collars rather than frock coats and 'boiled shirts'. Women were favouring new 'rainy day' skirts, with hems six inches from the ground.

While Winston was enjoying America, Jennie was supporting her country's position on its Venezuelan interests – the Monroe Doctrine. Originally articulated in President James Monroe's message to Congress in 1823, the doctrine was a principle of American foreign policy that called for an end to European intervention in the Americas, after the Latin American nations had won independence from Spain. It became a more important issue in the 1850s when Britain, which claimed sovereignty over several areas in Central America, specifically denied its validity. In 1895, American President Cleveland extended the doctrine's reach once more and demanded that Britain submit to arbitration over a boundary dispute between British Guiana (now Guyana) and Venezuela. The tense political situation became a full-blown diplomatic crisis. In December 1895, President Cleveland informed Congress that he planned to appoint an American commission to define the boundary in question, and that its decision would be imposed on Britain – by war, if necessary.

For a while, Americans in England became unpopular and some left for the continent. Jennie began instead a quiet but forceful campaign to promote the American political position, giving small dinners and private parties for her friends in London. Her influence, together with that of her American friends, was helpful in calming the potential crisis in Anglo-American relations – 'Lady Churchill was U.S. "Best" Ambassador' was the headline of one Boston newspaper.[4]

Winston witnessed some action in Cuba and wrote of his experiences for the *Saturday Review*. Eager to help her son, Jennie sent copies of the article to all her influential friends. Her contacts were priceless. In February 1896, she arranged for Winston to be accredited as war correspondent to the *Daily Telegraph*, where he covered action on the North-West Frontier in India, which he observed while still in the army. She later found him a publisher, Longman, and in 1898 he published his experiences as a book, *The Story of the Malakand Field Force*.[5] Winston was always short of cash, although Jennie helped him to turn his aptitude for journalism into a lucrative money-spinner. Jennie herself was also chronically short of funds, her only reliable income being the £2,000 a year from the rental of Leonard's mansion in New York. Her mother had left her nothing, and Randolph's money was in trust for her sons. She was, however, a skilled juggler of bank and insurance loans, and there were 'gifts' from her admirers and lovers to ease her frequent cash-flow problems. Her lifestyle was well beyond her means, but she was incapable of reining in her expenses. Yet in spite of her extravagance, Jennie worried about money. She wrote to Winston on 3 March 1897, 'Out of £2,700 [£186,000 in today's terms] £800 [£55,000] goes to you 2 boys [now aged twenty-three and seventeen], £410 [£28,000] for the house rent & stables, which leaves me £1500 [£103,000] for everything – taxes, servants, stables, food, dress, travelling – & now I have to pay the interest on money borrowed.

I <u>really</u> fear for the future.'⁶ There were rumours in London of her remarrying, but Jennie wrote to her friend Daisy, Countess of Warwick, denying this: 'Dearest Daisy, I am <u>not</u> going to marry anyone. If a perfect darling with at least £40,000 a year wants me <u>very much</u> I might consider it.'⁷

A 'perfect darling with £40,000' (£2.8 million) would have been a welcome asset. Jennie had once again rather imprudently invested some money with Moreton, who had 'just left on a journey, for the 500th time, to make a fortune'.⁸ She did not, however, allow her finances to depress her. She had many friends, and the Prince of Wales was a constant fixture in her life. When he was photographed in 1898 in his first motorcar drive, Jennie was one of his three passengers; and she was often his guest at Sandringham. There were also trips to Monte Carlo (where she gambled, fantasizing that she would one day win a fortune) and to France (where she met up with old lovers such as Bourke Cockran and the Marquis de Breteuil).

It was early in 1898, however, when the inevitable financial crisis finally arrived. Jennie needed to find £17,000 (£1.2 million in today's money) in order to pay off loans she had taken out from different insurance offices, which were now due, as well as to clear some pressing debts. Her security for this new loan was to be assurance policies on Winston's life as well as her own, for which he was now required to guarantee the £700 premiums. He was not best pleased to discover that she had undertaken this without consulting him beforehand:

> Speaking quite frankly on the subject – there is no doubt that we are both, you & I equally thoughtless – spendthrift and extravagant. We both know what is good – and we both like to have it. Arrangements for paying are left to the future. My extravagances are on a smaller scale than yours. I take no credit to myself in this matter as you have kept up the house & have had to maintain a position in London. At the same time we shall vy soon come to the end of our tether – unless a considerable change comes over our fortunes and dispositions. As long as I am dead sure & certain of an ultimate £1000 a year – I do not much care – as I could always make money on the press – and might

marry. But at the same time there would be a limit … I sympathize with all your extravagances – even more than you do with mine – it seems just as suicidal to me when you spend £200 on a ball dress as it does to you when I purchase a new polo pony for £100. And yet I feel that you ought to have the dress & I the polo pony. The pinch of the whole matter is that we are damned poor.[9]

Winston also wrote to his brother Jack in January 1898, asking him to share this financial burden with him, once he came of age. Jack agreed. Winston wrote of his relief the following month, adding: 'The only thing that worries me in life is – money. Extravagant tastes – an expensive style of living – small and diminished resources.'[10]

In spite of her musings about a suitor with £40,000, Jennie continued to pursue affairs with alluring but not especially wealthy men. She was still an attractive woman, who looked younger than her forty-odd years, able to appeal to much younger lovers. She befriended an officer of the Seaforth Highlanders, Major Harry Ramsden, a young man so handsome that he was known as 'Beauty' Ramsden. When his battalion was posted to Egypt, she decided to follow him there. Winston assumed that she was making the journey for *his* sake, to further importune Kitchener to deploy her son to the Sudan so that he could see some action. Dutifully, Jennie did send Kitchener a steady stream of messages while she enjoyed idylls with 'Beauty' at the Continental Hotel in Cairo and on a river-boat trip on the Nile. The affair ended on a sour note, however. When Harry had to rejoin his regiment at Wadi Halfa, Jennie saw no point in remaining on her own and travelled to Port Said to embark for the homeward voyage. She discovered, however, that her ship had been delayed for several days. She raced back up the Nile with the intention of reuniting with her lover, only to find him in his room embracing another woman, the wife of the army commander, Lady Maxwell. Jennie's temper was notorious and her outburst was apparently heard throughout the hotel. News of the incident reached the ears of the Prince of Wales, who was on holiday in the South of France. He found the whole episode highly amusing, and wrote to Jennie: 'You had better have stuck to your old friends than gone on your Expedition of the Nile! Old friends are Best!'[11]

This was not only typical of the Prince's sense of humour but possibly reflected his jealousy, too. Jennie was furious and drafted a cutting reply as soon as she arrived back in London. Leonie, who had hurried across the street to greet her, found Jennie still in her travelling clothes at her writing desk. Jennie recounted the story to her sister and read aloud her reply: '<u>So</u> grateful for your sympathy – as your Royal Highness knows exactly <u>how</u> it feels after being jilted by Lady Dudley!'[12] Leonie advised her not to send it. When Jennie insisted, Leonie offered to post it for her and secretly destroyed the letter. Jennie later composed further notes, which she sent herself to the Prince. He replied on 8 April 1898 from the Grand Hotel in Cannes: '*Ma chère Amie*, Many thanks for your two letters of 5th and 6th – I must ask your pardon if my letter pained. I had no idea *"que c'était une affaire si sérieuse!"* [that it was such a serious affair!].'[13] The sympathetic tone of the exchange exemplifies the close relationship between the Prince and Jennie. By the following week, all was forgiven, and Jennie arranged a dinner for him at her home. Winston had written an account of his experiences when observing the British army in action, subduing rebellious Pathan tribesmen in the Swat valley near the Afghanistani frontier. Wishing to make amends, the Prince warmly praised the book, which gratified Jennie immensely.

Winston was also pleased by the Prince's support, although he was disappointed that his uncle Moreton, who had been asked to correct the proofs, had made many mistakes and had altered the punctuation so as to significantly change the meaning of some of the book's passages. Choosing Moreton as proofreader was a youthful error, but in spite of it the book was still a great success. Jennie pressed for favourable reviews and used her considerable social influence to help sales.

Her efforts as a mother also extended to organizing employment for Jack, now aged eighteen. She asked her friend, the financier Ernest Cassel, to find a job in finance for her younger son in the City of London. Cassel was a great contact; he had been instrumental in financing the first Aswan Dam in Egypt, the Central Tube Railway in London, and the Atchison, Topeka & Sante Fe Railway in America, as well as the economic infrastructure of Argentina. He was a close friend of both Jennie and the Prince of Wales. Jack, although not keen to work in finance, accepted that *someone* in the family had to make money, and it might as well be him. With her duty done and both boys apparently settled at last, Jennie grew restless.

Parties and love affairs were pleasant, but not sufficiently stimulating for her. After spending an evening discussing her future with her friend and former admirer, George (later Lord) Curzon, newly appointed Viceroy for India, she later recollected:

> On the eve of their departure from England the Curzons paid a visit to the Duke and Duchess of Portland at Welbeck. I was of the party, and, sitting next to Lord Curzon at dinner one night, we got on a subject which, without my knowing it at the time, was fraught with great importance for me. In a despondent mood I bemoaned the empty life I was leading at that moment. Lord Curzon tried to console me by saying that a woman alone was a godsend in society, and that I might look forward to a long vista of country-house parties, dinners, and balls. Thinking over our conversation later, I found myself wondering if this indeed was all that the remainder of my life held for me. I determined to do something, and cogitating for some time over what it should be, decided finally to start a review.[14]

This was to become the *Anglo-Saxon Review*, a quarterly magazine (originally titled *The Anglo-American Review*). 'My ideas were of the vaguest,' Jennie later wrote, 'but they soon shaped themselves.' She chose the title because it was 'strong, sensible and solid'. She wished to produce a literary magazine that would be read and collected, 'published at a price which will ensure its respectful treatment at the hands of those who buy it'.[15] She chose magnificent covers, each a facsimile of a celebrated book of the seventeenth or eighteenth century; these were selected for her by Mr Davenport of the British Museum, who also contributed a short article. Lionel Cust of the

National Portrait Gallery supervised the illustrations. Jennie wrote to all the clever men of her acquaintance for contributions: Swinburne, George Bernard Shaw, Lord Rosebery, Cecil Rhodes, and others. She hoped to earn money from the publication. Winston wrote on 1 January 1899 from Bangalore that the *Review* would give her an 'occupation' and 'interest' and that it 'may also be profitable. If you could make a £1000 [approximately £70,000] a year out of it I think that would be a little lift in the dark clouds.'[16] Inevitably the publication soon ran into trouble: Jennie argued with the publisher, John Lane, with whom Winston had negotiated on her behalf. Winston had also collaborated with his mother on the preface for the first edition. It was a beautiful publication and Jennie worked furiously to make it a success, but it lacked a clear editorial direction and, at a guinea an issue (well over £70 in today's money), was too expensive to endure. Jennie had declared in her preface that the 'first object of every publication is commercial,'[17] yet the *Review* had only a short life.

In June 1898, Jennie was invited to stay at Warwick Castle by her friend Daisy, Countess of Warwick (who had long been the Prince of Wales' favourite mistress). The Prince had become increasingly difficult to please with his advancing years, and Jennie could still be relied upon to manage him at these events. Also in the party was a handsome twenty-four-year-old officer in the Scots Guards, George Cornwallis-West. He was just sixteen days older than Winston and had a traditional upper-class upbringing: Eton College, Sandhurst Military Academy, followed by a posting with the Guards. Jennie was immediately smitten, even though the relationship was unsuitable for many reasons, especially that Jennie was twenty years his senior. George, the only son of an ancient family, was heir to Ruthin Castle in Denbighshire and property of 10,000 acres. There was, however, little money left, and he was expected to marry an heiress. His two sisters had done remarkably well; the eldest, Daisy, had married the wealthy Prince of Pless, and Shelagh, younger than George, was to marry the very rich Duke of Westminster. Nevertheless, George was besotted with Jennie.

He fell passionately in love and that summer found it difficult to think of anything else. The first of several hundred letters that Jennie preserved was dated 29 July 1898 and was decorated with hearts: 'I am on guard again on Sunday but it will, I hope, be the Bank, which means I am free from 11 till 5.30 – I thought about you all yesterday & built castles in the air about you & I living together.'[18] Throughout the summer the couple contrived to meet at the same country-house parties. When George moved to London later that year Jennie received him at her home, wearing a loose Japanese kimono instead of the conventional whale-boned corset and gown. The young, infatuated lieutenant wrote ecstatically of the 'lovely Jappy gown'.[19] People, inevitably, began to gossip. George's parents thoroughly disapproved. His mother had made a scene, he wrote to Jennie, after two of her friends had told her of the relationship. George had become ill and taken to his bed. His father had a stern conversation with him about money, which he tried to ignore, being as hopeless about financial matters as Jennie. He wrote to her constantly, professing his undying love and rejoicing in their very satisfying physical relationship. 'Will you write me a line like the angel that you are,' he wrote after recovering from his illness on 13 July 1898: 'I have missed you so the last few days. I have a picture of you before me now one in this week's *Sketch* sitting at a piano. I have got such blues today. I want you to cheer me up badly.'[20] Then, the following week, 'Oh my Jennie darling I did so love seeing you today, how I do crave for you, and longed to rush out of the ranks & tell you so, when I saw you this evening, you are so much, so <u>very much</u> [underlined four times] to me sweetie.'[21] On 1 August, he wrote a line 'to tell you that I am thinking of you & that I love you darling'.[22] It was a very sensual affair, which shocked their social world. The Prince of Wales wrote to Jennie of his displeasure, telling her that she was being foolish and compromising her social position. She herself knew this to be true and told George that there could be no marriage, as he so desperately desired.

By the following June, in 1899, the affair was still going strong, and Jennie began to waver on the question of marriage. George was indeed a 'perfect darling', albeit lacking the requisite £40,000. She was lonely without him. He wrote to her of his love almost daily, although as well as expressing his intense ardour for her he also described, in excruciating detail, his hunting exploits: the quality of his guns, the number of birds or animals he had shot, what the conditions had been like for fishing, etc. His letters were boyishly enthusiastic, and if he was somewhat callow and immature, he was also loving. The relationship had clearly lost none of its passion. In August 1899, the couple decided to announce their engagement during Cowes week, where Jennie had met and fallen in love with Randolph twenty-six years before.

Public response was scathing: Jennie was the leader of Anglo-American society in Britain, a privileged and intimate member of the royal circle, and widow of one of the nation's most famous politicians. Instead of selecting a mature man who was her peer, she proposed to marry an improvident youth, whose family disapproved of his choice. One of the most forceful protests was made by the Prince of Wales, as George later recalled: 'I had been invited on board the Britannia at Cowes and the Prince of Wales took the opportunity of taking me aside and pointing out to me the inadvisability of my marrying a woman so much my senior.'[23] The Prince, as ever, was probably thinking more of himself than of her. Jennie was one of his favourite women; although he saw advantages in her being married, there were none in her being in a love match and unavailable to him. The colonel of George's regiment, Arthur Paget, who was a close friend of the Prince, requested a verbal understanding from George that he would not become engaged before leaving for the impending conflict in South Africa. George's father wrote to Winston, forcefully declaring the inadvisability of any future relationship between his son and Jennie, and asking for his support. Winston, although he regarded the match as imprudent, was reluctant to cross his mother and merely informed her of the letter, plus a subsequent one, stating that he had no wish to become involved in an argument with George's family. In a postscript to a second letter sent to his mother, Winston told her that he believed George would cave in under family pressure and that the marriage would not take place. A month after the announcement of the engagement, Jennie decided that perhaps she was indeed taking an imprudent step and told George that there would be no wedding. He was very upset, writing: 'Oh my little Missie I have been so depressed since we parted; to think that all our arrangements and little plans for the future, as man & wife, should have burst like a soap bubble.'[24]

Jennie, although wavering again, asked the Prince, with whom she was still rather cross, to find a good posting for George. To his delight, he was given, at the Prince's request, a position as aide-de-camp to Lord Methuen, who commanded the 1st Division, that was to sail out to South Africa. The situation there was deteriorating, and war seemed inevitable. The Transvaal, one of three republics that bordered the British Cape Colony, was among the most industrialized and wealthy nations on the African continent. It had been recognized in 1852 as an independent republic by Britain, which then attempted to annex it in 1877. The inhabitants, Boers of Dutch descent, sought independence, fighting the British successfully in a series of conflicts, in which they were victorious at Majuba Hill in 1881. That year, on 5 April, they proclaimed their self-government by the Convention of Pretoria. The discovery of gold in the Transvaal in 1886 generated an influx of mostly British 'outlanders' who came to harbour many grievances against the Boer administration, chief of which was their being refused the vote. Since the aborted Jameson Raid by the British in December 1895, the republic had been rearming heavily and a skirmish was anticipated. The many Britons who fervently believed in empire were determined to fight; Winston was among them. Many newspapers stirred up jingoistic imperialism, and the popular mood in England was one of belligerence and angry excitement.

Jennie made the initial contacts, and Winston the final arrangements, for a contract as war correspondent for the *Morning Post*. In early 1900 he set off for South Africa with eighteen bottles of ten-year-old Scotch whisky and six of very old eau de vie, as well as twelve bottles of Rose's Lime Juice Cordial. George's battalion officers were also well supplied – they had been cheered by Alfred Rothschild's gift of twenty cases of 1887 Perrier Jouet champagne. Officers leaving for the front stocked up on their favourite foods and liquors; Fortnum & Mason, the famous retailers on Piccadilly, instituted a special 'South African War Service'. Other well-known stores soon did the same. These gentleman officers took with them their own dressing cases and luggage, as well as their own shotguns, made by Purdy or Westley-Richards. They also took their hunters and their servants: valets, coachmen, grooms, and beaters. Although George was well kitted out (he took his polo pony, Toby) and was excited at the prospect of seeing some action, he was distraught at leaving Jennie behind. The British correspondent of a New York magazine wrote: 'When Mr. West started for South Africa, the tears were rolling down his face, while Lady Randolph, who was more or less in hiding at the hotel, as so many of his own relations had come to see him off – was quite prostrated with grief.'[25]

Jennie was now without both her son and her beloved George. She was unaware that Jack too was planning to enlist for the fight. The *Review*, or 'Maggie', as she called it (short for 'magazine'), took up much of her time and at this point was failing. She needed a new activity to absorb her considerable energies. Mrs A.A. Blow, the American wife of the manager of one of South Africa's richest mining syndicates, came to her with just the right idea. She suggested that Jennie organize an American hospital ship to care for the wounded in South Africa. Jennie was at first unsure; a large part of the American population supported the Boers and saw them as plucky fighters for their independence against the British. Some of the British were also against the war, but when she asked the opinion of her friends, they were encouraging about the project. So she turned to her sisters, who both enthusiastically agreed to help in the formidable task of raising the $150,000 required to equip a suitable ship with medical provisions, as well as a staff of four doctors, five nurses, and an additional forty commissioned officers and orderlies. Much of the sum was to be raised in America.

In London, Clara was more comfortable than she had been for many years. She now had her inheritance of £1,600 per annum from Mama, as well as the £2,000 a year that the Innishannon estate brought in. She could indulge her flair for interior decoration and furnished her drawing room very daringly in mauve, the latest fashionable colour.

What rendered the decor particularly distinctive, however, was the large stuffed head of a buffalo, shot by Moreton in Wyoming, that stared down at the mauve silk curtains. In 1900, once again to reduce outgoings, the house had to be let, on this occasion to Sir Osbert Sitwell, who brought his family to London to be painted by John Singer Sargent. His son, also called Osbert, was struck by the mauve colour scheme and by the modern electric fan. This was not all that caught his attention, as he later recorded: 'One other feature of the house is perhaps worthy of remark. Its owner's boudoir, in which we children were obliged to do our daily lessons, was lined with photographs of Winston Churchill at all ages up to the one he had at present reached.'[26] Like Jennie and Leonie, Clara was proud of Winston's every success. Just as Jennie was the undisputed star of the three sisters, so Winston was the acknowledged leader of their children. Throughout his life, he remained faithful to his aunts and cousins, who frequently turned to him for favours.

Clara was relieved to be in London with her sisters rather than at Innishannon, which she disliked. She did not want to go riding over banks, hated fishing, and was not at all taken with the native flora. To her frustration, Moreton spent what little they had on doubling the size of the gardens, while also introducing non-migratory quail from Virginia and rainbow trout from Canada. Most of the investments were wasted. Herons and poachers did for the trout hatchery, and the quails were eaten by hawks. Clara had tried to make the best of the house, but the discovery of rats' nests in cupboards (among other nasty surprises) had disenchanted her. The final straw was the cache of mummified human heads, found in a cupboard. These had no doubt been brought back by Moreton's brother Dick from his travels, but Clara was disgusted. She insisted that they be buried in the garden, with some holy words spoken over them. Her sons later dug them up again and took them gleefully to show their school friends at Eton.

Clara was pleased with the work and liked the responsibility of being on Jennie's glamorous fund-raising committee, with American society ladies such as Fanny Ronalds (still a close friend of Jennie's), the Duchess of Marlborough★, Mrs Joseph Chamberlain, Mrs Sidney Blow, and others. She wrote to Leonie of how busy she had been with meetings and with sending out cards to the committee. She had just lunched with Fanny Ronalds and Mrs Blow on their return from Windsor to present Queen Victoria with the list of subscribers. She also expressed her chagrin at having missed an occasion to meet the Queen:

> Fanny took down a whole list of the donations and subscriptions done neatly on vellum & tied with a red ribbon wh she gave to the Queen – who was more than gracious & kind to them both – but ... Jennie now says she ought to [have] proposed two others one of wh wd have been me – but she always thinks of things too late. What bad luck you & I have in that way. It wd have been such a thing to remember all our lives. Jennie says the Queen talked to her quite a half hour asking her about everything & who had helped her most on Committee. Jennie wanted to say 'My sisters were a gt [great] help to me' <u>but</u> she hesitated & the Queen said – the young Dss [Duchess] of Marlborough I am sure has helped you greatly – Oh yes said Jennie & then the conversation turned. Consuelo M [Duchess of Marlborough] who is about the most useless member of all!!![27]

Sadly, the nearest that Clara would get to meeting the Queen was to hear all about it from Jennie.

Both Clara and Leonie were as close as ever to their sister, and they both supported her unconventional romance. Leonie had written from Egypt, 'Be happy with that Darling George.'[28] She, too, was delighted to be involved in the hospital ship project. At this point she had further money worries, as the Madison Avenue house needed a new tenant and consequently her precious American income was threatened. Jack Leslie was in South Africa with his regiment, and she had sent Seymour away to boarding school the previous year. She had confided in Jennie in April

★ The American heiress, Consuelo Vanderbilt (named for her godmother, Consuelo, Duchess of Manchester) had married Randolph's nephew, 'Sunny' Marlborough, in 1895.

1898 that she had taken this decision because 'he can't get on with any tutor or nurse at home. I am so afraid they won't keep him, as he is so violent.'[29] Fund-raising with Jennie was a welcome diversion. Concerts, matinées, and other charitable entertainments were organized, and within two months far more than the required sum had been raised.

The crowning success of Jennie's campaign was an offer from the American millionaire and founder of the Atlantic Transport Company of Baltimore, Bernard Nagel Baker. He proposed to supply one of his company's transport ships, an old cattle boat called the *Maine*, for the duration of the war. This gift was all the more remarkable because he also offered to maintain the ship and crew at his company's expense. Jennie and her committee met almost daily, planning for military clearance and fitting the ship for its medical mission. Jennie decided that it would carry American nurses and that, to prevent any friction between them and the British officers, she would accompany them to South Africa. The campaign was not, however, without controversy. Slighted at not having been asked to take part earlier, the American hostess, Mrs Cornelia Adair, wrote to Clara and Leonie, demanding that they force Jennie to dissolve the committee before the ship left for South Africa. There was also malicious gossip about the real reason that Jennie wished to make the journey. One magazine commented: 'Every-one in London is wondering what Lady Randolph will do when she arrives in South Africa. It is well known that her one object in going out with the *Maine* was to follow Mr. George West.'[30]

Jennie was indeed eager to see her beloved, but in November 1899 she received bad news: Winston had been on a train that was ambushed by the Boers and was posted missing. She later received a letter from him telling her that he was safe, although being held in a Boer prison camp near Pretoria. At once she called on her influential friends to do everything in their power to have him released. George, also in the thick of battle, wrote her letters describing the harsh conditions and the fighting. She wanted badly to be near him. In mid-December, she learned that Winston had engineered a courageous escape. Jennie was relieved and proud. Her ship was now preparing for departure. Clara and her two sons waved it off, as did Jennie's family friend, Allison Vincent Armour, a member of the wealthy Chicago meat-packing family. The atmosphere was jubilant, but Jennie was despondent; she had just received a cable from George, informing her that he had been invalided (due to the serious after-effects of sunstroke) and was returning home. In a letter that she did not receive in time, he begged her to wait before leaving with the ship, or they would miss each other. Jennie, who would be forty-six within days of her departure, knew that she was putting her relationship with George at risk by not being in England when he needed her, but she wanted to do her duty. She also hoped to be able to see her sons. Jack had enlisted, so she now had both boys to worry about. The Anglo-American clash of ideas, methods, and personalities, as well as tensions in both the medical and the military communities, required a calming presence aboard the ship. She was undoubtedly the best person to achieve that.

Back in London the committee would continue to raise funds and organize the finances. Mrs Adair had graciously agreed to help; she wrote to Leonie that she was 'very glad' to have been made head of the committee during Jennie's absence. She told her how sad it had been to watch the ship's departure:

> I went to see Jennie off and it gave me such a pang to see her going off alone on that great ship with such uncongenial companions – but I do think it is a mercy she was able to go – all those conflicting elements will require smoothing down and directing and it is only she can do it until they get shaken down into their places. But when I saw that splendid floating Hospital sailing off I did think what enormous credit was due to all of you for carrying it out so successfully and to Mr. Baker for initiating it.[31]

The project had been a success, but Jennie paid a high emotional price. George flooded her with reproachful letters, accusing 'little Missie' of not loving him enough. She turned, as she always did, to her sisters. She begged Leonie to look after him for her, writing from the ship:

You may imagine that I did not feel over lively last night – I had a cable from George saying that he was invalided home & was probably leaving immediately – You must promise to see him, & write to me all he says – I am so devoted to him that it would be a terrible thing for me if I knew he blamed me for going – Heaven knows this is no pleasure – I <u>had to go</u>. Write to me fully – & look after George.[32]

George's father later discovered a telegram from Leonie to George, informing him of Jennie's expected return to England. Livid, he angrily accused Leonie of helping her sister 'in her insane infatuation for my son', asking her whether she seriously considered that such a marriage could 'possibly lead to the happiness of either'. He added bitterly that Lady Randolph was older than George's own mother. She would, he said, 'lose the name in which she is best known to the world and its rank and position and she will find herself married to a young man of such an impressionable nature that only a few weeks ago he proposed marriage to a young and pretty girl who refused his attentions'. Altogether he considered the business doomed. It was a 'marvel' to him that Lady Randolph could even contemplate such a step. He concluded by sombrely pointing out the inevitable estrangement from his family that George could expect if he went through with the ill-advised alliance.[33]

But Leonie stood by her sister, and George was determined. He met Jennie on her return; after a six-month separation, nothing had changed and he was still desperate to marry her. She was torn, wavering between marrying George and giving it up as a foolish notion. She knew that Winston was in love with Pamela Plowden, and expected both him and Jack to marry soon – which meant that she would be left alone. In 1900, Jennie decided not to return to South Africa and the couple finally announced their engagement in the *Daily Telegraph*. George was abruptly summoned to see his commanding officer, who informed him that if he married he would have to leave the regiment. Jennie, as usual, made use of her contacts and wrote to Lord Lansdowne, Secretary of State for War, who promised his support. The Prince of Wales, who had objected to the match for so long, also agreed to help. Furthermore, Leonie's intimate friend, the Duke of Connaught, offered to present the whole matter in a positive light to the Queen. With the support of her sisters and friends, Jennie made her bid for happiness. Things were to change, for her and the boys, as she explained to Jack, who was still fighting in South Africa:

> Now listen darling boy – I have thought over everything & have come to the conclusion that for <u>many</u> reasons – it would be unwise for either you or Winston to live with us once we are married – Knowing how fond I am of you both you will believe that I have not come to this conclusion hastily – It seems hard – & it gives me a pang every time I think of it – but I <u>know</u> it is the wisest plan – I shd like you & Winston to have rooms together, which I would furnish for you, & arrange your life as far as material comfort goes to the best of my ability – I need hardly say how <u>more</u> than welcome you will always be here – you cld look upon it as yr home for everything but sleeping.[34]

She concluded this rather harsh letter, written to a young man fighting on the front, with the admonishment that he must 'stand by' her. Both boys were of course old enough to lead their own lives, but they had no father and no home other than their mother's to call their own. Jennie was making a clear choice to pursue her own interests. She also wanted her children's reassurance that she should not feel guilty about putting her own desires first. She begged them both to support her decision and not to make her unhappy by withholding their approval. George thanked Winston fulsomely for his support, but both he and Jack were resigned rather than happy about the wedding.

It was a quiet ceremony, on 28 July 1900, at St Paul's Church in Knightsbridge. Jennie, now aged forty-six, married the twenty-six-year-old George wearing a 'chiffon gown of a pale blue shade over silk, elbow sleeves of transparent lace … skirt finely tucked and inserted with Cluny lace … round the hem of a lace flounce and underneath it frills and ruches of blue chiffon'.[35] On her head she wore a toque of tucked chiffon, Brussels lace, pale blue osprey feathers, and a diamond ornament pinned to the front. Around her neck was a pearl and diamond necklace. Many of the Churchills were in attendance, as were the Frewens and Leonie. The Duke of Marlborough gave Jennie away, and Clara signed the register. The American Ambassador Choate and several attachés attended, as did many society ladies, including Mrs Arthur Paget, Mrs Fanny Ronalds, Mrs Blow, Mrs Adair, and Mme Alice von André. Other guests included the Marquis de Soveral, Lord and Lady Londonderry, Lady de Grey, Lady Granby, Lady de Trafford, Count Albert Menadorff, Baron and Baroness Eckhardstein, and Lady Limerick. Years later, George recollected his disappointment that none of his family was present. Winston accepted the inevitable with stoicism and after the ceremony wrote to Jack, telling him that Mama had had a 'very pretty wedding', adding: 'As we know each other's views on this subject, I need not pursue it.'[36]

Clara gave the wedding breakfast for fifteen people at her home, at small tables decorated with roses. Moreton proposed the toast to the bride's health. There were telegrams and letters from well-wishers, and many presents, one of which was from the Prince of Wales, who called on Jennie before she left on her honeymoon to give it to her personally. She also received a magnificent pearl and diamond tiara from her friends, to recompense her for the fact that the Cornwallis-West family would not, as was traditional, make her a gift of the family jewels. Leonie wrote to their American cousin Eva Thompson, expressing hopes that the marriage would turn out well: 'He is a most charming man, <u>very</u> devoted to her. And as she is 15 years younger than her age, the difference between them need not be noticeable ... Now it is done, we all make the best of it.'[37] All of Jennie's family had decided to 'make the best of it', although Jack Leslie, writing to his wife Leonie from his regiment of the Grenadier Guards in Rhodesia, said with honesty that he was 'sorry to hear from you about Jenny [*sic*] marrying that ridiculous youth'.[38] He later wrote that he hoped George had 'survived the honeymoon'.[39]

At the end of July 1900, after Baby Lionel's christening, Leonie took her turn on the Motts' yacht for a cruising holiday along the south coast of England. In 1902 she and Jack were once again invited by the

Duke and Duchess of Connaught to accompany them on an official tour, this time to Egypt and India. The Prince of Wales commented to Jennie that he was 'much amused to get a letter fr [from] my Brother saying that he was asking Mrs. Leslie to India with Mrs Clayton indisposed (those are my words not his). He is quite right to have "two strings to his bow!"'[40] The party left in November and from Genoa travelled on the first-class battleship *Renown*, which had been specially fitted out for them, with a crew of 897 officers and men. Leonie's letters to her sisters described how much she had enjoyed the journey. From on board the ship at Aden, she wrote to Clara: 'Oh Clarinette it is all *so* heavenly – & I am *so* grateful for it all – I wish you could enjoy it all too!'[41]

Although not as snobbish as Clara, Leonie admired the royal family and venerated the British Empire. The trip was a marvellous opportunity to see the sights of India. They reached Port Said on 6 December and then travelled on to Cairo (which the Leslies had previously visited with the Connaughts in 1897) by special train. They paused at Tel-el-Kebir, where a British expeditionary force, led by Sir Garnet Wolseley, had routed Egyptian nationalist forces in autumn 1882. The duke walked around the graves, reading the names of many friends who had fallen in this famous battle. In Cairo they were greeted by the Khedive (Persian for 'Lord'),[42] ministers, and British officers before driving to the Abdin Palace, where they would stay. The agent, Lord Cromer, gave a large dinner in their honour; the following day the duke, accompanied by Jack Leslie, carried out a military inspection and held an investiture. Leonie accompanied the duchess, with an escort of Egyptian cavalry, to the Khoubee Palace, where they were received by the Khedive *Mère* (mother), surrounded by the women of the harem.

That evening, the royal party left by special train for Luxor. All the stations along the way were specially illuminated. Bands and large crowds welcomed the duke and duchess. When they arrived at Luxor, they embarked on one of the Khedive's yachts, the *Feirouz*, and the party cruised with other yachts in a flotilla up the Nile. From on board their luxurious craft, Leonie observed with fascination the river life of the Egyptians: the women filling their water pitchers and washing clothes, the curious mud villages, the camels, donkeys, and water buffalo. At every village, the people would come out to wave. When it was too cold to stay on deck, the royal couple and the Leslies would retire indoors to read or play bridge. At Aswan, one of the Khedive's bands played near their yacht and the Leslies accompanied the Connaughts sailing in one of the ship's boats. The following day they went by special train to the inaugural ceremony of the newly con- structed dam, which was composed of 2,000 yards of fine granite. They were greeted with 'God Save the King' and a guard of honour. The duchess laid the last stone of the dam, and the duke opened the lock gates. After the ceremony, the royal party made visits to the temples of Edfu and Karnak as well as to the tombs of the kings. After a stay in Cairo, they re-embarked at Suez to resume their journey to India.

Leonie described every moment of the trip to her sisters at home. From Bombay they travelled by special train to Delhi, where they were met by the Viceroy, Lord Curzon, and Lady Curzon; the Grand Duke Ernst of Hesse; the Governor of Bombay and Lady Northcote; the Governor of Madras and Lady Ampthill; the Commander-in-Chief, India, Lord Kitchener, and other officials; as well as the Nizam of Hyderabad; all the princes of India; the feudatory chiefs of Aden; the Khan of Khalor; and the representative of the Amir of Afghanistan. It was an extraordinary pageant, featuring magnificent jewellery and clothing of every hue. The Indian princes had tethered their caparisoned elephants outside the station, one of which the duke and duchess later rode in a procession, preceded by a herald and six trumpeters. At the end of February the party boarded a ship at Bombay to commence the return journey. In March, they reached Port Said, where mail awaited them. The duke learned to his dismay that his brother, Edward VII, had been unable to convince the government to make him, as he so dearly wished, commander-in-chief of the British armed forces.

In spite of his disappointment, the duke regarded this trip as one of the highlights of his life. In years to come, he often reminisced with

Leonie about their travels. Having tasted the delights of the royal progress, she admitted to the duke that she was 'rather dreading' the return to her home in Ireland. She was depressed at the thought and wondered when she would see her *Bon Ami* again.[43] 'Pat' was equally despondent – he would miss the three gentle taps on his door, which had been Leonie's way of saying goodnight. 'Though he thought of her by day and dreamt of her by night, he promised that he seldom thought of things which she would not have wished him to do.'[44]

In fact Leonie found that she had plenty to occupy her when she returned to Glaslough. Jacky had grown into a brilliant scholar who had won many prizes at Eton and was preparing to enter Cambridge the following year. Norman hoped to be admitted to the military academy at Sandhurst (which his cousin Winston had attended some years earlier). Meanwhile life in Ireland continued with its usual rhythm. Leonie locked herself into the drawing room to practise on her Bechstein piano, playing beautiful music – her son Seymour recollected bits of Wagner's *The Ring* and other pieces. He also remembered how she constantly smoked cigarettes, long before it was considered quite polite to do so. Lady Constance certainly found it a shocking habit and begged Leonie not to smoke in front of the children – advice she ignored, as Seymour remembered train journeys where he would have to hold a cigarette for her while she furiously scribbled letters and jumped out at stations to have them posted by the train guards.

Leonie and Jack often left his parents behind in Glaslough to spend time in London or Paris, or travelling with the Connaughts. Jacky and Norman were at Eton; Seymour was despatched first to Pettigo with his governess, then to a small boarding school in London. He was a sensitive boy who wrote years later of his mistrust of the 'Jerome impulsive demonstrations', sardonically remembering his Aunt Clara's welcome when he appeared at the end of term: '"Why you <u>Dear Thing</u>! how perfectly <u>lovely</u> to see you back from school! I can't <u>wait</u> to hear your news of it! Tell me <u>all</u> about it, sit on the sofa there and don't leave anything out!" Whereupon she turned to continue her correspondence.'[45]

Leonie was spending more of her time in London and was enjoying life. She was also seeing a great deal of the duke. Seymour certainly believed that he had been neglected as a child, but this may have been because he was so ill, and Leonie had to share her time between her other sons remaining at Glaslough. In the early 1900s she spent the school holidays there with the elder boys, frequently taking the baby, Lionel, with her to London. Seymour became an independent young man who determined to make his own way at an early age. He decided to become an electrical engineer – to general astonishment – and spent two years at a school where he was prepare for university entrance (known as a 'crammer'). He was then offered a place at London University. As he recollected with sadness in his memoirs, he never saw his elder brothers. Too busy to spend time with her third son, Leonie was usually to be found in the eye of the social whirlwind of London.[46]

CHAPTER TEN

Mortal Ruin

While Jennie dwelt in early marital bliss with the handsome George, and Leonie basked in the reflected glory of the Duke of Connaught, Clara languished at Innishannon. She had been despatched there to reduce outgoings. Money was once again scarce. Moreton was in London, seeing friends, working on his latest projects, and promoting with fervour his views on bi-metallism. Hugh and Oswald had been sent away to boarding school and stayed with their mother only during the holidays. They rarely saw their father, who took little notice of them anyway. He and Clara corresponded daily, and from time to time he sent her scraps of money. Sometimes the sums were small, an indication of their straitened circumstances. In May 1901, she wrote: 'Thank you for the fiver – it is very welcome.' Brede, the house she had fallen in love with at first sight, was now empty and she dreamed of moving there. Some of the necessary work was being arranged and she was so glad that Moreton had been able to pay the builder, wondering whether it was the last payment: '& now if we can only manage to arrange to finish the work there no matter how modestly what a pleasure it will be.'[1] Although she celebrated their twentieth wedding anniversary alone, her loyalty to her husband was still strong: 'Your dear letter this morning made me so happy – & your wire yesterday morning – though how I wish you <u>could</u> have been here with me. Yes, twenty years is a long time! & we have come through it bravely & well

– considering all our woes & troubles which I hope now will soon be over.'[2]

Despite her fluttery appearance, Clara could display mule-like determination. By 1901, she had decided that she really wanted a life at Brede, and it was to this future that she directed her efforts. She encouraged her husband to make this dream come true: 'for even if you can only just get enough to do Brede simply & modestly our being <u>together</u> there will remove my greatest worry & sadness – that life is running away, & we are so much apart.'[3] Clara yearned for a more stable life, yet she was still possessed by her mother's obsession with social status, behaving (and spending) as if the Frewen family were very wealthy. Their daughter Clare would complain years later of how depressing it had been to maintain this fiction of prosperity.

During the 1900s, Clara and Moreton were reduced to living hand to mouth. They were spending money on works at Brede, but Clara did not have enough to travel from Ireland to England to attend her mother-in-law's funeral and could barely manage to keep the family going:

> You sent me £5 wh went at once to Minnie [their servant] (whose mother is very very poor) & she wanted the money badly – & even then, there is more on her wages owing. Then you sent me £10-6-17 – 6 went to the butcher as soon as I got it cashed – he had been dunning me as he is a new man – that meant that I have in all £3 left … I am honestly trying to do the very best I know & am living as economically as I can.[4]

The Frewens neglected to pay their servants as a matter of course. Moreton once remarked that they preferred it, as it made them feel more like part of the family! Their staff were certainly tolerant and loyal, despite the unpaid wages. Yet in spite of their critical financial situation, Clara never once managed without domestic help. She was at heart still the young bride who had gone to Wyoming, incapable of buttoning her own boots. She had never cooked or done housework and had been brought up with the assumption that she would never need to. She had then married a man who did not expect her to do without a cook or housemaids. It never occurred to the Frewens to radically reduce their costly lifestyle; instead they reliedon on short-term, cost-cutting measures in the hope that Moreton would make good some day.

There were also treats. Moreton took Clara to America in 1902, where he was campaigning for bi-metallism in Washington DC. He wrote to Leonie of how happy Clara was and of how everyone was so nice to her. He was, as always, optimistic that business would improve: 'My dear it really looks as though I had struck a fortune this trip – but disappointments have not been infrequent and so I had better hold on until it materialises; but if it does sail home it is a vast fortune & we will all live in extreme opulence!'[5] Leonie knew better than to set much store by this declaration. The family had by now learned that Moreton's projects were risky and unlikely to deliver the great riches he so persuasively promised. One of the reasons that the Frewens were able to survive was that tradesmen and bank managers were impressed by Moreton's international celebrity. Demands for payment were often met by his solicitor's frosty reply that Mr Frewen had gone to America to lecture the Senate. Moreton shamelessly used notepaper from United States government offices to write to his creditors.

Clara had insisted that her two boys be educated at Eton, which the Frewens could ill afford. In 1900 the fees were 100 guineas, payable to the house fund, plus £10 per term to the school, £2 per term for 'use of furniture', and 20 guineas per annum for classical tuition. In addition, parents were asked to pay for extras such as music, art, school of mechanics and additional tuition, as well as subscriptions to the rifle volunteers, and for boating and cricket. There were also bills incurred at the bookshop and tailor, and a house subscription to cover costs such as tips to servants, prizes for competitions, and other expenses. Total costs came to at least £175 per year (about £12,000 in today's money).[6] Hugh had already endured what was to become a ritual humiliation of unpaid fees at his preparatory school, Speldhurst Lodge. The same pattern would occur at Eton. In addition, he had to suffer the negative comparisons made by his parents to his more brilliant cousins. Winston was already making his name as an intrepid journalist, and Clara and Moreton admired him greatly. Jacky was a dedicated student; he applied himself and achieved great academic success. Clara constantly compared Hugh unfavourably to them both, and in particular up-braided him for not working hard enough at school. Hugh's sister Clare, the only daughter of the eight children produced by the sisters, was a serious and emotional girl, who felt deeply on his behalf, writing to her cousin Jacky:

> Well – this is what I want to tell you, you know poor Hugh does not work very extraordinarily well at Eton – not as well as you do – and so Mother is always cramming <u>you</u> down his throat, if he is not friendly with you at Eton you will know the reason <u>why</u>. Of course it's Mother's fault, that's certainly not the way to make him like you, is it? She's always saying: 'Now look at Jackie [*sic*]! Look how <u>he works</u>! See what a lot of <u>prizes he brings back</u>, look what <u>good reports he has</u>!!' etc. etc. Poor Hugh is sick and tired of hearing your name, and so now, if Mother asks him something about Eton – or his marks – etc. he answers 'You had better ask Jacky Leslie's mother!' It's awfully mean of Mother, don't you think so? Once she said 'Well, I don't care Hugh. I met an Eton boy in London a little time ago, and I asked him about you, and he told me that you <u>didn't work one scrap</u>!!!!!' And Hugh is almost certain it's you! I'm sure it was Mother's make up, for <u>I</u> know you well enough to know you're not <u>sluggish</u> enough to do such a mean trick to Hugh as that, after you have been such friends last term, so if you could write me a nice letter explaining <u>if</u> you <u>did</u> say anything (and knowing you like Hugh) just say something nice for him. I would keep it, and show it to Hugh, and, if Mother says anything more I could just show it to her!! Poor Hugh is so unhappy.[7]

Hugh was indeed very unhappy and remained so for much of his life. Misunderstood and unappreciated by both of his parents, he grew bitter about his father's neglect. His youthful ambitions of becoming a poet were never fully realized, although as a boy he showed early promise. When King Milan died in 1900, Hugh wrote an elegy in his memory, which was complimented by the Prince of Wales. Clara carefully preserved the letter he sent, hoping that Hugh might one day be the future monarch's poet laureate. More often she felt dissatisfied by Hugh's development – and he was hurt by her disappointment. His sister Clare was also aggrieved, because her parents had such low expectations of her. Poorly educated, she was sent to a French convent at the age of fifteen, more, her mother suggested, to improve her character than her schooling. Fortunately, her cousin Jacky, who was the same age, was a faithful correspondent. They wrote to each other, as he had promised, all the time she was away, and his amusing letters cheered her. Jacky was very clever, but he was also subject to 'strain'. In March 1902 he was invalided home from Eton with a 'poor tired brain'[8] due to overwork. He later suffered from mental illness and in his adult life was often emotionally unstable. His mother found his problems difficult to understand. Leonie was such a firm advocate of the stiff upper lip that human weakness in her own family was intolerable to her. She constantly nagged her boys, exhorting them to look well and to do and say the right things. As a consequence, they found it very hard to unwind. Jacky especially was highly strung.

Leonie loved her nephew Winston tremendously, and the other cousins knew that he was the undisputed favourite. His aunts followed his progress as closely as did his own mother. Clare wrote to Jacky during the Boer War: 'Aunt Leonie is very busy, so she asked me to send you this paper, and also, Auntie asked me to tell you, to cut out and keep anything about Winston, or the hospital ship, in fact anything of interest.'[9] Winston was a star, and although he was liked by his younger cousins, they saw him little, as his world was far removed from their own. Oswald, too, had gone to Eton, although his parents had, typically, forgotten to put his name down. Clara rushed to the school and charmed the administrators into admitting him. He stayed for one year, before deciding to apply for the Royal Navy. When he was studying at a crammer in order to pass the assessment, he discovered that once again his parents had forgotten to enter him for the examination. Clara flew to see Lord Tweedmouth, First Lord of the Admiralty, and begged him to accept her son: 'It's not poor little Oswald's fault, it's mine; you <u>must</u> put it right for my sake.'[10] He agreed and in 1902 the relieved young man joined the *Britannia*, a wooden three-decker training ship, at Dartmouth naval training college.

The casual attitude taken by the Frewen parents to their responsibilities to their offspring, their servants and, indeed, to the world at large, was for a child both perplexing and often humiliating. All the children were eager to escape. Of the three, only Oswald (perhaps, as the youngest, the one who had had the easiest time) was able to achieve a close and warm relationship with his parents. He was tolerant of their foibles and at the age of sixteen even began lending his father money. Hugh and Clare, on the other hand, found that there was much to forgive and that such forgiveness did not come easily.

The Frewen children did, however, enjoy spending time with their Jerome cousins – Jack Churchill and the two elder Leslies especially. They were also very fond of their Aunt Jennie and Aunt Leonie. The families visited one another during the holidays. Regardless of the family's financial circumstances, Clara was always happy to welcome her nephews to Innishannon and, later, to Brede, which they all loved. Likewise, the Frewens enjoyed Glaslough and were frequent guests there. Clara often stayed with her sister as a cost-saving measure. When the Leslie and Frewen boys were at Eton, Clara took them all out when she visited, as did Leonie. Hugh (who bore his cousin no malice in spite of his mother's comparisons) wrote to Jacky in July 1902, organizing one such holiday visit:

> Mother told me to tell you that she wanted you here whenever you liked to come, and I propose you should come at once. Jack Churchill is coming sometime next week, & Hugh Warrender [a family friend] in the middle of September, & as you know we have only got 2 spare rooms. So if you come now you will be able to stay as long as you like, & then say after a fortnight, if Grannie Boo [Lady Constance Leslie, Leonie's mother-in-law] is still willing to have me, we could go back to Glaslough together.[11]

Moreton, a staunch supporter of empire, was still fully engaged in promoting bi-metallism; he was also a powerful advocate of protectionism and closer trading relationships between friendly nations. By the early 1900s the bonds that held the British Empire together were weakening, with Canada particularly espousing separatist ambitions. Moreton proposed a federation between Canada and the West Indies. He travelled back and forth between England and the United States to promote his trade theories, becoming well known by his sobriquet 'Mr Frewen of England'. For all his persuasive speaking and extensive network of contacts, he was still short of funds, although his financial ambitions remained as high as ever. His nephew Jacky remembered his 'happy phrase', which was: 'Don't talk to me about thousands'.[12] He talked in millions, while his household accounts were nil.

As always, appearances were maintained. In 1903, at the age of eighteen, Clare Frewen made her debut. At a fancy-dress ball given by the society hostess Mrs Adair, Clare wore a green dress, with her hair in two long braids, and carried a wreath of shamrocks round a harp to dance the Irish quadrille. She was not especially beautiful but she had blonde hair like her mother and was tall and slim like her father, with a lively personality and great charm. Oswald, who was at sea, recorded in his diary the following name-dropping news cutting: 'Miss Frewen – Mrs. Moreton Frewen's pretty fair-haired girl – is another American debutante of this year. Miss Frewen, who is a niece of Mrs. George Cornwallis-West, and Mrs. John Leslie (the latter a great friend of the Duchess of Connaught) is very popular with everyone she knows, and has the most winning manners!'[13] It is interesting to note that Clare was still considered to be an American, simply by merit of her mother's citizenship, despite her birth and upbringing in the United Kingdom.

Clara had, naturally, turned to her sisters for help with Clare's debut. The Frewens were at that time still living at the house just off Great Cumberland Street in London, which they had taken to replace Chesham Place. In 1903, 'Lower Jerome Terrace' was busy as the three sisters, all living on the same street, helped with preparations for Clare's coming out. Clare was the only Jerome girl of her generation, and her aunts lavished attention upon her. Jennie was particularly involved during Clare's first season. 'She became my second mother,' Clare later wrote. 'I had to go and see her every morning and read *The Times* leaders to her while she breakfasted ... Above all I must try to talk and smile and not look bored when anyone was introduced.'[14] Clare was embarrassed at her mother's and her aunts' all-too-obvious matrimonial ambitions for her, writing of her suitors:

> I was paralysed by the general attitude of society towards elder sons. I could not bring myself, however charming they might be (and who shall say that elder sons cannot be charming?) to talk to them without self-consciousness. There were at that time several conspicuous *partis* as people called them, and I could not get rid of the sensation that they knew that I was poor and that I knew they were marriageably desirable. I could not bear that they should think, or that anyone looking on should think, that I made the slightest effort to be unduly amiable. Rather than be suspected of such an attitude I was absurdly rude. If by any chance I did happen in spite of everything to get on rather well with such a one, I was irritated by the approval of my relations and by their effort to invite us together again – their swiftly rising hopes, and intense interest in the sequel.[15]

The aunts could indeed be a source of constraint and irritation. Clare's niece, Anita Leslie, remembered that Leonie was particularly adamant about following the rules and 'could give a terrific scolding on hearing that a girl had done something likely to "stop nice men from proposing marriage"'. She had strongly reprimanded Clare for walking a friend's dog in the park, *by herself*. Worse still, she had worn a chiffon scarf, which, Leonie said, *drew attention.*[16] As well as her reading duties, Clare was sent every morning to Aunt Jennie to practise how to do her hair. Jennie taught her the rules of society: 'Remember that you are not invited for your own amusement, but to contribute to the party.'[17] Her advice to her niece was most specific: 'pull in my waist and put up my hair'.[18]

That year, Clare fell in love with Wilfred Sheridan, a stockbroker whose annual income was only £500 (£34,000 in today's money) above his earnings in the City. Her father was furious, as she was expected to make a brilliant marriage to a wealthy man in order to help her family. She was therefore sent to Dublin for the winter season to try again. Her letters home indicated that she was having a fine time and echoed the letters of young Clara herself, many years earlier, reporting on the dances and pretty clothes. 'Darling Mummie,' she wrote on 8 February 1904. 'Before I tell you my news I will answer your letter, and start by thanking you <u>very</u> much for the ruby heart [King Milan's gift to her in her childhood, now reset as a ring] etc., they are much improved and *so* nice. It doesn't matter if you can't find the stays as I have bought a pair here, they are American stays, white, and really <u>very</u> nice ... I also got some pink shoes at the American shoe company here.' She had sat with Prince Arthur (of Connaught) at a ball, she reported, adding that he was 'so sweet, he talked volubly ... he was too nice for words'.[19] Young Clare was also not immune from the family habit of running out of funds as this letter to her mother shows:

> By the way, those £2 not turning up left me rather pinched, and I should never have been able to get down here without borrowing from Aunt L[eonie]. I came down 2nd class with Ethel, the return tickets cost (combined) two pound nineteen – I borrowed £2 for my boots, so when you see her in London <u>do</u> be an angel and pay her back, will you? ... If you are not too hard up, can you send me some money?[20]

This situation did not worry Clare too much; she was eighteen, pretty, and enjoying herself. She was also more sensitive and less self-centred than her mother had been at that age. She wrote cheerful letters home, urging her mother to be happy, and to think of all those who loved her.[21]

The situation at home was fraught. Too many bills were unpaid. Moreton was increasingly desperate to make a fortune. Years of talking big and maintaining a wealthy and optimistic façade had taken their toll. He expected all of his children to help with the family finances. He chose not to acknowledge that these finances were in essence his own debts, preferring to transfer the burden of increasing the family's prosperity to his offspring. When Hugh came of age, in 1904, Moreton went up to Trinity College, Cambridge, to see him, ostensibly to 'celebrate' his majority. What he really wanted was for his eldest son to raise a loan on the expectation of the Innishannon estate, which would come to Hugh on Moreton's death. Moreton thought that the mortgage would be sufficient to pay off the still-outstanding Eton debts as well as paying for Hugh's education at Cambridge. It was essential that Hugh should agree, argued his father, for Moreton had to satisfy a particularly pressing creditor, to whom he owed the alarming sum of £5,000 (£345,000 in today's money). The said creditor (whom Moreton did not name) was, he claimed, threatening Moreton with legal action if he did not find the money. In this Moreton was down-right disingenuous; the creditor was in fact his own brother Stephen. He did owe Stephen £5,000, from the days of the Powder River cattle business, and much more besides; Stephen was in particularly bad straits, having been invalided home from the war in South Africa, relieved of his command and placed on half-pay. But it is unlikely that Stephen, who remained on good terms with Moreton, would have put his brother through the bankruptcy courts, and neither he nor Hugh were told about the truth of the transaction. Years later, Hugh told the full story (with no anger or bitterness) to his cousin Jacky Leslie.[22]

Hugh signed the papers, borrowing £6,500 (£450,000 in today's money) on Innishannon; the agreement was that £400 (£27,000) would be spent on minor disbursements, £400 would settle Hugh's last bill at Eton, and £5,000 (£345,000) would be given to Moreton, to pass on to Stephen. The remaining £700 (£48,000) was to be put aside for Hugh's fees at Cambridge. Moreton also agreed to provide Hugh with £300 (£21,000) per annum after he left university. In fact, Moreton reneged on almost every part of the deal, treating his son in the very way he treated his other creditors, using evasion and duplicity to avoid repayment. Hugh had to leave Cambridge after two years because the money supposedly put in reserve had been spent by his father. The promised £300 a year never materialized, and Moreton 'forgot' his promise to provide it. It was remarkable that he had managed to wrangle this money from Hugh. Old Mrs Jerome had tried in every legal way possible to keep Innishannon from Moreton, but had failed to allow for his ruthlessness and for Clara's acquiescence in depriving her children of their inheritance. Moreton set off for America as soon as he had secured his money. He went to Washington, where he presented ten acorns from the old oak at the village green at Northiam in Sussex to his friend, President Theodore Roosevelt.[23]

This was all very prestigious, but it was not remunerative. The American agent for Moreton's disinfectant, Electrozone, was going bankrupt, so Moreton was pushing a contraption called the Hoffman engine, with little success. He was, by now, quite penniless, as he explained in a letter to Clara:

> I do not know which way to turn to send you what you require. I have twisted and turned in every direction, but I cannot see my way to good money without tearing my prospects, which are good, to pieces. Hugh has got £300 in reserve and I think if the worst comes to the worst he must discount one of those bills. This is a helpless letter. But in God's truth I am helpless just now. And yet I have made such a lot of good friends here, but I cannot safely use them yet; it will spoil all and get around in a moment what my position is. Burn this sheet the moment you have read it.[24]

Yet although there was so little cash, Clara still retained domestic servants and was continuing to landscape Brede. She told Hugh that she had spent £5,000 (£345,000) on repairs and renovations, much of it on her beloved garden. She had made garden rings and rose gardens, as well as two dams (both of which failed). She had also made preparations for a cast of a sculpture by the American, Augustus Saint-Gaudens, at a cost of £1,800. As a result, the gardens were spectacularly beautiful, and Clara instituted a tradition that well-known personalities should plant trees at Brede. She constantly lavished money on her home. Perhaps she felt it was all she had. The children were grown and leaving the nest, and Moreton was rarely there. In 1905, he decided to go to Africa with his friend Lord Warwick, with a view to prospecting territory in Kenya, at that time an almost completely unknown part of British East Africa. Moreton hoped to convince Warwick to buy up as much territory there as possible, and to advance the money to Moreton to do the same, with a view to then exploiting the timber forests of pine and red cedar. Moreton had to borrow the £2,000 necessary for his journey, which he convinced Hugh to underwrite, in exchange for forest land that Moreton would purchase for him. While he was away, the family faced yet another financial crisis.

In December 1905, Moreton wrote to a letter to Clara from Ravine, which demonstrates the complexity of his juggling of the precarious family finances:

> Darling ... I have just got your 'big budget' & was greatly distressed at that horrible mess resulting in the return of all those cks [cheques]. And I fear dear that it is your fault. I told you more than once to be sure & lodge all that money 'tomorrow morning' (Monday) at Morgans, & I fear you did not do it *that* is the only possible explanation. I sent to the L&C your ck on Morgans (look in your ck book & you will see the amount & write to Morgans for your cheques & you will I fear find it unpaid.) This ck I suspect Morgans dishonoured because you had not paid in the money to meet it. Thus this omission of yours to do this simple matter (& the consequences of which I had warned you) has resulted in dishonoured cks at both our banks. It is most distressing – the only other possible explanation is that the ck on Morgans sent by post to the L&C miscarried in the post: but this is extremely unlikely. I remember so well telling you 'pay it early to Morgans tomorrow or some of these cks will be in!' Write me at once & tell me whether this explanation of mine is right ... I understand the cable reference to 'scolding Hugh': he is in many ways unsatisfactory.[25]

A mere two weeks later, Moreton was encouraging his wife to take a trip to Malta with Clare. Hugh later recounted to his cousin Jacky the trauma that followed.[26] Hugh was the sole family member left in Britain when he received an urgent message from the family solicitor, who had received a telegram of distress from Clara, stating that she and Clare had run out of funds and were stranded on Malta. Hugh was the only Frewen he could get in touch with. The solicitor had arranged a loan of £400 (£27,000 in today's money) against Hugh's future American inheritance. The money was duly sent to Clara and Clare, so that they could continue their holiday. When Moreton returned from Africa early in 1906, he was unable to pay back the £2,000 (£138,000) that he had borrowed from his son to pay for the journey, which Hugh then also covered. These sums remained on his reversion until he inherited thirty years later. Yet his parents continued to criticize the young man. On 17 January 1906, Moreton wrote from East Africa that he was feeling optimistic about the prospect of finding a settlement there for Hugh, adding, however: 'I wish Hugh were a little more like Jacky, or that he could persuade Jacky to come with him.'[27] He wrote again two days later, stating that 'this wholesome new life will do him all the good in the world & knock all the poetic nonsense out of him'.[28]

Clara was not the only one who failed to consider the cost of a return journey. The venture to Africa had proved unsuccessful, because Moreton discovered that there was no means by which to export the timber from Kenya, as the transport infrastructure was non-existent. At the end of his trip, Moreton told Clara to send him £75 to buy his passage home. Home was now Brede or Innishannon, as the London residence had been given up.

But there were some happy times for the Frewens, who certainly enjoyed their share of family frolics. Oswald's diaries recount a typical episode one Christmas at Innishannon, in 1903: 'When turning in, Hugh & I went into Clare's room and ragged her. She got Mother to come in and help her, and Hugh & I hid in Mother's room. Ma & Clare came in & found Hugh. Hugh nipped out and got into Clare's room. Ma & Clare pursued. I got out of my hiding place, and: Ma & Clare in passage, Hugh & I in rooms: great fun.'[29] Hugh was then a young man of twenty, Clare eighteen, and Oswald sixteen. In December 1906, after Oswald had returned from his ship for Christmas, he recorded in his diary greeting his father and sister:

> At 9 Pa and Clare arrove. Hugh got behind the screen, and Ma & Nene [Susan Thynne, originally their nanny, now housekeeper] composed themselves in the drawing room. So did I, hiding myself behind the Times, as though I were reading it. Clare came in first, then Pa, and still I held up the Times, paying no attention. Then Clare said 'Well Hugh? Is that Hugh behind the paper?' Whereat I put the paper down, and there ensued a tableau. Hugh then emerged from the screen. Of course a v happy dinner.[30]

Good-natured amusements – such as hiding Ma's cigarette case, engaging in uproarious pillow-fights, and chasing each other – continued for years, in addition to more sophisticated entertainments.

Leonie, despite her exciting life in London, was not pleased by the life choices made by her eldest son, Jacky. He had pursued an academic career at Cambridge, where he was a successful scholar. After Eton, he had spent time in Paris, where he perfected his French, which was, like that of his mother and aunts, excellent. (Only Jennie failed to teach her children to speak the language to a high proficiency; of all the cousins, their command of French was the weakest.) Before moving to Paris, Jacky also spent time in Rome, at the Palazzo Volpe of his father's sister, Mary Crawshay. There he met ambassadors and European royalty, many of whom Leonie had also befriended.

After his stay in Paris, Jacky had gone up to Trinity College, Dublin, and then on to Cambridge. He entered King's College, where he read history. He was also increasingly drawn to the Catholic faith. He retained a strong interest in Irish politics and sympathized with Irish nationalist aspirations. Both his father, now a colonel in the British army, and his mother, Leonie, were horrified. Leonie saw his enthusiasm for Irish nationalism as a betrayal of his family, and his leaning to Catholicism as a rejection of their values. He summed up their relationship in his autobiography:

I was her first beloved and darling until my temper and moodiness gave my brother Norman the place of favourite ... Leonie used to compare her boy with Jennie's in words which I sorrowfully record: 'Jack and Winston have helped their mother in every way, even by not going to the University in order to work, and both absolutely adore her. I have done everything and given my boys everything and they don't seem to care for me at all'. There was just enough truth in this to leave me with remorse.[31]

Jacky's quest was for self-fulfilment. In his first year down from Cambridge, he visited Russia, where he stayed with his mother's friends the Benckendorffs, and then went to Louvain, in Belgium, to study scholastic philosophy. The following year he moved to the slums of the East End of London with a number of Cambridge Catholics where he received instruction in Catholicism and prepared to take orders. He then announced that he wished to convert to Catholicism and become a priest. It was a potent rejection of everything that his parents held dear; their entire social and economic underpinnings had been questioned and found wanting by their son and heir, previously so cherished for his academic brilliance. His mother was extremely upset. Her gentle and compassionate sister-in-law, Mary, wrote comforting words to the enraged Leonie on 6 April 1908:

I bleed for you – but listen dearest – I saw the boy this morning very thin & tired & gentle. He was so distressed to know he had hurt you in his way of telling you!! ie to ask you for his rosary! ... Listen dear. There is no use doing anything about the priesthood now. Do not say a word about that to him ... He has his mind full of preparations ... He is no longer anxious to be a Home Ruler or Sinn Fein. He says he quite agrees he should not enter the Irish priesthood or be under Irish bishops – I hope all that will come right ... His whole heart is with the poor. He said he could never be one of the people employed in making rich converts! He must work among the poor. It was the only thing he cared about. Leonie darling be comforted. It is not your fault. He has had every chance.[32]

Jacky had insisted that his name be changed to its Irish equivalent, Shane, and demanded that his family and friends address him accordingly. This was understandably difficult for his mother to accept, but his insistence was such that in the end everyone gave way.

Leonie's concern over her son's conversion to Catholicism was not merely personal. Her anxiety was that the heir to a Protestant estate should espouse the religion of the opposition. The Protestant Anglo-Irish ascendancy was crumbling and its privileged position within Ireland, both financial and political, was increasingly precarious. Successive Acts of land reform, and a sustained campaign for Irish independence, supported by the Catholic majority, had weakened the Anglo-Irish aristocracy, many of whom naturally resisted reforms that they believed were unfavourable to them.

In addition, the history was complex: Ireland had supposedly been part of a British unitary state since the Act of Union of 1800, and 103 Irish Members sat in the House of Commons at Westminster as Liberals or Conservatives. In the mid 1870s, Catholic emancipation, franchise reform, and the adoption of the secret ballot had led to the formation of a group of over fifty MPs, led by the Protestant Conservative lawyer Isaac Butt, who pressed for a modest form of legislative independence for Ireland. In 1875 this mild approach changed, when Charles Stewart Parnell, a charismatic twenty-nine-year-old landowner from County Wicklow (and also a Protestant), was elected on a Home Rule platform. He adopted highly effective obstructive tactics in the House, using long speeches and timetable-wrecking amendments, which successfully forced the Irish question to the top of the political agenda. Although English politicians loathed him, he presented a political alternative to the violent tactics espoused by the Fenian leaders who had been imprisoned or exiled after the failed revolutionary uprising of 1867. The Irish Republican Brotherhood, founded in 1857, was a secret society that espoused violence, rejecting constitutional attempts to gain independence as futile. There had been attempts to eradicate the Fenians, as they were known, but the brotherhood continued secretly and was a constant threat to British rule in Ireland.

In the general election of 1880, Gladstone's Liberals gained power, and Parnell became the undisputed leader of the 'Irish' MPs who now numbered over sixty. This new-found solidarity was exemplified in the land league movement. In 1879 the National Land League was formed, with the objective of securing basic rights for tenant farmers, including fair rents, free sale, and fixed tenure. Parnell became the president of the League, and there was much support nationwide for such reforms. Many Fenians also joined, and the result was a national campaign of mass agitation from 1879 to 1882, which forced the British government to pass a series of Land Acts. These Acts eventually abolished the old landlord system, which had sustained the Leslie family and their class for generations, transferring ownership of the land to those who worked on it. The process took some time, and unrest continued intermittently until 1923. This agrarian movement was used by Parnell to push for Home Rule in the 1885 election. In 1884, the Gaelic Athletic Association was founded to promote national games and, in 1893, the Gaelic League was created to revive the Irish language culture. These developments garnered enormous support throughout Ireland, except in eastern Ulster with its large Protestant population.

Gladstone, the prime minister, introduced a Home Rule Bill that was defeated in 1886. This setback, combined with Parnell's death in 1891, delayed progress further. Another Home Rule Bill was defeated in 1893. Political progress towards an independent Ireland was thus slow and, in spite of much support in Ireland and in England, without tangible success. Frustrated ambitions for Irish Home Rule grew more pronounced, and between 1905 and 1908 a new party, Sinn Féin (Gaelic for 'we ourselves'), was formed. Sinn Féin, which had close links with the Fenians (who still supported the violent overthrow of the British system), wanted Irish MPs to withdraw completely from the British Parliament and to establish an independent Irish government.

In the context of these turbulent events, Shane Leslie's desire to become a Catholic priest was viewed as nothing short of rebellion by his Protestant parents, who did not support even token reforms, let alone Home Rule. The Leslies had taken great care to preserve stability and tolerance at Glaslough, where both Catholics and Protestants lived on the family estate, in the village, and on surrounding lands. It was consequently difficult for local people, who respected the family, to rise against them in support of independence. The political became personal: in the election of 1885, some 750 Catholics, under great pressure from the nationalists, refused to vote against the Leslies – they stayed away 'for the sake of the family'. There was a scarlet-clad Monaghan militia, loyal to the British royal family, which camped for a month on the estate every year under Jack Leslie's command. Shane's Aunt Mary attempted to comfort his stricken parents by pointing out the advantages of Shane's philanthropic objectives: 'The turn his religion has taken of being a priest will save him from those dangerous destructive politics – & he can satisfy his heart as to the poor & be a great good happy philanthropist under control.'[33] Leonie was not reassured; Oswald Frewen wrote in his diary how she had 'flown' home from Malta at hearing the news that Shane was considering joining a monastic order. Oswald himself was sympathetic to his aunt's views: 'Considering he would have been a success in <u>any</u> walk of life, this is really sinful fanaticism, & wasting of good gifts.'[34] He wryly commented a week later that Shane was <u>not</u> going to be 'immured between 4 walls', but was, rather, to be a 'Dominican priest and do good among "the beloved poor children"'. So that's all right.'[35]

Shane next disappointed his mother and father with the decision to forgo his inheritance. He was planning to go into the Church and, even if he did not, he had no wish to take his place as heir to the estate. Leonie was angry and bewildered. Such a decision would upset the continuity of primogeniture, which allowed for predictable and planned estate management. It was as important for the community at Glaslough, which depended on the land for their living, as it was for the family that the continuity and stability of the estate be preserved. Leonie had invested years of her life in becoming a Leslie and had absorbed Protestant landed values and lifestyles as her own. In 1907, at their golden wedding anniversary, Sir John and Lady Constance had made over the estate to Jack. Now, Leonie and Jack had the responsibility for running it and supporting all of its dependants. It was planned that Sir John and Lady Constance would have all their expenses paid on a house at 22 Manchester Square in London, as well as an income guaranteed by Jack and Leonie. Although a younger son could if necessary take the place of the eldest son, the whole system was predicated on the commitment made by the eldest son and heir to its survival. Turning down the inheritance and its responsibility put the whole system into question. It was analogous to the royal heir deciding to forgo the crown.

Once again, Mary tried to help Leonie in her anger. 'I feel your grief beyond words,' she wrote in April 1908, '...what I cannot understand is that you should be so surprised. He had been chanting in his room for *years*.' She had clearly thought deeply about this unusual young man's reasons for converting to Catholicism:

> He has not been ever like other people – there was every sign. Here, he took a long solitary walk across the island to Iona. He gave a large sum to fishermen to take him across that stormy night. Why? That he might realise the, to him, joy of spending the night in a ruined chapel there. He ate several loaves of bread & walked back – barefoot. Is that normal? For it was to him a genuine treat. These signs have been numerous. Have you not been watching him do such things as we all have?

Mary urged her sister-in-law to be understanding: 'I think he *has* been true to his own nature. The chanting, the ecstasies, the stations & all the things that would bore us to death are to him great joys. Why not? The human spirit is inexhaustible in its variety.'[36] It was reluctantly agreed that Norman, Shane's younger brother, who was serving in the army, would take his place as the heir to the Glaslough estate.

Norman Jerome Beauchamp Leslie was tall and handsome, like his elder brother. Unlike Shane Norman was not bookish, although he did write poetry. He was a sportsman and, like his cousin Winston, a talented polo player who loved horses and gambling. Like his mother, he was an excellent musician and attended the opera whenever he could. In addition to good looks, brains, musical talent, athletic prowess, and charm, Norman had an enormous capacity for happiness. He enjoyed life and everyone, even the irascible Shane, loved his company. Norman was surprised by Shane's decision, but he stood by him. 'I am afraid Jacky's Lough Derg pilgrimage [a Catholic pilgrimage in Ireland] is not likely to help him much over there,' he wrote to his mother. 'I must say it is rather a pity to do these things in a locality where it is bound to cause ill feeling. However if he thinks it is leading him to a better state – well & good.'[37] Leonie found it easier to be proud of her second son, and because Norman was a ladies' man she took a sly pleasure in knowing that she was his favourite 'sweetheart'. In true Edwardian (or Jerome) fashion, he pursued women – when they were not pursuing him – and had many affairs. He was not, however, one for commitment, and he and his mother shared an almost classically Freudian relationship. In spite of this closeness, Jack was immensely proud of his second son, who had followed in his father's professional footsteps.

Army life suited Norman. He was posted to Malta in 1905, where he did little but play polo and attend dances. His letters home were full of horses, races, and matches. When the Frewens visited that year, he wrote to Shane, declaring that Auntie Clara had 'entered a second childhood here with considerable éclat, & dances hard at all the dances here, vice [sic] Clare, who sits out the whole time'.[38] He wrote frequently to Shane and Leonie, a habit since prep school. While he was at Eton, he and his mother had corresponded twice a week. She wrote newsy letters, telling him of all that was happening at Glaslough. In one, his mother described one of Prince Arthur's shooting visits to their lodge at Pettigo (Norman was fond of the Duke of Connaught, who had helped him in his career):

> I was <u>so</u> busy getting things ready here for the Duke's visit. You remember how very primitive every thing is here! & what with painting baths, putting new matting muslin curtains etc I had a lot to do. It went off very well. He brought a nice A.D.C. Capt Holland & the 4 guns got 50 brace in 2 days – Sat & Monday. The weather was fine & the walk in heather <u>pleasant</u>. Sunday however it <u>poured</u> – the

Pettigo people were very loyal & there was a torchlight procession –
Orange band & singing – & cheering the night of the Duke's arrival &
he came to the front door from the dinner table – and thanked them
& spoke to a Crimean veteran who is here. It all went off very well –
& the Muldoons made quaint remarks which Jackie [*sic*] will relate to
you. I took the precaution of their having seats to their trousers by
presenting them each with a suit![39]

Norman had so much fun in Malta that he found himself short of
funds and had to ask his mother for help. He was embarrassed and his
gratitude to her was laced with slightly rueful charm: 'Thank you so
much for the money,' he wrote. 'I don't like taking it from you, although
you may not believe it. All my fine ideas of being able to do everything
& never get into debt etc are knocked on the head, & I feel like the
ordinary "mug" of a subaltern, a source of worry to his relatives.
However, I hope it will be the last time.' His spirits were not much
dampened, however, and his letter continued with discussions about the
polo ('going strong') and his desire to attend the opera. In a letter two
years later he promised to take his mother dancing on his return to
London: 'Somehow you are much nearer my age than Marjorie Bagot
[his cousin] & many others I know, & there is no saying as to which I
would rather talk or go about with!'[40] It was little wonder that he was
his mother's favourite.

Norman's next posting was as ADC (aide-de-camp) to General Sir
John Maxwell in Egypt. He liked Egypt and got along well with
Maxwell. In June 1909, he wrote to his mother with enthusiasm: 'Day
after day goes on here with brilliant sunshine and no rain: it really is
wonderful. I don't think I shall ever tire of this place.'[41] He also regretted
that she was 'so depressed' at Glaslough and tried to cheer her by
expressing his wish to see the redecorations that had taken place.
Leonie and Jack had refurbished the house after Sir John and Lady
Constance had moved permanently to London. At last Leonie could
renovate to her own taste and the house was brought into the twentieth
century; decorators came from London to strip the shiny pitch-pine
and oak woodwork, and electric light, bathrooms, and central heating

were added.[42] But there were cutbacks as well. A new land agent had been appointed to help manage the estate, and the indoor staff were reduced from thirteen to seven.

Even with fewer servants, life at Glaslough continued on a grand scale. Entertaining royals was still de rigueur for Leonie, when the relaxed atmosphere would be replaced by pure formality. She would ready the house to perfection: a Union Jack was run up in their honour, policemen were brought in to patrol the grounds, and the servants and children instructed to behave immaculately. An exasperated Clare once commented to her cousin Seymour: 'I adore your mother, but really she is idiotic about royalties, most of them are so dull, what fun does she get out of them?'[43] The tremendous gratification that Leonie derived from royal company was captured later by her granddaughter, Anita Leslie, who once had a glimpse of several hundred letters from the Duke of Connaught, giving a detailed picture of royal life.[44] Many bore no stamp and were hand-delivered to Leonie every day. The attention made her feel special. Of the three sisters, Jennie, who moved the most freely within royal circles, was the least overwhelmed by blue blood.

Leonie loved the Edwardian formality, charmingly tinged with Irish whimsy, that reigned at Glaslough. Each evening, dinner was served at eight, on a polished table dressed with fine old Irish silver, a Charles II fruit basket, William and Mary candlesticks, plenty of Waterford crystal, and an Irish linen tablecloth. A tall arrangement of flowers had been introduced by Lady Constance, who joked that after many years of marriage, a 'cache-mari' (hide-husband), as she called it, filled with highly scented datura blooms, was an essential table prop.

In London, the weekly salons – 'entretiens de Léonie' – were attended by many well-known literary and artistic figures, and occasionally by royalty too. Ambassadors, diplomats, statesmen, as well as authors and artists, gathered for witty and intellectual conversation. Leonie and Jennie grew even closer as their lives became ever more similar. They shared confidences and gossip. Leonie, too, had an intimate royal friend and the ear of influential members of high society. She was also somewhat wealthier; although Leonie and Jack found that their overall family funds were decreasing, their own disposable income had grown slightly after taking over the estate.

Jennie was once again in the midst of political action. Now her battles were fought for Winston, who was carving out a promising political career. He fought a by-election at Oldham in July 1899 as the Conservative parliamentary candidate and lost. In October 1900 he stood again and was successful. In 1906, a few years after his election, he broke with the party and crossed the floor in the House of Commons to join the Liberals. Although criticized by some as opportunism, it was a good career move. When the government changed and the Liberals took power the following year, he became a junior minister. He was then appointed Under-Secretary of State for the Colonies in December 1906, at the beginning of which year he had published a fairly well-received biography of his father. Despite these successes, he still relied on his mother to help him. Her financial situation had marginally improved since her marriage to George (who told Shane Leslie that Jennie had even brought a stack of unpaid bills with her on honeymoon). It was customary for a new husband to settle his wife's outstanding debts, which George did. He continued to receive a small allowance from his father, and Jennie still had the income from the Madison Avenue mansion. While the newlyweds were away on a prolonged honeymoon to Belgium, France, and Scotland, Jennie received a letter from Winston, asking her to order new socks and handkerchiefs for him, and asking her to contact her friends, such as Lord Rosebery and Lord Wolseley, to enlist their help at the election at Oldham. He had even requested that his mother cut short her honeymoon in order to support his campaign. She complied.

Jennie wrote often to the Prince of Wales about Winston and forwarded the replies to him. In September 1900, just before Winston's election to the seat at Oldham, the Prince wrote to Jennie:

Ma chère Amie
    It is so very kind of you to have written to me when you are so busy

with Winston's election. Though understandably I am not a party politician I wish him all success.[45]

In addition, Jennie arranged lunches, dinners, and a variety of social opportunities for Winston to meet other political leaders.

Jennie also asked her friend, the financier Sir Ernest Cassel, for his assistance in finding her new husband remunerative employment. He organized for George to first gain some commercial experience by becoming an unpaid member of staff of the British Thomson–Houston Company, which was a contractor for the Central London Railway. After gaining some much-needed technical expertise, George was interviewed by the managing director and soon thereafter became chairman, not only of the company but of several other firms, as well as being elected a member of the advisory committee. The job was based in Glasgow, so George would travel south at the weekends to see Jennie, either in London or in the country. Their married life was almost a continuation of their courting days, allowing Jennie to look after Winston's interests during the week.

She enjoyed parties and was the star attraction at a theme party entitled 'British Society Beauties Dressed as Famous Men in History'. Dressed as a Spanish cavalier, she wore a costume complete with black tights, doublet, and hose, diamond buckles on her shoes, and a dark velvet cloak trimmed with gold. She carried a sword and a great diamond shone in her black sombrero, from which large feathers drooped. Her social status seemed assured as her renewed close friendship with the Prince of Wales, who became king in 1901, following the death that year of Queen Victoria, led to more royal honours. He quickly made Jennie Lady of Grace of St John of Jerusalem, and she was later invested with the Order of the Royal Red Cross in recognition of her work on the hospital ship *Maine*.

Winston's needs and requests after his election were constant; he needed Jennie to find him a secretary, he wanted a painting for a place on a wall, he needed a hostess for a function, he needed *her*. His only serious romantic attachment had been to Miss Pamela Plowden and it had ended with her decision to marry the future Lord Lytton. Winston found relationships with women difficult and leaned heavily on his mother for advice, which, when given, he deeply appreciated. When he took his seat in the House of Commons he sent his mother a cheque for £300 (£21,000 in today's money), declaring that in 'a certain sense it belongs to you; for I could never have earned it had you not transmitted to me the wit and energy which are necessary'.[46] Although Winston was by far the more outstanding of the two boys, Jack also needed his mother and stayed at her house (despite her letter suggesting he could not) after he returned from South Africa, where he had acquitted himself with honour.

In 1905, Jennie and George moved to Salisbury Hall, a beautiful, moated, red-brick Jacobean house near St Albans, and there gave weekend parties for their many friends: the Connaughts, the Curzons, the Manchesters, the Roxburghes, the Marlboroughs, and the Harcourts as well as, of course, the Frewens and the Leslies. Winston and Jack were also regular guests. In May 1907, the King came to stay. He had grown so stout that he could no longer manage stairs so the ground-floor rooms were rearranged to accommodate him. Accompanying him were his current favourites: among them Mrs Alice Keppel, Mr and Mrs William James, Consuelo Vanderbilt, and Prince Francis of Teck.

Jennie's frantic social life masked the cracks that had begun to appear in her marriage. George had a weakness for beautiful women and found it difficult to avoid temptation. Jennie was still attractive but when she reached fifty, her looks were not what they had been. She no longer rode, and the golf that she played with George was insufficient to keep her trim. She put on weight, and the fashion at that time for long clean lines was not as accommodating as the tight waists, huge skirts, and flounces of yesteryear. She clung to certain styles – white lace jabots, colossal velvet hats – that she knew were becoming, while relying more on her flashing eyes and ready wit. She had become an older woman married to a young, vigorous, and immature man. George wrote in an undated note that he was 'awfully worried as I feel you thought I <u>chassed</u> [*sic*] you. You know I didn't & that I'd sooner see you than all the others.'[47] They began to spend even less time together. George wrote in March 1906: 'Darling old Puss-Cat, I didn't mean to be beastly last night. But you will admit the events of the last few days have been somewhat disturbing. Just off to hunt. Bless you, yr loving Husband.'[48] George's sister Daisy, Princess of Pless, wrote in her diary in April 1907 that Jennie still loved George immensely, 'poor dear'. She commented that her sister-in-law was 'uncommonly nice' and 'still very handsome' but naturally the age difference was a 'sad and terrible drawback'.[49]

George was *very* young. In 1902, 'Sporting George' became one of the first Englishmen to acquire a motorcar and his letters that year indicate his obsession with 'runs' in the vehicle. He described breathtaking speeds and waxed triumphant over puncture-free journeys. George tried to apply himself to business, but his real passion was for sports. In August 1903, while Jennie stayed at Blenheim, he went horse racing at Goodwood in West Sussex, then home to his father in Wales where he shot snipe, grouse, golden plover, and teal. His letters to his wife were filled with long descriptions of his every hunting or fishing expedition. George was a young gentleman who lived for sport and pretty ladies. He was not a good husband for a worldly, ageing woman such as Jennie, who needed financial stability and emotional reassurance. She also needed an outlet for her still-considerable energy as well as a boost for her self-confidence, which was beginning to ebb. She wrote sadly and somewhat reproachfully to Leonie in May 1907:

I feel that I was cross & unreasonable the other day when I saw you – I am sorry – The fact is when I go to London – there are only 2 people I ever try to see, one Winston the other you – Both are often sad disappointments – one on account of work – the other on account of pleasure. I go away feeling sore at heart – I snatch a few minutes of Winston's society, by driving him to the Colonial Office, & the most you can offer me – are a few words uncomfortably (for me) at the telephone. But I have made up my mind – & shall not risk it any more – You know I love you & that when you want me I am to be found –

I like to think that you are enjoying yrself & making up for all those dull years when as you say yrself – your greatest excitement was to see me dress for a ball – Make the most of it while it amuses you – You looked very bright & happy last night Keep so – Yr loving Jennie[50]

Jennie was remarkably honest even about her sorrows. She acknowledged the pain and unhappiness of realizing that her best years were behind her, which coincided with Leonie's social triumph. Her younger sister, now aged forty-eight to Jennie's fifty-three, was more inclined than ever towards worldly pursuits and was rather caught up in her own popular success. Perhaps Jennie hoped to make Leonie feel a little guilty of neglect. Jennie was, after all, an intensely social being. Her nephew Seymour recollected an observation of his mother: that 'Jennie's room never has the chairs arranged except *en cercle* [in a circle], the lighting is dramatic but one can't read by it, luncheon is usually late and one is half-asphyxiated beforehand by the parlour maid burning incense in a large spoon. She has lovely bookcases but no readable books! She won't even play the piano alone, I have to go and play with her, four-handed!'[51]

Jennie was sustained by her ever-abundant optimism and her interest in Winston's career. In the election of 1906 she campaigned for him in Manchester and was horrified by the shouting of the suffragettes. In common with most women of her class and generation, she did not support votes for women and accused the suffragettes of damaging their cause with their shrieks and rants. Jennie was very pleased by Winston's victory, however, and in January 1906 wrote to Leonie of her excitement: 'This month has been very portentous for Winston. His book [the biography of his father], high office, now Manchester!'[52] In a later letter she responded to a comment from Leonie: 'I am amused by what you say about turncoats – I suppose it is a dig at Winston for going to the other side. There is no doubt it takes a big man to change his mind.'[53]

Jennie finally folded the failing *Anglo-Saxon Review* after ten issues, much to her regret and that of her dear friend Pearl Craigie, who had helped her with it. Without its planning to occupy her, she was somewhat forlorn and spent many evenings at the theatre or the opera with her son, Jack. It was around this time that she gave advice to Clare on clothes and other matters relating to her debut. She was full of good counsel for her sons and her niece but her own life was burgeoning with problems. George, who had set up his own financial investment business, had been swindled by a dishonest lawyer who left him £8,000 (over £500,000 in today's money) in debt. Jennie told Winston in November 1907: 'George hasn't been able to draw one penny from his business this year – so we have no nest egg to fall back on … It preys dreadfully on poor George, who is getting quite ill over it all.'[54] A few months later, in January 1908, Jack wrote to Winston that 'things seem to be going pretty badly in the home *ménage*. Poor George who has little stamina, has knuckled under to bad times and is in a bad way. I am trying to make him "buck up" against the bad times – but it is hard work.'[55] In April 1908, Jennie was delighted with the welcome news that Jack had become engaged to the Earl of Abingdon's daughter, Lady Gwendoline Bertie, known as 'Goonie' – a quiet girl with every attribute except money.

Jennie was keen for both her sons to marry, and she was very pleased when Winston, known to be awkward with girls, became smitten with Clementine Hozier, the daughter of Jennie's friend Lady Blanche Hozier. Blanche, an old friend, had led a colourful and highly scandalous life. Clementine (known as Clemmie) had survived a most unstable childhood amid great financial hardship. It was widely known that it was unlikely that even one of Blanche Hozier's four children was fathered by her husband Henry, who divorced her in 1891. According to her daughter and biographer, Mary Soames, Clementine never knew who her father was; candidates for her paternity included Lord Redesdale, Bay Middleton, and Blanche's own brother-in-law, 'Bertie' Mitford.[56] After the acrimonious separation from her husband, Clemmie's mother brought up her children in rented lodgings in England and France. Clemmie had learned to make her own hats and earned pocket money by giving French lessons. Remarkably Jennie, considered so worldly by so many, was pleased with the idea of her son marrying this penniless girl with somewhat doubtful antecedents. She told her friend Lady Crichton, 'my Winston is not <u>easy</u>; he is very difficult indeed and she is just right.'[57] Clemmie was also, by happy coincidence, Jack Leslie's god-daughter.

She and Winston were married on 12 September 1908 at St Margaret's, Westminster, in London, and Clemmie wore the veil of point lace that Jennie had worn at her own wedding to George eight years earlier. Jennie, now fifty-four, was attired in 'golden beaver-colored satin charmeuse ... finished with the widest of metal embroideries. The hat was of satin antique of the same color, with large velvet and satin-petaled lilies in metallesque coloring with bronze and silver centres, around the brim.'[58] Winston later wrote of his marriage: 'I married and lived happily ever afterwards,'[59] and to his mother, the day after the wedding: 'Best of love, my dearest Mama. You were a great comfort to me at a critical period in my emotional development.'[60]

In addition to being happy at home (although it is less clear that Clemmie was equally so, despite their mutual affection, according to their daughter Mary Soames),[61] Winston was successful at work and had become President of the Board of Trade in April 1908. Jennie, although happy to see her sons settled, was increasingly lonely. When George was travelling (which he did a great deal), Jennie would often stay with Clara, who was alone at Brede Place. The sisters no longer enjoyed the comfort of living in close proximity in London, although all three corresponded almost daily and stayed regularly at one another's houses. Clara's admiration for her glamorous sister was balm to Jennie's increasingly troubled spirits, while Clara loved hearing all the society gossip. Jennie's visits were a welcome distraction for both. Clara could forget momentarily about Moreton's fruitless ventures in Africa; Jennie could put her problems with George out of her mind and enjoy the tranquillity and beauty of Brede Place.

CHAPTER ELEVEN

The Last Duel

Brede may have been a sanctuary for Clara but it was also an extravagance that she held onto tenaciously in the face of all economic crises, many of which were self-inflicted. Her daughter Clare described Clara's recklessness in an incident that occurred in 1906. She and her mother had been stranded in the South of France when a family friend insisted upon giving Clare a fifty-pound note, which she had tried to refuse but had eventually accepted. She told her mother, who had been sobbing over their misfortune, whereupon Clara had wept on her daughter's neck, exclaiming, 'Oh, my poor child! My poor, poor child!' 'Then pulling herself together with an effort she suggested that we should go to Monte Carlo "just for the day, darling," and "have a little fling".'[1] Clare recalled insisting that they pay the hotel bill before leaving for the casino.

The Frewen children were growing up quickly. After an inauspicious debut – which had not resulted in a proposal from a wealthy suitor – and a winter season spent in Ireland, Clare was invited to visit her friend Princess Margaret, daughter of the Duke and Duchess of Connaught, who had married Prince Gustav Adolph of Sweden. When she returned to Brede, she planted a 'friendship garden', with flowers and plants sent by friends. Princess Margaret had given a great ox-eyed daisy, the Duke of Connaught various species of bamboo, Rudyard Kipling had sent rosemary and lavender, and George Moore fuchsia.

But conditions at home were, as Clare later wrote, 'distressful'. Moreton exhorted his family to 'never talk poor' and was adamant about the need to avoid bankruptcy to safeguard his long-held parliamentary ambitions. So they all struggled. Clare later wrote in her autobiography: 'From our childhood we had heard of bankruptcy as a kind of sword of Damocles hanging perpetually over our heads; so perpetually did it hang that Peter [Clare's pet name for Oswald] and I had often hoped it might fall and rid us of the suspense.'[2] Moreton would declare in front of the children that he would kill himself if made bankrupt while Clara avowed that bankruptcy must be avoided for as long as the boys were still at Eton and until Clare was married. All three children learned to recognize bailiffs and writs, written on blue paper and delivered to the front door. That aspect of their life was shaming and they hated it. Clare wrote:

> I always knew when things were getting acute, for then my father, either from incentive to economy, or in order to distract his mind from home affairs, would propose us by telephone to lunch with 'dear Duchess Milly,' or 'dear Lady Dudley,' to 'those dear Lonsdales,' or to 'the dear Whitelaw Reids' ... There were heaps of them, all 'dears' and they always seemed pleased to see us, probably because my father, even in his most tormented moments, was a very delightful person. I used to marvel at his mask to the world, and how he managed to preserve his spirits and not allow himself to be crushed by the endless struggle.[3]

Clare believed, and later wrote in her memoirs, that her father *had* made three fortunes in his life – in Australia, in India, and in Canada, each of which would have been sufficient to endow an average family for life. But Moreton was as unreasonably optimistic as he was extravagant and always believed that the really big money was just around the corner. His investments in wild schemes diminished his fortune even more than his and Clara's expensive lifestyle. Moreton's charm disguised his ruthlessness and, when applied with full force to his family, would convince them to give him any money they had. Clara had already signed away to Moreton everything she owned and now the three children were also pressed. Hugh wrote to his mother in 1907, explaining that he could not come to Brede for the weekend because he had to do business with Marshall, the family solicitor. He was worried about his father and wrote to his mother: 'He is just so hard up he doesn't know what to do, & so it is sweet of him isn't it to spare you the money up to town.'[4] That same year, Moreton planned a trap for Clare, who had now come of age and could be prevailed upon to sign away her future inheritance, as her brother Hugh had done. Clare described indignantly the occasion to Hugh:

Father made an appointment for me to see Marshall at 11 a.m. yesterday in order to <u>talk</u>, <u>discuss</u> and <u>consult</u> upon the project in hand. To my surprise he came with me – and then without any sort of warning tried to make me sign a document before I had ever talked, discussed or consulted and before I even knew what it was all about. I refused, naturally. And Marshall backed me up. Whereupon Father flew into a rage. I think if he had come to me and asked me kindly, and explained all it means to him, and appealed to my affection, I should not have hesitated. But thank heavens he did not, he lost his temper instead, and you know how unattractive and unreasonable he is in a temper. It made refusing considerably easier. He jumped down Marshall's throat until at last M. dips his pen in the ink, handed me the bill, and said 'I think, Miss Frewen, you had better do it for your father's honour' – or words to that effect!! But I refused, under the plea that I hadn't come to sign, but to discuss until I understood, and that I did not yet understand, so Marshall said 'Very well, I will not see you forced into signing against your will' and I went away and left Father there with a meeting of his creditors … Well, I went home. At 12.30 who should turn up but Father and Marshall. Well, there was I was at the mercy of those two men who talk Greek to me, not a friend, not a relative in London to help me … I felt miserable and lonely. Of course I signed … And that is the way I am made to sign things. It is <u>criminal</u> … I am frank to say that I was FORCED to sign – so there. As to Father's two thousand that he wants us three to raise for him, I will have

absolutely nothing to do with it. He can get it out of you and Oswald
if he likes. He won't get my help.[5]

It was a shocking way to treat a twenty-one-year-old girl and it is
extraordinary that Clara did nothing to help her daughter. She had
decided long ago to back her husband in all business matters and fully
expected her children to do likewise. Clare knew better than to rely on
her mother for support in standing up to her father, who was a
frightening bully when under pressure and unable to get his own way.
Although she yielded to her father's demands in the end, Clare's
attitude was strikingly different to that of her mother and brothers,
despite her youth. As she told Hugh, she wrote her father a remarkably
clear-eyed and composed letter:

> I told him also that I had no intention of following blindly what he
> told me to do, that I had both warning and example, and that if you
> had listened to the warnings of your relations you would not be in the
> position you are now – and that if Mama had not listened to him
> blindly we would not at this moment be in danger of losing our
> homes. He will find matters very different if he treats me as he treated
> you. If he goes to America I will come back to Mama, if he comes back
> I will remain away. I can live with Aunt L. [Leonie] till March – and
> then I have plenty of friends I can stay with – not to speak of relations
> ... My friends always dress me, so I am perfectly independent of
> Father, and he can't at my age make me come back if I choose to stay
> with my friends. Besides, I am young, I am liked, and I have the world
> on my side. There is not a soul among the people I live among who
> would not sympathise with me. They're all tired of his schemes ...
> Oswald must choose for himself – it is useless to help him, he would
> be beggared anyway and all of us beggaring ourselves with him will
> not help him. I am not going to do a single thing more than I have, try
> to keep Mama's furniture, that is all. Why did she ever sign? How can
> one help people who will not help themselves?[6]

What is all the more remarkable about Clare's trenchant analysis of her
family's predicament is her conclusion on the matter, which she

expressed in a letter written to Hugh a few hours after the first:

> I am sorry I wrote the hard letter about Father that I posted you this
> morning. I was wrong. I have been thinking it over and all bitterness
> has left my heart, and in its place reigns a supreme sadness. Poor Father,
> he does it all for the best, but it is <u>such a misguided</u> best. If only he
> would realise the futility of losing honour to save honour, of
> borrowing from Peter to pay Paul – of beggaring one's children and
> friends to avoid bankruptcy – of shunning bankruptcy to preserve the
> integrity of a name and the peace of mind. To have gone bankrupt
> three times would have been preferable, nay, more honourable, than to
> have gone on as he has gone on. No honour has been saved. The name
> has become a household name – some smile when they hear it, others
> say bitter things. In trying to mend matters he makes them worse. He
> is no business man. If only he would put it all in the hands of a capable
> business man and not interfere, instead of taking so much upon
> himself, things might go better. But no, he struggles on misguidedly all
> for the best – oh my God what a 'best'! And he cannot realise it. Don't
> feel bitter, Hugh dear, we none of us must. We must just realise that our
> help can be of practically no assistance to him, and therefore appear a
> little hard by refusing it … He has failed. Our lives are before us. Let us
> start fairly lest we, too, fail. Let us make of our lives what we can – the
> best if possible. We must not start too handicapped, neither must we be
> too optimistic. That is what made Father's life a failure.[7]

Early in 1908, Moreton travelled to America to promote his bi-
metallism views in the Senate. He had talks with President Theodore
Roosevelt and also spoke before the Committee of Banking and Currency. American politicians clearly did not know that Moreton was not
a politician but an agent, paid by silver interests – a fact he kept secret.
He then went to Bermuda in March with his friend Chester Beatty,
returning with the meagre sum of $50 ($900 in today's money). In April
an urgent summons from Clara reached him, requesting an immediate
transfer of $1,000 ($20,000) to her. The bailiffs were at Brede.[8]

Brede's restoration had been far more costly than originally anticipated, and Clara continued to spend money on landscaping the garden.

Through all the vagaries of Moreton's wheeling and dealing, she had clung to Brede. Relinquishing the house was unthinkable, just as it was unexpected to have it invaded by moneylenders and bailiffs. Earlier that year, Oswald had relished outings in London and trips to the theatre with Ma, followed by jolly suppers at the Carlton Hotel. There were shopping expeditions to Harrods and Hatchards bookshop, lunches at Claridge's, trips to the Zoo, and more plays and dinners. In January 1908, for his birthday, the family went to see *The Scarlet Pimpernel*. Cash flow had slightly improved thanks to Oswald's signing that same month to take on a debt of £1,050 (£62,000 in today's money). He was waiting for a naval appointment and Clara was trying, through Winston, to have him assigned to the royal yacht.

The year 1908 proved, however, to be an *annus horribilis* for the Frewen family. The money finally ran out: Clara's American income, the family's only reliable funds, had by April been spent by Moreton in his business speculations, and their three children had been tapped dry. Generous friends and family had already given – many of them more than once. Jennie and George were suffering financially, as were Leonie and Jack, who now found that agricultural revenues were dwindling, yet still had to bear the Glaslough expenses as well as provide an income for Jack's parents, living in style in London. The bailiffs who appeared at Brede were preparing to take away furniture and personal belongings. Clara held her head high. When Clare and Oswald returned one day from making calls, they found a new butler at the door and reproached their mother for hiring a servant when there was no money. 'Hush,' she told them, 'he's a bailiff – but very nice.' She had agreed to pay him ten shillings to answer the door and polish the mirrors.[9] Clara wrote to Moreton, who was in New York:

> I am having a terrible time – bailiffs came to Brede ... & although I assured them there was a bill of sale they went to the extent of coming last Saturday to say that <u>if</u> I did not pay the wretched £18 before 2 o'c – they <u>wd</u> post bills up on our front door ... I had to go into Hastings find the most respectable pawnbroker & pawn my diamond ring for wh I got £30 ... Then Clare is very ill with measles – poor Oswald

having taken 2 twos (splendid) [exam results] has come home ... & of course he had to know all about the bailiff etc – too humiliating ... Tomorrow Lowless & Co send their men here to make catalogue, & I am going to be up all night to pack & take away little valuables to <u>me</u> like Milan's box etc. The sale takes place by auction on 4th May – I shall see all my little treasures go one by one. Jennie says she will buy in a few small things for me if she can but you know how hard up <u>they</u> are. I am doing my best, but it is heartbreaking & I never felt more down ... I must tell you all these things so that you know the position – but oh <u>how</u> glad I am you are doing so well – only how everything takes time ... Goodbye no time – not a moment for more, your distracted but loving old wife – God bless you.[10]

This letter was typical of Clara: supportive and loving but also complaining about real hardships. Her reference in this letter to King Milan's box was likely an intentional jab at Moreton for leaving her in this position and a reminder of the life she might have had as the Queen of Serbia.

Moreton responded with sympathy but promising little: 'This is the saddest letter by far I have ever had in all my life, my sweet old thing,' he replied. 'All your pretty things that we both loved, and that I could not protect: and you are so brave and dear.' Then Moreton turned bitterly on his children, who had already suffered so much and on whose behalf Clara had waxed indignant. 'But you never ought to have been in this horrid gulf. I feel that it never need have been ... If the three children had stood together instead of listening to Leonie, they could have made a loan of £3000 on their reversions, fairly secured by the Brede improvements and lease, and they could have protected you and themselves from this awful disaster.'[11]

Such a defence was disingenuous at best. Moreton was claiming that he could capitalize on the money that he and Clara had spent on Brede by using the enhanced value provided by the improvements as security against loans against their future inheritances taken out by his children – a tenuous idea. By the time the bailiffs arrived, Hugh had already advanced £8,500 (£500,000 today), which would eventually increase by another £20,000 (over £1 million). When his father made Innishannon over to him (in order to avoid paying the heavy insurance premiums, on which the mortgagees insisted), Hugh assumed an estate burdened by a debt of £26,000 (£1.5 million) for which he, as 'owner', had to pay £1,300 (£77,000) per annum in interest. Oswald had also incurred, as his sister had so accurately predicted, a debt of £1,050 (£62,000) when he came of age. Later that year he committed himself to a further £4,000 (over £250,000).

Hugh, Oswald, and Clare were all at Brede to comfort their mother and to help in the crisis. Moreton, who was in the United States, did not witness the misery. Oswald recorded that valuers came in April and made them 'a little uncomfortable'. A week later, on 30 April 1908, he wrote in his diary: 'Apparently the oak here is worth 750 in mother's and my rooms alone and has got to go to the hammer. If I don't say much it is not because I don't feel it.'[12] On 4 May, Hugh and his mother went to town to sell the furniture from Great Cumberland Place – the last of the furniture saved by Clara Jerome from the Paris Commune in 1871. The trauma proved too much for Hugh, who departed for Africa a month later to try to make his fortune.

The sisters rallied round. Jennie and Leonie each bought some of Clara's special trinkets and mementos and gave them back to her. This was a hardship for both of them: George's business ventures were bringing in nothing, and no money had yet been received for the sale of the Glaslough lands in 1905. The Leslies feared that they could borrow no more to run an estate that was producing no income and might have to close it down altogether. Nevertheless, they asked Clara to let them know which items she particularly needed to save and did what they could. Other friends also helped, and many of Clara's favourite pieces were returned to her.

On his return from America when the worst was over Moreton went to London to meet Mandarin Tong-Shih-Yi of the Chinese Ministry of Finance, who was in England to gather information and advice on stabilizing the Chinese currency. It was ironic that Moreton, whose household contents had just been auctioned, was considered a financial expert in many political and diplomatic quarters. Clare went to stay with Aunt Jennie, who won £140 (£8,300 today) on the races (a source of income on which she relied throughout her life). Jennie sent her sister Clara £5, with instructions to come to London for a week, with hotel expenses to be paid by Jennie. There would be parties, as well as a wedding to attend, and Clare was insistent her mother should come: 'now you <u>must</u> do this, & not thrawl [*sic*] my plans … you looked ill & you <u>must</u> get a change.'[13] Clara was often ill during this period and needed increasingly to be cared for. This Moreton could not, or would not, do but Clara was never abandoned by her sisters or her children.

Jennie's advantage over her sisters in her marriage settlement had been compensated for by their mother's will, and the three sisters were now on a fairly level financial field. None of them had enough money. Leonie was in many ways the better off, but the Leslie family was experiencing hardship, and she had very little discretionary income. Jennie relied on George, whose talent for business was now in considerable doubt. Both Leonie and Jennie wanted to help Clara but it was not within their means to do so. It must have been immensely frustrating for them to watch Moreton fritter away capital on schemes that never came to anything. Despite evidence of Moreton's financial mismanagement, they remained loyal to the Frewens. Leonie travelled down to Brede after the auction with the trinkets that she and Jennie had managed to purchase for Clara, bringing her son with her, the eight-year-old Lionel, who, like all the boys in the family, immediately fell under Uncle Moreton's spell. Although now well into his fifties, Moreton rode like a fiend and could still climb a tree with speed and agility. Lionel was entranced by his uncle's sporting tales and, inspired by his feats of derring-do, caught a few large fish, nearly a foot long, in a pool that he came upon in the forest. When he returned with his proud haul, he was met with dismay, as the grown-ups informed him that he had caught rainbow trout from a hatchery that Moreton had established at Brede, which had been stocked from the one he had put in place at Innishannon in 1897. Moreton, relatively untroubled by the fiasco, merely suggested that they have them for dinner. Leonie later remarked that they were eating what was probably the most expensive fish she had ever had.

Moreton was feeling cheerful; he had managed to raise more money on Oswald and Clare's expectations. By the end of the year, both children had come to accept with relative equanimity the demands made on them by their father and simply gave him what he wanted without argument. Oswald recorded how in November 1908, in the same year that the bailiffs had come to Brede, he and Clare went with their father to the American Consulate in Bishopsgate and took out loans against their future inheritances: 'we signed away patrimony recklessly to the extent of £3¾ and 4,000 respectively, in sanguine expectation of getting about £1100 each … & with the devout hope of getting £200 pocket money each.' The situation had by this time reached near-comedic proportions for the unfortunate pair: 'Clare swore the affidavit as though it were the wittiest joke ever perpetrated!'[14]

In what would become a pattern of role reversal, Clara's children started looking after their mother, who was then only fifty-seven, long before she could be considered elderly. Clare took her mother to Capri for a break in spring 1909, which she described to her cousin Shane:

> I wish you could come and see us. We are living – Mama & I – a Bohemian life in the most divine spot. I heard of it through a poet: Herbert French, and rented it for three months, & a cook, & then told Mama & so here we are. She needed a change & I wanted solitude & warmth & peace – to write … We have been here a month, & hope to remain until the first of May – then to Naples, & from Naples back to England by sea. You can imagine how I love every moment of it. Mama too is happy, rather like a lizard in the sun! Relations at home do not understand – Aunt Jennie writes (not often!) of the doings of fashion, it seems too strange to read of such doings here. We are in another world, & England is a faint dream, & friends & family are fanthoms [*sic*], except Oswald, who writes about 4 times a week from Portsmouth & is always in my thoughts.[15]

While Clare and her mother escaped financial worries as best they could, Moreton launched another ambitious project soon after learning that he had just missed becoming a millionaire once again. Some twenty years previously he had purchased, at a low price, 1,000 acres of swampland south of Duluth, on ground at the head of Lake Superior. He had recently sold the land to raise some ready cash, just before the swamp was drained for the founding of the city of Superior. The investment, had Moreton held onto it, would have shown a very substantial profit. Similarly, he sold at this time his shares in the Broken Hill silver mine in Australia. He had purchased these shares cheaply, when it was believed that the mine was nearly exhausted of silver and practically worthless. The discovery and the success of the Ashcroft process had changed that, as the remaining ore that could be extracted from the Broken Hill mine was now very valuable. Too late for Moreton, the shares in the mine subsequently shot up in value.

Just after his return from Kenya in 1906, Moreton had travelled to the United States in expectation of a small coup in gold mines. While he was waiting for the shares he had purchased to rise, he went to Canada to see his friend the Viceroy, Albert, Lord Grey. While there, he accepted an invitation from Charles M. Hays, President of the Grand Trunk Railway, to accompany him on a trip to the west of Canada, following the rail line that the Grand Trunk Pacific Railway was in the process of building. Prince Rupert harbour, on the north coast of British Columbia, was to be the line's western terminus. The port was situated 550 miles north of Vancouver and some forty miles south of south-east Alaska. Hays believed that Prince Rupert was to be the San Francisco of the North and the British Empire gateway to the Far East. He was so taken with Moreton's exaggerated accounts of the millions that he claimed he was about to make on his timber in Kenya that he offered him 1,000 acres of Prince Rupert land at $100 an acre, on which he was offering a discount of 25 per cent. The offer additionally stipulated that Moreton would market the new terminal, which was to be both a shipping centre and a port that would eventually, it was hoped, rival that of Vancouver. There were witnesses in the saloon car where the deal was done, but no contract was signed. This was to cause Moreton his last and greatest heartache. The following year, Hays confirmed the agreement at the Savoy Hotel, again in front of witnesses. Moreton threw all his energy into selling the land to friends and acquaintances in England by talking up the Prince Rupert investment opportunity, convinced that this was his last opportunity to make a fortune. He was certain that he would make enough to retire on, writing in January 1909 to Shane (who had purchased some of the land on Moreton's advice) that he had got some real estate on the Pacific, 'which is the best sort of nest egg & which will presently allow us to restore nice old Brede carefully & to "live happily ever afterwards"'.[16]

With Hugh in the Colonial Service and Oswald at sea, Moreton also looked to Clare to improve the family fortunes. Both he and Clara wanted their only daughter to marry well; Clara believed, like her own mother, that a brilliant marriage was the best ambition a woman could have, while Moreton saw his daughter as another means by which to improve his income. Clare, not unnaturally, rebelled against this pressure. Her desire for independence – to spend time in Capri and to write – was given short shrift by her father. Although he could not forbid her to make the journey as by then he had, once again, left for America, he wrote to her angrily from New York:

I have read your long letter over again, the first one from home and it satisfies me less and less … It is self from beginning to end! … you have missed great opportunities. I have never pointed them out to you for the reason – a bad reason – that I am extremely proud and to suggest to my child that she might have helped me immensely, and can, is frankly disagreeable to me. You are a beautiful woman with a mental equipment, which, rightly employed, might have helped infinitely. God forbid that you should angle for men whether old or young … but if you would look around and make useful and not merely Bohemian or ornamental friends, I might, and thus you and your mother and Oswald might have been much further along the road![17]

Clare was indignant at her father's attitude, yet resigned herself to her position. She agreed to marry a man she did not love, Baron Heercken, a wealthy Dutchman. 'My mother was so pleased,'[18] Clare later recorded; Clara looked forward to visiting her married daughter who would live in a castle with its own moat. She travelled with Clare to London, to break the happy news to her sisters. They were to stay with Jennie who, by coincidence, had included in her dinner party Wilfred Sheridan, the impecunious stockbroker with whom Clare had fallen in love five years previously, following her debut in 1903. He was still handsome and unmarried. The engagement to Baron Heercken had not been announced and, by the end of the evening, it was clear that it never would be. Wilfred proposed and Clare said yes. An incurable romantic, Jennie was overjoyed, but Clara was worried what Moreton would think. She was right: Moreton was very displeased. A penniless son-in-law, who had to work for a living, was not what he had envisaged for his only daughter.

But there was little to argue about; the couple were in love and Wilfred was hardly unsuitable. Although he did not have much money, he was a gentleman and of the English aristocracy, from a family of great literary talent. Clara quickly overcame her initial disappointment at the loss of a chateau and wrote to Oswald:

> My precious one
>
> Only think of it! Clare is engaged! & to Wilfred! ... Oh they are so happy & Clare is perfectly radiant & looks lovely & says she is so glad she is going to marry a charming Englishman & live in dear old England! & always be near us & the Puss! [pet name used by the Frewens for both Clare and Oswald] Isn't it splendid! You know what a dear he is – he tells us he is making £1500 a year in the City wh makes it possible, also he is heir to Frampton Court – although that does not make him nicer – but pleases the Aunts! Who are delighted...
>
> I love you mon petit cheri,
>
> *Ta maman qui t'aime* [your mum who loves you][19]

It was Wilfred's parents who were disappointed, for there was not enough money left in the family to run Frampton Court. In marrying an impecunious girl, Wilfred would be forced to work to support the family, to educate his children in the right schools, and to pay for maintenance of the estate. After he inherited the family seat, there would be insufficient income to run a townhouse, or to travel, or to indulge in any luxuries. The Sheridans had hoped their son would do better. Wilfred and Clare were happy, however, and made their plans. It was to be a fine society wedding, and congratulations poured in from their many friends. They were an attractive couple who knew the right people and were invited everywhere. Wedding presents began to arrive at Jennie's house. Lady Naylor Leyland lent Clare and Wilfred her enormous house overlooking Hyde Park, not only to display the many gifts, but also to use as a venue for the wedding reception. They were married on 15 October 1910, in a ceremony attended by all London society. Among the guests were the Prime Minister, Herbert Asquith, Princess Margaret, and Clare's aunts and their families, including cousin Winston.

It was a magnificent occasion, but the usual Frewen tragi-comedy took place behind the scenes. Clare, who was staying at Lady Leyland's house, later described her wedding day:

> At last: 'The greatest day of your life, dear', as my mother called it …
> At eleven o'clock my wedding dress arrived, brought in a wooden bandbox by a small errand girl, accompanied by a representative of the firm [Worth]. Braided footmen and an aged butler opened wide the double doors to receive them. Then the authoritative young female announced that the dress could not be left until it had been paid for, not by cheque but in cash. This graceful message was conveyed by a footman to a housemaid, who in turn delivered it to my mother's maid, who told it to my mother. Not all the cajoling or threatening or insulting could deter the grim young female, who was 'merely carrying out orders', so while my mother – apoplectic with indignation – dressed hastily to go out to the bank, the errand girl sat on the bandbox in the middle of the marble hall.[20]

At the reception, the family's lawyer, Arthur Marshall, sat in a downstairs room to which all of Moreton's gatecrashing creditors were directed.[21] These complications could not diminish Clare's happiness in marrying the man she loved. When the canon said in his address that a successful couple must have 'common interests and common friends', Wilfred whispered to Clare that they would be all right, as he had 'lots of common friends'.[22]

Undeterred by the ongoing financial crises engulfing his family, Moreton decided that his next move would be to pursue his long-cherished political career. Although he had hoped to become a Member of Parliament after he had secured his fortune, he felt sufficiently confident in the Prince Rupert venture to throw his hat in the ring. Under the sponsorship of Independent Nationalist MP Tim Healy, he was elected unopposed in December 1910 as a Member for West Cork. When Healy failed to be elected in another constituency, Moreton resigned so that Healy could take his place. Moreton, whose mother was Irish, and whose family had owned property in Ireland for years, was a passionate advocate of Home Rule who believed in seeking accommodation with the Unionists. In January 1909, he wrote to Shane (a Nationalist who did not seek such accommodation with the Unionists) of his reasons for getting involved in Irish politics:

> But I am going to give you a lusty kick if you dare to warn me off as a 'carpet bagger'. Not much! … My father's father was for many years member for Athlone. My father though an English MP was in right of an Irish domicile & six thousand acres in two counties, Irish; my mother born in Kildare had not a drop of any but Irish blood in her veins. I am in the commission of the Peace for two Irish counties, & sad is the flight of time nearly senior magistrate for Galway! Being an avowed Home Ruler; having talked about it on English platforms for quarter of a century (and before Gladstone found salvation) I am not eligible for an English 'Unionist' seat, & as a Protectionist of quite equally early avowal, the 'other fellows' will not harbour me! … It would really interest me to learn & vastly puzzle you to say why any man on your benches is more entitled than am I to sit on those benches?[23]

His main political activity was to secure donations in the United States to support Home Rule conciliation, where he was a superb fund-raiser for the Irish cause.[24] Fighting funds flowed from the east coast cities, where many descendants of emigrants earned their living and raised their families, brought up on stories of the famines. Newspaper engravings of starving and ragged children in hillside huts played straight to the homesick consciences of the Irish populations of New York, Boston, and Philadelphia, who were relatively unconcerned about whether the money was spent to succour poor families or to fund the violent campaign against the English. These American funds gave Irish nationalism new, increased leverage. The British political establishment realized with dismay that they had a new enemy: Irish nationalists in America, who were hostile and well funded. Unlike the Nationalists, who refused to contemplate making provision for Ulster's separatist aims, Moreton believed that by working for conciliation and compromise with Ulster, he could help achieve Home Rule for Ireland with the consent of its entire population. In the United States he met his old friend (and Jennie's former lover) Bourke Cockran, who was a very active supporter of Irish independence.

Winston by now also upheld a form of Home Rule for Ireland, as did the Liberal prime minister, Herbert Asquith. By 1912, Winston and other leading British politicians had accepted that it was feasible and even desirable to pass a Home Rule Bill. Political discussion in London focussed less on the old question of real Irish intentions and the danger of ultimate separation from Britain, and more on the practical problem of creating a legislature. It would be an Irish legislature, with an Irish executive for purely domestic Irish affairs. The imperial Parliament in Westminster would be reserved for matters that affected the crown, such as war, the army, the navy, international treaties, the imposition of most taxpaying (in the early days) and, for the first six years, control of the Irish Constabulary (with the exception of the Dublin Police, control of which was to pass to the Irish executive immediately). The Bill was endorsed by Irish Nationalists such as John Redmond, who led the Irish Parliamentary Party, as well as influential Nationalist politicians John Dillon (who, with Redmond, was at the centre of all Home Rule negotiations between 1910 and 1916) and William O'Brien (who opposed the 3rd Home Rule Bill, however, because he was against the partition of Ireland). At this time, all of these supporters accepted the supremacy of an imperial Parliament.

The successful implementation of local government in Ireland (following the 1898 Local Government Act), and the fact that the majority of Irishmen owned their own farms, had moderated people's views on both sides of the divide. There was broad acceptance for Home Rule, and Redmond's support for the Bill was echoed across the Atlantic. The only remaining opposition came from the mainly Protestant province of North-east Ulster, where Unionist politicians led by Sir Edward Carson (and supported by the Conservative leader Andrew Bonar Law) were vehemently against the new Parliament. Carson set up the Ulster Volunteer Force to oppose Home Rule, in which Jack Leslie served as a lieutenant. To counter the threat of Protestant violence sponsored by the Ulster Volunteers, the Irish Volunteers, largely controlled by the Irish Republican Brotherhood (or Fenians), were set up in Dublin. These groups were technically unarmed militias and not armies (at least until 1914).

On 28 September 1912, Sir Edward Carson and his allies organized a day of protest. In Belfast all shipyards and factories were closed and the day was devoted to securing signatures for a covenant that would resist Home Rule. After religious services in the churches, Carson led a procession, holding the faded yellow banner that was said to have been William III's from the Battle of the Boyne in 1690.[25] They marched through the streets to Belfast town hall, accompanied by an escort of 2,500 men wearing bowler hats and carrying walking sticks. At the town hall, Carson was the first to sign the pledge refusing to recognize the authority of a Home Rule Parliament. For the rest of the day, tens of thousands of men and women streamed into the town hall to sign, many in their own blood. Within days, a total of 218,206 Ulstermen had signed the Covenant, in addition to 228,991 women who had signed a parallel declaration. The Covenant, also known as the Solemn Pledge, was based on sixteenth- and seventeenth-century Scottish precedents, established to preserve and advance the Protestant Reformation in the British Isles. Some supporters felt that the religious dimension to this political pledge was misguided. Among these was Leonie, who wrote to Moreton of her belief that it was a mistake for some of the clergy to make the Covenant a religious statement, although she wondered whether their support 'wd secure nonconformist vote in England against H.R. [Home Rule], wouldn't it?'[26]

On 1 January 1913, Carson moved an amendment to the Home Rule Bill in the Westminster Parliament to exclude all nine counties of Ulster. In doing so he was supported by the leader of the Conservative Party, Andrew Bonar Law. Carson was adamant: 'We all know,' he declared, '...the vast majority of our fellow countrymen who are Nationalists in the South and West of Ireland will have Home Rule if this Bill becomes law, and that we shall not have the power to stop it. All we propose to do is to prevent Home Rule becoming law in our own part of the country.' William O'Brien replied for the Nationalists, saying that they would go to any lengths to meet the demands of the Ulstermen – 'with one exception – that is, the partition of our country'.[27]

Winston had become Home Secretary in February 1910. His vision of Irish Home Rule for a united Ireland differed from Moreton's aim of a federal Ireland (administered in separate units), which accommodated the Unionists. Moreton had written to his nephew from America in March 1910, castigating him for his Irish policy and ending: 'I know a good deal more than I can afford to write just now. Here, thanks to your propaganda, no man feels safe.'[28] Winston replied to this by cable, saying simply: 'Many thanks for your letter I never mind political criticism from those who are my real friends.'[29] Like many British politicians, Winston had previously disapproved of Home Rule, declaring in his campaign for the Oldham seat in 1899: 'All true Unionists must ... be prepared to greet the reappearance of that odious measure with the most strenuous opposition.'[30] By 1910 he had altered his views and agreed that it would be safer to give Ireland Home Rule.

The Irish question was no longer, he stated, 'fierce and tragic guise ... Rebellion, murder and dynamite, these have vanished from Ireland.'[31] By 1912, Winston had also modified his ambition for a united Ireland to accept a compromise over Ulster.[32] Within less than two years, however, the outbreak of the First World War in August 1914 would suspend reform on Irish Home Rule in Westminster.

Winston's political star was in the ascendant, although he had made many enemies along the way. He was widely regarded as a traitor to his class and a man of overwhelming ambition. Still, he was full of optimism for the future. He was happily married, whilst still close to his mother. When Jennie decided to publish her memoirs in 1908,[33] Winston advised her to avoid hurting anyone's feelings. She did this so adroitly that the published book, *The Reminiscences of Lady Randolph Churchill*, was charming but quite unrevealing about her love life or her relationships with her sons. Jennie had taken a great deal of artistic licence over the facts and the book was less an accurate autobiography than a pleasant fiction. It was well received, however, and she was encouraged sufficiently to write a play. In addition to providing amusement, her writing brought in much-needed income. George's business had suffered with the financial panic in New York in 1907, which had been caused by the failure of the respected Knickerbocker Trust and the Westinghouse Electric Company. These had led to a series of business collapses, stock market plunges, and a massive run on America's banks. The US Treasury injected millions of dollars into the banks to try to save them, but many of them were ruined. George's firm never really recovered from this setback. As always in times of trouble, he fell ill and spent much of 1907 laid up in bed. His throat infections and sinus trouble would always flare up when he was stressed.

Jennie was spending more time away from her husband. In the spring of 1907, George's sister Daisy, Princess of Pless, made reference in her diary to George, 'with whom everything is not quite as he would wish it'.[34] Winston was concerned about George's inability to cope with setbacks. In 1906, he and Jack had lent George money (which was subsequently repaid by George's wealthy brother-in-law, the Duke of

Westminster, who was known as Bend' Or). In an effort to economize, Jennie and George gave up their house, Salisbury Hall, and moved back to London to live at the Ritz, which had opened in London in 1905. Whenever money became too short to ignore, all three Jerome sisters would rent out their houses, let the servants go, and move to an hotel. Incredibly, this was actually a cost-saving measure, although it might have been more effective if they had chosen a hotel less luxurious than the Ritz.

Jennie also tried to find ways to earn. In 1909, she bought, re-decorated, and sold a house at such a profit that even Winston was impressed. 'I was so glad to hear of your excellent stroke of business,' he wrote.[35] Winston had long ago decided on two maxims regarding money, both of which he observed throughout his life: one, that needs and not resources should determine his spending; and, two, that in the absence of funds income must be increased, rather than expenditure decreased. It was therefore important to find a reliable means of generating income and he was full of admiration that his mother had managed to do this:

> The utility of most things can be measured in terms of money. I do not believe in writing books which do not sell, or plays which do not pay. The only exceptions to the rule are productions which can really claim to be high art, appreciated only by the very few. Apart from that, money value is a great test. And I think it very creditable that you should be able after two or three months' work, which you greatly enjoyed, to turn over as large a sum of money as a Cabinet Minister can earn in a year.[36]

Jennie became a grandmother twice in 1909 – to Jack and Goonie's son John, and to Winston and Clemmie's first child, Diana. She was also cheered by the success of her play, *His Borrowed Plumes*, which starred Beatrice Stella Campbell. The actress, better known as 'Mrs Pat', was a theatrical star who had risen to fame in 1893 with her role in *The Second Mrs Tanqueray* and who had subsequently played all the great female leads, from Juliet to Lady Macbeth. She was graceful and beautiful, with long black hair and a husky voice. Her husband, Patrick Campbell, had been killed in the Boer War, leaving her with two children (her daughter often shared the stage with her). George alleged in his memoirs that he had met the actress for the first time in 1909, although a letter from Clara to Moreton a number of years earlier referred to George's 'little flirt with Mrs. Pat Campbell'.[37] George later claimed that he had first met Mrs Pat in the winter of 1909, when she 'became a constant visitor to the house', adding: 'Besides being a very beautiful woman, she was a brilliant conversationalist, and had a keen sense of humour and a ready wit.'[38] Whether or not George's assertion is true, Jennie was amiably disposed to Mrs Pat and was delighted when she agreed to star in the drama, writing to Leonie in June 1909, 'Mrs. Pat has really been an angel & the play wld not exist without her.'[39] *His Borrowed Plumes* was a play within a play. The heroine, represented by Mrs Pat, has written the scenario of a novel, which she then shows to the 'other woman', who steals not only that but the heroine's husband to book. She gives him the manuscript, which he unwittingly uses as the basis for a play of his own. In the last act, with the audience within the play calling for the author, he makes peace with his wife and announces the truth: that he has been masquerading in 'borrowed plumes'.

In an ironic twist, George and Mrs Pat fell in love during rehearsals (if not before, during their earlier flirtation), although Jennie, pre-occupied with her production, did not seem to notice. The play opened in July 1909 before a grand audience at the Hicks Theatre in London. Winston, of course, attended, in a box with his mother and stepfather. Mrs Patrick Campbell later wrote, 'At the first performance everybody who was anybody, and who could procure a seat, was present.'[40] In the audience were the Dowager Duchess of Manchester, Prince Francis of Teck, Grand Duke Michael of Russia, the Duchesses of Marlborough, Rutland, and Roxburghe, Earl Howe, Lord Elcho, Lord Charles Beresford, and Mrs Asquith, among many other personalities. The production received mixed reviews and was seen more as a society event than an artistic endeavour. *The Times* critic wrote on 7 July:

when mundane ladies produce original modern comedies out of their own original modern and quite charming heads, all the other mundane ladies who have written original modern comedies themselves, or might have done so if they had chosen, or are intending to do so the very next wet afternoon, come and look on. These are the occasions that reconcile one to the theatre. For a sudden feminine glory invades it and transfigures it, so that it becomes an exhibition of beauty and elegance; the very latest dialogue on the stage is accompanied by a *frou frou* of the very latest Paris fashions in the stalls.[41]

The play made no money, but Jennie was happy. As Mrs Patrick Campbell wryly noted, 'An exaggerated importance gradually grew around the production, owing to Royalty and many distinguished people being interested in it.'[42]

Jennie had always loved the theatre: like her father before her she enjoyed spectacle on a grand scale. Riding the wave of her success, she hoped to create a national theatre in London and helped organize a National Theatre Committee, which was largely responsible for raising £30,000 (nearly £2 million in today's money) to buy a site opposite the Victoria and Albert Museum in South Kensington. When the National Theatre Committee merged with the Committee for a Shakespeare Memorial Theatre later that year, the new group asked Jennie to chair the executive committee. She agreed and held the first meeting at her sister Leonie's London house. The immediate need was for funds, so Jennie proposed a Shakespearean Memorial National Theatre ball at which the 600 guests would appear in Shakespearean or Tudor costume. She herself would go as Olivia from *Twelfth Night*.

The gala was a welcome distraction from the trials of her personal life. Money was as ever a constant problem, and her arguments with George were now frequent. His relationship with Mrs Campbell made a bad situation worse. George and the actress were now openly spending time in each other's company, and his absences from the marital home had become more and more prolonged. Jennie wrote a letter to her mother-in-law in August 1910, the draft of which has survived, complete with its original erasures (quoted in parentheses). Jennie described her relationship with George:

> You know that our relations have become very strained (on my part) nearly to breaking point. As he is your son – your only son – & I am sure in your own way you love him – I implore (of) you to think out (for him) <u>without any consideration of me</u> – what is best for <u>him</u> – He can have his freedom if he wants it – free to marry Mrs Patrick Campbell or anyone else he thinks would make him happy – I have done my best & have failed – (There is much that I could say but I will refrain). In respect to money & extravagance (of) with which he has reproached me there is absolutely nothing to choose between us. In fact if our mutual finances were looked into I think mine would come out the best – I (make) seek no excuse for my own shortcomings – they are many – (we are but human but in many ways I can claim to have done my best but) I have loved him more than anyone on earth & have always been true & loyal.[43]

Once again, as at their father's death when they gave up their inheritances, and as at their mother's remarriage when Winston waived his allowance, her sons came to her financial rescue. Jack wrote a comforting letter, and he and Winston sent £100 to help her.[44] In April 1911, both sons met their mother to discuss the issue of separation. Afterwards Winston wrote from the Home Office in Whitehall to George. He did not mince his words:

> Dear George West
>
> I have seen my mother and Jack & am now I think better able to form a judgement than when I met you. I have advised my mother not to seek by any means to renew relations with you after the way you have treated her for the last two years. As to her final course she must be guided by legal opinion. She harbours no resentment against you. The immediate circumstances however require to be discussed between us. The public manner in which you advertised your desertion has created serious difficulties for both of you quite apart from the unnecessary affront to her. Your joint financial position must be

considered in regard to the maintenance of credit, the sudden withdrawal of which might be ruinous to both of you. The sale or disposal of property in which you are jointly interested must be effected in such a way as to prevent needless loss as much as possible. Wheater [George's business partner] also, who I have always respected, has a claim to be taken into account. I have asked my mother to prepare me a note to assist me in discussing with you the disentanglement of your joint affairs. Your return to London next week would appear desirable and I should be willing to meet you at a business interview on Thursday or Friday at an hour which can be settled later by mutual convenience. This seems to me to be better than an immediate recurrence to solicitors and I therefore make the offer. Perhaps you will let me know what you decide.

Yrs vy truly,

Winston S Churchill[45]

On 20 June, Jennie attended the ball she had organized to synchronize with the coronation of King George V, which took place two days later. The death in May 1910 of her old friend and confidant Edward VII marked the end of her visits to Sandringham. She was not an intimate of George V or his wife, Queen Mary.[46] It was the end of an era, and it coincided with other fundamental changes in the political landscape of Britain.

The Liberal government was pushing through social and tax reforms. In the 'People's Budget' of 1909, the Chancellor of the Exchequer, David Lloyd George, proposed graded and increased income tax as well as a 'supertax' on large incomes, designed to target the landowning class. The budget aroused great debate before it was passed in the Commons, only to be summarily rejected by the House of Lords. The Lords objected to those changes that were unfavourable to the landed classes, whose interests had been protected by Edward VII before his death. The Liberals subsequently pressed for a reduction in the power of the Lords. Reform was required; trade unionism was on the rise, with membership increasing from 750,000 in 1888 to 6.5 million by 1918. The rapid growth, combined with dissatisfaction about working conditions, exploded in strike action between 1910 and 1914. The printers' strike of 1911 led to the establishment of a new workers' daily newspaper, the *Daily Herald*, edited by George Lansbury.

Winston, although Home Secretary, was not closely involved in the discussions over House of Lords reform. He was hoping to leave the Home Office for the Admiralty. A diplomatic incident had occurred in Agadir, off the coast of Morocco, which the French were about to declare as their protectorate. A German gunboat had deliberately provoked the French and consequently Winston had become focussed on military matters.[47] When Prime Minister Asquith asked him to become First Lord of the Admiralty in October 1911, he left home affairs to concentrate on foreign policy, an increasingly critical mission, as Germany threatened and war loomed on the horizon.

Despite his new responsibilities, Winston was never too busy to take care of Jennie's complicated finances. When he had relinquished, at her remarriage, the £500 per annum allowance that she and his father had intended for him and had defrayed the loan that she had taken to pay for Jack's and his own allowance prior to her remarriage (which he and Jack received from 1897 to 1900), he had advised his lawyers that in return he wished for an undertaking from his mother to make provision for her children, should George's financial position improve. In fact George was close to bankruptcy by the time he and Jennie separated in 1911, and Winston's main concern was that his mother should not be dragged down with her philandering husband. The letter that he wrote to her on 13 April 1911 reads remarkably like one from a parent to a child rather than the other way round:

Dearest Mamma,

I am quite sure it would not accord either with your dignity or yr happiness to seek by any promise of relations or circumstances to induce George to return to you. You would not wish to hold him in a thralldom & such a condition could not last & wd only be cruel to both of you. I agree with you that the immediate disentanglement & rearrangement of yr affairs shd be effected before any avoidable publicity is given to your rupture. I have written George a letter a copy of wh is enclosed herewith. Please prepare me with Jack the statement of yr joint financial position from yr point of view. It is not necessary to consider yet what ultimate course shd be taken, and it is important not to disclose in any way yr intentions … We must know exactly how the law lies before <u>any</u> step is taken. In the meanwhile please do not write to George. There is great strength in silence, & that strength is often proportioned to the difficulty of preserving silence. I hope I was not rough in my manner last night. My heart bleeds for you & I am only trying to find & guide you upon the course wh will secure the peace & honour of yr life. Do ponder over this: *you* cannot keep even the smallest household under £1000 a year. This will leave you almost nothing for all the things you want to do. On the other hand if you can at any rate for the present abolish household expenses you will have more pocket money & more freedom than you have had for many years.

Ever yr loving son,
Winston[48]

Jennie was an optimist and, like her sister Clara, had the agreeable facility of putting her worries behind her. In spite of Winston's advice, when George asked to move in with her again, she accepted, although he moved out again quite soon thereafter.

During those difficult final years, Jennie was drawn to other, more pleasant, activities. She conceived an ambitious plan to raise more money for her theatre project, a replica of an Elizabethan town, where people from the twentieth century would enter the sixteenth. With the help of Sir Edwin Luytens, who had redesigned the Albert Hall for the ball, they chose Earls Court in West London as the site. The plan was to alter the dilapidated buildings and build new ones in the Elizabethan style. A vast capital sum was required for the project, and Jennie managed to persuade Cox's Bank to donate £40,000 (nearly £2.5 million in today's money). Other wealthy friends also made contributions. In January 1912 the London *Daily Mail* referred to Jennie as 'the busiest woman in London': 'She has always been energetic. It is in her American blood. When she first came to England, as Lady

Randolph Churchill, she gave London Society a fillip. Never has she been content to travel in a groove. But just now, she has in hand a scheme which is by far the biggest she has ever evolved.'[49] The *Daily Express* was no less in awe of her energy, drawing a direct link between her accomplishments and the success of her son Winston:

A handsome, fashionably-dressed lady, with striking dark eyes and a notably strong chin, is standing in the hall the size of a railway station with half a dozen men. The lady is talking. The men are listening. She asks them questions, terse, straight to the point, and the answers are given equally directly. She is Mrs. Cornwallis-West, the originator and tireless director of the 'Shakespeare's England' Exhibition at Earl's Court [*sic*]. There is nothing amateurish about Mrs. West's management of this great Exhibition. There is nothing casual. Her staff are all experts, but she directs ... As one talked with her and realized the enthusiasm with which she has approached her work and the complete grasp that she has of all the details, one began to understand how very much Mr. Winston Churchill is the son of his mother. He may have inherited his political genius from his father, but he certainly owes to his American mother the superb energy and thoroughness with which he astounded the Board of Trade, appalled the Home Office, and is delighting the best elements at the Admiralty.[50]

It is interesting that both of these articles refer to Jennie specifically as an 'American'.

There is no doubt that her talents as an impresario were stupendous. She persuaded a number of the nobility to don their family armour for combat jousts. To celebrate the opening of the exhibition, Jennie hosted a series of parties at the Mermaid Tavern for friends and European royalty. Her family and many friends helped with the 'Tourney', as she called the jousting competition, which Queen Alexandra attended. Jack Leslie and Hugh Warrender acted as 'The Martiall's Men', and Sunny Marlborough, as well as Randolph's nephews, Lords Ashby St Ledgers and Tweedmouth, were jousters. Clare Sheridan was a 'Wayting Ladye' and among the Queen's train were Lady Diana Manners (later Cooper) as well as Vita Sackville-West and Violet Keppel (who would enter upon a notorious love affair some six years later). Daisy, Princess of Pless, played the Princess Errant and her escort was Jennie's former lover, Count Charles Kinsky. In their train were Prince Christopher of Greece, Prince Bentheim, the Hereditary Duke of Mecklenburg-Strelitz, and the Spanish Duke of Alba. Jack Churchill led the Parade of Knights and George brought up the rear. Winston did not participate, no doubt feeling that the First Lord of the Admiralty could support the exhibition in a more dignified manner. In spite of the attractions, including sideshows, a scenic railway, and an international circus, the exposition still lost money.[51]

While these festivities were taking place, Jennie's marriage had all but fallen apart. George had become critical of her. In a satirical novel he published in 1930, entitled *Two Wives*, a character called Lady Carsteen is a thinly veiled caricature of Jennie, a society woman with an exaggerated idea of her own importance. He found Jennie's inability to manage money increasingly frustrating, a failing that C.B. Cochran, a boxing promoter (and later a successful theatre producer) who worked with Jennie on the Shakespeare exhibition, also noted: 'Her ideas were wonderful. It was money that perplexed her. She threw it around like water.'[52] George observed that Jennie had no appreciation for the cost of things yet when she wanted something she just had to have it, without even asking the price. The Elizabethan pageant was a case in point – a splendid success that lost money. An Elizabethan ball held ten days later was equally magnificent, but its profit was tiny. Jennie was good at organizing events, and her previous fund-raising efforts, such as playing at concerts, were profitable. But the balls and parties that she orchestrated generated little surplus, because she spent too much on them.

George was also deeply envious of her success. When the end of the marriage finally came in December 1912, both parties agreed that arrangements must be made quickly, to avoid further hurt. Jennie believed that he wanted a divorce because he hoped to marry a younger woman and have a family. Jennie had her faults, but lack of generosity was not one of them. In the face of her humiliation, she wished George well: 'When this & our financial difficulties are settled,' she wrote to him on 29 December 1912, 'a new and I hope prosperous life will be open to you – Make use of it in the best sense – & your happiness & prosperity will be my best reward for the sacrifice I am making in giving you up.' She sadly added: 'No one knows better than you what that sacrifice means to me – for I have loved you devotedly for 12 years. You have been ever in my thoughts & this love will only die – with me.'[53] Jennie held her head high during the divorce proceedings and garnered much sympathy. George went to Brazil with his sister Daisy, and Mrs Campbell pursued a flirtation with the playwright George Bernard Shaw, who was in love with her. Jennie changed her name back to Churchill.

Just before the decree became absolute in April 1914, Jennie learned that George intended to marry not a young heiress, as she had imagined, but instead Mrs Pat Campbell, who was twelve years older than George and in dire financial straits herself. Jennie felt the betrayal deeply, and her family were furious with him. Moreton wrote angrily to Clara: 'So that beauty George West is to be married on Tuesday to Mrs Pat Campbell ... Full fathom five they dive to a joint folly.'[54] Even George's sister Daisy sent Jennie telegrams, begging her to withdraw her consent to the proceedings. After the divorce was made absolute, she cabled: 'Jennie dearest you did your best it's awful and he will regret just read news in paper am miserable hope see you soon much love Daisy.'[55] George, waiting for the final documentation to come through, was desperate to keep his leading lady happy and calm before she opened in her new play, Shaw's *Pygmalion*. Jennie wrote to George, reassuring him that he would soon have his liberty:

> The d.n. [decree nisi] will be made absolute on Monday and I understand that you are going to be married on Tues. You need not fear what I may say for I shall not willingly speak of you. And we are not likely ever to meet. This is the <u>real</u> parting of the ways. But for the sake of some of the happy days we had together – should you ever be in trouble and wanted to knock at my door it would not be shut to you.

I am returning you my engagement and wedding rings – I say goodbye
– a long, long goodbye.

Jennie[56]

She simply would not give in or break down publicly. Her sisters were sympathetic. Leonie wrote before the decree nisi to lend her support: 'Dearest – you have done <u>all</u> you could, and we can only <u>deplore</u> the folly, if he commits it, of marrying Mrs. P.C. I know how generous & noble you have been – and how you made the sacrifice, hoping it wd be for his good.'[57] When Leonie discovered that the marriage had actually taken place, she wrote again: 'You take it in the right way. You are very fine – courageous – and human.' She confided that she felt 'hateful and revengeful', and that Jack was 'very disgusted' but that Jennie had the more admirable response: '<u>yours</u> is the right spirit – no animosity – no bitterness, just = Fini =.'[58] Leonie wrote often to tell Jennie again that she thought it was 'disgraceful' of George to have put her through such an ordeal. 'I resent it for you,' she declared, 'altho you are big & noble enough to forget it.' She was uncompromising in her condemnation of George and Mrs Campbell: 'He should never have come into yr life. And as for Her – well there is nothing too bad to describe my feelings about her – the only consolation, is that she will have a pretty bad time of it, if she cares for him – & serve her right – there.'[59]

Leonie had anxieties of her own. In the same week that their old friend, King Edward VII, had died, Norman, her favourite son (and now heir), was due to fight the last duel engaged in by a serving officer in the British army. Leonie could hardly believe that her son could have been so foolish. In 1910, while in Egypt under General Maxwell, he had exchanged letters with Princess Shevikar, the wife of a distinguished Pasha. Her husband, Ysoury, was renowned both as a polo player and a superb swordsman. When he discovered a love letter, he sent it to General Maxwell and demanded satisfaction from the officer. Maxwell gave Norman twenty-four hours to leave the country, while Ysoury's challenge was studied by a small committee in London, comprised of

Sir Ernest Cassel, Lord Charles Beresford (both close friends of the Leslie family), and Lord Cromer. Leonie turned to the Duke of Connaught for help, but there was no avoiding the consequences of Norman's indiscretion. The committee agreed that the duel must be fought. If it were fought in Paris and kept absolutely quiet, Norman, if he survived – Ysoury had declared that he would kill him – would not have to resign his commission. Jack Leslie, a better swordsman than his son, offered immediately to fight in his stead. Norman refused, however, and instead trained intensely with his father during the four-week grace period before the encounter with Ysoury. It was a strict rule of honour that, as the guilty party, Norman could not attempt his adversary's life, but must merely defend himself.

Leonie was adamant in her determination to keep the indiscretion within the family. Duty came first, followed by an obligation to hide unpleasantness. Her son Seymour wrote that his mother's 'Edwardian recipe' was simply: 'Never talk of money, illnesses, children or <u>servants</u>.'[60] She channelled all her anxiety into ensuring that the event remain shrouded in secrecy. Seymour recorded: 'Leonie imposed a strict security – her motto was always *Cache ton jeu* [hide your game] … "no one was to know, it would be all over if the Press learnt of it".'[61] Sir Ernest Cassel was prevailed upon to lend his house in Paris for the duel, and Leonie tried to find a new posting for her son. In April 1910, General Sir Ian Hamilton wrote to her with some possibilities:

> I have looked into the state of the Battalions of your Son's Regiment, and find that if he resigns his appointment as Aide-de-Camp forth-with, he can be absorbed at once. This would save his being placed on 'a rate of pay equal to half-pay' which is what he would fall to if he resigned at a time when there was no vacancy. Without any injustice to anyone I can post him to Dublin, and if you were particularly keen about it I would try to post him to Bordon, although there is a 2nd lieutenant who has actually prior claims. There is no vacancy in India, and of course Egypt for him is taboo…
>
> Let me know as soon as you can about this.[62]

Norman and Ysoury met on 15 May, each accompanied by a second and a surgeon. Norman was attended by Docteur Henri Blanc from the Hôpital de Lagny, who presented him with a bill of 100 francs (£4, or £250 today). The duel lasted an hour and a quarter. Norman retired with honour after parrying successfully until Ysoury over-lunged, severing the muscles in two fingers. Norman was extremely fortunate. His commander was unforgiving, however, and because he had selfishly brought the regiment into dishonour, he was under no circumstances welcome to return. His fellow officers were told that Norman had left suddenly to see his mother, who was ill; only a handful of close friends knew the truth. After the duel, Norman was shipped to the Battalion of the Rifle Brigade, serving in India. He was characteristically light-hearted about the whole affair, exhorting his mother to follow his example and make little of the event, writing beforehand:

> There is absolutely no fear whatsoever, it is only rather a pity that the affair is turning out to be such a screaming farce ... Don't even pretend to be worried, because there is absolutely none the whole talk of danger is too idiotic, but at the same time I don't intend to miss. Remember this is the finest opportunity to shew everybody your pluck, so mind you do.
>
> Bless you,
> Norman[63]

Like his mother and father, Norman was a great believer in showing 'pluck' and Leonie was gratified by his stiff upper lip and strong sense of decorum.

The following year, in 1911, Leonie received some exciting news. Enthused by the Gaelic revival, Shane had travelled to America for a lecture tour, wearing the trademark saffron kilt that he would sport for the rest of his life. During his visit, he fell in love with Marjorie Ide who was in America visiting her elder sister Anne, now the wife of Jennie's one-time beau, Bourke Cockran. Marjorie was the beautiful and rather spoiled daughter of a statesman who had been Governor of the Philippines and Samoa, and who was now the American Ambassador to Spain. Worldly and sophisticated, she had often acted as hostess for her father. She was also huge fun. Brimming with self-confidence, she loved parties and dressing up. Her unusual and exotic childhood had left her afraid of nothing, and she bore on her shoulder a tattoo of a snake curled around a dagger, the work of Samoan natives (her sister Anne had a tattoo of a lizard, the work of natives of another village). Marjorie had reputedly turned down over one hundred proposals of marriage; Shane, tall, moody, terribly handsome, and tremendously talented – a man who had forsworn women and planned to become a priest – was a challenge that this girl could not resist.

Leonie travelled to New York that same year to meet her son's fiancée. Marjorie, who had left for Madrid to prepare her trousseau, was due to return shortly to spend time with Shane as well as to meet his parents. From New York City, Leonie wrote to Marjorie, still in Spain. It is a remarkably modern and considered letter that bears reproduction here at length:

> It has all been such a surprise, that it has taken some days for me to understand. I have tried to think it over very sensibly – from all points of view – and it now seems quite clear to me. It is <u>entirely</u> a question of how much in earnest <u>you</u> really are – for of Shane's deep affection there can be no question. *If* there is <u>any</u> doubt in yr mind, for God's sake give it all up – and tell him <u>now</u>, while I am with him.
>
> If, on the other hand you know yr own mind & heart – if you have <u>seriously</u> considered the sacrifices this marriage will entail – if you are ready to face the discomforts of living in a small way – if you are <u>sure</u> – then indeed I will do all in my power to make things easy … You know that I worship Shane, and that my happiness wd be, that he kept to his high ideals and still managed at the same time to do some practical work. If you love him, you can help him *so* much – and have an interesting life with him. When I married 27 years ago, we started on a very small income – but I enjoyed every day of the year – because the things that matter to me are <u>not</u> the things that money can give. If you are the same, I am sure you can make a great success of it all – and

I can promise you a warm welcome from all the family – and a home in Ireland, whenever you are tired of the world & want peace & quiet! ... Only <u>be sure</u>.[64]

Leonie emphasized the financial sacrifices (a word she frequently used) that Marjorie would be called on to make, because Shane had given up his inheritance, a decision that could not be revoked. He had an annual allowance of £200 (about £12,000 today), which was insufficient to support a family. Leonie was so eager to help her son that she agreed to make over to him and Marjorie a portion of her own American income (£800 per annum).

Unfortunately, the engagement ran into difficulties. Shane had a nervous breakdown while lecturing in Chicago. Although Leonie did her utmost to hide his mental weakness, claiming he was 'overtired', Shane was temperamentally unstable and prone to collapse. Leonie prepared to take him to The Cedars, the New York home of Bourke and Anne Cockran, where he could recover.

In Madrid, Marjorie heard the news and became frantic. She wrote to Moreton, who had congratulated her warmly on her engagement (Moreton, by astonishing coincidence, had met Marjorie years ago when she was a child in Samoa), expressing her concerns:

My farewells were said, my trunks packed and I was leaving for Paris last night when the cable came from home, telling of Shane's illness. It seems that he had the grippe and didn't half take care of himself, went to Chicago in the midst of it (as far as I can make out from the cablegram) and is now seriously ill at Bourke's with a nervous breakdown. As you can well imagine, I am nearly distracted with grief and anxiety. So he is far away and so helpless at this time of all others. I feel as if I must get on the first and fastest steamer and go to him but Anne [Cockran] cables that the doctors say that I mustn't, that he must have complete rest and quiet and the marriage must be postponed until autumn ... You, knowing Shane so well and how wonderful he is, can realize how much he would mean to a woman who really understood him and loved him as I do. And how I thank God, no matter what happens now, that I waited for Shane instead of marrying some man whom I half liked.[65]

Despite the doctors' orders, Leonie believed that Shane would recover more quickly in his fiancée's care. She wrote to Marjorie, urging her to come to New York and support Shane:

> I can't tell you how distressed I am to think you should have all this anxiety & sadness just at the moment you were announcing yr engagement, and were enjoying all the excitement of it. We have felt for you – it has really been very tragic. I know Anne has written to you fully about Shane's illness – and how the doctors think it will take a long time for him to recuperate and that the wedding should only take place in the autumn. I don't think they realize how much of his weakness is due to nerves – and my own idea, is that when I take him down to the Cedars tomorrow, he will begin to mend at once – and get strong quickly. I feel somehow, that if you were there your presence would help more than anything to cure him – & if he mends slowly, you will feel less anxious with us, than away. Is the trousseau very important? Couldn't you order just a few nice things – and come, & then let us decide about the wedding when you are here? Whatever you wear, he will think you beautiful – and you can always get more later.

Seymour was planning to travel to the United States at the end of April, she added, and hoped that he and Marjorie could travel together. They could bring some of the wedding gifts, including two rugs that Norman was sending from Persia. Leonie was having a necklace made for her future daughter-in-law, she wrote:

> mounted with some stones I had from my mother, for you – the designs have just come – from [the jewellery designer] 'Chaumet'. He has a house in Paris & in London. You might go & see him as I shall be returning the design I have chosen, next week. They take ages to set stones, but I am hoping they will have it finished in time. I thought you might like to wear the 'tassel' part by itself on a high gown. I do hope you will like it – my sister Jennie helped to choose the design.[66]

Shane recovered and in June 1912 the happy pair were married at The Cedars in New York. Having acquired a lively and well-connected American daughter-in-law, Leonie felt that the sacrifice of some of her American income was worthwhile, although the overall financial picture was worrying. The Leslies shared the problem faced by Irish landowners whose property had been purchased under the provisions of the Wyndham Act of 1903. The Wyndham Act (or Irish Land Act) followed land reforms beginning in 1870, which aimed to increase tenants' ownership of the land they farmed. It guaranteed that the annual repayments made by farmers on land purchases would be lower than the rents they had been paying (government funds would make up for any difference). The Act had an additional appeal to landowners in that it provided a 12 per cent government bonus calculated on the value of the estate. It also ensured that these payments would be made in cash (this provision was in fact delayed) and allowed landowners to retain demesne farms on their estates, now mortgaged to the Land Commission (a body set up by the Land Act of 1881 to fix rents that would be binding on landlord and tenant), on favourable terms.[67] In 1912, the Leslies were only just beginning to receive the promised payments from the government for the estate. What money they had was invested in stocks that were declining in value.

For years the Leslies and other landowners had lived on the income produced by land that they owned and rented out to tenant farmers. Now, they received a capital sum for their land, which they needed to invest wisely to generate sufficient revenue to run the estate and to pay all the family expenses. For families like the Leslies whose revenues were modest, it was a potential disaster. Leonie hoped that, now that he was married, Shane would withdraw from any radical republicanism, as the political situation in Ireland had worsened further. She wrote to Jennie in 1913 that an instructor (Protestant) had been 'mauled' in Dungannon (by Catholics) and was unconscious for two days – but that there had been no reprisal allowed from the Protestants. 'Feeling gets worse every day on both sides – and it is all very painful, but all foreseen by anyone who <u>knows</u> Ireland. Few people in England do.'[68]

Moreton continued to travel to the United States to raise money, most of which went towards the nationalist Irish regional newspaper, *Free Cork Press*. In 1913 he raised £4,000. He eventually grew disenchanted, however, when the paper would not support his conciliatory ideas on partition for Ireland.[69] He now preferred to focus more of his attention on his Prince Rupert investments. On 9 April 1912, the Frewen solicitor Arthur Marshall had met the Grand Trunk solicitor, and the agreement was made final between Moreton and the company concerning the Prince Rupert lands. The papers were sent to Montreal to await the signature of Hays, the company's president. Hays planned to return to America on the maiden voyage of the *Titanic*, thus becoming one of the 1,503 passengers who drowned when the ship hit an iceberg. A few weeks after the tragedy, Smithers, the new president of Grand Trunk who had previously assured Moreton that the agreement would be honoured, now wrote to tell him that his counsel had advised that Moreton had no claim on the lands. Moreton, who believed that he had finally made his fortune, felt as though the Fates had sunk the *Titanic* – and his hopes – on purpose. His lifelong dream had been snatched from him. It was not to be borne and he wrote a furious letter to the Grand Trunk Company. When his friend Lord Albert Grey discovered its contents, he rebuked Moreton for its tone, writing on 12 December 1912:

> I do wish you would not post business letters without talking them carefully over with your friends beforehand. It was a real shock to me to find you had sent it. If you wanted to prevent the Grand Trunk adopting your proposal you should not have allowed your temper to express itself in the way you did. Again let me beseech you not to be your own solicitor. The wonderful, delightful facility with which you handle your pen or typewriter is a danger of which you ought to be afraid.[70]

Lord Grey, a true friend, generously advanced Moreton the fees for the legal battle his friend insisted on undertaking. In court he managed to salvage from the Grand Trunk Company a smallholding in Prince

Rupert, on the outside of the perimeter of the best property, not on the inside as he had originally been promised. Still, Clara calculated that his share was worth £250,000 sterling, an enormous amount of money then (and, indeed, today, when it would represent £15 million). He continued to argue his case for better land and was angry that he had – once again – been forced to liquidate some of his holding to pay his debts.

While longing for more prosperous times, Clara was cheered by her elder son Hugh's marriage, rejoicing in his choice of bride. Maria Elena Camilla Nunziante di Mignano, or Memy, as she became known, was the daughter of an Italian duke. Oswald bitterly recorded his feelings as the second son in a sour diary entry on the eve of his mother and sister's departure for the wedding in Rome:

> Pa writes imploring me to be 'damned careful' in affairs matrimonial – he's frightened because Hugh is marrying, & so proving to him that his sons are marriageable, & Ma writes that she & Clare are going to Rome Jan 7th. I feel rather jealous ... he gets that, & Peamarsh estate, & £400 a year [which in fact he never received], & his engagement ring (which I would be too proud to accept as a gift from someone else, even my Mother) – the entire XX Century fatted calf of the Prodigal Son, while I who have never given them one instant's anxiety, & have been as true to them as blade to hilt am constantly being warned by one Parent not to marry 'till I feel the rising tide of a good income under my keel' (said income to be carved out by myself), & the other Parent says 'I intended writing you a long epistle, but have been Xmas shopping all day' – who for, Heaven knows, I don't even receive a Xmas card, & she hasn't wished me a merry Xmas yet.[71]

Oswald was jealous of his brother Hugh, just as he was jealous of Clare's affection for her family and of his parents' affection for his siblings. As children, Hugh, Clare, and Oswald had been close, the last two in particular. Since Moreton was never at home, and Clara left the children in the hands of the servants, the three had been abandoned very much to their own devices. While Hugh was away at school, Clare and Oswald suffered at the hands of a vicious French governess, who beat them regularly. Clare has left a description of her: 'She had a red face and very long greasy hair that descended to her ankles, and which in the process of braiding she coiled several times around her neck.' Clare and Oswald, aged six and seven were, as Clare explained, 'given entirely to her keeping, morally, spiritually and physically'. The children hated her. Five years of 'appalling torture' followed, which resulted, Clare said, 'in all kinds of psychological idiosyncrasies, most of which are perhaps worth while, for a friendship of love was cemented between Peter [Oswald] and myself which has proved the only stable reality in a world of disillusions.'[72] That Clare recorded this in 1927, years after her marriage, indicates the strength of those sibling bonds. When one night Clare tried to tell her mother that Mademoiselle had abused them, she was beaten even more viciously and the helplessness they both felt drew them unnaturally close. As a consequence, Oswald suffered all his life from jealousy over his sister's affections.

Although there was much family fun as the Frewen children grew older, they were as youngsters starved of their parents' care, and all three were emotionally stunted, finding intimacy with others difficult. Clare was fortunate in Wilfred, who had a strong personality. They argued fiercely, but he provided Clare with much-needed stability. When their second child, Elizabeth, died in early infancy, Wilfred shook his wife out of her despair and made her embrace her life and responsibilities.

Hugh would not be so fortunate in his choice of partner. Memy was a Catholic, and the sermon at their wedding was sternly delivered by a priest who warned of the danger of 'mixed' (religious) marriages. Yet in the early months of their union Hugh and Memy were in love and happy, as Hugh described to his cousin Shane from the Hotel de Russie in Rome: 'Thank you so much for your letter, congratulations, & advice. I know that you who are my oldest friend and with whom I have been brought up & educated, feel with me as a brother. I can't tell you how happy I feel; Memy & I are like two children without a care in the world. The old saying that the course of true love never ran smoothly does not obtain in our case.'[73]

Memy was warmly welcomed by the family when they returned to Britain after the wedding, but within the first year of their marriage, she and Hugh were increasingly in difficulties. They also suffered serious financial problems. The summer of 1914 seemed, however, positively idyllic to the Frewen family. Visitors came to Brede to enjoy the gardens. Moreton felt more prosperous and relaxed now that the Grand Trunk Company had agreed to honour his agreement and he could thus purchase the outer perimeter lands at the previously negotiated discounted price. He just had to find the money to do it. Meanwhile, there were picnics and walks. When Leonie and her son Lionel visited in May for a big family party, Oswald noted that his aunt was 'looking extremely handsome, & full of vivacity'.[74] Shane and his wife Marjorie joined the party for lunches and excursions. Oswald recalled that he and Shane, both ardent nature lovers, had discovered a nuthatch's nest in a nesting box. The following day Clara found a wren's nest. Aunt Jennie also came to stay for a weekend that summer. These were joyful family times. Oswald was particularly elated to be made a director of the new company set up by his father to exploit the Prince Rupert lands, writing that he felt more confident of the future as a result. Such happiness and high hopes did not last, however. With war looming, Oswald left on 2 August, not for Prince Rupert as he had hoped, but for Southampton to join his ship, the *Lookout*.

The following evening, the Foreign Secretary Edward Grey looked down from the Foreign Office in London at the lamps being lit in St James's Park. Turning to a friend standing beside him, he said: 'The lamps are going out all over Europe; we shall not see them lit again in our lifetime.'[75]

CHAPTER TWELVE

The Lamps Go Out in Europe

The First World War was a seismic event that left few British families unscathed. Following the declaration of war on 4 August 1914, sons of the upper classes were among the first to go to the front, and the death toll in this group alone was enormous. By the end of 1914, six peers, sixteen baronets, ninety-five sons of peers and eighty-two sons of baronets had been killed. Although the majority of aristocrats who went to war returned home, the losses sustained by British and Irish peers and their sons were proportionally higher than those of any other social group. Their rate of attrition was one in five, while the comparable figure for other social groups was one in eight.[1] All three sisters realized that their children were vulnerable. Jennie, Clara, and Leonie braced themselves for bad news as they watched the horror unfold. They each had a son who would see battle: Jack Churchill, aged thirty-four; Hugh Frewen, aged thirty-one; and Norman Leslie, aged twenty-eight. Other concerns paled into insignificance, as Leonie wrote to Jennie in August 1914: 'The man who bought our house isn't paying us yet – & it complicates! But all one's private affairs seem nothing – just this terrible war – & all that is happening, which we get now & then, indications of. <u>Do</u> write – <u>please</u>.'[2]

Jennie had long believed that war was inevitable, because Winston thought so. His days at the Admiralty had been spent in readying the fleet. Now that war had begun, Jennie never saw her son, who was tearing around the ports visiting the ships. He had founded the Naval Air Service and was himself a trained pilot. Soon after war broke out, Lord Kitchener, Secretary of State for War, asked Winston to oversee Britain's aerial defence. Winston immediately moved thirty-nine aeroplanes, fifty-two seaplanes, and a few small airships to France, where the Naval Air Service set up bases near the enemy lines. Jennie was hungry for information about the war's progress and, when his time allowed, snatched a few minutes with her son. She wrote to Leonie in September 1914 that Winston had told her of a fierce battle raging (on the continent) with 1,500 casualties already.[3] The lists of the dead and injured rolled in, with columns of small type recording them in each day's paper. It was becoming apparent that the conflict might be long and very bloody.

Britain had entered the war with the Triple Entente (the British Empire, France, and Russia) against the Central Powers (Germany, Austria–Hungary, and their allies). The conflict was sparked by the assassination of the Archduke Franz Ferdinand, heir apparent to the crowns of Austria and Hungary, by a Serbian nationalist in June 1914. Tensions had been rising for years, however, due largely to Britain's escalating military rivalry with Germany. German attempts, encouraged by Kaiser Wilhelm II, to build a fleet to rival the Royal Navy, together with Germany's determination to undermine Britain's ties with France and Russia after 1905, had convinced some British statesmen that the Germans had ambitions to dominate Europe similar to those cherished by Napoleon. Britain's war aims were to thwart these objectives, to achieve victory in Europe, and to preserve the empire. The British government was keen, therefore, to bring about a peace settlement that would not only significantly weaken Germany but also ensure that neither of Britain's allies became so powerful that they could threaten British interests in Europe, Africa, or Asia.

The plan was relatively straightforward: the British Expeditionary Force (BEF), the best-equipped and best-trained force that had ever left British shores, would sail to France and help the French and Russian armies. It was never intended to be the key British contribution to the war effort, as the French and Russian forces were believed to be sufficiently powerful to defeat the Germans with only a small amount of British army support. Britain's major contribution would be two-fold. The Royal Navy was to blockade the enemy and the British government was to supply funds to her allies. This strategy, which played to Britain's strengths – naval and economic – and was named 'the British way in warfare' by military historian Basil Liddell Hart,[4] was predicated on the ability of the allies to fight with minimal British military assistance. Most of the British population famously believed that the conflict would be short and decisive: in the famous phrase, 'over by Christmas'. But just four months into the war, it was obvious that this strategy would not work, because the assumption of a short war was incorrect. The British government and people had to accept that they needed to do far more to defeat Germany, whose troops were now occupying large tracts of French territory.

Young men were dying in their thousands, and few families were spared. Leonie, the wife and mother of a soldier, tried to be courageous when Norman left for France, but she told her cousin Kitty Mott that her son had 'vanished into space'. She had spent 'a few moments with him every day' while they were in Cork, before his departure, and they had 'parted very simply – no heroics – but I expect his heart felt all crumpled up, like mine did'.[5] Leonie made every effort to be brave, as she knew Norman wished her to be. He had made his arrangements calmly, as he explained in one of his letters to her:

Dear Ma,

...Now please keep this letter – all my affairs are in order – my valuables & a letter for you re my debts & assets, & small presents to some friends, & a general summary of my insurance policies, Nitrogen shares etc, will be found in my green despatch box locked – this will be sent to Glaslough with my other luggage. I have got the key on me – in the event of my death you may open it by force & it will explain exactly what I want done. You will benefit by my death over & above my small debts, as I am insured for £1000. But the paper inside the box will explain you everything, if I die. Great hurry here & a lot of work with the reservists pouring in. I'll wire you as soon as I receive definite instructions – I hope to come through London.

NL[6]

The British forces under Sir John French had begun landing from 11 August 1914 at Le Havre, Boulogne, and Rouen. By 23 August one cavalry[7] and four infantry divisions were deployed on a front of twenty miles. The BEF infantry were ordered to hold the Mons–Condé canal and successfully resisted the German attack, although outnumbered by six divisions to four. That evening, however, the news came that their French allies had fallen back, and on the morning of 24 August the BEF began a general retreat during the next fourteen days to the outskirts of Paris. The counter-attack at the Marne in September by French and British forces resulted in driving the Germans back to the Aisne River, where both armies settled into trench warfare. By the end of a year whose terrible battles included those at Ypres in October and November, all that had been achieved was thousands of deaths and 475 miles of continuous trenches, running from the North Sea to the mountain frontier of neutral Switzerland. Neither side advanced more than a few miles over the next three years and the losses were huge. It is difficult to obtain exact figures for the total number of casualties, but estimates on the Western Front reach 5 million dead and up to 12 million wounded (although these numbers can only be an approximation).[8] Total war losses have been estimated fairly consistently at 8.5 million killed (not including those who died from disease and malnutrition).[9] Millions were also wounded; the number of British wounded is estimated at over 1,500,000.[10] The trenches were filled with sick men. Officers usually took the lead in the attacks and were killed by snipers as they led their men forward. The casualties were horrendous.

Norman Leslie led his unit with courage. He was killed on 19 October 1914 in the very early days of the war. He was last seen charging up a railway embankment near Armentières when he was shot by a sniper. In his hand was his sword, given to him by the Duke of

Connaught, which was recovered and returned to his mother many years later.

When the news broke, Jack Leslie was alone with Shane's wife Marjorie in Glaslough and Leonie was in London. Shane wrote to his wife: 'A day of misery and tears. I was too late to break the news to Mother – but Winston and the War Office verified it and we turned round to face the horror. I broke it to Lady Constance, Sir John and Elsie (Norman's cousin). We have arranged a memorial service for Monday and on Tuesday mother will come to Ireland. Cheer father up: I am afraid it will be terrible for him.'[11] Shane, who had a strong sense of duty, wanted to help his family through their grief. He wrote encouragingly to his father:

> I grieve to think of your lonely sorrow in Ireland. Mother is bearing up well thanks to her friends. Lionel is with her and she scarcely realizes. I will bring her over next week. I spent a miserable morning breaking the news to relatives and inquiring at the War Office. I can hardly feel worse but I know I shall – I wish indeed it was myself and not him that [was] taken. But words fail and I can only remember that pride will overcome sorrow. He could not have died more nobly and his name will live forever.
>
> Your affec son,
> Shane[12]

In the words of his younger brother Seymour, living in Schenectady, New York and working for General Electric, Norman was the only 'fully adjusted' member of the family.[13] Leonie, who had not heard from him in days, was stunned at the news. The loss of her beloved son was an emotional blow from which she never really recovered. His room at Castle Leslie, with its ageing photographs of his youthful loves and his polo ponies, was left untouched. Every year Leonie would put rosemary for remembrance on his bed. His death also had other ramifications for the family, as Norman was the heir. The ownership of the estate passed back to his father, who was charged death duties on an inheritance that Norman never lived to receive. (Jack Leslie refused to pay them for the remainder of his life. Shane had to settle the outstanding amount, with interest, after his father's death.)[14]

A week after Norman's death, Seymour wrote a letter of condolence to his father:

> I think you might care to have a line from me to tell you how I feel & <u>understand</u> that you have lost, as it were, a close & intimate friend – one whose interest in <u>Glaslough</u> and all the things of life that <u>you</u> care for, was a constant pleasure to you. You need (& you shall find) all Shane's & my affection at this moment. I only saw Norman for 48 hours in the last 4 years, yet I had been looking forward, on my return, to years of comradeship & mutual interest – he <u>was</u> so keen on everything. I know Shane's affection will be a revelation to you. But he is not very practical or businesslike, so if you or Ma want me, just cable anytime. My dread now, is that they will want <u>you</u> on active service before long?
>
> Yr affectionate Seymour[15]

Norman's death had occurred only two months into the war, and society had not yet become accustomed to the daily losses. The newspapers carried full reports and a memorial service was held in London. Among the large congregation were Lady Constance Leslie, Major Murray (representing the Duke of Connaught, who was still one of Leonie's closest friends and now living with his wife in Canada, where he was serving as Governor-General), the Russian Ambassador and Countess Benckendorff, the French Ambassador, the Marquis de Soveral, the Countess of Kerry, Priscilla Countess Annesley, the Earl and Countess of Cromer, and the Countess of Londesborough, as well as many others. Leonie was supported by her son Shane and followed by her two sisters. Moreton and Lionel were also there. Another service was held at Glaslough, conducted by the Lord Primate of Ireland, Revd John Davidson. He read part of a letter that Norman had sent to one of his lady friends a few days before war was declared:

> Try and not worry too much about the war, anyway. Units, individuals, cannot count. Remember we are writing a new page of history. Future

generations cannot be allowed to read the decline of the British Empire, and attribute it to us. We live our little lives and die, and to some are given chances of proving themselves men, and to others no chance comes. Whatever our individual faults, virtues, or qualities may be, it matters not, but when we are up against big things let us forget individuals, and let us act as one great British unit, united and fearless. Some will live and many will die, but count the loss not. It is better far to go out with honour than survive with shame. I cannot believe we will not fight, it would be too utterly shameful. If it is so, I would rather resign and fight as a volunteer for France.[16]

The words were widely reported in the newspapers following his death and it was some comfort to Leonie that she could take pride in her courageous son, whose words now reached a wider audience. Mary Crawshay, Jack's sister, wrote to Leonie that she felt the letter was 'like the stone chosen by young David & flung unerringly at the giant. His youth is part of it & made his vision so clear, his words so direct.'[17]

Leonie and Jack received hundreds of letters of condolence penned by friends and acquaintants, from the local population of Glaslough and Pettigo, where 'Master Norman' was greatly liked, to members of high society such as the Beresfords, the Castellanes, the Connaughts, the Caledons, and the Marquis de Soveral. Margot Asquith, wife of the prime minister, wrote of their joint sorrow. Norman's relatives were devastated at the loss of this happy, handsome young man. Jack's sister Olive wrote to Leonie that she had only ever loved three people: Murray (her husband), Leonie herself, and Norman: 'How we are going to get on without him I don't know.'[18] Norman's cousin Elsie Hope, now Countess of Kerry (and later Marchioness of Lansdowne), was heartbroken:

> Darling Auntie Leo,
>
> I think of you so constantly, & no words can ever tell you what I feel. There are no words for such a grief as this. Dear Auntie Leo, all the happiness of my childhood seems to be connected with Norman, as I look back upon it. How dull it seems to think we shall not see him any

Leonie in Dublin with nephew
Winston, c. 1881.

Clara Frewen with her children
c. 1888: Hugh (standing), Clare (seated)
and baby Oswald in his mother's arms.

Jennie with her sons, Jack (left) and Winston c. 1889.

A family portrait, *c.* 1889. *From left to right, seated*: Clara Frewen with Oswald, Jacky Leslie, Mrs Jerome with Clare Frewen, Jack Churchill, Hugh Frewen, Norman Leslie in Leonie's lap. *Back row, standing*: Jennie Churchill, Winston Churchill.

Leonie with three of her sons *c.* 1900. The 'sailor boys' Norman (left) and Shane, and baby Seymour in Leonie's lap.

From left to right: Leonie, Jennie's friend Hugh Warrender,
Jack Leslie, Jennie and a convalescent Winston.

Clara Frewen, dressed for a ball
as a French aristocrat *c.* 1901.

Brede Place, Clara's beloved country house.

The Royal Yacht at Cowes. Jennie, seated left, never missed the Cowes Regatta, attended often by her cousin Kitty Mott, right.

Winston Churchill.

Aboard the hospital ship *Maine*, *c.* 1899. Jennie, seated centre, and the team of American nurses and British officers with whom she would journey to South Africa to help the wounded of the Boer War.

Jennie's Elizabethan Pageant, 1911. Leonie is standing, left.
Seated are Clara, left and Jennie, centre.

Leonie Leslie *c.* 1908.

Norman Leslie in uniform, 1914.

The eccentric radical Clare
Sheridan with her children,
Richard (left) and Margaret
c. 1920.

Jennie, in her sixties, photographed by her niece, Clare Sheridan.

more. Dearest, my heart aches & aches for you & Uncle Jack. I could not say a word to him when I saw him but he must know what I feel.

Your lovingest Elsie[19]

For years Shane had refused to conform to his family's plans for him and he stubbornly resisted attempts to control him. Yet he took his responsibilities seriously. An important task was to find his brother's body in France. He set out in December, describing his quest in a letter to his mother:

Darling Mother

Last Friday afternoon I found the place where Norman had been temporarily buried. He lies about a mile behind the trenches occupied by his regiment and within sound of the guns of both armies whose shells pass daily above his head. As I stood by the head of his grave a fierce attack developed on the right and the sky was ripped with the flashes of the guns, while a gigantic German searchlight threw the surrounding countryside into sepulchral relief. His grave seemed to rock with the thunder of the gunfire ... I thought it best to encoffin his remains so that it would be possible should you ever wish it to bring him to Glaslough ... and proceeded with a squad of Rifle Brigade men to open his grave. Some planks had been placed over his body so that uncovered he looked just as he had been. His clothes were unsoiled and clean ... We lifted him into the coffin and returned him to the same position. I lifted the bandage from his mouth sufficient to see his teeth and to touch the one he broke with a billiard ball at Deep dene 15 years ago. Then I knew it was he. To fit him into the coffin it was necessary to take off his boots. I did not cry till I saw that lonely pair of boots on the field for they had the shape and look of so many other pairs of his I had seen outside his room ... as he had died in them I placed them at the foot of the coffin and took a bootlace away with me. For you I cut a lock of his hair which I enclose in this letter and some flowers which the daughters of the village doctor had laid on his grave ... The writing on the Cross over his grave will probably fade but by these signs you will one day know it is he – there is a tin with his name on it buried at the head and at the foot are his boots and upon the coffin is a large crucifix … I cannot describe how calm and peaceful he was … he seemed as one who had reached his appointed end with credit and dignity … When it was dark I said the prayers for the dead and called to him by the name that I only used to call him. Nine times I called – and there was no answer … I spent two days in the trenches of his old regiment and learnt exactly how it all happened. He had been doing extremely well and at the battle of the Marne was looked upon as their coming officer … his last night on earth was spent at Chapelle d'Armentières in some buildings where the chalk marks are still visible. He was sent down the railway with his men to locate the German guns. At a level crossing a mile down the line he crossed three or four times in order to get a good view. Matters were critical as there were Germans between his Company and the next. One of his men told me that but for him they would have been all captured. He crossed the line again and this time he was shot from a signal box. He was hit above the navel and said 'Good God' once but sank instantly. He was buried on the Tuesday following …

    Yr affectly,

    Shane[20]

Leonie was grateful for Shane's words and relieved that he had found his brother's body. The tragedy drew them closer, as her letter revealed:

What a wonderful pilgrimage. I have followed you every step – in my heart's mind – to Armentières. How comforting to me, his Mother, that you should have knelt by his grave – that you shd have had that beloved body of his put into safer wrapping, that it may not be disturbed. I don't feel that Norman is there, but I loved that dear manly form – flesh of my flesh – and I would have it resting in peace – and I know now that you saw it – and were the last to gaze on it. Darling Jackie, you & Norman are very like fundamentally – and altho yr outlook on Life was different, I can only think of the one, coupled with the other – from the earliest days, when 2 little sailor boys were toddling near me. Thank God I still have one of you – and that all is Love between us.[21]

The Leslie family comforted themselves with the fact that Norman had died a noble death, defending what they believed was an honourable cause. Shane wrote to his brother Seymour that Norman had died a hero: 'From what I have seen of this war I can only say that his end was as glorious as blessed. Better to be stricken down in action than maimed and tortured like rats in a gin. Better die fearlessly in the open air than rot from typhoid in a pestilent hospital. There are many worse things than dying young in battle.'[22] At the age of thirty, Shane tried to emulate his brother's bravery by volunteering to drive an ambulance in France behind the lines. Jack sent him off with a soldier's advice: 'Wrap yourself up as much as possible and sleep whenever you have a chance. Run into no danger unnecessarily & always before you leap look for your line of retreat or defence.'[23]

Norman's many friends were also deeply saddened by his death and wrote to Leonie, who found comfort in their words. One of them was Norman's friend and fellow soldier, Paul Kennedy:

What – during the 8 years that I knew him – I loved him for more than almost anything else was that – in spite of the fact that in whatever company he was in he always stood out as the most brilliant & charming person there – he never forgot his old friends however dull they might be in comparison & however far or long, distance or time had separated them. This was all the more wonderful in one who as a natural result of his brilliant brain & charming character had a larger circle of friends than anybody I have ever seen or can imagine. Though he had only been a few months in the 3rd Bn he stood out head & shoulders above all the others in it. Everything centred round him ...
I like best to remember him for his frank fearless eyes & generous spirit. His joie de vivre made everyone round him cheerful & happy.[24]

Leonie was dignified in grief and found solace in making small sacrifices, such as giving up sugar in her tea. For many, such privations were not by choice. Soon after the outbreak of war, the German navy had attempted via submarine warfare to halt the flow of imports to Britain.[25] By the end of 1916, German U-boats were destroying around

300,000 tons of shipping per month, figures that increased in 1917, when sugar, meat, and potatoes were in particularly short supply, and panic-buying led to food shortages. In January 1918, the Ministry of Food responded by introducing sugar rationing, followed by rationing of butcher's meat, in order to guarantee supplies. To help with the war effort, Leonie worked as a volunteer in a YMCA canteen in Victoria Station. Washing dishes and serving tea to soldiers departing for the front made her feel useful.

The Frewens meanwhile had more self-inflicted problems. Oswald had written a letter to his mother, describing the British naval action off the island of Heligoland on the north German coast. On 28 August, Commodore Reginald Tyrwhitt, commanding what came to be called the Harwich Force, and Commodore Roger Keyes, commanding the 8th Submarine Flotilla, engaged the Germans and sank one destroyer. When German reinforcements appeared, three additional British battle cruisers under Admiral Sir David Beatty's command arrived and sank three enemy ships, leading to a decisive British naval victory. Without his son's knowledge Moreton had had Oswald's letter published in the *Morning Post* as part of his strategy to criticize naval command. Commodore Tyrrwhitt was very angry, believing that Oswald himself had sent the letter to the newspapers. In it, Oswald had called the skirmish a 'massacre' because of the Royal Navy's superior numbers, implying that the British press had exaggerated their prowess in battle. He was in serious trouble and cousin Winston, as First Lord of the Admiralty, had to intervene on his behalf. Commodore Tyrrwhitt had requested Oswald's removal from the flotilla, but Winston had argued that the debâcle had been Moreton's fault. Winston also informed the commodore that Oswald came from a 'literary family' and that the letter had been genuinely personal, with no political motive. Tyrrwhitt reluctantly agreed to let the matter drop.

Having had lunch with Clemmie and Winston, Clare described to Oswald how their cousin had taken the affair in good spirit. He had told her that Oswald's letter was very good and that, given a blue pencil and three seconds, he could have made it publishable! Winston agreed that Moreton had been to blame, and Clare shared his thoughts with Oswald:

'I call it very hard indeed on the boy, your Father ought never to have done it without first asking Oswald if he might.' I then told him that you & Tirret [*sic*] had met, & parted friends, & that seemed to please W. awfully. I also said you had promised your Captain you would write no more descriptions home, so the result of Papa's action was a dead loss to the family. Winston's eyes twinkled, & he said 'You tell him to write them to *you*.' They were both delightful to me, & Winston is so keen, so enthusiastic, so confident, it does one good to have seen him. He *is* clever, he *has* got personality! I wonder why people hate him so, he has so much charm when he wishes, perhaps he doesn't always wish? He says we shall have a million men in the field in the spring – so I said 'Don't you think it will be all over by then?' 'Good God no!' he exclaimed. He then said the atrocities were worse even than we thought, & that, re, the British Prisoners in Germany who are working in the fields – orders have been given to 'work them so hard as to render them useless' & Winston's voice quivered with passion as he said it; & he added, fiercely: 'If I could get hold of the Emperor, I would make him answer to me in person for every outrage that has been committed.' What seemed to infuriate him most was the Kaiser's reference to 'our contemptible little army'. However it was really the best thing he could have said, for it's brought in more recruits than anything else.[26]

Clare was also anxiously waiting to see whether Wilfred would, as he threatened, join up. Hugh had volunteered to go to the front. He and Memy's passion had not weathered well and after the birth of their first son, Roger, the couple were experiencing further difficulties. Much of this was due to their deteriorating financial situation. Moreton had reneged on his promise of the £400 a year to the couple and they were constantly short of money. Oswald was bitter about his sister-in-law and wrote angrily to Clare, on whom he continued to lavish his affection:

Angel child

…Yes, they are an 'acquisitive' lot, those foreigners; in my humble opinion, it is not the daughter standing by her poor old dad who is the snake-in-the-grass, but the alien daughter-in-law who means to batten on her new-found relatives, furnish her house at their expense, & then go & *let* it. They are a hard proposition, that pair. I wish old Hugh would be either wholly good, like you, or else wholly bad. I can't keep on loving him one day & being angry the next, it is *so* tiring! … What do they mean all the time by Hugh's 'going East'? Is it merely barrack-room jargon for Flanders, or is he really going East – to Constantinople? I have not been so excited over <u>anything</u> in the war yet, as our attack on the Dardanelles … Oh darling one, I'm <u>longing</u> to see you again. <u>What</u> fun. There'll never be anybody like <u>you</u>, anywhere. In my wildest flights of fancy I've never imagined <u>anybody</u> to be more 'as nice' as you![27]

Clare was profoundly confused by her emotions. She did not share in the general war fever around her. In September 1914 her mother, now sixty-three, came to stay at the cottage that Clare shared with Wilfred and their young daughter, Margaret. A second daughter, Elizabeth, had been born in 1913 and died, tragically, in her first year. Clare was devastated and began her first attempts at sculpture to escape her grief. Clara was full of anti-German feelings and slogans from when she had fled Paris and the Prussians in 1870. She insisted on visiting the Empress Eugénie, now an old woman living in retirement at Farnborough. After giving them tea, the Empress took them into her private room to gaze at a portrait of the Prince Imperial, with whom young Clara had danced at Compiègne. The two women stood reminiscing over the sparkling heydays of the Second Empire.

But Clara could not escape the horrors of the present for long. Within a few short weeks of his enlistment into the Royal Naval Division, Hugh was sent to Antwerp. On his return for leave some months later, he was given short shrift by Memy, who had been living in freezing conditions with their baby at Brede. Hugh was then posted to Gallipoli. He found on his return after being wounded that Memy had left him to live with her mother in Mignano, in Campagna, Italy.

At the beginning of 1915, thirty-four-year-old Wilfred announced that he had enlisted as a private in the City of London Territorials. Clare was very worried, as the high casualty rates were well known by then. She felt that Wilfred's volunteering was unnecessary – married men were not being called up, nor was anyone over thirty. But he believed, as did so many of his countrymen, that this was 'a war to end war'. He told his wife that 'there are moments when the individual belongs to the State and not to the family, and this is the moment'.[28]

Five months later, Wilfred was promoted to lieutenant and transferred to the Rifle Brigade. Clare discovered then that she was expecting another child. In May 1915, Wilfred sailed for France with his battalion, while his wife waited anxiously at home. He was home on leave in August, but had to return to the front before the child was born, as officers were being recalled quickly in preparation for the Battle of Loos. Clare went to stay with his parents at Frampton Court to await the arrival of her baby, and each day she and Wilfred's mother waited for news. On 20 September, a baby boy, the son and heir, Richard Brinsley Sheridan, was born. Clare, euphoric, wrote to tell Wilfred. His hurried reply spoke of his joy, but after that there was silence. He was killed just a few days later.

His mother was the first to learn of the death of her only son, but did not tell Clare until she had sufficiently recovered from Richard's birth. 'My mother-in-law, ashen, white-faced, frail and ghost-like in her white dressing-gown, sat by my bedside day after day and answered my enquiries evasively,' Clare later wrote. 'There was no letter, there had been a battle, she admitted, and the posts were still disorganized. Her heroism was magnificent, her courage during those days when she hid from me – until I had regained strength – the news that he was "missing".'[29] The letters and telegrams of condolence began to pour in, including a letter from her cousin Winston:

Clare my dear
   I am so sorry for you. I know there is nothing I can write can ease

a single throb of your immense sorrow, or soothe a moment of your loss. In the face of this terrible event I feel by how fond I am of you, how we have always been friends since you were a little tot, how good you have always been to me, how devoted Jack is to you, & how near you are to all of us & we to you. God help you is my prayer. I greatly admired Wilfred, he was so handsome, so sparkling so heroic. Your life with him must have been one of the most beautiful and most perfect events which has taken place in this world. Be sure it will renew itself in some form wh is outside our comprehension in other states of existence. Rejoice also in the past wh is a reality and a possession wh can never be taken away. Rejoice also in the new life which you can guard & cherish – servicing his image & carrying on his honourable name ... Once more God bless you dear little Clare. Clemmie & I will pray that you may at last find some comfort & serenity.

Your loving cousin,
Winston[30]

Clare was now alone, with a toddler and a newborn. She was comforted by a letter that her husband had left for her before departing for France:

You will only read this if I am dead, and remember that as you read it I shall be by your side: you will know that I shall be saying to you – 'Now pull yourself together.' There is nothing to cry about, only is there a great happiness in that he did not fail and that he has done the big thing; he has got into his eleven; he has won his colours; it is up to me to be proud of him and glad for him and not to weep. My head is up, my chin is out and I take my step forward into my new existence knowing that he is watching and approving.

Remember that all over England are broken hearts and ruined lives, remember that one splendid woman, such as you are, refusing to weep, and hugging her soul with pride at a soldier's death, will consciously or unconsciously stiffen up and bring comfort to these.

Remember also that my death is only an iota and that others have died and will die as I have done. Only by your strength and power can you gain me distinction and cover me with glory. No one is to wear mourning and if they hold a memorial service I want it to be helpful and not 'morne' … I can leave you nothing, darling, except the memory of years, and you know what our life together has been. Surely if perfection is attained we have attained it.[31]

Clare cherished these brave words, but she had little else. Wilfred's employer, the City firm in which he had invested all their savings, had gone bankrupt. Wilfred's parents, who were elderly, were accustomed to living on their fixed income, which was already becoming inadequate with increased taxation and higher costs of living. Moreton wrote to Wilfred's father, asking for help for his daughter, but was refused. Clare was reluctant to impose on her own parents, who were themselves hard up.

Leonie rescued her niece with an invitation to stay at Glaslough. She needed the company, she said. Shane was now living in America. After he had left to do ambulance work early in 1915, he had then gone to help in the Dardanelles. While there, he had had another nervous breakdown. Leonie had decided to take him to America where he could join his wife Marjorie, who had gone home to live with her sister for the duration of the war. Leonie relied on her sisters for practical assistance. Jennie helped to organize the trip and sent her clothes for the unexpected journey – a silver tea gown and parasol. Leonie expressed her gratitude and her hope to see Shane safely settled. She would then return: 'the journey back will be grim & lonely. However – I'm like you luckily, & can always summon up courage.'[32] Leonie was amused, she wrote, to note that an American doctor travelling in their train carriage was admiring a picture of Jennie in a copy of *Tatler* magazine.

She returned from America some weeks later, relieved to be able to tell Jennie of Shane's improvement, as well as to offer her thanks once more. Although Leonie did everything she could to help her eldest son, she was always disappointed by his mental instability and felt that he let himself and others down. Shane's father-in-law, Henry Clay Ide, took quite a different view and wrote a letter to Leonie in which he subtly reproached her:

I did not show to Shane the letter which you wrote to me largely about him … [he] cares immensely for your good opinion and affections. I hope you will pardon me for saying that I do not at all agree with you in this subject. Shane is not a 'slacker' … He did his best to serve his country in any way he could, in France, in England and in his enlistment for the Dardanelles. He did it all without a penny of compensation for time or equipment … His eyes & his nervous makeup rendered it impossible for him to do [fight] in the field … I never saw a man more thoroughly patriotic and anxious to die for his country than he was and in a field where he could render important service in ascertaining Irish sentiment in this country and reporting it.[33]

Shane was no soldier, but after recovering from his breakdown, he began working to improve British-American relations over the Irish question while he was in America. It was a task that required tact and intelligence. Leonie had considered Norman her 'best friend' and had so loved his easygoing temperament, as well as his moral acuity. Shane was complicated and, although his mother loved her sensitive, highly strung son, she found him hard to fathom. Despite his efforts to please her, their conflicting characters and their history of difficulties meant that relations were often strained.

Leonie's attentions now turned to Clare and her two children. The two women had always had a close relationship; all Leonie's nieces and nephews were fond of her and she was Winston's favourite aunt. If she was perhaps a little hard on her own children, and especially Shane, she was very understanding with her sisters'. When they turned to her for help she never let them down. When Hugh was injured and returned from Gallipoli to hospital in London, Clara felt unable to go to meet him – instead she sent him a wire. Leonie found out which hospital he was in and visited him, taking him fresh peaches and toilet soap. Hugh wrote to Shane that his mother's gesture had brought tears to his eyes.

The war continued to exact a terrible toll. In 1915, Winston hatched a plan to use naval power in the Dardanelles to relieve the stasis that had, in his opinion, frozen all the main war fronts. The idea was to force a passage through the Dardanelle straits in Turkey and to insert a fleet into the Sea of Marmara, which could then advance to the Golden Horn, intimidate Constantinople, and thus press the Turkish government to sue for peace. A further advantage would, in his view, be accrued because he believed that the fall of Turkey would bring Greece, Bulgaria, and Romania into the war on the Allied side.

Instead, the plan was changed and the view of the commander in the eastern Mediterranean, Admiral Carden – that the Dardanelles could be forced by naval power alone – prevailed. Many errors of judgement, both tactical and strategic, by commanders in the front line as well as in the War Council back in London, contributed to the failure of the plan. The naval invasion was stopped before the peninsula could be taken, and by the time of the amphibious invasion two months later, the Turks had rearmed and fortified their positions. Terrible losses were sustained, and the end result was trench warfare: precisely what the plan was designed to avoid. Quite a few of the mistakes made were Winston's, and many turned against him. The defeat caused a political crisis and Winston bore the brunt of the venomous criticisms made of the Dardanelles plan. He left the Admiralty to become Chancellor of the Duchy of Lancaster, a position with no executive power. It was a dreadful time for Winston and Clemmie, who were shunned by many. Clementine told Martin Gilbert, Winston's biographer, some fifty years later, 'I thought he would die of grief.'[34]

Winston decided that he would prefer to fight honourably for his country rather than continue, ineffectual and discredited, in government. In November 1915, he resigned his new office and arranged to join his regiment of the Grenadier Guards in France, where he was quickly promoted to command the 6th Battalion Royal Scots Fusiliers. He returned regularly to London to keep up with the news there. In 1916 his friend Lloyd George took over as prime minister; Winston joined his Cabinet as Munitions Minister the following year. Throughout the war, Winston received first-hand descriptions of combat from his cousins Hugh and Oswald, who sent regular accounts of their experiences. Oswald was gratified that his naval expertise had proved valuable to Winston, in an unfamiliar but welcome turning of the tables. Hugh wrote full accounts of his time at Gallipoli, to which Winston replied encouragingly:

> I hope you realise how much we who stay at home feel we owe you all: and with wonder & admiration we watch your feats of arms & endurance. Everyone is so brave & daring nowadays that these qualities are scarcely noticed at the front; but at home we feel in a real sense your debtors. You have been having gt experiences and I rejoice you have so far come safely through them ... My confidence in our ultimate complete victory is undimmed.[35]

His brother Jack, who also returned with experiences of Gallipoli, proved a stalwart and useful ally, as was, indeed, his mother.

Jennie worked hard during the war, organizing buffets for thousands of soldiers at railway stations and helping at a convalescent home in the country for wounded soldiers. She also raised money, as well as acquiring staff and space, for an American Women's War Hospital at Paignton in south Devon, of which she was chairman of the executive committee. She became head matron of a London hospital, at Lancaster Gate. In addition to her war work, Jennie was earning money by doing one of the things she did best – writing. She was commissioned by *Pearson's Magazine* to write a series of articles, which were later collected into a book entitled *Small Talks on Big Subjects*. Her first article appeared in the September 1915 issue and concerned marriage in wartime. She wrote on topics she knew best, such as 'Extravagance', women's rights (on which she had softened her attitude and which she now supported), and friendship, trying to keep her essays light and amusing, as well as informative.

She was also a good influence on Winston. She had been furious when he was forced to resign and later suggested he begin painting again, which he had learned to do as a boy, as a way to relax. He began by experimenting with a children's paintbox, and the following morning bought a complete set of oils and an easel. Painting, one of the few subjects at which he had excelled at school, soon absorbed him. He was a consummate painter – the artist Sir John Lavery told Jennie that he could take it up as a profession.

When Winston left to join his regiment in France, Jennie reminded him to take care: 'Please be sensible. I think you ought to take the trenches in small doses, after 10 years of more or less sedentary life – but I'm sure you won't "play the fool" – Remember you are destined for greater things ... I am a great believer in your star.'[36] She tried to take her mind off her anxiety by seeing more of her daughters-in-law, with whom she had good relationships. The little presents of cash that she regularly gave them contributed towards their housekeeping expenses.

Jennie was also greatly cheered by a new admirer: Montagu Porch, whom she had met in 1913 at Hugh's wedding in Rome. He had been the British Resident in Nigeria – a post assigned to him by Winston in 1906 – where Hugh had befriended him. He had found Jennie very attractive; she thought him congenial and good company. At thirty-eight, Porch was three years younger than Winston. After graduating from Oxford, he had served in the Boer War, following which he had travelled on an archaeological expedition through the Sinai Desert, before his assignment in Nigeria. He fell in love with Jennie in 1914 and she did not discourage his attentions. Now a lieutenant in the Nigerian Regiment of the Cameroons Expeditionary Force, he was back in England on leave, and he and Jennie saw a great deal of each other. He was not the only young man to keep her company.

Jennie hated being lonely. In spite of her apparently vigorous social life, she had lapsed after her divorce into uncharacteristic self-pity, writing in very disillusioned terms to Leonie in July 1914:

I wish we could see more of each other. Life is so short and we both so down the wrong side of the ladder! The fact is that we are both 'Marthas' instead of 'Marys' and allow things which do not really count to take up our time and to keep us apart. We pander to the world which is callous, and it only wants you if you can smile and be hypocritical. One is forever throwing away substance for shadows. To live for others sounds all right – you do, darling!! but what is the result?

You are a very unhappy woman all round! As for me every effort I make to get out of my natural selfishness meets with a rebuff. My sons love me from afar and give me no companionship even when it comes their way. The fault is undoubtedly with me. Every day I become more solitary and prone to introspection which is fatal.[37]

Jennie complained to Leonie that she had no one to go to the theatre with and that she was depressed at growing old. It was difficult, she admitted, at her sixtieth-birthday dinner, to go into a room and know that she was no longer the most beautiful woman in it. After she had reproached Clemmie and Goonie for abandoning her, Goonie and the children moved in with her for a while, but Jennie needed more. She was still full of energy. She decided to let her hair go grey to stunning effect. She had plenty of admirers (including Hugh Warrender, who hoped to marry her) but many of them had gone to the front. She wrote them long letters of encouragement, but felt neglected. Her nephew, Seymour Leslie, frequently called, only to find her in tears. He was unsympathetic: 'No husband, no lover. She has become a trial.'[38]

She tried her best to stay busy. She sold her house on Brook Street for a handsome profit and bought a new one in Westbourne Street, near Hyde Park. Its interior was soon transformed. She was the first to use yellow curtains to catch the sunlight, and she made door handles out of old silver watchcases. She was original and tasteful, using tinted light bulbs to provide softer and thus more flattering light, and place mats instead of lace tablecloths on gleaming mahogany tables. After the war began, she was the first in London to replace her footmen and waiters – needed at the front – with maids. She designed a smart uniform for them: tight-fitting black cloth jackets with lapels, cut off at the hips, and a plain black skirt. Under the new jacket, the maids wore a starched white collar, a black bow tie, and a waistcoat.

Montagu Porch wrote to her throughout the war, visiting her in London when on leave in 1916 and again in early 1918. She was grateful for his attentions, especially as 1916 and 1917 were difficult years. She had always been particularly proud of her legs and dainty feet, and loved pretty shoes. But at that time, she suffered a bad infection in one of her toes, which had to be amputated. To add to her cares, her house on Westbourne Street was burgled and many of her precious mementos were taken. Among them were gifts from Edward VII, Queen Alexandra, and George. Jennie made light of her loss, claiming that the burglars had done her a favour, as she would no longer have the trouble of looking after so many things.

Clara was also having a difficult time. After the idyllic summer of 1914, by 1917 her world seemed to be falling apart. Moreton was still arguing about the Prince Rupert settlement, because he needed more time to find the money to exercise his option to buy the land set aside for him. If he could buy it at the agreed favourable price, he could then resell it a profit (totalling, in his view, £250,000). But as usual he did not have the funds. Clare, meanwhile, had begun a career as an artist. After a precipitate engagement with the very young and very wealthy Lord Wilton, she had suddenly changed her mind and began sculpting to make her living, taking a studio in St John's Wood and accepting commissions from friends. Moreton, who thought the enterprise undignified, had told his daughter that he could not keep her and that she and her children cost him more than the contribution of her widow's pension. He was extremely annoyed that she had not chosen a life of riches with Lord Wilton and refused to visit her in her studio. Clara did not believe her daughter would 'stick it out for a fortnight'.[39] Clare wrote to her mother, pleading for a more sympathetic hearing: 'Darling Ma, Not a word from you about the studio & Pa (as I long ago expected) writes a protesting letter against it ... But you must be tolerant. It is not an unworthy work because you do not care about it, any more than Pa's bimetallism is unworthy because I cannot understand it.'[40]

Clara was no more happy about the situation of her son Hugh. Before departing for Campagna, Memy, furious at not having enough money, had started to sell the furniture. Moreton was taken by surprise by a spirited young woman who had the cheek to defy him, as he complained in a letter to Leonie: 'The trouble is she [Memy] bought a lot of furniture did not pay for it & then proceeded to sell it here in the village – which of course "outruns the constable". So she had to give a promissory note & as I <u>had</u> to endorse it – that is how it happens.' Moreton was concerned about what would happen, following the end of the war: 'Hugh is here; very quiet – but what possible future is ahead for him. The best objective if it can be realised would be a consular [appointment] somewhere; but I am sure she [Memy] would never stick it.'[41] Clara also worried about Oswald, who was still with the navy. She was pleased, however, by Winston's safe return from France and his new appointment to the Cabinet. From a modest house in Regent's Park in London that she and Moreton had rented, she wrote to her nephew at the good news: 'A thousand congratulations & many congratulations to dear old England to have got you back again.'[42]

In 1916, Sir John Leslie, Leonie's father-in-law, died at the age of ninety-three. It was an unsettled time in Ireland. In that year, the Irish Volunteers (a technically unarmed militia, largely controlled by the Irish Republican Brotherhood), led by Patrick Pearse, and the Irish Citizen Army, led by James Connolly, staged a rebellion against the British. The Easter Rising, as it was known, was put down and the British government took the decision to execute the leaders, leading to widespread public outcry. In America, Shane was appalled; as he tried to explain to anyone who would listen in England, the executions were alienating the Americans, whom the British were trying to persuade to join them in the war against Germany. The death sentences led to much bitterness on all sides. Moreton took great exception to the American perspective. Bourke Cockran, Shane's brother-in-law, made a passionate speech decrying the British, which outraged Moreton. He wrote to Shane:

> The reports in the New York Herald of the Carnegie Hall meeting and Bourke's speech there, fill us with amazement. Never before did any political incident hit me half so hard. I have known Bourke for over thirty years & have fought his battles, and always before success-fully, at a hundred tables; but this time I am quite done. 'They were men of spotless lives – these men whom England has butchered. The

best of Ireland has been shot down like dogs by British soldiery for asserting immortal truth'. The men who were executed were men who were in open alliance with Germany & opening the ports of Ireland to armed invaders with thousands of spare machine guns ... The half dozen chiefs of this <u>most vile</u> rebellion were shot. What sort of a rebellion was it? Five wounded <u>Irish</u> soldiers from the Flanders front were on a Tram car; one was shot dead; the car itself was riddled with bullets, & a woman with a baby in her lap was shot dead inside. The four wounded Irish soldiers advanced toward the mob & said 'would you shoot your own women in that tram'; the immediate reply to which was that each of the four was murdered ... And yet these are the people who find in my old friend an apologist, & when wholesale & unprovoked murder – murder for loot, is rife in the streets of <u>their own Capital</u> which they attempt to burn – Bourke calls on the President 'to assume the glorious role of defender of the human race'! I have few older friends than Bourke; but with what face can I ever again meet him on friendly terms here or in America.[43]

Moreton considered himself a sympathetic friend to Ireland and was a supporter of Home Rule. But like many other Britons, he was shocked at the decision by the Irish Volunteers (with 180,000 members) not to join in the war effort against Germany and Austria. John Redmond, leader of the Nationalist Party, had encouraged all Irishmen to enlist in the British army, in the hope that this would sustain British support for Home Rule. His call was answered by the majority of the Irish Volunteers, but also rejected by a minority of 11,000 of the members. This caused a split within the group. The majority broke away to become the National Volunteers (many of whom went on to enlist), while the radical nationalists remained as the Irish Volunteers. They saw the conflict with Germany as an opportunity to break free from British rule, and some actively supported Germany. Moreton was equally unimpressed by the American response to the war and declared that Britain could 'go it alone', sentiments that he expressed to his nephew Shane in another letter of June 1916:

Do not worry in the least degree about the Irish voter in the US.
Over here ... we have reached a superb indifference as to his methods
of voting. From now on the British <u>Empire</u> armed to the teeth is a
very big show indeed ... What is going to happen in Ireland just these
days I do not know; but we are truth to tell most heartily sick of her,
& the more she bellyaches & misbehaves the less the consideration she
will receive in the new big Constitution after. It was a most short
sighted policy that – when she refused national service. The anti-
Home Rulers here welcomed it, & the Shinn [Sinn] Fein murderers,
because they saw it would reduce the modicum of consideration that
Ireland would receive when the Empire Convention assembles.[44]

Jack Leslie was also disappointed at the Irish failure to fully support
Britain, writing to Shane, just weeks before the Easter Rising, that the
country was full of 'seditious literature' and that men interested in
enlisting were talked out of it. He had some Catholic recruits who had
asked to be transferred to another battalion as 'their friends shy stones
at them when they go home for belonging to a Protestant battn.
[battalion]. Party feeling is as rife as before the war & nobody thinks
what it will cost him to lose the war.'[45] Anglo-Irishmen like Jack Leslie
could not believe that Irishmen would not support Britain in the
struggle with Germany. In fact, some 206,000 Irishmen on both sides
of the religious divide volunteered and fought with great bravery in the
war. After the executions of the leaders of the Easter Rising, nationalists
such as William O'Brien capitalized on Redmond's discomfort,
declaring that the latter's moderate position with regard to Britain
caught him in a cleft tree. There was fear on the pro-Home Rule side
of having alienated American support.

In the midst of all the trouble in Ireland, Leonie was as usual
constantly fussing over the boys, which Jack Leslie (Shane's son and her
grandson) felt had made them all very highly strung. Her current
obsession was sixteen-year-old Lionel. Never a keen student, he was at
a loose end, and his mother wanted to organize his future. Leonie
eventually decided that a course at Trinity College in Dublin would be
just the thing for him and took him there for an interview in May 1916.

His brother Seymour, who had returned from the US earlier that year and was working for Vickers Armaments while living with Aunt Jennie in London, was unimpressed by his younger brother and wrote to Shane that Lionel 'has become very gross ... [he] has no imagination, religion, emotion, application nor enthusiasm.'[47] Young Lionel, he confided to Shane in a later letter, was a becoming a source of worry:

> Lionel (aged 16, looks 18) discovered the other night, spearing a suspended pillow, & explained he was practising bayoneting! His heart (though not his intellect) is in the right place. He has taken your place as our Great Family Problem. Yes indeed. He is irrepressibly good natured, thick-skinned, truthful, absentminded, <u>indolent</u>, & deplorably unimaginative. Has none of that <u>enormous</u> interest in things his brothers possessed.[48]

Lionel's only interest seemed to be in fighting. By September, however, Seymour found him much improved and slimmer as well as very 'militarily inclined', something he felt should be applauded:

> I'm all for encouraging his one ambition – it's <u>something</u> – I know countless English boys who aren't keen about <u>anything</u> & don't know <u>what</u> they want to be. Lionel has decorated his room with the ancestral duelling pistols, spurs, & guns, nailed to the walls! He <u>will</u> wear [a] khaki hat, & when motoring thro' Sinn Fein districts, Mother throws a green & white scarf over it, to his indignation; as, otherwise (she explains unconvincingly) the hostile natives might puncture the tyres! ... [When we] Motor through 'Augher, Clogher & Aughnacloy' – at each charming view, Marse [Master] Lionel says '<u>What</u> a fine place for a machine gun emplacement'; whenever a bird or other poor beast appears '<u>What</u> a shot'![49]

The Leslies did not always agree with one another on political issues, but there was much affection between them. Shane, an ardent nationalist, recollected sharing rifles with his father, swopping them over for training with the Ulster Volunteers, led by Jack, and the National Volunteers with whom Shane had previously drilled. What helped ease any possible tensions that this might have caused between them was that all the Leslies believed the war to be just and that it had to be fought. Sir Jack was helping to train the reserves in Ballyshannon, although he was too old to enlist; Seymour was working all hours in armaments; Shane was busy writing in America, trying to garner support for the war and encourage American entry into the conflict; and Leonie was doing volunteer work in London.

Particular problems in Ireland during the war were caused by continued nationalist agitation for independence and the British response to the rebellion. Martial law was imposed as a result of the Easter Rising. Sir Jack wrote to Shane of the situation some months later:

> As I said before Ireland is quiet and Martial Law has been dropped for months though it has not been officially withdrawn, nor can it be after what took place. Searching for arms was mildly enforced for about 3 weeks only after the rebellion & the real hardship to the inhabitants under Martial Law i.e. quartering troops on the inhabitants was never dreamt of. There has never been a rebellion put down so mildly before … Do look on case of Ireland without sentiment & consulting the pages of ancient history … Never has Ireland been so rich or so prosperous. The coasts are defended for her from the barbarians and her own men an enormous majority of them sit at home & grumble … The haven of hatred & discontentment is engendered from the day that those delightful little children whose heads we pat in the cottages are handed over to the Nationalist School master who educates them to hate their benefactor England. This germ is then fostered by a selfish priesthood whose interest it is to keep up ignorance thereby making sure of their own lead of the people & their own opulence. A lot they care for the people … They the priests do not want H.R. [Home Rule] at heart, because they exist by discontentment.[50]

Shane continued to work in America, and he and all the family celebrated when America joined the war in April 1917. Seymour wrote with jubilation to Marjorie:'The entry of the U.S.A. (equal in resources to about 9 Englands), & the Russian Revolution has shocked us into speechless bewilderment – these events are beyond words, & fill us with joy. The entry of the U.S. is particularly gratifying, for obvious reasons, to you & me ... Thank God for this wonderful Thing.'[51]

Violence returned to Ireland after the 1918 elections, when the radicals of Sinn Féin comprehensively defeated the Irish parliamentary party. The Sinn Féin representatives then constituted the first independent Irish Parliament, or Dáil, in Dublin on 19 January 1919. The new government was headed by Eamon de Valera. Two days later, on 21 January, the Irish Volunteers (who had increasingly become known as the Irish Republican Army, or IRA) ambushed a Royal Irish Constabulary group in County Tipperary. These and other guerrilla attacks, together with the British response to them (and to the Dáil), led to the War of Independence, which lasted from 1919 to 1921. The Irish forces, led by Michael Collins, struggled for two years before a truce was agreed. These were dark days.

Leonie sought to find the right words to comfort her son Shane, who was distraught at the violence and heading for another nervous breakdown. In a letter of December 1918 she wrote:

Darling, do not feel too sad about Ireland. Every country is going through great upheavals this coming year. In Ireland where the population has been better fed these last two years than ever before in its history – they are really, believe me, all enjoying existence more than ever in their lifetime before. You see all the poor people better clad – all the fields tilled – prosperity on every side – their sport & fun seems to be politics. Half of them do not know what it is all about – but they like the excitements ... Personally, yr Father & I wd support <u>any</u> form of Govt that helped them towards law & order ... They have been allowed great freedom, of thought & action, they should unite in obtaining some 'mid way' secure form of self govt. It will come, I am sure ... when they have agreed on a form of Govt you will step in – & help. I am worried, when you say you are near a nervous breakdown. Turn yr thoughts to other things for the present & reserve yr help for later ... As to your <u>own</u> work during the war, my dear, you have done yr best. As Norman said 'to some the chances come'. You have had no chance of winning V.C. or giving yr Life but you <u>have</u> helped in the cause of Humanity, in bringing better understanding between people – and what more could you have done?[52]

As Ireland entered into a bleak period, Britain was joyful. The First World War was at an end. In October 1918, Germany accepted President Woodrow Wilson's terms and, on 11 November 1918, there was dancing in the streets in London and Paris. Oswald recorded the parties in Trafalgar Square, which the Frewens attended – even Clara, who danced and sang with the crowds until midnight. Winston and Jack Churchill were safe; Hugh was alive and, after a brief reconciliation, he and Memy had had a second son. Clare was living in a studio with her two small children, trying to earn a living, and had begun a series of love affairs. After surviving the war, Oswald prepared to go back to sea. The Leslies tried to regroup at Glaslough to recover from the conflict abroad and to see out the conflict at home. Seymour was in London and Lionel in Dublin. Leonie and Jack awaited with eager anticipation the arrival from America of Shane, Marjorie, and their two children. Leonie wrote of how she longed for the days when her son and his family would live at Glaslough permanently.

On the morning of the armistice, Winston was alone in his room at the Hotel Metropole, overlooking Northumberland Avenue. As the eleventh-hour deadline approached, he recorded his thoughts: 'Victory had come after all the hazards and heartbreaks in an absolute and unlimited form. All the Kings and Emperors with whom we had warred were in flight or exile. All their armies and fleets were destroyed or subdued. In this Britain had borne a notable part, and done her best from first to last.'[53]

CHAPTER THIRTEEN

After the Deluge

Clara and Moreton gave up Ormonde House, in Regent's Park, in 1917, after which they lived at Brede, with trips up to London, when they usually stayed with Leonie. Money was, as always, short, but Clara continued to ignore it and spent freely on her exceptional gardens. According to her great-grandson, Jonathan Frewen, Clara worked closely with the experts at the Royal Botanic Gardens and by 1920 had amassed a significant collection of rare plants. Under her stewardship, Brede had become a masterpiece of landscaping. In a last attempt to carve out some profit from the Prince Rupert scheme, Moreton decided that he and Oswald should travel to Canada to see whether some commercial opportunity could be salvaged. He still did not have the capital to buy his allocated land. (Oswald had retired from the navy in good standing in September 1919 and returned home to help his parents.) Clara, now sixty-eight, was becoming increasingly eccentric, her girlish ways and fussy manner seeming somewhat incongruous in the modern world. She was incapable of punctuality, had no organizational skills, and relied on family or staff to accomplish tasks for her. Oswald described the journey to the funeral of his uncle, Edward Frewen, in London, which provides a vivid picture of what Moreton and Clara had become:

Called at 8 instead of 7.15. No taxis. With one or two camel-protests from Ma, Pa she & I walked to St John's Wood Church carrying, the one a large bandbox containing a wreath, another another smaller bandbox containing a hat for Aunt Nan, & the third Pa's travelling bag containing wines & a tongue for the Funeral lunch. No 'buses, so we took the Tubes. Pa, bag-in-hand, paid 6d for the tickets in a lordly way, left me to ground my bandbox, take off my gloves, & extract 1½d from an inner pocket to pay the rest, & was surprised at the delay involved. Arrived at Baker Street, with a genial 'This way' he strode to the Escalator. I escorted Mamma, she complaining of lumbago, Charles [a servant], the early hour, the many parcels, the skimped breakfast, Charles again, Pa's idiosyncrasies in desiring to go by Tube, the time wasted in not going by Bus, the paucity of taxis, Charles again, the size of her bandbox ... at that moment the escalator moved under her feet, 'inaperçu', & her complaints took a new & altogether more vehement turn, & only ceased when all her energies were <u>essential</u> for the terrible ordeal of getting <u>off</u> the escalator. By then Pa had got onto the platform, the train had come in & <u>we</u> were barred off while it went out. On the other hand, Ma had forgotten her lumbago & half her other complaints in her indignation over the escalator, & <u>now</u> over strap-hanging. I left Pa to bring her along, at Trafalgar Square, & forged ahead to get the tickets. Pa & she entered the station <u>not</u> via the Booking Office & there was more 'business', as the stage would call it, over the tickets. Altogether a very sporting train-catch, even for the Frewens, especially for a Funeral.[1]

Just after the war, Hugh had bought a small hotel in South Kensington, in London, as a business investment. After working there and then selling it on a year later, he followed a business opportunity in Mesopotamia (modern-day Iraq). With two children, Roger and Jerome (known as Romey), and Memy, his estranged wife, to provide for, he was looking constantly for ways to improve his circumstances. Although his parents could give him no money, he relied on them to look after Romey, who lived with them at Brede. Roger lived with his mother, who shuttled between England, Italy, and Switzerland.

The trip to Prince Rupert was not a success, and Oswald returned home empty-handed. Moreton stayed on in Canada and had to write to Clara urgently at the end of 1919, requesting permission to draw her quarterly allowance in order to pay for his fare to return home: 'I will wind up my letters for 1919 with a line of love for my sweet old wife. There never was a greater darling and I love her more each year. You have been so brave and good and gallant.'[2] He always knew the right thing to say to his Kali. Clara welcomed him home warmly and Moreton, now sixty-six, immediately launched himself into a new scheme: to regenerate the empire's finances by settling ex-servicemen in the virgin lands around the Peace River in Canada. They would grow wheat and save Britain £50 million a year in subsidies, he believed. The plan led nowhere.

Oswald decided at that point to join his brother Hugh in Meso-potamia. Knowing that Moreton would consider his departure a betrayal as he was still angry with Hugh over a past disagreement. Oswald wrote on 1 May 1920 that he had decided not to tell his parents about his decision, as Pa might take against it because of the connection to Hugh. Oswald also knew that if he stayed, his small savings would disappear. 'Pa borrowed another £50 [£1,350 in today's money],' he wrote in his diary, '& whether I spend £200 [£5,400], which is about the price, in going to Baghdad & back, or stay here & parcel it out to him makes little odds, except that Baghdad <u>ought</u> to return me my money with much interest, & I don't think the other will.'[3] He was, for once, adamant in standing up to his father and informed his parents of his decision to travel to Mesopotamia.

Clara was encouraging to Oswald, perhaps knowing that this was her son's chance to make something of himself, but Moreton blustered angrily about lack of family loyalty and made venomous attacks on Hugh who, he said, had done no good in his life. Oswald listened patiently, but that night he wrote of his true feelings in his diary. His remarks demonstrate a profound insight into his father. As Oswald rightly surmised, the real problem was that Hugh had ventured out on his own:

Hugh's past is irrelevant as I am in no sort of partnership with him, but
if it were: he was private secretary to Girouard [High Commissioner of
the British Northern Nigeria protectorate] for a longer term than any
other man; he was spoken of in glowing terms by Temple his chief; he
took the highest prize extant in Hausa [in Northern Nigeria]; he
joined up at the very beginning of the war, although married; for as
long as it lasted he made a success of his hotel; & he left it to take up
this good job which he found all for himself … [Pa] has started
borrowing from me now that Ma has none & he has discovered I have
(he has had £135 this last month) & is as [financially] embarrassed as
ever. If I stay I shall see first my deposit account go, then he will get me
to raise on my securities. I raised in 1908, & again later, some £5,000
[or £350,000 today] on my prospects ([which were] £14,000) & for a
whole year after, his every letter told me the matter was on his mind.
Then – silence. Ever since I have known him he has been on the verge
of a vast fortune. His unit is £100,000, mine £1. He scorns anything
that involves work, he disdains anything under £10,000 nett or 20 %
commission. Solid sober business is beyond him … In despair of his
making good, seeing the idea of selling Brede taking root & flourishing
in his mind, seeing the possibility of Mumkins dying & my having to
support him on a third of her income – less what I have alienated [*sic*]
for him –; seeing myself at 33 earning nothing, a non-starter, I have
embraced the first opportunity of getting into harness, to prove my
grit, to prove my intelligence, to prove or disprove my business ability,
to make a little money to give Mumkin a few luxuries at her latter
end, to keep a roof over Pa's head should Mumkin die, & to enable me
to marry & perpetuate the name & make provision of my latter end –
& this cartload of bricks descends on me![4]

The 'cartload of bricks' referred to the barrage of bitter criticism that
Moreton had loosed upon his departing son. In contrast, Oswald was
warmed by his mother's sympathy – she had been a 'perfect brick',[5] he
recorded, and had risen to the occasion magnificently. Oswald left for
Mesopotamia with high hopes on 15 May 1920 but when he returned
home on 2 August, he had no fortune and no prospects. He was

surprisingly buoyant, however, having enjoyed the trip and much appreciated seeing his brother. He accepted philosophically that there was no future for him in the Middle East.

Earning a living continued to be a major preoccupation and Oswald constantly calculated his finances. He knew his patrimony would be a pittance and was living on the £300 (£8,400) a year that Clara had proposed to give him; he was prepared to accept her offer because he had raised nearly £6,000 for his father, with no prospect of its return. He had given up hope that Moreton would succeed in anything. His father had started with £15,000 (£1 million), he recalled, and in forty-seven years had reduced that to a loss of £7,750 (£220,000), for which Oswald was now responsible. Both Hugh and Clare had jumped clear as best they could, so Oswald had to assume his parents' financial liability because their own credit was exhausted, and they would have lost Brede if he had not. Brede was the family's only anchor and they were all deeply attached to it. Oswald recorded in his diary on 3 May 1920: 'Pa terrifies me with vague talk of "selling the dear old place".'[6] He and his mother knew that without Brede there would be nothing at all. Clara clung tenaciously to the house and Oswald supported her fervently. Although he was determined to find the means to save it and support himself, the financial picture was worsening. In June 1921, the family solicitor rang to say that there was a judgement on Clara and Oswald, for backing a promissory note of Moreton's for £260 (£7,280). The least that the creditors would accept was the full amount of Clara's income from America in June, some £600 (£16,800). They also received the news that the Receiver of the Grand Trunk Railway Company wanted all the arrears owing on the Prince Rupert property, which was still being held in Moreton's name but for which they had received no payment.

Clare had managed to avoid becoming embroiled in all these family problems. She had thrown herself into sculpture, training with Jacob Epstein and landing some prestigious commissions. Apart from her parents, the rest of the family was encouraging; both Jennie and Winston (of whom she produced a clay bust) agreed to do sittings, as did many friends. Clare also embraced a bohemian lifestyle that included many love affairs, which she confided in Mama, on condition that she would not tell Moreton. Whenever the children wished to exclude their father, they wrote to their mother in French – a language that she still spoke as well as English. Moreton loathed foreigners – except for Americans – and looked down on any language other than his own. Clare's letters spoke of a handsome American officer who showered her with gifts and loved her with a physical passion, telling her gossip-loving mother not to be shocked. 'Those are things we keep to ourselves,' Clare wrote; 'if I didn't tell you no one would know, but I know you love hearing about these things!'[7]

Winston's great friend, F.E. Smith (Lord Birkenhead), was another of her lovers and she went on cruises with him, often accompanied by Winston, who pretended to be a chaperone. Winston visited Clare's studio regularly, enjoying casual suppers with her bohemian friends, with whom he found he could share his artistic side. They discussed painting, on which he had pronounced views. Clare recorded the conversation in her memoirs:

> Given the brain-power, it was possible, he thought, to switch it on or off at will, as he did for instance from politics to painting, as Michael Angelo [sic] could from sculpture to poetry, and Leonardo da Vinci from painting to engineering ... He told me one evening as he leaned against the mantelpiece, after dinner, that: 'In my next incarnation (!) I mean to be a woman, I mean to be an artist, I shall be free, and I shall have children!!'[8]

Clare had fallen in love with Lord Alexander Thynne, brother of the 5th Marquis of Bath and a Tory MP. Although theirs was not an exclusive relationship, she was heartbroken when he was killed at the front in September 1918. The family wanted to see her settled. Jennie and Leonie had advised their niece to marry wealth (which neither of them had done), Jennie warning Clare to be discreet and Leonie whispering her habitual warning, 'cache ton jeu' (hide your game). Clara grew increasingly anxious while her daughter was entangled with Lord Birkenhead, who was also Lord Chancellor, writing to Leonie:

The poor darling does not realise how people enjoy saying unkind things. It is getting to be quite a scandal but Jennie just laughs – she says Clare needs that sort of man to perk her up. I begged her to ask Winston to speak to F.E. about it but she says he does not care. He adores Clare, thinks she can do no wrong after all she has suffered and he is <u>devoted</u> to Lord B. – you know how he always stands by his friends. So whatever scandal these two create together is in Winston's view <u>no</u> scandal – they are 'splendid', and whatever they feel like doing is 'perfect'. So there it is.[9]

All of London knew that Clare was promiscuous – but she did not care. According to her niece and biographer Anita Leslie, Clare had lunches with her Aunt Jennie, during which she 'received lectures concerning the importance of secrecy in love affairs'.[10] However, she had long ceased listening to any of her elders. She saw Moreton as a failure, whose advice was worthless, and she believed Mama was affectionate but lacking in sense. She loved and respected 'Tante Léonie', but Leonie could only remonstrate gently and offer advice. Jennie's words of caution were unceremoniously laughed at; Clare found it hilarious that her aunt, with her notorious reputation, should dare to offer any counsel at all. Clare had become a headstrong woman, battle-hardened and sophisticated in the ways of the world.

Nevertheless, the whole family was taken completely by surprise when Clare disappeared on a secret trip to the Soviet Union in 1920. She had been much taken with the Bolsheviks in London, befriending Commissar Kamenev and becoming his lover. She thought revolutionaries were alluring and accepted unhesitatingly when Kamenev invited her on a visit to Russia, with the lure of an opportunity to sculpt Lenin and Trotsky. It was an extraordinary thing to do at a time of such great civil and political unrest. The Bolshevik Revolution of 1917 had been violent and bloody; the Tsar and his family, cousins of the British king, had been murdered in 1918. Far from becoming a democracy as Lenin and other leaders had promised, the new Soviet Union was a brutal dictatorship. The country had certainly been in dire need of reform. After Russia lost the Crimean War in 1856, Tsar

Alexander II acknowledged that his country had fallen far behind other European nations, with an economy still dependent on agriculture and manpower provided by serfs – peasants tied to the land with practically no rights. With Alexander II's reforms, the serfs were freed, and general education for the population, until then quite absent, was improved. After the Tsar was assassinated in 1881, however, the new Tsar, Alexander III, reversed many of these reforms. The miseries endured by the population continued, and a further revolt took place in 1905. The new Tsar, Nicholas II, issued a declaration that promised reforms, including civil rights and a national parliament, or Duma.

The new government did not, however, keep its promises, and elections were secretly controlled so that reformers were not elected to the Duma. Opposition to the government continued, although the outbreak of the First World War temporarily halted revolt. As members of the Triple Alliance, together with Britain and France, Russia immediately mobilized its troops to defend Serbia from Austria. But it was proving to be increasingly difficult to motivate and control an already discontented Russian population. The economy was near to collapse, and many people in the cities were starving. In March 1917, riots broke out in St Petersburg (which had been renamed the more Russian-sounding Petrograd at the start of the war). Instead of firing on the rioters, the troops joined the revolt. The Tsar was forced to abdicate and his government advisers resigned. The Provisional Government, however, continued to prosecute the war. The leader of the Bolshevik Party, Lenin, exiled in Switzerland, was determined to return to his homeland to claim power and had no intention of allowing Russia to remain at war once he had done so. It was the Germans themselves – needing a regime that would seek peace – who offered to send him through Germany itself into Russia, in a sealed train. He arrived in Petrograd in April 1917. Six months later, he had seized control of the government in what became known as the October Revolution.

This new government signed the peace treaty with Germany in

March 1918 and moved the capital farther east, to Moscow. Banks were put under state control, and Church property was confiscated. Not all Russians supported the Bolsheviks, however, and a bloody civil war broke out later in 1918, between the anti-Communist White Russians and the Bolshevik Red Army. In 1921, the White Russians were defeated. Millions died during this violent struggle and millions more emigrated.[11] There was great fear in parts of Europe, including Britain, that the Bolshevik revolution would spread – as was its avowed intention. Winston Churchill was one of the new regime's most fierce critics. He loathed the Bolsheviks, writing of them some ten years later: 'not a wounded Russia only, but a poisoned Russia, an infected Russia, a plague-bearing Russia; a Russia of armed hordes smiting not only with bayonet and with cannon, but accompanied and preceded by swarms of typhus-bearing vermin which slew the bodies of men, and political doctrines which destroyed the health and even the soul of nations.'[12] Prime Minister Lloyd George did not share Winston's iron determination to root out the evil of Bolshevism. He knew how war-weary the British were; over three quarters of a million men had died in the war and, with the worldwide outbreak of virulent influenza just after the end of the conflict, millions more were threatened. Winston, however, was immune to the prime minister's reticence. He wanted the West to overthrow this 'pestilent' ideology and to use British soldiers still on the continent to help the White Russians to do it. They were unsuccessful and Winston's part in the debâcle reinforced his enemies' view of his lack of sound judgement.

Clare chose not to confide her plan to go to the Soviet Union to her cousin, now Minister for War and Air, for obvious reasons. But Shane, with his left-leaning sympathies, was aware of it, as was her devoted brother Oswald. Shane agreed to say nothing to anyone until Clare had been gone for a week. She sent her apologies to Lord Birkenhead, on whose yacht she was meant to be spending the weekend, and travelled with Commissar Kamenev to Sweden. She stopped en route to visit her friend, Crown Prince Gustav, who rather bemusedly supplied her with biscuits and cigarettes for the remainder of the journey. A visa allowed her entrance to Estonia and thence to Russia. Clara and Moreton were unaware that anything was amiss. On 19 September 1920, Clara wrote to Jennie: 'Where is Clare? I'm told the rumour in London is that she has gone off – with Kamenev!!! Ha! Ha! Honestly, I was told this seriously. People don't know what to talk about, do they?'[13] She was not amused to learn the truth when Moreton opened a letter from Clare to Oswald that arrived at Brede two days later. Oswald was immediately sent for and described his arrival that same day in his diary: 'Found Pa – I can only call it raving, & will try to forget the things he said – & Ma "inexpressibly shocked". I turned her off for bed with the consoling announcement that Kamenoff [*sic*] had <u>shaken hands</u> with the Prime Minister of Great Britain.'[14] The Frewens were mortified. Clara tried to make people believe that Clare had simply gone to Sweden to do a bust of Prince Gustav, but she expressed her distress to her sisters. 'Moreton, Oswald and I thought best to keep Clare's doings to ourselves but Jennie writes me that rumours are going about London,' she wrote anxiously to Leonie, 'we think we must tell <u>you</u> and <u>Jennie</u> what is happening – no one else.'[15]

Leonie was, as ever, concerned primarily with ensuring that the damage was limited. When newspapers started to print stories, she advised her sister Clara to remain dignified, saying that Clare had done 'nothing dishonourable'. 'She is misguided but it is not for <u>Family</u> to turn against her. Darling, if I <u>may</u> advise you – say <u>nothing</u> – or as little as you can. Put on a brave face and act just as if everything was all right and very likely things <u>will</u> turn out all right.'[16] She wrote to Jack's sister, Olive Guthrie, attempting a light-hearted tone: 'I expect you have heard of Clare's mad escapade of going off to Russia to do Lenin's bust? … I know you will be a good friend to us all and make light of it. When we meet we can both damn her to our heart's content.'[17]

While Clara found it difficult to take her sister's advice and put on a brave face, Moreton was livid. According to Oswald, who went to see Jennie, Winston was also displeased, especially as he had pressed so hard for anti-Bolshevik military intervention in Russia. Winston had a meeting with Shane, in which he criticized his cousin for his part in

Clare's escapade. Shane recounted their discussion to Clara, who lost no time in relaying the exchange to Oswald. He described his mother's account in his diary:

> Her account of Winston and Shane and their 'awful row' was so grotesque that I simply couldn't look her in the face, and even in this I was not suffered to suffer in my own way, for I found her saying 'and Winston just looked at him like this – LOOK AT ME DARLING – like this.' What Winston had said to Shane and how Shane's head had hung lower and lower and how finally he had got up and said he couldn't remain any longer, and how Winston had refused to shake hands with him, all had been embellished in the telling, but to have a sort of Movie addition with Ma 'featuring' Winston was too much.[18]

Moreton wrote to Shane of his anger at what he saw as a betrayal: 'Now a word about your indiscreet oath to give her a week's start. Is an oath of that kind binding? … And after a scene with Winston you divulge at dinner to the three worst women gossips in town that she had not started for Stockholm to sculpt the Crown Prince but with Kamenev to see Lenin in Moscow … Depend upon it that is why Winston is so angry with you.'[19] Shane thought the brouhaha most amusing. Jennie was angered by Shane's levity and wrote to Leonie: 'Can't you tell Shane to keep his mouth shut. He goes around holding dinner tables with his own special account – making a joke of everyone except himself in the telling. I can't get hold of him. He's your son. Restrain him.'[20] Yet even in Clare's absence, Jennie and Leonie attended the opening of her exhibition on 12 October at Agnew's.

Shane and Clare corresponded while she was in Russia, and he advised her to behave with caution upon her return. It was sound advice. Typically Clare had disregarded the implications of her behaviour for others. On 11 October, she wrote to Shane from Moscow, telling him that while she sculpted Lenin, she would describe her family to him: 'he thinks we are funny sort of cousins for Winston to have! Winston is apparently the best hated man in England, & to my mind they greatly exaggerate his power & importance.'[21] A week later she responded to Shane that she was sorry that he had borne the brunt of the family's disapproval, although she believed that by the time she returned, 'it will all have calmed down ... I do not gather on what basis the family is so upset. Is it for my safety? I am safe. Is it moral? There is no scandal. Is it political prejudice? I have come on no political mission. I am 35 and a working woman. I have come where there is work.'[22] Clare's great facility was to ignore what did not suit her. But she was right to claim that the commotion would pass.

Once the furore had died down, Clara came to see her daughter's trip as exciting. True, the scandal had been hard to bear, but it began to seem very dramatic, especially as Clare was now writing articles about the experience in *The Times*. Clara wrote to Shane, who was by then fully rehabilitated and forgiven for his part in the deception:

> Thank you *du coeur* [from the heart] for your dear letter to *me* congratulating on Clare's safe return. It *is* wonderful that she is actually home – & that I shall see her in the flesh tomorrow! Meantime I have been reading her Times articles which I am frank to say thrill me! I do hope she is appreciative & grateful to <u>you</u>, for all you have borne for her sake! As far as I am concerned, I shall never forget Shane dear, your thoughtfulness kindness & affection to me, in writing to tell me all you heard & could, to comfort me in my anxiety. You are a real dear.[23]

It was as well that Clara took pleasure in the thrills of Clare's life, because it became ever more exotic. In the 1920s Clare espoused free love with her radical politics. She planned to pursue a career in journalism. Like the rest of her family, Clare wrote well and for the rest of her life was able to earn substantial amounts from her published work, newspaper articles, and books. Although the family learned to accept her eccentricities, she was often hard to defend. She claimed that Trotsky was charming and delightful and that her Bolshevik hosts had been perfect gentlemen, she had no qualms about returning home from Russia covered in gifts of sables. Observers said she was an apologist for murderers and an opportunist who wore furs stolen from those the Bolsheviks had dispossessed. At this point a trip to America seemed like a good idea, a useful bolthole to escape the less forgiving elements of London society after her Russian adventure.

When Clare was refused a visa because of her reputation as a Bolshevik sympathizer, Aunt Jennie solved the problem by prevailing on the Foreign Office to help. As usual, Jennie was able to get what she wanted, and Clare departed for New York in January 1921. Despite the problems that Clare's flit to Moscow had caused Winston, Jennie was a stalwart who believed firmly that family always came first. Clare saw her aunt for the last time, on her departure to America, when Jennie came to the station to wish her farewell. She looked so beautiful, Clare recalled: 'She put her arm through mine as we walked down the long platform and said: "Remember, if you are not happy come straight back, we are all here to open our arms to you".'[25] Having always admired Aunt Jennie's honesty and loyalty, Clare treasured the message that her aunt gave her the night before she left, reminding her that she had a 'powerful family' who loved her.[26] Her aunt Leonie agreed that some time away would be beneficial for Clare and tried to explain how the family felt:

> You are wise dear thing to go off for a few months, but remember we all love you and want you back soon … Take my advice darling Clare on one line only try to be a little more underline. It is quite permissible to think a man is wonderful in any way you like – but one does not talk about it … remember that to Jennie and me you are very dear – our only niece – that is why we get so wrought up over you. One doesn't trouble except with people one really loves. And remember also that you are the nearest thing to a sister that Winston ever had – and apart from the embarrassment you can cause him when your unusual doings are associated with his name – he can be deeply wounded. So don't do that again.[27]

Leonie was right about Winston. He had been very divided about Clare's flight to Moscow. Deeply hurt by Clare's disregard for his position and by her lack of trust in not warning him in advance, he also loved his cousin, who was indeed the closest he had to a sister. As the consequences of the trip continued to reverberate, he wrote to her from Whitehall in January 1921:

Private

My dear Clare,

I do not feel that you have just cause to reproach me. You did not seek my advice about your going and I was not aware that you needed any on your return. Anyhow it was almost impossible for me to bring myself to meet you fresh from the society of those whom I regard as fiendish criminals. Having nothing to say to you that was pleasant, I thought it better to remain silent until a better time came. But that does not at all mean that I have ceased to regard you with affection or to wish you most earnestly success and happiness in a right way. While you were flushed with your adventure I did not feel you needed me: and frankly I thought I could not trust myself to see you. But no one has felt more sympathy or admiration for your gifts and exertion than I have, and I should be very sorry if you did not feel that I would do my best to help you in any way possible or that you did not count on my friendship and kinship. But note at the same time please that you have those other friends and have to train your words to suit their interests. I hope your work in America will be successful and you will come back in a few months with a healthy gap between you and an episode which may then have faded and to which we need neither of us ever refer.

Your affectionate cousin,

Winston[28]

Clare stayed at first in New York, where she gave lectures about her trip to Russia. She then travelled on to California, where she embarked on a highly public affair with the movie star Charlie Chaplin, with whom she went camping in the desert. Clare's maid Louise informed Oswald that Clare had also taken a younger man in New York as a lover before Mr Chaplin. (In spite of her many declarations of being a working woman and political radical, Clare, like her mother, had never lived without a personal maid.) Her many lovers over the years were often men whom she sculpted and in time they made an eclectic list:

Bernard Baruch, Benito Mussolini, Kemal Atatürk, among many others
– most of them either extremely rich or politically powerful. Leonie
wrote sadly to Oswald: 'All that matters is that her affairs should not be
made public and make Winston look foolish – he loves her you know
– we all do. It's the war that has broken her up – she <u>can't</u> be an
ordinary widow and she <u>won't</u> be an ordinary wife. Only Wilfred could
control her.'[29] After some years of travelling and sculpting, Clare decided
in 1924 to settle in Constantinople, where her friendships with the
Russians gained her the reputation within the expatriate British community of being a Soviet spy.

Clara gave up trying to control her wayward daughter, who simply
refused to take advice. There was enough for her to worry about at
Brede. In March 1921, Moreton's guaranteed options on the Prince
Rupert land had finally expired, as he had been unable to find the
£50,000 (nearly £1.5 million today) required to exercise his purchasing rights. Also in 1921, Fred Stenning, their agent at Innishannon –
whom Moreton had brought over from Rhodesia twenty-five years
previously to run the trout farm operation – was murdered by Irish
nationalists, in front of his wife. After Stenning had been threatened by
letters signed 'The Black Hand', Moreton told him to stop collecting
rent, but this did not save him. The Frewens were upset and alarmed.
Moreton vowed never to set foot in Ireland ever again. He wrote a
strong letter to the *Daily Telegraph*; the following day his house at
Innishannon was torched. After their neighbour in Innishannon,
Colonel John Peacocke, was also brutally murdered, Moreton again
wrote to the *Daily Telegraph* of his disgust:

> For forty years I have believed that for England's sake Ireland should
> have 'Home Rule' and that in spite of ourselves the federal system of
> Home Rule would save us, as Redmond so often assured me in the old
> days it would. But what a disillusion is mine. For years past I have
> watched the baser elements in Congress – the Frank Walshes and
> Cohalans – capturing the Irish vote by denouncing the 'old
> Oppressor,' and so surely as the sun rose the next day on their
> maledictions some dear fellow like Colonel Peacocke, 3,000 miles

away, or my two gallant police-sergeants, are murdered in my lovely valley of the Bandon. Such has been the bloody sequence, paid for in American dollars. And these Congressional murderers, did they know it, just as surely murdered John Redmond, as they have now murdered John Peacocke. I cannot believe that decent Americans will continue to listen placidly and continue to be accessory before the act to murders such as these. I, at least, wash my hands of it all, even though my recantation comes too late to save John Peacocke.[30]

Moreton was now sixty-eight years old and his health was poor. In July 1921, he had a large cyst removed from his neck. Oswald organized the operation, Leonie provided lunch, and Shane a bed at his house in London. Clara's health was not especially good either. Her eyesight was failing, and in October 1921 she broke her leg. Neither she nor Moreton felt confident in the future, nor were they contented with the past. Oswald was thirty-four, living with his impoverished parents, with no job and no prospects. Cousin Winston had been prevailed upon once more and this time was asked to help his Frewen cousin find employment. After the Russian debâcle, Prime Minister Lloyd George had transferred Winston to the Colonial Office from which he had only been able to obtain a position in East or West Africa for Oswald. It was a job and an income, but it would mean exile. Oswald was deeply disappointed and recorded: 'He was very friendly & affectionate, & solicitous about Ma, & I bottled myself up till I got home, when the disappointment overcame me & I burst into tears.'[31]

The end of the war had brought some happiness for Jennie. After her divorce, she had reverted to the name Lady Randolph Churchill. She was still trying to establish a better financial footing with income from her writing, although she was not especially successful. Her son Jack wrote, urging her to use restraint: 'you have over £2000 a year … We have begged you so often to live within your income – which is not a very severe demand. Your income is larger than mine in most years and you have nothing whatever to keep up.' He was worried about where it would end: 'Unless you are able to do so and if you start running up bills again – there is nothing that can save you from a crash &

bankruptcy.'[32] She was much cheered, however, by her admirer, the forty-year-old Montagu Phibben Porch, who had won her heart and then her hand. Montagu was from an old and wealthy landed family in Glastonbury, although he himself was not well off. There had been a scandal in which one of his sisters had been convicted of poisoning her husband in China; her sentence had been commuted and she had returned to live with her mother in Bath. Montagu, however, was a quiet, old-fashioned, courteous man who offered Jennie sincere affection. He had written to her after Hugh's wedding, expressing his admiration of her, and Jennie had replied to him while he was on military service in Nigeria. After a correspondence, during which Jennie discovered dry humour and quiet courage in this dapper man, he arrived in London on leave during 1916. They spent a great deal of time together before he returned to Africa. In the spring of 1918, Montagu arrived for another visit, and Jennie invited him to travel with her to Glaslough, to visit her sister. They had a fine time in Ireland. After English rationing, Jennie and Montagu tucked into full breakfasts of bacon, eggs, porridge and cream, followed by dinners of leg of lamb, and other hearty meals in the beautiful house on the lake. It was there that Montagu proposed marriage.

Leonie was happy to see her sister looking so well and urged her to accept Montagu. After their two-week stay, Jennie and Montagu became engaged, which was something of a jolt to the family. Jack wrote to his mother on hearing of the engagement:

> What a surprise! ... Whenever I go to war you do these things! I feel sure that you have thought it all out carefully, and that you are certain that you are acting wisely. I know the last few years must have been lonely for you. With both of us married it was inevitable that you should be alone ... If he makes you happy we shall soon be friends ... Now, my dear, you know that no one can make any change in our love for one another, and it will be something to know that you are no longer alone.[33]

On 1 June 1918, the couple married at Harrow Road Register Office, with Winston, Clemmie, and Goonie present. Winston and Jack Leslie were witnesses. The family was happy for her. Even Randolph's youngest sister, Lady Sarah Wilson, attended the wedding. This time, Jennie decided to keep her name and she remained Lady Randolph Churchill for the rest of her life. On a visit to Blenheim after the marriage, she signed as 'Lady Randolph Churchill', writing in 1919 to Leonie that she had had a talk with her trustees about her name, as she wanted 'so much to have it regularised'. She felt that she was entitled to keep it: 'As you know I have worked war-work since the beginning of the war, *arduously* and have never had the slightest recognition and it wd. be a great favour if the King gave me permission (by receiving me) to stick to my name which as you know my boys have asked me to.' She declared that she had 'no snobbish feeling about it', but that she had 'made a name for herself' and it was 'undoubtedly an asset'.[34]

Jennie, now sixty-four, was once again happy. She and Montagu lived in her beautifully decorated house on Westbourne Street. She told her friend, the novelist George Moore, that as Montagu had a future and she a past, they would be all right as a couple. There was much catty London gossip, but Jennie declared that she did not care. She later claimed of her marriages that her second had been romantic but unhappy, and her third happy but not romantic. 'Montie' was steady and loyal, and he worshipped her. He had returned to Nigeria after the wedding, where Jennie could not follow him for the remainder of the war. In July 1919, shortly after the conflict ended, he resigned from the Nigerian Civil Service and returned to London to be with Jennie. He sold some of his land in Glastonbury, and Jennie bought a house in Berkeley Square as an investment, to renovate. She decorated it with her usual flair and sold it at a very good profit.

Following Montagu's return from Nigeria, the couple embraced a busy social life. Jennie danced and threw parties. Although he was the younger by twenty years, Jennie was the live wire. Montagu took the social whirl in his stride, enjoying his high-spirited wife. They travelled through France, visiting her friends. They met exciting people at parties – Stravinsky, Picasso, Ravel, Proust, and James Joyce – some of whom later visited the couple back in London. Shane Leslie recalled how entertaining Montagu found it all. Jennie, in turn, was grateful to have a devoted man by her side. She still organized small dinner parties to help Winston's career, but Clemmie was now in charge of that part of his life. Jennie continued to take a close interest in Jack, but he was happily married and needed his mother less than before. Montagu, however, needed and depended on her. Jennie continued to spend just as she always had, and their finances took an alarming dip. In 1921, Montagu decided to return to Africa to make some money. He was also tiring of the unkind comments being made about him in the fashionable London salons. Unfortunately he had few qualifications for a career; after discussions with Winston and Jack, they agreed that Africa was a land full of potential and a place he knew well. To help their mother, her two sons agreed to finance Montagu's trip. In March 1921, he travelled out to the Gold Coast (now Ghana) where he had high hopes of making a quick fortune, fully expecting Jennie to come out and join him as soon as he had found a house.

Before leaving, he took Jennie to meet his mother, who had not attended the wedding. Montagu was the last of his line and, in marrying Jennie, who was past childbearing age, he would leave no heir to follow him. Their meeting was brief but Montagu was unmoved by his mother's disapproval. He loved his wife, who loved him in return. He found a note from her in his pocket as he left for Africa: 'My darling, Bless you and *au revoir* and I love you better than anything in the world and shall try to do all the things you want me to in your absence. Your loving wife, J. PS Love me and think of me.'[35] He would never see her again.

Although Jennie was once more alone life was interesting again. She went flying in an aeroplane and acted in a film for charity.[36] She danced all the new dances and read all the new books. In the spring of 1921, she accepted an invitation to visit Rome from her friend Vittoria, Duchess of Sermoneta. She, Winston, and Clemmie first went to France, where they stayed with the Laverys at Cap d'Ail and where Winston did some painting. The duchess later collected Jennie to take her on to Rome. There she found the life very sparkling, she wrote to Leonie, and enjoyed the races, dances, and shopping. Not surprisingly, she also 'bought some lovely things',[37] including a pair of dainty slippers. The duchess recollected that they had done a great deal of sightseeing and shopping during their visit: 'We ransacked all the curiosity shops and Jennie bought profusely; her zest in spending money was one of her charms. She was still a handsome woman, her dark eyes had lost none of their sparkle with the passing of years and the shape of her face was always admirable ... her beauty was of a dark southern type.'[38]

After her sojourn in Italy, Jennie accepted an invitation to visit her friend Lady Frances Horner, at Mells Manor in Somerset. One day during her visit, when Jennie was wearing her new Italian slippers, she fell down a staircase. She was unable to move and the doctor was called in from the neighbouring town of Frome. He diagnosed a simple fracture of both bones above the left ankle. These were set and Jennie was taken home in an ambulance two days later, accompanied by a doctor and a nurse. Montagu was sent the news and wrote immediately from Coomassie, on the Gold Coast, telling her that he could 'hardly pull myself together to write you some words of comfort and sympathy'. He was 'terribly upset', he added, and worried that she might never be able to dance again. But he reassured her that he would love her 'very much to make up for all the pain and anguish' that she had suffered. Montagu was grateful that she was comfortable in her own home with her sons near by, as well as her sisters and many friends. Like everyone else, he believed that her recovery would be swift. He explained that he could not leave his business: 'Darling, I am ready to come to you any day – this I have cabled to you. But my business would suffer v. much – my business that has turned out an amazing success.'[39]

Within two weeks, however, gangrene had set in; Winston was summoned and he immediately called in a surgeon, who declared that he would have to amputate the leg at once. Jennie's sang-froid did not desert her and she told the doctor calmly to make sure that he cut high enough. He amputated her leg just above the knee. Montagu learned of the dreadful new development and wrote a long letter over a period of several days. He could not sleep and was sick with worry:

> My sweet precious Darling only now that you are maimed & tortured I know how much I love you – you poor Darling are in pain – Terrible suffering you must be going through while I am here powerless to help & comfort you. My head aches, my eyes pain me, my throat is swollen with passion and despair – I am ill … Jennie Darling I will help you to bear all this. How can I ever love you enough – I will be very good to you, considerate & faithful – I could never be disloyal to you now. Bless you sweet Darling – I send you all my love & kisses & more kisses for the poor little place where the stitches are.[40]

Clara was an emotional wreck at her sister's plight and useless in the emergency. Oswald recorded that she had come to London to see Jennie, afterwards visiting him at Clare's studio house, where he was living while his sister was away:

> She came, tired & with jagged nerves all over, wrought up frantically, having been sitting up at Aunt Jane's [Jennie's] for two nights & gotten her a hospital bed from Heal's (to that extent, at least, she had been practical). She talked & mimicked <u>wonderfully</u> – quite unnaturally – till about 7 when she went back to Aunt Jane's (Aunt Jane has had her left leg amputated above the knee; wherefore the Churchills announce the loss of a <u>foot</u> – <u>so</u> Churchillian!)[41]

Oswald was referring to the Churchill propensity for understating negative news. Clara wanted to be at Jennie's side as much as she could and to share in her sister's pain. Oswald wryly observed that his mother loved drama and threw herself emotionally into every crisis. He described the madness in his diary:

> if poor little Jane [Jennie] is suffering physically, its nervous reflection on Mumkin is intensified. Anything one can say to steady her merely sounds brutal, heartless, & unsympathetic, & I long ago discovered that it is <u>fatal</u> to sympathise with her over anything: she merely uses the sympathy as fuel to add fire to her own torments. All her misery is from

within … Ma sits next to the hall at Westbourne Street conjuring up a vision of an amputated leg the whole time, & fearful lest she be not sufficiently miserable to prove her love for her sister. She can be of no use to anyone & can't see Jane. Aunt Leonie came in while I was there, & if Ma was 70 % distraught, Leonie was most certainly 95 % prostrated. Lacking the key to the riddle I thought her incoherent. She wished to ring up doctors, told Jack Churchill she didn't know 'which one to sit with', inveighed in general against strong young women who leant on her for support, & went out, borrowing £1 from Ma, 'to send a cable'. She was grey-white & far beyond scenes or hysterics, & like a spent wave on a level beach. Hardly had she gone when Shane appeared, hoarse & hollow-eyed. Jack C. (the only element of imperturbable sanity in the place) motioned me to escort him home as he was manifestly distraught.[42]

Leonie, too, was overwhelmed with the pandemonium. Her daughter-in-law, Marjorie, was about to give birth to her third child and had just learned that her father had unexpectedly died in America. Both Marjorie and her sister Anne, who had come to be with her for the birth, were devastated. Leonie, usually so reliable, could think of nothing but Jennie. Fortunately, the amputation was a success, much to everyone's relief. Jennie was on the mend and was soon able to receive visitors. She was positive and courageous, greeting her friend Eleanor Warrender by saying: 'You see, I have put my best foot forward to meet you.'[43] Winston cabled to Montagu on 23 June that all was well. Montagu was reassured, although still concerned. He wrote to Jennie that he was still 'suffering agonies of anxiety' and that he was 'often frantic with apprehension and fear'.[44] He had no one, he declared, in the world save her to love. He was working hard to build a future for them, and the business that he had established in Africa was doing well. He wrote to Jennie on 27 June that he had arranged with the Inland Revenue Authorities to pay their income tax by instalments, with the last instalment paid in January 1921, after which Jennie would have her entire income, free of tax.[45] Jennie knew how it would distress her husband to be away from her at this critical time. She was aware, however, that he was worried about getting his business in order before departing for England (he was also trying to raise the money to pay off the mortgage on their London house on Westbourne Street). She sent him a cable on 28 June to reassure him, telling him that she had received his letters and that she was fine.

Messages poured in from Jennie's many friends and acquaintances, all sending good wishes for her recovery. She enjoyed her visitors, but she was still suffering, as Oswald recalled: 'Brought up a nice bunch of yellow lilies for Aunt Jane & took them round in the afternoon. The butler said she was getting on well & was, indeed, seeing people, so I sent up to ask if she would see me, & she <u>did</u>! Aunt Leonie there. She looked her old self, asked after every individual member of my family, even Romey, & was very sweet, but kept grimacing with pain.'[46]

The following morning, 29 June, Jennie awakened in high spirits and ate a good breakfast. She enquired after Marjorie, whose baby was due that day. Then suddenly, without warning, she began to bleed profusely. The main artery in the amputated leg had haemorrhaged. Jennie cried, 'Nurse, nurse, I am feeling faint,'[47] and then slipped into unconsciousness. She was in a coma by the time Winston and Jack arrived. Leonie was in a hospital room with Marjorie, who had just given birth to a son, Desmond, when she was notified of Jennie's condition. Shane, Anne, and Bourke Cockran were also with her, and Bourke immediately drove Leonie to Westbourne Street, where Jennie was barely breathing. She died some moments later. It had happened so quickly and unexpectedly that no one could quite believe it. Oswald described the events in his diary:

> Marjorie … produced a 9lb. boy within 5 minutes either way of the tragedy, & Aunt Leonie was with <u>her</u>. Winston came round in pyjamas & a motor-car, & Jack at once. Both arrived before the end, but neither before final unconsciousness … Leonie & Jack Churchill were afraid of Ma's breaking down & my highest mission in life (or death) was to look after <u>her</u>.[48]

Jennie was sixty-seven years old.

CHAPTER FOURTEEN

Last Journeys

That June morning Clara was on a train journey to London, not yet aware that her sister had died. Oswald rushed to the station to meet her. The press had already learned of Jennie's sudden death, and the family were desperate that Clara not read of it first on news boards. Oswald was late and missed her arrival by five minutes, however, and Clara saw the boards posting her sister's death while leaving the station in a taxi. At Jennie's home in Westbourne Street, Oswald caught up with his mother, racked with grief. He stayed by her side, later accompanying her and Leonie to see their sister's body before the coffin was closed:

> I had never seen her before without puckers round her mouth, & powder on her nose, & flashing eyes full of vivacity. Here the mouth had set, not in a Cupid's bow but in a crescent, corners drooping, grim as a warrior chief, the nose emerged aquiline, the wax-like complexion was sallow, the brow noble. It might have been the body of a Roman Emperor or a Redskin Chief; the only woman it called to my mind was my formidable grandmother who died in 1896 [1895]. We all saw the likeness: Ma, Aunt Leonie, Winston. Leonie & I made to leave, but I saw Mumkin on the verge of a breakdown of the first magnitude, so broke back to warn her how bad it would be for Jennie if she let herself go, & she kept me by her & sat calmly on the sofa for some 10 minutes.[1]

Winston and Jack stood side by side at the moment when their mother was brought down the stairs in her coffin. On the following day, 30 June, Winston wrote to the Duke of Connaught, the surviving brother of Jennie's close friend Edward VII:

Sir:

Your Royal Highness's most affectionate letter about my dear Mother has profoundly touched my heart, and I thank you Sir, most earnestly for it, and even more for the lifelong friendship of wh. it is the expression.

It was a cruel disappointment & blow to have this fatal event, just as we were entitled to believe that the immediate danger was surmounted. But since it was to be, I am thankful that her sufferings are at an end and that she sleeps after her life of sunshine and storms.

She looked beautiful yesterday in her coffin. Since the pangs of the morning thirty years had rolled from her brow and one saw again her old splendour of features and expression, without a wrinkle or a trace of pain or weariness she lay as if carved out of marble in the heyday of her beauty.

Poor Leonie had a fearful day yesterday with this intense grief and also her own anxieties. She showed all her greatest qualities.

Once more I thank you Sir for all the kindness you have shown to me and mine.

And remain Your Royal Highness's devoted servant,
    Winston S. Churchill[2]

The funeral took place at Bladon, near Blenheim, on 2 July 1921. Jennie was to be buried next to Randolph, in the churchyard. The funeral train departed from Paddington Station. On board were Jennie's sons and their wives; her sisters; Jack Leslie; her nephews, Shane and Seymour Leslie, and Oswald Frewen; as well as Lord Blandford, Eleanor Warrender, and a few other close friends. Oswald described the occasion in detail:

Got Mumkin to Paddington just at 9.30, which I told her was the train-time. (Actually it was 9.45 so there was no fluster). They had a saloon & 2 corridor compartments in a special reserved coach, & I think Aunt Jennie was in another saloon, in which we had tea on the return journey. Jack Churchill, alone, was in the saloon, & I, thinking Aunt Jennie was to come there, thought it better to persuade Ma to sit in one of the compartments, where there were Hugh & Eleanor Warrender, Lord Howe, & the doctor responsible for her demise. Anyway, she wanted to wander & was restless, & presently returned to me, very kipped, saying Leonie had refused to let her into the Family Saloon, where she had a right! I don't really suppose Leonie had done anything of the sort, the saloon would have been very trying, & the Warrenders were a much better 'atmosphere' than the Churchills & their wives. However I soothed her as well as I could … Winston came through the corridor, questing, till he found her & made a fuss with her, so she was quite reconciled!…

On arrival at Oxford Winston ushered Ma & me into the leading motor, & we headed the procession to our glee; Ma's because she was getting the honour due to the elder sister, mine because the Leslies & Churchills were eating our dust instead of we theirs…

There was a blazing sun, a little quiet gentle country church, a sympathetic parson, boys' & women's voices only in the choir, & the grave was lined with white roses & pale mauve orchids … altogether it was quite a bright little service…

We all walked over to Blenheim after the ceremony & had a 'picnic lunch as there were no servants' … After lunch Winston took Hugh & Eleanor [Warrender], Ma & me, round the gardens.[3]

Even in his distress, Winston was kind to the fussy and melodramatic Clara. He sought her out in the train, made sure that she was given precedence on arrival, and later took the time to show her round the gardens at Blenheim. The Frewens were not an easy family. Clara was demanding and often querulous, while Oswald had a cynical way about him that at times was doubtless grating. Moreton had lost everyone's money on countless occasions, and Clare was proving to be turbulent. The Churchills and Leslies were in many ways compatible and at ease with one another – hence the seating arrangements in the funeral train.

Aunt Clara may have been a trial, but her nephews and surviving sister treated her with respect. 'I am so thinking of you,' she began a letter to Winston on 5 July, after the funeral, '& write a few words to tell you, how touched I am for all your gentle courtesy, & thoughtfulness of me on Saturday, when you were suffering such sorrow yourself.' She was appreciative of the memories created that day. 'All was so beautiful,' she added, 'the simple service in the dear little old Church – the beautiful hymns – the beautiful music – all the wonderful flowers from those who loved her – And the sunshine – and Magnificent Blenheim. These Memories will abide with me forever.'[4]

Leonie was pragmatic in her loss. On the same day as her sister Clara, she wrote to Winston at the Colonial Office that she was 'getting things straight' at Jennie's home. 'They will be taking an inventory of furniture tomorrow. I shall be there. Everything will be locked up after this – and despatch boxes better come to yr house.' She only wished to help, adding, 'I don't want to take up yr time – if there is anything you want done – just send me word.'[5]

Clare Sheridan wrote in typically self-absorbed fashion from Mexico City:

Winston dear

You know, that your loss is just as much my loss. She was a second mother to me. I loved her with all my heart, and shall never have such another loyal friend. No one knows better than you do our devotion for one another. The tragedy of it is horrible to think of. I can't write you more – I am so so miserable.[6]

In addition to sending flowers for Jennie's funeral, George Cornwallis-West wrote to Winston, claiming that he 'never had anything in my heart for her but affection & admiration'. He realized, he added sadly, that 'the greatest mistake I ever made in my life was in allowing myself to be persuaded into a separation from her'. It was a decision, he ended grimly, that he had 'lived and am living to bitterly regret'.[7] Jennie had never borne George a grudge and had written to him in June 1919 with typical generosity: 'in your heart of hearts, you must know that I never could have but kindly feeling towards you. I never think of you but to remember all the happy days we spent together – I have forgotten everything else.' She had added, 'Peace is an essential of life – & if you have that, you are on the fair way to happiness. Life is frightfully hard, one's only chance is within oneself.'[8]

Newspaper coverage of Jennie's death, both in England and in America, was extensive. In Britain, leaders and articles appeared not only in the major titles, such as *The Times*, *Daily Mail*, *Daily Express*, *Daily Telegraph*, *Daily Chronicle*, and many more, but also in regional papers such as the *Aberdeen Free Press*, *Liverpool Echo*, *Bournemouth Daily*, *Bristol Evening Press*, and countless others. A picture of her in her youth, featured in the *Daily Sketch*, was captioned: 'Lady Randolph in her prime when the great ones fell under the spell of her beauty and vivacity.'[9]

The American papers were full of the news.[10] The *Boston Globe* headline read: 'Mother of Winston Spencer Churchill: She was Miss Jennie Jerome of New York City'. All around the nation, newspapers reported the death of one of America's most famous exports. 'Daughter of American was long a powerful influence in London Political Life,' claimed the *Boston Traveler*. The *Philadelphia Inquirer* told of 'An American Girl in British Politics', while the *Boston Post* boasted that 'Lady Churchill was U.S. Best "Ambassador".' Tributes appeared in all the New York papers, such as the *New York Times*, *New York Tribune*, and *Evening Post*. There were also features in papers nationwide, such as the *Pittsburgh Chronicle*, *Savannah Press*, *Nashville Banner*, *Providence Tribune*, and the *Indianapolis News*, whose headline on 29 June was 'Famous Woman Dies after Brief Illness'. The articles all made the point that an American had made a significant impact on British politics. Jennie had been married to a well-known British politician, and her son Winston was clearly on the way to making a name for himself. By then he was sufficiently important for the *Seattle Intelligencer* to write of Jennie's death, 'American Born Mother of British Minister Succumbs to Heart Failure.'

Jennie never lived to see Winston become Britain's greatest prime minister, despite having had high hopes of her eldest son. When she died, her sons were devastated. Shane Leslie wrote to Clare that, at the funeral, 'Jack and Winston were like widowers.'[11] Winston many years later kept a cast of his mother's hand on his desk (it had been at Glaslough with the Leslie family, and Leonie's grandson Jack Leslie brought it to Winston in 1948). It was almost identical to Winston's own hand.[12] Moreton summed up their loss in a letter to Leonie: 'God takes her to himself: what a part and a large part she must ever be in the bright visions of your past life & of darling Claras ... the other two of the sisterhood how you both miss her & Clara most of all – because hers had become a lonely life & full of trouble.'[13]

It was an odd existence for the three Frewens left at Brede. Hugh and Memy had now divorced, although she maintained good relations with the family. Romey continued to live at Brede with his grandparents, cared for by his nanny. By 1922, Moreton was almost permanently ill and required constant care. His infirmity was a terrible strain and when Hugh returned, impoverished, from Africa, the household was not a happy place. Oswald decided to study law, and apply for the Bar. Winston, who was again called on to help, provided his cousin with a character reference. Oswald had left a section of his reference form blank and, to his delight, Winston added the statement: 'He is my first cousin & I have been in close touch with him continuously. He was a good officer in the Royal Navy present at several actions, writes well, & has shewn himself a good & devoted son.'[14]

Oswald regularly accompanied his mother to London for periods of respite from Moreton at Brede. Moreton's illness made him believe that he could only use the toilet in his brother's house on the estate at Brickwall and he insisted on being taken there every time he needed to pass a 'motion'. Seeing her ebullient, strong husband so reduced upset and unnerved Clara, and she relied on outings to the Chelsea Flower Show, lunches with Leonie, and tea with friends for relief. Clare, who had returned from America, also spent time with her family in London. By staying at her club and lunching with Leonie or friends and acquaintances, Clara managed to live as though she had money. In fact her financial situation was dire. Hugh had no money at all; as Oswald waspishly wrote, he could not even afford to pay for his own cigarettes and would charge them to the Frewen account at the village store. To make matters worse, Hugh was in love with a girl from a neighbouring village, Rosalind, a local beauty only eighteen years old, who did not know her father, but whose mother's husband was the road-mender. Despite the twenty-year age difference, Hugh secretly married Rosalind in November 1922. Oswald went to enormous lengths to prevent Clara learning of the unsuitable marriage. At the time, Clare was away in Rome, sculpting Mussolini. When, in December, Oswald finally broke news of the marriage to his mother, he explained that Hugh and Rosalind planned to emigrate to Australia and have Romey join them there as soon as possible.

When Clara discovered the deception, she was appalled and refused to meet Rosalind. She wrote her son a letter, referring to the marriage as a tragedy. Oswald also wrote to his brother, stating that his first duty was to his mother, who was too upset to come to see Hugh leave for Australia. A ludicrous day ensued that December in London, just before the couple's departure from England. Shane and Marjorie gave a small reception for them, which Clara and Oswald, who were in London, refused to attend. Leonie had agreed to meet Rosalind and Hugh privately the previous day, but would not attend the party. Although Hugh spent his last day in London trying to see his mother, Clara declined to admit him. As far as she was concerned, not only was Hugh penniless, but he had married a village girl and made the family a laughing stock. Her eldest son left for a new life in Australia without a farewell from either his mother or his brother. Before departing, he did, however, make his peace with his father. Hugh believed that the main reason for their strained relations was Moreton's shame at the debts with which he had encumbered his eldest son. All bitterness was now forgotten: 'We met in a spirit of mutual forgiveness,' Hugh recorded, 'and parted for the last time the best of friends.'[15]

Clara contrived to ignore the worsening situation with Moreton at Brede. His behaviour had become intolerable and he refused to zip up his trousers properly, at Brede or at Brickwall. Still he laboured at his typewriter, working eight hours a day, fighting off bankruptcy writs and trying to earn money from journalism. In the spring of 1922, after he had a minor stroke, Oswald and Clare tried to persuade their mother that he could no longer be cared for at home. Oswald repeatedly tried to explain to Clara that there was not enough money to pay for seven servants to cater for her, Moreton, and Romey. He was appalled by his mother's plan to hire a night nurse as well as a day nurse, at four guineas a week apiece. Oswald and Clare investigated nursing homes and were very worried to learn the cost: twelve guineas a week would leave very little on which to run Brede. Clara's American income had to cover £650 (£18,200 in today's money) a year for the nursing home, £300 (£8,400) for Memy as her divorce settlement,[16] £300 promised to Oswald, as well as Romey's schooling, the servants' salaries, and the upkeep of Brede, not to mention her own personal expenses. It was impossible, yet Clara refused to countenance cutting household costs or finding a nursing home for Moreton. Instead, she bickered with her children and with the nurses, leaving Oswald and Clare to scrape together what they could. Jordan Mott cabled £100 (£2,800) from America, but the amount was insufficient to pay their many debts. Clara refused to worry about money; she had decided that what was important was to secure a knighthood for her husband before he died, and she instructed Oswald to do what was necessary to obtain one.

Finally, in July 1923, Moreton was sent to a home, where the kind nurse who looked after him found him 'hilarious'.[17] This was but one problem solved, however, and as this diary entry shows, Oswald was at his wits' end:

I am here to get Pa out of Brede Place. Ma's income has spent from £1800 to £2100 each half year since Jan. '22, & as it only amounts to £2400 a year at most, it is obvious it cannot go on so. Lord Milner has put up £500, Clara Hatzfeldt £300, the Huntingtons £400, & I £1000 in that time ... Ma is trying, with the frenzy of a she-bear for her whelps, to retain 3 things ... Pa, Brede & Romy [*sic*]. If she were normal she could sell Brede & keep Pa, & possibly even Romy, in a tiny house. But she is 72 & incapable of the effort. Again, if she were rational she would send Romy to Hugh, but she won't. This house would cost all of £400 even to 'shut up', she keeps in it for herself, Pa, Romey, 2 nurses, cook, kitchen maid, housemaid, parlour maid, & nursemaid in permanence, Stone, Edmunds & Walter in attendance on it, Memy, Roger, me & sometimes a guest, periodically. In addition she has made herself legally liable for £300 to Hugh in exchange for his breaking the Innishannon entail on behalf of Pa.[18]

Clara resigned herself finally to the inevitable loss of some of the servants, but not without complaints. She had become bitter and resentful, and Oswald bore the brunt. Hugh was far away in Australia and Clare refused to allow her mother's unhappiness to impinge on her own life. She had just bought a house in Prussia, where Oswald began to join her regularly for trips throughout Europe on his motorcycle, which he named Satanella. Clare indulged her wanderlust, moving to Constantinople in 1924, and then to Algiers the following year. Oswald travelled with his sister when he could, on much-needed breaks from the terrible financial situation at Brede. In November 1923, Oswald received a letter from the bank, stating that the Frewen account was overdrawn by £807 (over £22,000); he negotiated a further overdraft and Clare gave him £200 (£5,600) to help. It was then that Marshall, who was still the family solicitor, delivered his bombshell to Oswald: his father owed over £100,000 (nearly £3 million), with creditors all over the world, and there was no hope of further credit. It was only a matter of time before the money completely ran out. Brede would have to be sold.

Time had run out for Moreton, too, and he died quietly in September 1924, aged seventy-one. It was not unexpected, and his death came as a relief to the family. Clara was without her children for the funeral, as both Oswald and Clare were motorcycling across the Ukraine and could not be reached in time. When Moreton was a child, a phrenologist had fingered his skull and deduced: 'large self-confidence and very little regard to what others say or think of him. Energy to outstrip his fellowmen in any dangerous or hazardous pursuit.' In a prescient assessment, he added: 'And when speaking he will draw a graphic and vivid description of things he has heard and seen and paint them in glowing colours.'[19] Moreton had lived a life in which joy and expectation had always been followed by sorrow and disappointment. Clara had been his partner for better or very much worse for over forty years. 'My poor darling went home last night,' she wrote to Leonie on 2 September 1924. Clara was always more concerned with posterity than the event itself: 'He looks so beautiful I can't tell you what a memory it will be for always.' Leonie had to send her seventy-three-year-old sister, who signed her letter 'your stricken but courageous old Clara,'[20] the money to settle her hotel bill.

Brede was all that was left to Clara. Her main preoccupation for some years had been to hold onto it, despite Oswald's firm insistence that it would have to be sold. Clara continued her steadfast refusal to acknowledge the severity of her financial situation. It was easier to criticize her children; she also began to blame Moreton for taking her money.[21] All her life Clara had been spoiled and had successfully ignored unpleasantness. She would likewise ignore the necessity of quitting Brede. In November, just after Moreton's death, Oswald discovered that his mother had spent an additional £228 (over £6,000), which she could not account for – leaving them £730 (over £20,000) overdrawn and with the maids' wages unpaid. He gave notice immediately to the housemaid, parlourmaid, and cook. By his calculations, they owed £1,270 (more than £35,000). Oswald decided that the house at Brede should be temporarily shut up on 1 December 1924.

Clara was sent to winter in Switzerland with Romey, returning the following April. The Frewens had become paupers; Travers Jerome (Leonard's nephew and Clara's first cousin) sent them $1,000 (worth about £7,500 today) from America in July 1925, and Clare sent money when she could from her house in the desert at Biskra in Algeria, where she was living with her children.

But the difficulties did not end there. Hugh was struggling with his second family in Australia, during a depression. He did not have enough money for food, clothing, or even medical emergencies, and was pathetically grateful for the small cheques that Shane and Clare sent as often as they could. In February 1928, he cabled requesting urgent help as they were destitute after floods. Oswald was furious, but Clara insisted that they cable £20 (£830 in today's money) and arrange a guarantee with Marshall as Hugh had asked. It was many years before Hugh's situation improved. Clare's earnings from art and letters left her somewhat better off, even though she had two children to support. Oswald, who had been unable to translate his legal qualification into a lucrative career, finding his independent nature uncomfortably curbed by the discipline exercised by his firm, was left running Brede on a shoestring and coping with his increasingly querulous mother (who refused to sell the house). He managed to generate some income through his writing, but it was insufficient to run the household.

Clara's life now assumed a pattern: winters were spent in Switzerland, at the Hôtel Richelieu or Hôtel Bristol, to save money on upkeep at Brede and to avoid paying tax on her American money in Britain. There, she looked after the three boys who were at boarding school at Glion sur Montreux: Hugh and Memy's son Roger, Clare's son Dick Sheridan, and Shane's son Jack Leslie. Although she enjoyed seeing the children, Clara resented being away from Brede and moaned constantly to Oswald (and others) that she was being 'forced' into exile. Romey was finally sent to Australia in November 1925 to join his father and family, and would never see his adoring grandmother again.

Clara could not understand that these harsh measures were the only way to keep Brede and she accused Oswald of unreasonable financial stringency. She even told Leonie that he mistreated her. Her sister helped as best she could, sending her money and gifts whenever possible. Leonie herself, however, was not well off, as much of the capital that the Leslies had received from selling their land had been invested, on their friend Sir Ernest Cassel's advice, in Russian shares, which had become worthless after the revolution. The Leslie family finances never recovered from this setback. Clara complained, but she also had adventures; she went on trips with Oswald, who wrote travel articles for newspapers and magazines, and she visited Clare in her desert home at Biskra – decrying the entire time the heat, the food, and the lack of comforts. In spite of their continued differences, Clare was faithful to her mother and often invited her to visit. They were frequently at odds over their attitudes to money. Clare had been shaken at Wilfred's death to find herself practically destitute with two young children and she never forgave those who failed to help her at that time, including her father. She also resented her mother's lifelong assumption that she was entitled to a luxurious life, free from financial anxiety. Clare did not hesitate to air her views and favoured a very direct approach with her mother. 'Well you ought to be pleased to think you have been of use this winter!' she wrote in February 1927, adding:

> It is not often you can help, but you <u>have</u> helped tremendously … I
> expect you are rather glad to be back in Suisse, where there are fewer
> expenses, less 'living-up' to rich friends – etc. The Motts to whom I
> telegraphed twice on your acc. never answered a word or sent love. I
> expect you have given me & Peter [Oswald] dreadful reputations to all
> your friends – & they think we are neglectful brutes, who take all your
> money whereas if they knew the truth, & of how Peter is struggling to
> borrow money for you to live on – etc – & as for me – no one helps
> me. I am as you know, as I have been for 11 years living on my wits –
> & I can only manage to fend for myself & my children – & whatever
> my 'duties' may be to my mother I am unable to attend to them.[22]

In February 1928 more of the furniture at Brede had to be sold. Oswald noted that Clara wept at parting from items that had once belonged to her mother and to Jennie. The French pieces were now gone – as were the remains of the great Jerome fortune. Clara, although in poor health, travelled regularly to Glaslough to see Leonie and to save money. She had been having trouble with her eyes for some time and later in 1928, while she was in Ireland, her bad eye became worse. She had to have an operation, during which it was removed. This was an improvement, as the pain in the defective eye had produced strain in the other, resulting in poor sight. Oswald asked Winston, now

Chancellor of the Exchequer, to send her a telegram. Winston, ever considerate to his aunt, wrote her a letter from the Chancellor's Office at 11 Downing Street, telling her how pleased he was to hear that her eyesight had improved overall as a result of the operation. Clara returned to Brede in January 1929 with Barney, a female servant paid by Leonie to help Clara manage the household. Within a week, Barney wrote to Leonie, informing her that she wished to give notice. Clara demanded to know why and Oswald recorded the reply in his diary:

> Ma demanded her reasons in detail, & after persisting, got them. Barney declines to be spoken to like a dog. To which Ma says 'I can never have been rude to you, it was *you* who were rude to me, I'm famous for being so sweet' … Leonie had, I think 'arranged' that Barney should 'run' Brede at 'so much per week'. It might be done, of course, especially if, as Ma has told Barney, there were no debts in the world & Ma had £1000 a year clear. But as, in addition to $5,000 to Jim Dennis, there is £475 owing to Memy & £88 in local bills, & £375 in Income Tax, and £16 in the Bank to meet it with, Barney doesn't feel it is a fair deal. In case this & the cold of Brede were really behind Barney's resignation I said 'Would you care to try living abroad with Ma on so much a week?' to which Barney replied 'I couldn't live with her under any circumstances.' The fact is that Ma is too strong to be treated as an 'old lady', she will demand, in an XVIII Cent. [Eighteenth-Century] way, unremitting service throughout the day – literally. May shall hold her face towel while she washes her face, Barney shall read to her, or write at dictation all the morning. Even while she's playing patience Barney must be in the room with her.[23]

Clara's letters to Oswald were alternately threatening and cajoling: 'Brede, Brede was everything to me,' she wrote, 'oh how I long for it so – Can't it be?' She then continued: 'We could live so happily – & I know Leonie wd contribute.'[24] When these pleas were resisted, she accused Oswald of stealing from her, leading Leonie to suggest that Winston should audit their accounts. By now Oswald was at the end of his tether. Mother and son lived a precarious, beleaguered existence, punctuated with moments of affection. In May 1930, Winston came to tea and, to Clara's delight, planted a tree in her 'celebrity' tree grove. As they walked back to the house, Oswald told his cousin that this was the first visit he had ever made to Brede. Oswald was 'shattered' by his 'simple answer': 'My dear Oswald, it's the first time I've been asked!' Oswald was further surprised by his cousin: 'when I said I wanted to write mornings & go & look after my fields etc. afternoons, he countered "No, it's the other way about; *I* lay bricks all day & write in the evenings" – "Oh, I <u>can't</u> write when I'm tired", I said – "And <u>I</u> can't write when I'm sober" retorted the Great Man!'[25]

These happy occasions were rare. In June 1930, Clara complained about their financial situation to the family solicitor. Oswald countered by trying to explain to her how little money there was – he was building a small house on the property for himself that would be inexpensive to run. He pointed out that they could not afford the staff nor the maintenance at Brede, nor could they pay their income tax, especially as Clara had been spending money on 'jaunts' up to London. The discussions were frequent and bitter. Oswald was depressed and Clare was exasperated; she accused her mother of being responsible for her own financial predicament and continually proposed that Clara give up Brede altogether and live with her, thus saving them both money. Clara refused, which made Clare furious: 'You have a genius for making a martyr of your self & helping no one,'[26] she wrote in February 1932. Clare was also worried about Hugh – she had received a letter in January 1932, saying that he was living in a tent, on the dole, growing potatoes.

Clara did still have some moments of happiness: occasional fond letters from Clare, a trip taken on a motorcycle with Oswald, letters and gifts of dainty food and embroidered handkerchiefs sent with love from Leonie. In August 1933, Oswald, Clara, and Hugh's son Roger travelled to Paris for a holiday and to spend Christmas with Clare, who was living there. While in Paris in April the following year, eighty-three-year-old Clara had a heart attack and was rushed to the American Hospital in Neuilly. Oswald travelled to France immediately and took her back to Brede. Because of the damage to her heart, she could not stay there so, in spite of her protestations, Oswald transferred her to a nursing home in St Leonards in Sussex. Clara was still obsessed at the thought of losing Brede and in December 1934 demanded Oswald's promise that he would never sell it, adding, 'Well anyway you won't sell it while I'm alive.'[27]

Clara's heart was weak and she lingered on for a few weeks only. She died peacefully a month later, in the nursing home, on 20 January 1935. There was a flattering amount of attention paid to her passing, which was in some ways the passing of an era. A notice in *The Times*, an obituary in the *Daily Telegraph*, and many letters referred to her life as an example of Victorian social history: her early days in the West and as a prominent society hostess in the 1890s. References were made to her famous daughter, Clare Sheridan, as well as to her restoration of Brede. The notice in the Peterborough column of the *Daily Telegraph* summed up her life: 'Mrs. Frewen never took quite the same prominent place in society as her more brilliant sisters. She was, however, a well-known figure in the political and social circles of her time.'[28] Clara's death was the end of a way of life for her long-tried youngest son, who wrote bleakly of the funeral in his diary on 22 January 1935: 'And it was borne on me that I was not only burying my Mother, but Brede Place.'[29]

Leonie was now the last survivor of the Jerome sisters. Her life had been more comfortable than Clara's, but it had not been easy. Ireland had recently been dominated by violence, begun during the War of Independence of 1919–21. It was not until December 1921 that a treaty was signed, partitioning the country and giving twenty-six counties independence. The six counties of Ulster were granted their own parliament in Belfast in 1920 and remained within the United Kingdom, reflecting the wishes of the Protestant majority who lived there. The establishment of the Irish Free State was, however, opposed by many. There followed a civil war between the new government of Ireland and those against the treaty, led by Eamon de Valera, who rejected the partial surrender evidenced by partition. He and other hardliners fought for a unified, independent Ireland. The civil war, which ended in May 1923, was a brutal beginning to independence, claiming the lives of many Irishmen. This brief, ugly war would have enormous political repercussions, determining alliances and attitudes for years to come.

The conflict made life extremely difficult for those who lived in Ireland, as Marjorie Leslie discovered. She had moved from America to Glaslough with Shane and their two children after the war. In 1920, she took her daughter Anita to a golfing and seaside resort in Bundoran, in Donegal, some seventy miles away from the Leslie estate. When they arrived, they discovered that there were no staff at the large hotel and that a black hand had been painted over the entrance: a Sinn Féin warning to leave the premises. The night that they arrived, the train station at Bundoran was blown up, leaving Marjorie and the other guests stranded in the town. Anita later wrote that her mother had tried to find a telegraph office, but the post office and all the shops were closed. There were no trains running and no means of sending a message. The following day, a house was burned down in the town. Soon after their return to Glaslough, Marjorie left for London with her children. Ireland was now considered 'dangerous for children', but Jack Leslie resolutely stayed on. All around him, the big houses were being torched, but he refused to be intimidated. Leonie supported him.

Throughout these black times, Shane and his father disagreed politically. Sir Jack was a Protestant landlord of the old school, benevolent but conservative, respected by all who knew him. Family lore has it that in 1920 some armed men were parading in Glaslough village and, when told of this, Sir Jack strode down to inspect them. As the oldest living British Grenadier officer, he took it upon himself to compliment what he assumed were Ulster Volunteers on their turnout. Sir Jack was deaf and notoriously vague, so he never noticed that the lads were IRA commandos. They were apparently so bemused by the courteous gentleman that they left him and the estate alone. Shane was a Catholic and an ardent Nationalist, yet he and his conservative father contrived to live together amicably, arguing but not fighting. During 1921–2, Shane was involved in the peace talks between Michael Collins and the British negotiators, held at Sir John Lavery's studio. The Leslie family claim that Winston Churchill, a friend of both Michael Collins and the Laverys, pressed for a commitment from Collins that his favourite aunt's house would never be a target for the arsonists. Whatever the reason, the Leslie family home at Glaslough still stands.

While all around her was chaos, Leonie maintained calm in her home. None of their servants left and life in the big house continued much as if no battles raged outside its protective walls. Leonie was unimpressed by the polemical politics around her and remained pragmatic. Always a moderate, she advised caution and restraint. She had softened her position on Home Rule and unlike her husband had refused to sign the Covenant. When Jennie and others in London criticized the Unionists, however, she defended her adopted homeland.

Leonie's lifelong motto of 'cache ton jeu' (hide your game) was applied particularly to the political troubles in Ireland, where discretion could help keep one's house standing and one's life safe. She still maintained a vivid interest in the world around her and felt constrained within the narrow horizons of Glaslough. Throughout her married life she had enjoyed the gaiety and intrigues of London and Paris, alongside the pastoral charm of Ireland. Now that she was increasingly restricted to County Monaghan (although they still had the house in London on Cumberland Place), she was bored and longed for society outings and friendships. Although initially shocked, she took vicarious pleasure in her niece Clare's escapades.

Clare, in her capacity as a journalist, was present in Dublin when the Irish civil war began in June 1922. The war was fought between two factions of the republican movement that disagreed over acceptance of the Anglo-Irish treaty of 1921, which was widely supported by the population. The pro-treaty side was led by Michael Collins, who became chairman and Minister for Finance of the Provisional Government, responsible for the establishment of the new Irish state (the Free State). The majority of the IRA were, however, against the treaty and became known as the Irregulars. They established a number of armed strongholds in Dublin, including the Four Courts building, which housed the state's Supreme Court and High Court, as well as many of its public records. On 28 June, the Free State forces, which had been set up with the help of the British government and were led by their commander-in-chief Michael Collins, launched an attack on the Four Courts and other buildings occupied by diehard republicans. They captured the republican positions in the city, although when engagements of this type were repeated throughout the country it led to a guerrilla war. Michael Collins was killed on 22 August 1922 during an inspection tour of the South. The conflict was finally won by the Free State government in April 1923, when the republicans gave up their arms (but not their objections to the new state). When Clare later discussed the destruction of Ireland's historical documents with Winston, he commented: 'Well a State without archives is better than archives without a State.'[30]

Leonie introduced Clare to her many influential friends, such as Lord D'Abernon, the financier and art collector who became Britain's Ambassador to Germany; Fridtjof Nansen, the famous oceanographer and now Norwegian delegate to the League of Nations;[31] and Count Mensdorff, the Austrian delegate to the League, who had been the Austro-Hungarian Ambassador to Britain before the war. Clare wrote from Geneva, where she was composing articles for the New York newspaper *N.Y. World*, thanking her aunt for introductions to these important men who had granted interviews to their dear friend's niece. Clare shared her aunt's ability to observe dispassionately. On the murder of Michael Collins, she wrote: 'I couldn't believe it. But – it fulfils what I wrote in an article, that the Irish historical record is one of murder & treachery, & disloyalty. And in the end they always sacrifice their chiefs.'[32] Shane's wife Marjorie was shocked at Clare's response to the tragedies she witnessed and did not care for her. Clare, untroubled, would comment frequently that none of the younger women in the family liked her. Leonie, however, was always a close ally. She understood Clare's need for stimulation, because she shared it. When the Four Courts fell in Dublin, with all the bloodshed, Leonie had just arrived by train from Glaslough, where she was meant to be resting following the diagnosis of a heart tremor. Clare was horrified to see her, but Leonie insisted that the boredom would kill her. She had been at Castle Leslie for two months, she declared, and needed distractions. They hired a jaunting car (a horse-drawn carriage) to follow the angry crowds around the city, then adjourned to the Shelbourne Hotel for a restorative cup of tea.

The upheavals convulsing the country encroached on the Leslies directly. The Leslie lodge at Pettigo, where Leonie had once so proudly entertained the duke, was forcibly occupied by Sinn Féin, who left it in a filthy state. The lodge was then commandeered by the Staffordshire Regiment, who mounted a wireless apparatus on the roof. Sir Jack wrote to Shane that at Pettigo religious hatred was 'worse than ever'. He distracted himself by painting and playing lawn tennis. Leonie, he wrote, was 'courageous but fidgety & argumentative otherwise very well'.[33] To add to their difficulties, some of the Leslie land documents had been destroyed in the Four Courts, which further delayed payments owed to them for land bought fourteen years previously. Jack and Leonie decided to take a holiday in Wales to forget the violence around them and to allow Leonie to recuperate from her heart complaint. She was tired and anxious, writing to Marjorie: 'It seems mean to be here in England, safe, & among happy people. I left so many desperately unhappy people in Ireland – it is all so terrible & sad over there – such a nightmare. Everyone I saw, broken hearted – or terrified.'[34]

Leonie's pragmatism extended to the changes that took place around her. When she stayed at the Viceregal Lodge in Dublin in 1922, she remembered the days when she had danced at the castle and felt 'happy and young!' The place was full of memories, she wrote to Marjorie, '& now it has been handed over to Mr Collins! Well – the old order passes – one must hope the new order will be good for the good of all.'[35] Like many people, she had been saddened by the murder of this handsome and charismatic leader. Hugh echoed the thoughts of countless British when he wrote to Shane that they were 'all overcome with horror at the death of Michael Collins. What is to be the fate I wonder of this vindictive, headstrong and undisciplined people? Charming, brilliant, and emotional, they seem wanting in every essential of cohesion or ordered government.'[36]

Leonie believed, like her husband, that they must endure the difficulties, which for years they did. In many ways life continued at Castle Leslie as before. A few servants were let go, grounds were no longer maintained, and standards in general were not quite as high, but their lifestyle was still quite comfortable. Leonie took breakfast in bed, brought to her by her maid. Like her nephew Winston, she would stay there for most of the morning, going though her mail and writing letters. Leonie was a prolific correspondent. She took interest in both the general and the detailed events of her day, the personal as well as the political. However, she did not share in her letters any thoughts that could damage the family. Although she had inherited the Jerome temper – her outbursts were known as 'tantrums' at Glaslough – she never stayed angry for long and usually controlled her feelings with iron mastery.

In 1928, Clare published her autobiography, *Nuda Veritas*, in which she wrote of her aunt that she 'was more tolerant than Jennie, a strange mixture of the worldly and the philosophical'. Clare loved Aunt Leonie but was also able to observe her dispassionately:

> In public she was witty and brilliant. Alone with me she was almost a sage disguised; she gave me 'direction' and saved me from drifting along the path of doubt and cynicism. Her advice was profound. I thought she might have been a very great woman had she had the chance or had she trusted herself. But the world had either buffeted her too much, or perhaps not enough. She had led a strangely repressed life, but she was too proud to resent it and had too much humour for self pity.[37]

Leonie overlooked the transgression implicit in the memoir's publication because she liked hearing about Clare's successes. She also took pleasure in Winston's political achievements. She was thrilled when he was made Chancellor of the Exchequer in 1924. The whole family was impressed, and Clare wrote to Leonie from Constantinople, where she was living, 'I was so interested about Winston. Of course he <u>is</u> a very loveable person.'[38] Leonie admired Winston but continued to find her own eldest son exasperating.

Shane was a talented writer and a good poet, and his political efforts had helped the cause of Irish nationalism, yet little that he did impressed his mother. She was, by contrast, fond of Marjorie, who was pretty and fashionable, keen on parties and society. When Leonie learned in 1925 that her son and his wife were experiencing marital difficulties, she reprimanded her son and encouraged him to make more of an effort to please his wife. Shane, no longer the ascetic he had once been, had engaged in some rather wild entertaining in London during his wife's absence, at which Tallulah Bankhead was a favourite and frequent guest. A handsome and lively raconteur, renowned for his high spirits and clever wit, Shane was much in demand in 1920s London society. At first, Marjorie was only too happy at this transformation in her husband, who had previously been so preoccupied in the engine room of Irish politics. She loved to dance, and her long legs were shown to greater advantage as skirts grew shorter and heels higher. Shane's many female admirers were, however, hard for her to bear, as were his obvious attentions at parties to what she called his 'band of alley cats'.[39] She was jealous, and he was not prepared to curb his excesses.

Leonie disapproved strongly of divorce, as her granddaughter later wrote:

> Our grandmother Leonie was appalled at the word divorce, not for religious, but for social reasons. She had been reared in an era when the revelation of marital unhappiness was considered disgraceful. Whatever happened, the outer forms must be adhered to for the family's sake. And after a lifetime of careful watching, Granny Leonie had formed the opinion that the most uncongenial temperaments could adjust as soldiers do to enforced companionship. She upheld the old Edwardian principles that within the iron strictness of social demands humans remained human. They must be allowed freedom for disciplined amours that upset no one. Divorce upset everyone. The

family was riven. Children knew. Servants gave notice.[40]

Marjorie, who felt that action was called for, left her husband and moved with her three children, Anita, Jack, and Desmond, to Paris early in 1925. She was grateful to have her mother-in-law so clearly on her side. 'I find him <u>much</u> changed – very sweet and nice,' she reported to Leonie from Paris in February 1925 when Shane had come to see her, 'and best of all <u>self-controlled</u>.' The couple had had some good talks, she said, and discovered that his 'casual treatment' of her at parties, which she resented, was at the root of their troubles. If he could just be 'considerate of me publicly', they could get on perfectly. She was glad that she had let Shane visit her in Paris, Marjorie continued, 'in spite of rather amusing but painful complications here. Yes – it is indeed hectic!'[41] Further accounts were sent from Paris. Marjorie took Leonie very much into her confidence and kept her informed of developments: Shane had come and gone and was now taking a 'walking holiday' – across Hungary! She needed her adored Leonie's counsel:

> I don't know <u>what</u> Shane is doing. He tells me nothing in his occasional letters. It is a rather unsettled and unsatisfactory condition – as I can't see any definite life for the future – and I do want to get settled somewhere. Anyway – this playing hard and being flattered – just to forget is all very well – but I am not built that way to have that satisfy me indefinitely. What do you think? If he only knew – & cared – enough to put up a good fight & get me back – it would be so different.[42]

Leonie advised patience. Shane was much better now, she told Marjorie, and his lady friends were 'harmless'.[43] The couple were reconciled and Marjorie moved back to London at the end of 1925, taking the children with her.

The wild parties now began again in earnest. Anita recalled a 'Baby Party' with a costume theme for the adult guests. Her mother wore a romper suit and her father was arrayed in one of his daughter's nightgowns, which had been torn and stitched over his shirt and shorts, with blue ribbons tied on the shoulders and a blue sash round his waist.

That night, Shane came home in an ambulance. Although he never touched alcohol, festivities and the presence of others made him exuberant. In the course of rollicking party games, he had mimicked a child taking diving lessons while standing on a table. He had slipped and broken his collarbone.[44] The injury failed to slow the couple down and they continued to enjoy an active social life. During the day, Shane worked hard at his writing. In addition to his poetry, he published novels at this time: *Doomsland*, about his Irish childhood; *The Oppidan*, about Eton College; and *The Cantab*, about his experiences at Cambridge University.

Leonie took a close interest in her son's marriage, because she saw it as her responsibility to ensure that he did nothing foolish or regrettable. In addition, she was responsible for the couple's finances. When Marjorie had left for Paris in 1925 to decide whether or not to divorce Shane, Leonie had corresponded with her over the monetary arrangements.

> Will do finance as you suggest. I suggested [to Shane] you should agree on his drawing cheques on Lloyds up to £200 in a year – (at the rate of £50 in 3 months as his writing is precarious). As he gets £750 from U.S. from me – that leaves you £550 – from him.
>
> Do you think that fair? You have the £550 & yr own money & keep the children as you have full control over them. They can stay with Shane at Glaslough 2 or 3 months in the summer, you being very welcome any time you can come.[45]

But although Shane and Marjorie were reunited, their marriage was no longer an entirely happy one. As Leonie had advised, they settled down together in London to make the best of things, but there were regular outbursts. Not everyone in the family felt that Leonie's influence was benign. Clare, in particular, believed that emotional honesty was more important than maintaining appearances. In September 1931, she wrote to Shane from Brede before returning to the North African desert:

> I have seen Marjorie & heard her outpourings, & your Mother & hers. I have told your mother that I think it is very immoral of her to try &

hold you together against your wills. Both she & Marjorie have ruined you. Your mother crushed your political career & your wife your literary career not that your literary career hasn't been successful, but it has nearly cost you your reason. Both of you will be happier apart, you ought to devote all your thought to your work & live in the clouds of your imagination, forget that you were ever married & count the world well lost.[46]

Leonie, on the other hand, believed in maintaining relationships, even after the fire of passion had been extinguished.

Her own marriage was warm and courteous without being passionate. In 1917, the Duke of Connaught had turned to Leonie for comfort when he had lost his wife. Throughout the next twenty-five years they remained intimate and the duke never remarried. When he retired in 1921 to a villa at Cap Ferrat in the South of France, Leonie travelled to see him there and bask in the sunshine in the lovely gardens. She and Lady Essex, who lived near by, helped him to choose the chintzes for his new home. Leonie closely followed the duke's friendships with the other ladies whose company he enjoyed and was prone to possessiveness when he seemed to favour one in particular. According to Anita Leslie, she would rapidly depart for his villa whenever there were signs of an intimacy developing between him and one of his lady friends, in order to prevent an unsuitable alliance.[47] After a rather uncharacteristic outburst of hers, he wrote to her, declaring that his feelings for her were 'those of the most intense affection, the deepest sympathy and the greatest respect'.[48]

According to his biographer, Noble Frankland,[49] the duke cultivated many friendships and flirtations with the American women who caught his eye: 'Prince Arthur [the duke] knew that he had many faults and that among them was his tendency to keep falling in love. Probably Leonie, inadvertently, was herself partly to blame for this. Her absolute discretion … her patience and tact and her wisdom and reliability may have so far enhanced Prince Arthur's instinctive liking for American women, as to tempt him to trust them all.'[50] As well as being a frequent visitor to the duke at his home in France, Leonie also regularly attended dinner parties with the duke when he was in London. Up until the 1930s, the duke sent his electric brougham (carriage) once or twice a week to collect her for dinner at Clarence House. She often found these dinners rather dull, especially when only members of the royal family were present. On these occasions stiff formality was observed, and the next day she was often heard to murmur: 'Rather hard work – such silence – all Royals except me.'[51] From 1898 to 1936 she spent nearly every Whitsun at the duke's home at Bagshot Park in Surrey. A loving correspondence between them continued for years, but by 1930, Leonie had started to find the seventy-year-old duke's company less entertaining. Although only ten years older than she, he became very slow and deaf, whilst Leonie, who remained trim and sprightly, revelled in the company of smart young men such as Somerset Maugham and Noël Coward.

But Leonie had not spent all those years drumming a sense of duty into everyone in her orbit only to abandon her old friend, especially royalty, simply because she was not amused. Without the patina of power and prestige, the duke was just someone whose society had become rather dull. When accompanying her on one of these 'slightly soporific' duty calls, her granddaughter saw how irritable Leonie became and believed that she was indeed bored by the duke.[52] During the visit, Anita admired his tartan dressing gown and later expressed a desire for one herself. Her grandmother responded sharply: 'You'll do no such thing, nothing looks shabbier than tartan. We're all sick of that old dressing-gown. He is so obstinate about it.' Following her grandmother's fit of pique, Anita wryly commented: 'For once her advice had not been taken.'[53]

CHAPTER FIFTEEN

Four Roses from Four Sons

Despite the frustrations of her relationship with the ageing duke, Leonie continued to take pleasure in the triumphs of her friends and family. In 1933, her close friend, Frances Horner, published her book of memoirs, *Time Remembered*, and Leonie wrote enthusiastically to congratulate her. She looked forward to seeing her in London, she wrote: 'What a lovely talk we will have in front of the fire.'[1] She still received guests at home in Glaslough, and welcomed her children and grand-children there. Her neighbours, Lady Caledon and her sister Lady Charlotte, often visited Leonie. However, after 1923 and the division between the Irish Free State and the Six Counties of Ulster, the Caledons lived in a different country. Part of the five-mile wall that ran around the Leslie estate (which was in the Irish Free State) was now a border. This border was on bog land and beyond it was Northern Ireland, part of Great Britain and thus under different laws, with different currency, stamps, and food prices. The bog itself was a political boundary and ordinary citizens were restricted – whether walking, bicycling, or riding a horse – to using a little adjoining 'unauthorized road' between the two estates. Only priests and doctors were permitted to drive cars along it. This was the reality of the division of Ireland in 1923. Societal attitudes were slower to change. Anita Leslie remembered that Lady Caledon travelled by train to London, grandly refusing to buy a ticket from the bewildered ticket collectors, and would give vague explanations that the train ran through Caledon land. Moreton and Clara used a similar argument to travel to London by train from their local station, Robertsbridge; they bought third-class tickets, if indeed they purchased tickets at all, but would sit in a first-class carriage. For years, Moreton's surprise and affront were apparently sufficient to send the hapless ticket collectors scurrying.

Life at Glaslough was not as grand as it had been in its heyday of Lady Constance and Sir Jack, but Leonie and Jack still lived in considerable style. Clare Sheridan's daughter Margaret remembered staying there and recollected with some wonderment that after breakfast at 'The Big House', the head gardener, Mr Bryce, would arrive to enquire which dress her ladyship intended to wear for dinner, so that the flowers in the dining room, picked from the garden and arranged daily, might match the colour of her outfit. Leonie and Jack clung to these traditions while embracing modern conveniences such as electricity (installed in 1919) and gramophones. Visitors often felt that they were walking into another, more tranquil and more civilized era. The grand piano, together with leather-bound books of music, occupied a room filled with Italian paintings, facing the beautiful lake. Grapes and peaches grew in the hothouses, and sweet-smelling lilies and heliotrope grew in the gardens, which were surrounded by fields and woods. For many, Glaslough was an enchanted castle where time stood still. The Leslies were proud of their demesne and of their long tradition in Ireland. This independence had been celebrated by their family for centuries; a list found of all the landowners who had been ready to accept bribes and peerages if they voted for the Union of 1800 (forced through by George III) recorded that Mr Leslie had resisted any such inducements. Against the name of the unbribable Mr Leslie of Glaslough the king's agent had recorded: 'Wants Nothing.'

Friends and family were as ever the most important fixture in Leonie's life. Days with Winston were a special treat. He loved spending time with his family and truly relaxed when they were all together. Leonie wrote to Marjorie of a happy day of frost and bright sun, spent with him and Clemmie, together with Goonie, Jack, and all the children, at Chartwell, Winston's country house: 'After luncheon Jack C. & Winston cut down trees, & came in exhausted to tea – after which we all danced with the children & played hunt the slipper. Winston is charming in his own home – the House is very comfortable – & the views, over the valley (their own valley) very beautiful today.'[2]

London was as ever an attractive alternative to rural life at Glaslough. As finances were still a constant concern (Leonie's American income was crucial to their lifestyle), the large London house at Cumberland Place eventually had to be sold. Jack and Leonie bought a smaller house and then, later, a two-storey flat on Eaton Square. Leonie, aged sixty-six in 1925, still slim and energetic, attended London parties and social events with relish. She was proud of her sash and the decorations that she wore on her bosom, in particular the Order of St John of Jerusalem, which she had received in 1920, in recognition of her contributions to charitable works. She still loved lively society and would divert money that was badly needed to make repairs on the estate to pay for metropolitan amusements. Like Lady Constance, she held onto her small luxuries for as long as she could, enjoying tea parties and trips to Paris well into her seventies. She was particularly devoted to embassy parties, which were in full swing until diplomatic tensions grew in the 1930s. Leonie stopped attending receptions at the German Embassy when the charming Baron Hoesch was replaced by the far less aristocratic Joachim von Ribbentrop, who threw lavish events for which huge bouquets and luxuries would be flown in specially.

Her many letters to Marjorie were encouraging. 'I hear of you looking very beautiful,' she wrote, 'so I know things are right. Nobody's life is "all smooth" and I think you have as much [*sic*] good things … as anyone I know – & you enjoy life.'[3] Leonie hoped that Shane and Marjorie would learn to accommodate one another. Compromises in a marriage could be made, she firmly believed, and the façade maintained. Unfortunately, Seymour was still unsettled. He had left England at the end of the war to work for the manufacturer Vickers in Spain, selling buses built on site from leftover parts. In 1923, he returned to London and then left for the Soviet Union to sell grain elevators to the

Russian government. On his return he opened a small specialist bookshop in London, called the Chelsea Book Club. He also spent time writing and his avant-garde novel, *The Silent Queen*, was published by Jonathan Cape in 1927. Leonie, whilst proud of her son's accomplishment, was less than keen on its subject; the eponymous 'silent queen' was in fact a noiseless lavatory, invented by an American millionaire, and the novel described many of the Leslies' friends and acquaintances. Although the reviews were favourable, Seymour had no desire to write another novel.

Leonie was equally unimpressed with Seymour's next venture. In 1927, he became a fund-raiser for Queen Charlotte's Maternity Hospital, then a small and little-known institution. After his novel was published, he had struggled to find work. Although he had answered the hospital's job advertisement in *The Times*, he assumed that, with no experience, he would never get the post so after the interview he crept quietly home, only to discover that the board had telephoned to offer him the position. Leonie's response was typical, described here beautifully by her son:

> My mother had just replaced the receiver and turned to me, mingled amusement and concern on her face. 'The Lying-In Hospital has just rung you up. Oh my <u>dear</u>, what on earth have you been up to? But of course it's obvious! Why didn't you tell me sooner? Our doctor may know of someone who could arrange to prevent, if it is not too late? But are you sure it isn't a trick to get money?' and already Leonie was revelling in the contemplation of yet a new family crisis, one of those 'Mysteries' of hers.[4]

She was relieved to hear the explanation, but not altogether pleased about the job, which she was glad to hear was only for three months, saying 'No one need know.'[5] In fact, Seymour stayed on for twenty-five years, during which time he played an essential part in building London's first large maternity hospital. He was key in raising the finance that allowed the breakthrough in antibiotic treatment that would save thousands of lives.

He was further inspired to revive 'Queen Charlotte's Birthday' as a modern fund-raising ball in 1932. George III had begun the tradition of a birthday ball around 1780, to celebrate his wife's birthday on 19 May.[6] Lady Howard de Walden, a member of Seymour's committee, thought it a splendid idea and suggested that twelve debutantes, dressed in white, should enter, pulling a giant cake lit by 188 electric candles (one for each year since Charlotte's birth in 1744). The ball was a huge success and soon became a tradition; over the years the number of debutantes increased from 12 to 240. More than any other subscription ball, Queen Charlotte's Birthday became a fixture in the London social calendar. Seymour, now happily established in his job, also wrote a column about London society for *Vogue*, entitled 'Our Lives from Day to Day', tongue firmly in cheek.

Leonie was more pleased when Seymour decided in 1929 to marry the Yorkshire-born Gwynneth Rawdon (known as 'Timmie') whom she liked very much. She wrote to her sister Clara that her son had 'chosen very wisely'. Timmie was, she said, 'your & my sort − & very unselfish − & very pretty − & rather old fashioned'.[7] The couple had settled sensibly in a small and cosy flat in London and Leonie approved of the young people living within their means. Glaslough was, of course, always available to Leonie's children and their families for restful holidays. The birth in 1930 of Seymour and Timmie's daughter Jennifer added to Leonie's satisfaction that her exuberant son had finally settled down.

Lionel, who was very much younger than his three brothers, was proving to be more of a problem. Shane and Norman had left home when he was still very small, and Seymour had lived apart from the family because of his illness. Spoiled and quite undisciplined, Lionel was sent down from Eton for being 'unteachable'. The final straw was a poem that so enraged his teacher that his pen split the page in two while he was marking it in disgust. The offending piece ran:

Juzz buzz Fuzz
Fuzz Buzz Wuzz.[8]

It was conspicuously very far from the academic achievements of the talented brothers who had preceded him. Leonie hired a tutor and suggested forestry as a career. She was at her most tender in the letter that she wrote to Lionel after it became clear that he would have to leave Eton:

> Lionel Darling
>
> Thank you for your nice letter. I am sure you have tried to work – and if you have not succeeded, it is that you need more help in yr work, like Mr Thorn's supervision, so I think you will have to leave Eton, and go to some nice place in the country with a tutor. Let me know when you come up for Long Leave. We will talk over these plans for the future – and I am quite sure we will find some honourable occupation for you when you are older, to work hard at. It would be interesting to learn about Forestry wouldn't it? I am longing to see you again and give you a good hug. I hear the Dogs are well at Glaslough. I am hoping we can take you there with the tutor for Xmas.
>
> Bless you,
>   Mother[9]

After the war, however, he was accepted for a place in Trinity College, Dublin, where he reputedly reduced his heating bills by cutting up his floorboards for fuel. The college fines book also records a penalty of £2 for 'firing an air gun in New Square and missing the Junior Dean'. Lionel next decided to join the Cameron Highlanders regiment. The trying sound of his bagpipe practice permeated Glaslough until he departed with his regiment for India in 1922, from whence for the next four years he regularly sent illustrated letters to his parents. He then decided to resign his commission and to *walk* home from India. He crossed the Himalayas, exploring Tibet and parts of China, meeting en route a beautiful Burmese girl with whom he fell in love. Leonie's disapproval when she heard the news was immediate. Margaret Sheridan, then fifteen, who was staying with the Leslies at Castle Leslie when he returned home, wrote excitedly to her mother about the affair:

She was the daughter of a chief, up in the mountains. He was the first white man she had ever seen. Apparently she was perfectly divine, lovely figure, ivory coloured skin, almond shaped eyes, and so on … He wrote home impassioned letters about her, and really wanted to marry her. But I gather the old chief was dead against it, and Lionel left his Burmese mountains, with a temporarily broken heart … Only don't say I told you so, because the matter is being hushed up. Leonie thought it perfectly disgraceful, and she is the only one who knew about it, except Anita, who told me.[10]

Leonie was kind to Margaret, the daughter of her much-loved niece, but could not resist giving her advice and unfavourably comparing her to Anita, her granddaughter. Leonie's heart was warm but she could be interfering. Her sons knew that her catchphrase, 'Do you mind if I say something?' always prefaced the offering of her opinions. Although Margaret was happy living in the desert at Biskra with her mother, Leonie tried to persuade her to make more conventional life choices. Margaret wrote in exasperation to her mother:

This morning I went in to say good morning to her before breakfast as I always do, and we fell into discussing my future. I was told, that at the age of twenty I must marry some nice Englishman, with a lovely place in the country in order to help the family, and that she had already a nice husband in view for me, only would not tell me who … I just said 'yes, yes, how lovely, of course, that's the only thing to do' and so on. But when I thought about it after I got nerves in an infantile way. You won't let them make me marry some dreadful Englishman, with a bloody house in the country, will you meema? I should commit suicide if they did … However I shall not disillusion Leonie till the time comes. But I don't see where the 'helping the family' part would come in … ?[11]

Margaret missed little and she understood Leonie well. The Leslies' longevity posed problems for those waiting in line. Leonie and Jack did not achieve control of Glaslough until 1907, when they were both well into their forties. Now Shane and especially Marjorie waited impatiently for their turn to run the house.

In the meantime, two highly strung, strong-minded women lived on the estate, each vying for dominance. Margaret wrote to Clare of the goings-on:

> It is most amusing, to watch Marjorie and Leonie, and what they say and do. When I go into see her in the morning, Leonie always begins by criticising and running down all Marjorie's guests, and when I go into Marjorie I always hear bitter complaints concerning Leonie's guests. Then, too, when they both come down stairs, Leonie puts a book on one table, and Marjorie picks it up and moves it to another table, and puts some bibelot in its place. Then Leonie puts it back again and Marjorie glowers. Then, they are always going at each other about their clothes. Leonie objects to Marjorie's jumper, and so it goes on. Too funny for words.[12]

Margaret called them the 'crazy Leslies'. They were certainly eccentric, despite Leonie's best efforts at a well-ordered family life. Lionel was commissioned to write stories for *Tatler*, which were later published in 1931 in a book, *Wilderness Trails in Three Continents*, for which cousin Winston provided the introduction. However, these efforts did not please her; she was, according to Margaret, 'sniffy' about it. Leonie would have preferred her sons to lead less unusual lives. Margaret described in another letter a gift she had received from an Arab friend, which perfectly illustrates Leonie's conventionality:

> I must tell you something so funny that happened yesterday. I came down to dinner wearing Habib's little watch. Leonie saw it and asked who gave it to me, I said 'Oh Habib Lotfallah' her face fell, but I, with devilment gleaming in my eyes, said 'I think he is one of the most charming men I know, don't you?' 'Pass me the salt dear' said Leonie. This morning she called me into her room and said, as she handed me some green beads, 'Here is a necklace for you darling, it will make a change from always wearing that watch'. I can't help laughing when I think about it. Poor Habib![13]

Leonie's life at Glaslough and in London was by the 1930s in sharp contrast to that of Clara, who was unhappily spending much of the year abroad in a Swiss hotel. In 1932, Shane wrote to Oswald from Sussex, anxious about Clara who had complained to him at length of her discontent. She had also expressed her disapproval of the book Shane had written that year, which included a chapter on Moreton: *Studies in Sublime Failure*. Shane's letter sums up the Leslie family's feelings about Clara rather well: 'Where are you leaving your mama? She is equally on all our nerves and on our consciences. I feel so sorry for her and hope she will be peaceful at Biskra. She ought to have quiet and happy years but she has no element of quiet in her. I am sorry the book upset her but she must realise that Moreton belongs no longer to his family but to the personal history of his times.'[14]

Leonie spent time with her sister in Paris in 1934, when Clara was visiting Clare and Leonie was helping to launch Lionel, who had decided to become a sculptor. Clara remained in Paris after her sister had left and was staying with Clare when she had her heart attack. When Clara died in the Sussex nursing home the following year, Leonie, aged seventy-six, had been ill herself and unable to attend the funeral, so she sent Shane in her stead. Now the surviving matriarch of the family, Leonie forgot no one. She sent letters and gifts to Clara's son, Hugh, in Australia, and to his son Romey, who now reverted to his given name, Jerome. Hugh by then had had four other children by his second wife, Rosalind (a fifth had died as a baby), and was still struggling desperately. Shane also sent his cousin gifts and money, and always remembered Jerome. The cousins had been brought up to cherish their family links and they assiduously kept in touch.

Rumours that Clare was a Soviet agent had not dampened Winston's affection for his cousin, although the government intelligence services stated their belief that she was a spy. Clare's file records a visit paid in 1925 to Winston, who was Colonial Secretary, by Admiral Sir Hugh Sinclair, chief of the Secret Intelligence Service (MI6): 'CSI today interviewed Winston. Winston informed him, in answer to his question about Clare, that he was not prepared to go bail for her. He was prepared to believe anything CSI told him about her.' The file also records that, as late as 1942, MI5 was still intercepting Clare Sheridan's post.[15] It is possible that Clare *was* being paid by the Russians. She was indiscreet and so lacking in judgement and critical self-awareness that she might easily have convinced herself that the money was payment for her work as an artist, rather than for spying against her country.

On a personal level, Winston gave her the benefit of the doubt. Although Clemmie did not care for Clare, nor wish to entertain her, Winston continued to see his cousin on his own – but family gatherings between the Churchills and Frewens were rare. In September 1933, Clare and her son Dick were invited to lunch at Chartwell. This was the first time Dick had met his Churchill family, as Clare wrote to Shane. In this significant letter, she described Winston's distrust of Hitler:

> On Friday we motored over to lunch with Winston as Berney Baruch [one of Clare's lovers while she was in the US] was also going to lunch there & said he wanted to see Dick. I proposed myself & Winston very amiably let me come. Just ourselves, & Clemmy [*sic*] & Randolph [Winston and Clemmie's son]. Dick had never seen his Churchill relations before & was much amused. R. and Winston simply wrangle together – Randolph adopting the attitude of the 'bright young people' & Winston rather sound & ponderous became so exasperated he just told Rand to shut up! Par moments the conversation was interesting – Winston declares emphatically there will be a European war in 3 years …
>
> P.S. I forgot to tell you that what impressed me most about Winston is his vibrant hatred of Hitler – to such an extent that he actually said he would join hands with Soviet Russia if necessary to 'down' Germany and you know what <u>that</u> means from Winston – Apparently Pilsudeski is having a conference with Russia, which W. says is very significant. He says Europe <u>must</u> unite to keep Hitler down – that he's the most dangerous thing that ever happened.[16]

Through Winston and her other political contacts Leonie felt very much in the know. Being in the Duke of Connaught's circle also helped to keep her informed. In November 1936, King Edward VIII made known his intention to marry an American divorcee, Wallis Simpson. The decision prompted a crisis: such an alliance for the King, as 'Supreme Governor' of the Church of England, was deemed unacceptable by Prime Minister Stanley Baldwin. In order to marry Wallis, the King abdicated in December 1936 and left for France, where the couple were married the following year. Throughout the scandal, Leonie was, naturally, taken into the duke's confidence. As a close friend of Edward VII, she had been treated with friendly courtesy by his son, George V. She recounted to her granddaughter Anita how Queen Mary, George V's widow and the mother of Edward VIII, had taken tea with the duke and Leonie at Bagshot Park before the abdication. As Leonie had known Edward as a young man, the Queen Mother urged Leonie to drop some tactful hints to him about the unsuitability of the relationship. The next day Leonie and the duke drove over to Fort Belvedere, where Edward was staying with a group of friends, including Wallis Simpson. After tea, they all went for a walk. On returning, Mrs Simpson had sat down and held out her feet to the infatuated King, with the order: 'Take off my little muddy shoes.' Leonie, to whom it was clear immediately that the situation could not be changed, said: 'It's no good trying to stop that sort of thing. He likes it.'[17] Marjorie, however, supported her fellow American and, according to her daughter Anita, claimed that Wallis was both 'respectable' and 'soignée', commenting that it did not matter about bringing down a throne as long as no one became 'piggy'(greedy).[18]

After Clara's death, Leonie felt responsible for her sister's children as well as her own. She wrote to Hugh that he should reorganize his (modest) American investments inherited from his mother, which provided him with a very small income. Hugh was touched by her interest and in March 1936 wrote to Shane:

Some time ago you sent me on a letter from Aunt Leonie. How splendidly she writes – such a wonderful balance between head & heart: you must be so proud of her. I too was proud of my dear mother [Clara] & loved her to distraction; she was so sweet, romantic, and so original. But unlike yours, she was <u>all</u> heart. She could never make an effective contribution to any serious discussion. She was a baby all her days. This was what made her so intensely loveable. Her thoughts were always instinctive, and instinct is but the sum of all our prejudices. Your own mother reacts to convention. That is inevitable. But the conventions she cherishes are borne along in the chariot of reason, thus giving direction & purpose to even formless traditions.[19]

Leonie was also concerned about Clare, who in January 1937 was devastated by the death of her son Dick of appendicitis, just a few months after his twenty-first birthday. First she had lost Wilfred and now their only son. That year, she decided to take another spectacular trip to try to recover, planning a visit to the Indians in the American West. Her cousin Winston, who had lost his own infant daughter Marigold many years previously, saw Clare before she left. He embraced her, saying: 'There are no words. Just know I love you. And go to those Red Indians. I am sure you will learn something further.'[20] The peaceful landscape of mountains and plains certainly restored her equilibrium, and she learned to carve wood, returning with crates of carved Red Indian faces. When Winston saw them, he exclaimed that they were all heads of their cousin Shane, with his high cheekbones and half-closed eyes. In 1942, Winston allowed Clare to sculpt his head. As he never got up before twelve noon (even during the war), she came to him in the morning while he was still in bed. He used to sleep in the underground shelter, which had become the night-time annexe of the prime minister's residence at 10 Downing Street, doing his work and receiving guests from his bed. Clare grew frustrated trying to capture him, as he refused to keep still or to give up his cigar. She was ready to abandon the project, but one morning managed to seize a few uninterrupted hours and finished the piece very quickly. Winston wrote warmly that she had produced 'a very fine piece of work'; he would 'certainly like to have a replica of the head in bronze' and would send a cheque (always appreciated by his perennially impecunious cousin) straight away.[21]

As the dark undercurrents of war flowed through London, Leonie was, as ever, very well informed. Seymour recollected how she frequently rang him from her flat, speaking in French, with an 'exaggerated discretion'.[22] In April 1939, at the age of eighty, Leonie had been to Chartwell to visit Winston, who had told her that he had seen Chamberlain and told him that their ships were 'dangerously dispersed'. She relayed this to Seymour, adding: 'His French is so bad, Jennie never troubled to have him taught.'[23]

Just before the Second World War broke out, Leonie returned from the Derby horse race one afternoon to dress for the opera when she tripped over a telephone wire, breaking her leg. The bone was soon set in the London Clinic with the new 'Petersen Pin'. Seymour described how his mother's room there filled with flowers and fruit from her friends and acquaintances until she laughingly complained and begged him to take some of them away. She then went home to Castle Leslie for the duration of the war.

Lionel meanwhile had fallen in love with Barbara Enever, an artist whom he married after war broke out. They eventually settled on the Isle of Mull with their daughter, Leonie, who was born in 1944. Lionel was happy; he sculpted and wrote poetry. He also became an expert on the Loch Ness and Loch Fadder monsters, publishing a book on the subject. In addition he apparently had considerable gifts as a mystic and was appointed 'Arch Druid of the Western Isles'.

During the war, Marjorie and Seymour's wife Timmie, together with their children, also moved to Ireland to be at Glaslough with Leonie and Jack, who were by then in their eighties. Although technically in the neutral Irish Republic, the estate was on the border, so members of the Leslie family fighting in the war could visit by travelling to Northern Ireland (part of Great Britain) but had to change into civilian clothes (usually in the changing room of the next station in the north) before entering the republic. It was an odd situation; on the Irish side there was plenty of food, but no coal, white flour, petrol, or mustard. In the next 'northern' village, they were subject to the British restrictions of total war: blackouts, air-raid alerts, and severe rationing, including clothing. It was not long before a mutually beneficial smuggling system developed and such barter, as long as they were small and non-commercial, was ignored by the authorities. After 1942, American soldiers were quartered on the Caledon estate, Leonie's nearest 'northern' neighbours, and she would frequently drive in the old one-horse brougham to visit the officers there. The American soldiers were warned that it was a court martial offence if they crossed the border into Eire; but they could be spotted, recalled Seymour, walking in single file through the bog, in search of bacon, eggs, and whiskey in the Glaslough village inn. The 'Two Irelands' were a source of considerable confusion to the soldiers.

Shane and Marjorie's son Jack had joined the Irish Guards. He was captured at Boulogne and taken prisoner by the Germans in May 1940, being held at a camp in Bavaria. Lionel was posted to Italy; Shane was running the Home Guard in Sloane Square in London; his daughter Anita was in Beirut; and his other son Desmond was training for the Royal Air Force in Florida. Letters flowed in from all sides and were exchanged between Leonie and her two daughters-in-law, all anxious for news. Winston continued to send frequent messages to his favourite aunt and Leonie became an important source of information. There was an Irish censor, due to what was dubbed 'The Emergency' (despite the country's official neutrality). Many Irish citizens crossed the border to enlist, however, to fight the Nazis; and Ireland as a whole largely supported the Allies, especially after the Japanese bombing of Pearl Harbor in December 1941. Leonie would go over the border with her letters to a 'northern' post office to avoid two sets of censorship. She drove over in her one-horse carriage, and her son recollected that as she passed the American GIs stationed on the Caledon estate, she would make the 'V for Victory' sign with her hand to the young men.

Leonie's strength, however, was on the wane. Although she was resolutely optimistic about the war and refused to countenance defeatist talk, she slowly began to fade away, living in her bedroom, even leaving her letters unopened. On his last visit, she had prevailed upon Seymour to ensure that the family vault was not damp and, to check, he was lowered into it horizontally, reporting that he had found a bone-dry crypt in good order. Leonie found this very amusing. On 21

August 1943, she slipped away peacefully at the age of eighty-four. Family members found it hard to believe that she was gone. Bereft, her husband Jack followed her only months later. Clare wrote of her sorrow to Shane: 'This is just a line to say how glad I am to hear that you were with her at the last. To have the links of birth & death is very significant. As for myself I shall miss her, & more than I missed my mother. Only she & I know what we have been to one another.'[24] Shane's aunt Olive Guthrie, who had also loved Leonie, wrote to him in sympathy:

> I feel so much for you … There was something tragic to me always in the way she wished to please you, & that you were almost the only person she was tactless with. Too much attention can be as bad as not enough…
>
> I am sure having had you with her, to see her off on her last journey must have atoned for everything. I remember her saying after some little coolness between you 'I believe he is really fond of me & I know he will miss me when I die'.[25]

Like her sisters, Leonie had little to leave behind save her memory. She bequeathed what remained, as well as the small balance of the American trust, to her two younger sons, Seymour and Lionel, as Shane's son Jack was due to inherit the Glaslough estate. Her legacy was in her warm words and cool advice, offered to any who needed it. She was a woman of heart and mind, wise and thoughtful. With her death, one of Winston's last links to the past was gone. On 1 August 1943, he wrote his last letter to her before he departed for Canada: 'You have sent me a lot of charming messages which have cheered me greatly on this long journey. They give me, what no one else can give me, the link with my youth and with my mother.'[26] A quote from the 'Spectator' column in the *Irish Independent* after Leonie's death stated that she had told the journalist that Winston was her favourite nephew 'because he is such a fond family man'.[27] Leonie had also been very proud of her famous relative, wiring to him in September 1939, 'Feel safer now you are at Admiralty.'[28] The strength of the bond between Winston and his aunt was illustrated in Shane's letter to Seymour, on 24 August, after their mother was buried. He wrote that he had placed in Leonie's coffin his last poem for her, the wooden cross from Norman's grave at Armentières, and 'between her fingers a silver coin Winston sent her for luck when she sent him scissors for his birthday some years ago'.[29]

She was also buried with four roses, three red and one white; as Shane wrote, 'Four roses from four sons.'[30] Like both Clara and Jennie, Leonie's greatest achievement was her children. They were clever and attractive, unusual and engaging. Her influence on them was enormous, and her encouragement and high standards drove them to ever greater accomplishments.

Epilogue: A Beautiful Affection

At the forefront of the transatlantic matrimonial alliances made between 1870 and 1914, but not themselves heiresses, Clara, Jennie, and Leonie married for love, and their marriages were a disappointment. They did not, however, walk away from their troubles. Consuelo Vanderbilt left the Duke of Marlborough in 1906 after eleven years of marriage (and the birth of two sons), while other unhappily married American women took refuge in highly strung nerves and poor health. Pauline Whitney, married to Almeric Paget, spent her life shuttling back and forth to spas, supposedly to revive a weak heart; Ethel Field, married to naval hero David (later Lord) Beatty, suffered such depressions that she neither slept nor ate for days at a time; and the famous Nancy Langhorne Shaw, who wed Waldorf Astor in 1906, was plagued by constant illnesses and afflictions in the early years of her marriage (before she discovered the beneficial effects of 'good works' and politics). The Jerome sisters, unlike these titled Americans, remained active as well as, unusually, staying loyal to their spouses. On 24 October 1909, the *New York American* ran a two-page article headed 'How Titled Foreigners Catch American Heiresses' and went on to cite forty unhappy marriages.[1] The Jerome sisters never complained publicly of the choices they had made. Instead, they endeavoured to make the best of their circumstances and helped each other to do so.

Clara coped with a very difficult husband by denying the humiliating realities of her life. Although she made many mistakes and often exhibited abysmal judgement, she held her head high, supported her husband unflinchingly, and raised, more or less adequately, three children. She created a landscape at Brede that is still recognized as a masterpiece. Jennie, like Clara, also made many unfortunate decisions, but she was warm and generous, and rose above her circumstances with a charm and courage that was universally acclaimed. Leonie used her tact and dignity to secure a place in a family in which she had originally been unwelcome and she touched the lives of all those around her with her wisdom and compassion.

Not only did these three women cope with the tribulations of their lives and loves, but they did so while maintaining their prized social status. Many aristocratic wives in Britain after 1870, faced with material decline, were placed in a particularly frustrating position. With no outlet for a professional career, such as politics (practised unevenly by Randolph), or business (practised very badly by Moreton), or the army (practised gallantly by Jack), the Jerome sisters found that the responsibility for ensuring that the domestic sphere retained its accustomed elegance fell upon them. Appearances had to be kept up. The children had to be properly (and expensively) educated; daughter Clare had to make her debut. It was all the more important to women of their class to adhere to these standards because they had so little else beyond their social position. Their story thus illuminates what it meant to be a female member of the British aristocracy during its decline, when incomes were falling but lifestyles were slow to follow the downward spiral.

In this light, Clara, Jennie, and Leonie managed rather well. They maintained lifelong loyalty to their husbands and each produced remarkable children. Winston's genius and impact are celebrated and he continues to be recognized as one of the greatest figures of the twentieth century. Shane, Norman, Seymour, and Lionel Leslie were all accomplished writers; on the Frewen side, Clare Sheridan was a renowned artist and writer, while Hugh and Oswald were also authors.

The Jerome sisters also exercised their many talents – literary, musical, and artistic. Jennie wrote extremely well and published articles, two books, and two plays as a means of generating income when there was none (especially as reducing expenditure was, for her, never an option). She and Clara had a genuine gift for interior design and decorating that was constantly admired. All three sisters were superb musicians. They played the piano wonderfully; Leonie and Jennie remained at a very high standard almost to the end. Leonie, in particular, had an exceptional knowledge of composition.

The Jerome sisters' lives are also significant because they were close to almost all the major historical forces of their time, from Mrs Astor's New York to the end of the Second Empire in France; from the Wild West of Wyoming to the Marlborough House set of Edward VII in London. They were buffeted by the Boer War, the Irish Troubles and Home Rule, as well as two cataclysmic world wars. They were witnesses, from a privileged (albeit somewhat tenuous) position, to the glory days of the British Empire.

On a human level, Clara, Jennie, and Leonie were determined and robust women who knew what they wanted and followed their desires. In a world and at a time when women were much circumscribed, they were restricted to channelling their abilities into social achievement; their lives as a result were dominated to a large extent by their relationships. Within these severe limitations, however, Clara, Jennie, and Leonie were very skilled, befriending the great men of their day, raising talented children, supporting their marriages, and living life to the full.

'What a beautiful affection it was that united those 3 sisters,' wrote the Duke of Connaught to Leonie's sister-in-law, Olive Guthrie, after Clara's death in 1935.[2] It was indeed a beautiful affection – strong and deeply sympathetic – that weathered for eighty years life's misfortunes as well as its joys and united these three sisters, so different, yet so attached, with a bond broken only by death.

A Note on Purchasing Power

A number of sources were used to convey pound and dollar amounts in present-day values and to convert these currencies where required. Calculations for the purchasing power of the pound were taken from 'Inflation: the value of the pound 1750–2001', House of Commons Research Paper 02/44, 11 July 2002. Between 1861 and 1901, £1 was worth nearly £70 in 2001 values. Exchange rates between the US dollar and the pound sterling were calculated using data provided in *Exchange Rate between the United States Dollar and the British Pound, 1791–2000*, by Lawrence H. Officer in Economic History Services, a website maintained by Miami University, Wake Forest University, and EH.net. The exchange rate between 1874 and 1876 was approximately $5.50 to £1 sterling; from 1877 to 1939 (with exceptions in 1920, 1921 and 1932) the rate remained remarkably stable at around $4.80 to £1.

Other conversion calculations were made based on data also provided by Economic History Services, calculated using the consumer price index, available from the following internet address: www.eh.net.hmit/compare/. The approximate current-day values of quoted figures are shown in parentheses following the historical figure in the text.

A Note on Sources

In addition to the original material held by the Churchill College
Archives Centre, the Irish National Library, and the Leslie and Frewen
families, a number of books about the Churchill, Frewen, and Leslie
families were consulted in the research for *Fortune's Daughters*.

Jennie Churchill published a memoir in 1908, under her married
name of Mrs George Cornwallis-West, entitled *The Reminiscences of
Lady Randolph Churchill*. The work provides a gratifying amount of
detail, as well as indications of Jennie's views and personality. There are,
however, a number of inaccuracies, quite apart from the fact that Jennie
chose not to reveal details of her personal relationships. She admitted to
leaving much out, prefacing the memoir: 'But there may be some to
whom these Reminiscences will be interesting chiefly in virtue of what
is left unsaid.'[1]

There are also four biographies of Jennie Churchill: by René Kraus
(*Young Lady Randolph*, published in 1944); Ralph Martin (*Jennie: The
Life of Lady Randolph Churchill*, published in two volumes in 1969 and
1971); Anita Leslie, Jennie's great-niece (*Jennie*, published in 1969); and
Peregrine Churchill, Jennie's grandson, with Julian Mitchell (*Jennie,
Lady Randolph Churchill: A Portrait with Letters*, published in 1974).

The work by Kraus is of little interest as it contains numerous factual
inaccuracies. The biography produced by Ralph Martin is its exact
opposite and has been meticulously researched. He has used many

original letters to support his work, and I have made use of these quotations. He has not identified these quotations by date, so I have referred to them as citations. Anita Leslie has had access to family documents as well as to oral history, and has created a well-written account of her great-aunt (in addition to her biographies of Leonard Jerome, Clara Jerome's husband Moreton Frewen, and their daughter Clare Sheridan). She did not, however, give sources for her many quotations, which cannot therefore be identified by date or provenance. Where I have made use of these, I have cited them from her text. Peregrine Churchill and Julian Mitchell have made use of original correspondence that has been dated and identified by provenance in their biography. Where I have used excerpts from their work, it has been quoted from their text and identified by date.

Finally, Jennie's correspondence and documents, which now form part of the Chartwell Collection are held at the Churchill College Archives Centre in Cambridge, where they may be consulted. These archives are of great interest and have been extensively used for this book.

The biography of Jennie's first husband, Lord Randolph Churchill, by his son, Winston S. Churchill, as well as those by Roy Foster, Lord Rosebery, and Robert Rhodes James, were all helpful. The biography of Winston S. Churchill written by his son Randolph S. Churchill provides many letters that are correctly dated and identified, making this a useful work. Biographies of Winston S. Churchill by Roy Jenkins, Martin Gilbert, and Piers Brendon were all also very helpful, as indeed was Winston's own autobiography, *My Early Life*, published in 1930.

The memoirs of Jennie's second husband, George Cornwallis-West, entitled *Edwardian Hey-Days*, were published in the same year and provide a limited but at times interesting glimpse of their marriage.

There are two biographies of Clara's husband, Moreton Frewen, as well as the chapter 'Moreton Frewen' in *Studies in Sublime Failure* by Shane Leslie (Moreton's nephew – and Anita Leslie's father). The latter focusses on Moreton's professional life and is of limited use here. Anita

Leslie's biography, *Mr Frewen of England* (1966), provides welcome information on Clara's life, which is otherwise poorly documented. Anita Leslie did not, however, give sources for her quotations, which often cannot be dated or identified by provenance. They have been cited in my text when used. In his excellent biography of Moreton Frewen, entitled *The Splendid Pauper* (1968), Allen Andrews made considerable use of original material without giving sources for his quotations, which, when used, have been cited in this text as they appear in his book.

There are no published works on Clara Frewen or Leonie Leslie. Anita Leslie's biography of her great-grandfather, Leonard Jerome (*The Fabulous Leonard Jerome*, 1954), was very helpful in providing information on the family up to 1891, when Leonard died. Her auto-biography, *The Gilt and the Gingerbread* (1981), was also a useful resource. The family archives made available by the Frewen and Leslie families were invaluable for more information on Clara and Leonie. In addition, the extensive Leslie archive collection, now held at the National Library of Ireland in Dublin, contains a large collection of Leonie's correspondence with her family and friends, including letters to and from her sisters. In the absence of secondary material on Clara and Leonie, the original archives held here and by the families were indispensable.

Leonie's sons Shane, Seymour, and Lionel all published books. Shane was the author of fifty-three works, of which the autobiographical *The Film of Memory* (1938) and *Long Shadows* (1966) provided me with many insights. Seymour's memoirs, *The Jerome Connexion* (1964), were of much interest, as was Lionel's *One Man's World* (1961). In all of these books, original quotations were unsourced and have been cited when used in my text.

The memoirs of Clara's husband, Moreton Frewen, *Melton Mowbray and Other Memories* (1924), are informative but contain almost no material about his family. The memoirs of Clara's son, Oswald Frewen – *Sailor's Soliloquy* (1961) and his unpublished diaries, in which all the entries are dated – were of great help and have been quoted here.

Clara's daughter, Clare Sheridan, wrote a number of books about her life, of which *Nuda Veritas* (1927), *To the Four Winds* (1957), and *My Crowded Sanctuary* (1945) were the most useful for this biography.

Notes

INTRODUCTION, PP. xiii–xix

1 King Papers; Jennie Churchill to Clara Frewen, November 1894.
2 The Spencers all descend in the male line from Sir Robert Spencer, who was made Baron Spencer by James I. The 2nd Lord Spencer's son, Henry, was created Earl of Sunderland. In 1699, the 3rd Earl of Sunderland married the daughter of the military genius, John Churchill, Duke of Marlborough. After the death of their son, the 4th Earl of Sunderland, the next son, Charles, succeeded to the earldom. The lack of a Marlborough heir meant that the dukedom and the Blenheim estates passed to the eldest surviving nephew, Charles Spencer, 5th Earl of Sunderland. In 1817, he decided to include the surname of Churchill to commemorate the Battle of Blenheim. The full family name is therefore Spencer-Churchill, although most family members were known as 'Churchill'.
3 Cited by Ruth Brandon, *The Dollar Princesses*, p. 4.
4 A Frenchman of aristocratic descent visited America in 1897 and published anonymously a memoir of his experiences and impressions. See *America and the Americans: From a French Point of View*, pp. 34–7.
5 See David Cannadine, *The Decline and Fall of the British Aristocracy*, p. 9.
6 Within this elite group, there were forty-two families who were very rich indeed, owning more than 100,000 acres, such as the Buccleuchs, the Devonshires and the Northumberlands.
7 John Bateman, *The Great Landowners of Great Britain and Ireland*, pp. 472–3.
8 The 41 Scottish and 101 Irish peers were not entitled to sit in the House of Lords. Only those with an English title could do so.

9 David Cannadine, *The Decline and Fall of the British Aristocracy*, p. 11.

1: MRS ASTOR'S NEW YORK, PP. 1–23

1 Leonard Jerome to Clara Jerome, 6 May 1889, cited by Ralph Martin in *Jennie: The Life of Lady Randolph Churchill: vol. I: 1854–1895*, p. 321.

2 Cited by Ralph Martin in *Lady Randolph Churchill, vol. I*, p. 20.

3 Clara Hall's name was in fact Clarissa, like her mother, but she changed it to Clara when she married in 1849 and was known as Clara for the rest of her life. To avoid confusion, I have referred to her as Clara throughout the text.

4 Records show two spellings for the name: 'Wilcox' or 'Willcox'.

5 Leslie Papers, NLI, L/5/17; Hugh Frewen to Shane Leslie, 18 August 1956.

6 Leslie Papers, NLI, L/2/8; Norman Leslie to Leonie Leslie, 4 November 1912 [?].

7 Clarita changed her name to Clara some years later, when in her twenties.

8 See Frederic Cople Jaher, 'The Gilded Elite: American Multimillionaires, 1865 to the Present', p. 196, in W.D. Rubinstein (ed.), *Wealth and the Wealthy in the Modern World*, pp. 189–276.

9 Stephen Fiske, *Offhand Portraits of Prominent New Yorkers*, cited by Ralph Martin in *Lady Randolph Churchill, vol. I*, p. 21.

10 Reported in the New York *Herald*, 5 March 1891, a story of reminiscence on Jerome's death, in Ralph Martin, *Lady Randolph Churchill, vol. I*, p. 21.

11 Ward MacAllister, *Society as I Have Found It*, p. 157, 349.

12 Anita Leslie, *The Fabulous Leonard Jerome*, p. 41.

13 Anita Leslie, *The Fabulous Leonard Jerome*, p. 47.

14 Ralph Martin, *Lady Randolph Churchill, vol. I*, p. 22.

15 Cited by Eric Homberger in *Mrs. Astor's New York: Money and Social Power in a Gilded Age*, p. 31.

16 Ralph Martin, *Lady Randolph Churchill, vol. I*, p. 28.

17 Dixon Wecter, *The Saga of American Society: A Record of Social Aspiration 1607–1937*, p. 154.

18 Anita Leslie, *The Fabulous Leonard Jerome*, p. 65.

19 Cited by Ralph Martin in *Lady Randolph Churchill, vol. I*, p. 23.

20 Cited by Anita Leslie in *The Fabulous Leonard Jerome*, p. 72.

21 Ralph Martin, *Lady Randolph Churchill, vol. I*, p. 25.

22 Ralph Martin, *Lady Randolph Churchill, vol. I*, p. 27.

23 Frederic Cople Jaher, 'The Gilded Elite', in Rubinstein (ed.), *Wealth and the*

Wealthy in the Modern World, p. 199.

24 Mrs George Cornwallis-West, *The Reminiscences of Lady Randolph Churchill*,
    p. 3.

25 Mrs George Cornwallis-West, *The Reminiscences of Lady Randolph Churchill*,
    p. 2.

26 Mrs George Cornwallis-West, *The Reminiscences of Lady Randolph Churchill*,
    p. 2.

27 Edward Robb Ellis, *The Epic of New York City*, p. 326.

28 Cited by Edward Robb Ellis in *The Epic of New York City*, p. 328.

29 Cited by Anita Leslie in *The Fabulous Leonard Jerome*, p. 57.

30 Richard O'Connor, *Courtroom Warrior: The Combative Career of William
    Travers Jerome*, p. 14.

31 Anita Leslie, *The Fabulous Leonard Jerome*, p. 82.

32 Mrs George Cornwallis-West, *The Reminiscences of Lady Randolph Churchill*,
    p. 1.

33 Cited by Ralph Martin in *Lady Randolph Churchill, vol. I*, p. 30.

34 Cited by Richard O'Connor in *Courtroom Warrior*, p. 13.

35 Cited by Ralph Martin in *Lady Randolph Churchill, vol. I*, p. 30.

36 Cited by Anita Leslie in *Jennie: The Life of Lady Randolph Churchill*, p. 12.

37 Anita Leslie, *Jennie*, p. 5.

38 Chartwell Collection (Char), Churchill College, Cambridge:
    Char/28/1/20; Leonard Jerome to Jennie Jerome, 20 November 1868.

39 Char/28/1/22; Leonard Jerome to Jennie Jerome, 2 February 1869.

40 Char/28/1/22; Leonard Jerome to Jennie Jerome, 2 February 1869.

41 Mrs George Cornwallis-West *The Reminiscences of Lady Randolph Churchill*,
    p. 3.

2: THE COURT OF EMPEROR LOUIS NAPOLEON, PP. 24–40

1 Mrs George Cornwallis-West, *The Reminiscences of Lady Randolph Churchill*,
   p. 4.

2 Between 1880 and 1924, over 26 million people arrived in America for the
   first time, nearly all transported in passenger liners. See Rob McAuley, *The
   Liners*, pp. 36–7.

3 Mrs George Cornwallis-West, *The Reminiscences of Lady Randolph Churchill*,
   p. 4.

4 Mrs George Cornwallis-West, *The Reminiscences of Lady Randolph Churchill*,

p. 5.

5 Mrs George Cornwallis-West, *The Reminiscences of Lady Randolph Churchill*, p. 6.

6 Mrs George Cornwallis-West, *The Reminiscences of Lady Randolph Churchill*, pp. 16–17.

7 Mrs George Cornwallis-West, *The Reminiscences of Lady Randolph Churchill*, p. 6. Clara allowed Jennie to use 'her' stories of the imperial court for Jennie's reminiscences.

8 Clarita Jerome to Clara Jerome, 12 November 1969, cited by Clare Sheridan in *To the Four Winds*, p. 15.

9 Clarita Jerome to Mrs Clara Jerome; cited by Ralph Martin in *Jennie: The Life of Lady Randolph Churchill, vol. I*, p. 39.

10 Cited by David Duff in *Eugénie and Napoleon III*, p. 197.

11 Mrs George Cornwallis-West, *The Reminiscences of Lady Randolph Churchill*, p. 27.

12 Mrs George Cornwallis-West, *The Reminiscences of Lady Randolph Churchill*, p. 31.

13 Cited by Anita Leslie in *Jennie: The Life of Lady Randolph Churchill*, p. 23.

3: 'TO MEET: RANDOLPH', PP. 41–61

1 Peregrine Churchill and Julian Mitchell, *Jennie, Lady Randolph Churchill: a Portrait with Letters*, p. 19.

2 Cited by Peregrine Churchill and Julian Mitchell in *Jennie, Lady Randolph Churchill*, p. 19.

3 Jennie's description of her courtship with Randolph is surprising sketchy in her *Reminiscences*, and she left only a short memorandum of it in her papers. See Peregrine Churchill and Julian Mitchell – *Jennie, Lady Randolph Churchill*, p. 19; Ralph Martin, *Jennie: The Life of Lady Randolph Churchill, vol. I*, pp. 61–2; and Anita Leslie, *Jennie: The Life of Lady Randolph Churchill*, pp. 22–37.

4 Cited by Anita Leslie in *Jennie*, pp. 24–5.

5 Cited by Ralph Martin, *Lady Randolph Churchill, vol. I*, p. 62.

6 Randolph Churchill to Jennie Jerome, 16 August 1873, in Peregrine Churchill and Julian Mitchell, in *Jennie, Lady Randolph Churchill*, pp. 19–20.

7 Jennie Jerome to Randolph Churchill, 17 August 1873, in Peregrine Churchill and Julian Mitchell, *Jennie, Lady Randolph Churchill*, p. 20.

8 Randolph Churchill to Jennie Jerome, 18 August 1873, in Peregrine

Churchill and Julian Mitchell, *Jennie, Lady Randolph Churchill*, pp. 20–21.

9 Randolph Churchill to Jennie Jerome, 19 August 1873, in Peregrine Churchill and Julian Mitchell, *Jennie, Lady Randolph Churchill*, pp. 21–22.

10 Randolph Churchill to Lord Marlborough, 20 August 1873, in Peregrine Churchill and Julian Mitchell, *Jennie, Lady Randolph Churchill*, pp. 23–25.

11 Cited by Ralph Martin in *Lady Randolph Churchill, vol. I*, p. 72.

12 Cited by Ralph Martin in *Lady Randolph Churchill, vol. I*, p. 72.

13 Duke of Marlborough to Randolph Churchill, 31 August 1873, in Peregrine Churchill and Julian Mitchell, *Jennie, Lady Randolph Churchill*, p. 32.

14 Duke of Marlborough to Randolph Churchill, 31 August 1873, cited by Ralph Martin in *Lady Randolph Churchill, vol. I*, p. 72.

15 Randolph Churchill to Jennie Jerome, 7 September 1873, in Peregrine Churchill and Julian Mitchell, *Jennie, Lady Randolph Churchill*, pp. 33–5.

16 Randolph Churchill to Jennie Jerome, 10 September 1873, in Peregrine Churchill and Julian Mitchell, *Jennie, Lady Randolph Churchill*, p. 35.

17 Mrs Clara Jerome to Leonard Jerome, cited by Ralph Martin in *Lady Randolph Churchill, vol. I*, p. 71.

18 Clara Jerome to Randolph Churchill, cited by Ralph Martin in *Lady Randolph Churchill, vol. I*, p. 71.

19 Leonard Jerome to Jennie Jerome; cited by Anita Leslie in *Jennie*, pp. 27–8.

20 Clara Jerome to Randolph Churchill; cited by Ralph Martin in *Lady Randolph Churchill, vol. I*, p. 71.

21 Leonard Jerome to Jennie Jerome, 8 September 1873, in Peregrine Churchill and Julian Mitchell, *Jennie, Lady Randolph Churchill*, pp. 64–5.

22 Clara Jerome to Randolph Churchill, 29 September 1873, in Peregrine Churchill and Julian Mitchell, *Jennie, Lady Randolph Churchill*, p. 65.

23 Jennie Jerome to Randolph Churchill, 16 September 1872, in Peregrine Churchill and Julian Mitchell, *Jennie, Lady Randolph Churchill*, pp. 44–5.

24 Randolph Churchill to Jennie Jerome, 18 September 1873, in Peregrine Churchill and Julian Mitchell, *Jennie, Lady Randolph Churchill*, pp. 46–8.

25 Jennie Jerome to Randolph Churchill, in Peregrine Churchill and Julian Mitchell, *Jennie, Lady Randolph Churchill*, pp. 49–50.

26 Duke of Marlborough to Randolph Churchill, cited by Ralph Martin in *Lady Randolph Churchill, vol. I*, p. 79.

27 Randolph Churchill to Jennie Jerome, cited by Ralph Martin in *Lady Randolph Churchill, vol. I*, p. 78.

28 Jennie Jerome to Randolph Churchill, 30 September 1873, in Peregrine Churchill and Julian Mitchell, *Jennie, Lady Randolph Churchill*, p. 66.

29 Jennie Jerome to Randolph Churchill, 3 October 1873, in Peregrine Churchill and Julian Mitchell, *Jennie, Lady Randolph Churchill*, pp. 67–8.

30 Leonard Jerome to Jennie Jerome, 7 October 1873, in Peregrine Churchill and Julian Mitchell, *Jennie, Lady Randolph Churchill*, p. 68.

31 Char 28/2; Jennie Jerome to Randolph Churchill, 26 September 1873.

32 Randolph Churchill to Jennie Jerome, cited by Ralph Martin in *Lady Randolph Churchill, vol. I*, p. 83.

33 Char 28/93/33–6; Jennie Jerome to Randolph Churchill, 1873.

34 Ralph Martin, *Lady Randolph Churchill, vol. I*, p. 90.

35 Hugh Montgomery-Massingberd, *Blenheim Revisited: The Spencer-Churchills and their Palace*, pp. 105–7; and Gail MacColl and Carol McD. Wallace, *To Marry an English Lord: The Victorian and Edwardian Experience*, p. 125.

36 Randolph Churchill to the Duke of Marlborough, cited by Ralph Martin in *Lady Randolph Churchill, vol. I*, p. 91.

37 Anita Leslie, *Jennie*, p. 35.

38 Randolph Churchill to the Duke of Marlborough, cited by Ralph Martin in *Lady Randolph Churchill, vol. I*, p. 91.

39 Leonard Jerome to the Duke of Marlborough, cited by Ralph Martin in *Lady Randolph Churchill, vol. I*, p. 93.

40 Duke of Marlborough to Randolph Churchill, cited by Ralph Martin in *Lady Randolph Churchill, vol. I*, p. 94.

41 Leonard Jerome to the Duke of Marlborough, cited by Ralph Martin in *Lady Randolph Churchill, vol. I*, p. 93.

42 Ralph Martin, *Lady Randolph Churchill, vol. I*, p. 94.

43 Ralph Martin, *Lady Randolph Churchill, vol. I*, p. 96.

4: THE PRINCE OF WALES AND THE MARLBOROUGH HOUSE SET, PP. 62–91

1 Mrs George Cornwallis-West, *The Reminiscences of Lady Randolph Churchill*, p. 57.

2 Mrs George Cornwallis-West, *The Reminiscences of Lady Randolph Churchill*, pp. 58–60.

3 Cited by Anita Leslie in *Jennie: The Life of Lady Randolph Churchill*, p. 39.

4 Mrs George Cornwallis-West, *The Reminiscences of Lady Randolph Churchill*, pp. 60–1.

5 Mrs George Cornwallis-West, *The Reminiscences of Lady Randolph Churchill*, p. 39.

6 Anita Leslie, *Jennie*, p. 42.

7 Mrs George Cornwallis-West, *The Reminiscences of Lady Randolph Churchill*, p. 37.

8 Virginia Cowles, *Edward VII and His Circle*, cited by Ralph Martin in *Jennie: The Life of Lady Randolph Churchill, vol. I*, p. 102.

9 Clara Jerome to Mrs Clara Jerome, cited by Ralph Martin in *Lady Randolph Churchill, vol. I*, p. 102.

10 Jennie Jerome to Mrs Clara Jerome, cited by Ralph Martin in *Lady Randolph Churchill, vol. I*, p. 101.

11 Gail MacColl and Carol McD. Wallace, *To Marry an English Lord: The Victorian and Edwardian Experience*, p. 212.

12 Mrs George Cornwallis-West, *The Reminiscences of Lady Randolph Churchill*, pp. 47–8.

13 Cited by Ralph Martin in *Lady Randolph Churchill, vol. I*, p. 103.

14 Mrs George Cornwallis-West, *The Reminiscences of Lady Randolph Churchill*, pp. 48–9.

15 Clara Jerome to Mrs Clara Jerome, cited by Ralph Martin in *Lady Randolph Churchill, vol. I*, p. 104.

16 Mrs George Cornwallis-West, *The Reminiscences of Lady Randolph Churchill*, p. 37.

17 Clara Jerome to Mrs Clara Jerome, cited by Ralph Martin in *Lady Randolph Churchill, vol. I*, p. 108.

18 Jennie Churchill to Mrs Clara Jerome, cited by Ralph Martin in *Lady Randolph Churchill, vol. I*, p. 109.

19 Jennie Churchill to Mrs Clara Jerome, cited by Anita Leslie in *Jennie*, p. 42.

20 Randolph Churchill to Mrs Clara Jerome, 30 November 1874, in Peregrine Churchill and Julian Mitchell, *Jennie, Lady Randolph Churchill: A Portrait with Letters*, p. 75.

21 Winston S. Churchill, *My Early Life: A Roving Commission*, p. 73.

22 Winston S. Churchill to Randolph Churchill, 8 October 1887, in Randolph S. Churchill, *Youth: Winston S. Churchill 1874–1900*, p. 97.

23 Martin Gilbert, *Churchill: A Life*, p. 33.

24 Winston S. Churchill, *My Early Life*, p. 4.

25 Jennie Churchill to Randolph Churchill, 17 January 1876, in Peregrine Churchill and Julian Mitchell, *Jennie, Lady Randolph Churchill*, p. 83.

26 Ralph Martin, *Lady Randolph Churchill, vol. I*, p. 178.

27 Gail MacColl and Carol McD. Wallace, *To Marry an English Lord: The Victorian and Edwardian Experience*, pp. 70–1.

28 Jennie Churchill to Mrs Clara Jerome, summer 1874, cited by Ralph

Martin in *Lady Randolph Churchill, vol. I*, p. 109.

29 Clara Jerome to Mrs Clara Jerome, June 1875, cited by Anita Leslie in *Jennie*, p. 46.

30 Clara Jerome to Mrs Clara Jerome, 16 June 1875, cited by Anita Leslie in *Jennie*, p. 47.

31 Clara Jerome to Mrs Clara Jerome, 12 June 1875, cited by Anita Leslie in *Jennie*, pp. 48–9.

32 Clara Jerome to Mrs Clara Jerome, cited by Ralph Martin in *Lady Randolph Churchill, vol. I*, pp. 112–13.

33 Conversation with Sir Jack Leslie, March 2004.

34 Char 28/5/1, 5/2, 5/3; Randolph Churchill to Jennie Churchill, 1, 21, and 23 April 1875.

35 Randolph Churchill to Jennie Churchill, 4 July 1876, in Peregrine Churchill and Julian Mitchell, *Jennie, Lady Randolph Churchill*, p. 99.

36 Char 28/5/15; Randolph Churchill to Jennie Churchill, 18 January 1876.

37 Randolph Churchill to Jennie Churchill, in Peregrine Churchill and Julian Mitchell, *Jennie, Lady Randolph Churchill*, p. 82.

38 Char 28/5/29; Randolph Churchill to Jennie Churchill, 18 April 1876.

39 Cited by Anita Leslie in *Jennie*, p. 45.

40 Ralph Martin, *Lady Randolph Churchill, vol. I*, p. 112.

41 Char 28/96/73; Jennie Churchill to Randolph Churchill, 1877 [?].

42 There are a number of accounts of the Aylesford scandal, and one of the best can be found in Peregrine Churchill and Julian Mitchell, *Jennie, Lady Randolph Churchill*, pp. 87–104.

43 Jennie Churchill to Randolph Churchill, 20 April 1876, in Peregrine Churchill and Julian Mitchell, *Jennie, Lady Randolph Churchill*, p. 92.

44 Jennie Churchill to Randolph Churchill, 20 April 1876, in Peregrine Churchill and Julian Mitchell, *Jennie, Lady Randolph Churchill*, p. 93.

45 Cited by Anita Leslie in *Jennie*, p. 55.

46 Jennie Churchill to Randolph Churchill, 30 June 1876, in Peregrine Churchill and Julian Mitchell, *Jennie, Lady Randolph Churchill*, p. 96.

47 Randolph Churchill to Jennie Churchill, 30 June 1876, in Peregrine Churchill and Julian Mitchell, *Jennie, Lady Randolph Churchill*, p. 97.

48 Cited by Peregrine Churchill and Julian Mitchell in *Jennie, Lady Randolph Churchill*, p. 103.

49 Cited by Ralph Martin in *Lady Randolph Churchill, vol. I*, p. 120.

50 Mrs George Cornwallis-West, *The Reminiscences of Lady Randolph Churchill*, p. 68.

51 Mrs George Cornwallis-West, *The Reminiscences of Lady Randolph Churchill*,

p. 68.

52 Mrs George Cornwallis-West, *The Reminiscences of Lady Randolph Churchill*, p. 69.

53 Cited by Anita Leslie in *Jennie*, p. 56.

54 Mrs George Cornwallis-West, *The Reminiscences of Lady Randolph Churchill*, p. 69.

55 Mrs George Cornwallis-West, *The Reminiscences of Lady Randolph Churchill*, p. 70.

56 Jennie Churchill to Randolph Churchill, cited by Anita Leslie in *Jennie*, p. 58.

57 Mrs George Cornwallis-West, *The Reminiscences of Lady Randolph Churchill*, p. 73.

58 Viscount D'Abernon, *Portraits and Appreciations*, cited by Ralph Martin in *Lady Randolph Churchill, vol. I*, pp. 125–6.

59 Winston S. Churchill, *My Early Life*, p. 5.

60 Jennie Churchill to Randolph Churchill, [n.d.], in Peregrine Churchill and Julian Mitchell, *Jennie, Lady Randolph Churchill*, p. 107.

61 Randolph Churchill to Jennie Churchill, 15 August 1881, in Peregrine Churchill and Julian Mitchell, *Jennie, Lady Randolph Churchill*, p. 109.

62 Mrs George Cornwallis-West, *The Reminiscences of Lady Randolph Churchill*, p. 79.

63 Char 28/6/23; Randolph Churchill to Jennie Churchill, 25 January 1879.

64 After some dispute in the 1960s and later, this has become the generally accepted view.

65 Randolph also provided equally for both boys in his will.

66 Char 28/102/19; Jennie Churchill to Randolph Churchill, [1876].

67 Jennie Churchill to Mrs Clara Jerome, cited by Ralph Martin in *Lady Randolph Churchill, vol. I*, p. 136.

68 Allen Andrews, *The Splendid Pauper*, p. 46.

69 Clara Jerome to Mrs Clara Jerome, 1875, cited by Allen Andrews in *The Splendid Pauper*, p. 37.

70 Clara Jerome to Mrs Clara Jerome, 1875, cited by Allen Andrews in *The Splendid Pauper*, p. 37.

71 Clara Jerome to Mrs Clara Jerome, 1875, cited by Allen Andrews in *The Splendid Pauper*, p. 38.

72 Clara Jerome to Mrs Clara Jerome, 1875, cited by Allen Andrews in *The Splendid Pauper*, p. 38.

73 Cited by Anita Leslie in *The Fabulous Leonard Jerome*, p. 239.

74 Cited by Anita Leslie in *The Fabulous Leonard Jerome*, p. 215.

5: THE WILD WEST, PP. 92–120

1 Jennie Churchill to Clara and Leonie Jerome, cited by Anita Leslie in *Jennie: The Life of Lady Randolph Churchill*, p. 67.

2 Jennie Churchill to Mrs Clara Jerome, cited by Ralph Martin in *Jennie: The Life of Lady Randolph Churchill, vol. I*, p. 145.

3 Moreton Frewen to Clara Jerome, 1879, cited by Allen Andrews in *The Splendid Pauper*, p. 54.

4 Moreton Frewen to Clara Jerome, 1880, cited by Allen Andrews in *The Splendid Pauper*, p. 54.

5 Moreton Frewen to Clara Jerome, 1880, cited by Allen Andrews in *The Splendid Pauper*, p. 55.

6 Moreton Frewen, *Melton Mowbray and Other Memories*, cited by Ralph Martin in *Lady Randolph Churchill, vol. I*, p. 147.

7 Moreton Frewen to Jennie Churchill, cited by Ralph Martin in *Lady Randolph Churchill, vol. I*, p. 147.

8 David Cannadine, *The Decline and Fall of the British Aristocracy*, pp. 360–2.

9 Cited by Allen Andrews in *The Splendid Pauper*, pp. 16–17.

10 Cited by Allen Andrews in *The Splendid Pauper*, pp. 28–9.

11 Moreton Frewen to Clara Jerome, 19 November 1879, cited in Allen Andrews, *The Splendid Pauper*, p. 12.

12 Allen Andrews, *The Splendid Pauper*, p. 57.

13 Cited by Allen Andrews in *The Splendid Pauper*, p. 59.

14 There is little correspondence or other record of the youngest Jerome sister before her marriage in 1880. Her granddaughter, Anita Leslie, who knew her well (and was nearly thirty when Leonie died), received many of her confidences, which she used when writing her books about her family (including biographies of Leonard Jerome, Jennie Churchill, and Moreton Frewen).

15 Anita Leslie, *Edwardians in Love*, p. 200.

16 Leslie Papers, NLI, L/1/3; Leonie Jerome to Clara Jerome and Mrs Clara Jerome, 24 April 1879.

17 Leslie Papers, NLI, L/1/2; Leonie Jerome to Mrs Clara Jerome, undated, April 1879 [?].

18 King Papers; Charles Fitzwilliam to Leonie Jerome, 7 October 1881.

19 Cited by Anita Leslie in *The Fabulous Leonard Jerome*, p. 254.

20 King Papers; Charles Fitzwilliam to Leonie Jerome, 1 January 1882 [?].

21 King Papers; Charles Fitzwilliam to Leonie Jerome, 23 May 1882 [?].

22 Leslie Papers, NLI, L/1/2, [n.d.].

23 Jennie Churchill to Mrs Clara Jerome, cited by Ralph Martin in *Lady Randolph Churchill, vol. I*, p. 149.

24 Mrs George Cornwallis-West, *The Reminiscences of Lady Randolph Churchill*, pp. 101–2.

25 Mrs George Cornwallis-West, *The Reminiscences of Lady Randolph Churchill*, pp. 144–5.

26 Clara Frewen to Leonie Jerome, 24 August 1881, cited by Anita Leslie in *Mr Frewen of England*, pp. 66–7.

27 Clara Frewen to Mrs Clara Jerome, 24 August 1881, cited by Anita Leslie in *Mr Frewen of England*, p. 66.

28 Moreton Frewen to Clara Frewen, cited by Allen Andrews in *The Splendid Pauper*, p. 72.

29 Moreton Frewen to Clara Frewen, cited by Allen Andrews in *The Splendid Pauper*, p. 73.

30 Moreton Frewen to Clara Frewen; cited by Allen Andrews in *The Splendid Pauper*, p. 74.

31 See David Cannadine, *The Decline and Fall of the British Aristocracy*, pp. 406–20.

32 Char 28/98/24–5; Jennie Churchill to Randolph Churchill, 3 January 1883.

33 Char 28/98/3–6; Jennie Churchill to Randolph Churchill, 1883.

34 Char 28/1/2–3; Mrs Clara Jerome to Jennie Churchill, 6 August 1883.

35 Char 28/1/5–6; Mrs Clara Jerome to Jennie Churchill, 23 November 1883.

36 Char 28/1/5–6; Mrs Clara Jerome to Jennie Churchill, 23 November 1883.

37 Leslie Papers, NLI, L/1/4; Leonie to Jack Leslie, 7 February 1883 [?].

38 Leslie Papers, NLI, L/1/4; Leonie Jerome to Jack Leslie, 8 February 1883 [?].

39 Leslie Papers, NLI, L/1/4; Leonie Jerome to Jack Leslie, 6 August 1884.

40 Char 28/1/7–9; Mrs Clara Jerome to Jennie Churchill, 8 August 1884.

41 Leslie Papers, NLI, L/1/5; Jack Leslie to Jennie Churchill, 30 August 1884.

42 Char 28/1/7–9; Mrs Clara Jerome to Jennie Churchill, 8 August 1884.

43 See John Bateman, *The Great Landowners of Great Britain and Ireland*.

44 R.F. Foster, *Modern Ireland 1600–1972*, pp. 375–6; and S.J. Connolly (ed.), *The Oxford Companion to Irish History*, p. 297.

45 R.F. Foster, *Modern Ireland 1600–1972*, p. 378.

46 Shane Leslie, annotation in the Leslie copy of John Bateman, *The Great Landowning Families of Great Britain and Ireland*.

47 Leslie Papers, NLI, L/1/5; Sir John Leslie to Leonard Jerome, 5 September 1884.

6: GLASLOUGH, PP. 121–146

1 Leslie Papers, NLI, L/1/3; Leonie Leslie to Clara Frewen, October 1884.
2 Char 28/1/10–11; Mrs Jerome to Jennie Churchill, 22 December 1884.
3 Cited by Anita Leslie in *The Fabulous Leonard Jerome*, p. 259.
4 Anita Leslie, *The Fabulous Leonard Jerome*, p. 260.
5 Frewen Papers, Shane book; pp. 152–3.
6 Char 28/1/10–11; Mrs Clara Jerome to Jennie Churchill, 22 December 1884.
7 Cited by Anita Leslie in *Jennie: The Life of Lady Randolph Churchill*, p. 93.
8 Piers Brendon (Keeper of the Churchill Archives Centre, Cambridge), *Winston Churchill: A Brief Life*, p. 12.
9 Ralph Martin, *Jennie: The Life of Lady Randolph Churchill, vol. I*, p. 161.
10 The original Conservatives, known as Tories, were Irish guerrillas who attacked the English. The name Tory was applied – insultingly at first – to royalists who opposed the Exclusion Bills of 1678–81, which would have allowed the Duke of Monmouth to accede to the British throne in place of the Catholic James II. The Tories, suspected of Jacobite sympathies, were excluded from power from 1714 to 1760; they then held office almost continuously until 1830.
11 Richard (Dick) Frewen to Moreton Frewen, cited by Allen Andrews in *The Splendid Pauper*, p. 91.
12 Moreton Frewen to Clara Frewen, cited by Allen Andrews in *The Splendid Pauper*, pp. 92–3.
13 Moreton Frewen to Clara Frewen, cited by Allen Andrews in *The Splendid Pauper*, p. 93.
14 Moreton Frewen to Clara Frewen, 1887, cited by Allen Andrews in *The Splendid Pauper*, p. 101.
15 Moreton Frewen to Clara Frewen, 1887, cited by Allen Andrews in *The Splendid Pauper*, p. 101.
16 King Papers; John Leslie to Leonie Leslie, 21 November 1886.
17 Char 28/7/67–8; Randolph Churchill to Jennie Churchill, 27 September 1875.
18 Leslie Papers, NLI, L/1/9; Leonie Leslie to Eva Thompson, October 1885.
19 Leslie Papers, NLI, L/1/9; Leonie Leslie to Eva Thompson, 11 October 1887.
20 R.F. Foster, *Lord Randolph Churchill: A Political Life*, p. 167.
21 Cited by Roy Jenkins in *Churchill*, p. 15.
22 Mrs George Cornwallis-West, *The Reminiscences of Lady Randolph Churchill*,

p. 91.

23 Cited by Ralph Martin in *Lady Randolph Churchill, vol. I*, p. 168.

24 Mrs George Cornwallis-West, *The Reminiscences of Lady Randolph Churchill*, p. 104.

25 Cited by R. F. Foster, *Lord Randolph Churchill: A Political Life*, p. 258.

26 Moreton Frewen to Clara Frewen, cited by Allen Andrews in *The Splendid Pauper*, p. 105.

27 Moreton Frewen to Clara Frewen, cited by Allen Andrews in *The Splendid Pauper*, p. 109.

28 Moreton Frewen to Clara Frewen, September 1887, cited by Allen Andrews in *The Splendid Pauper*, p. 111.

29 Moreton Frewen to Clara Frewen, 1887, cited by Allen Andrews in *The Splendid Pauper*, p. 112.

30 Moreton Frewen to Clara Frewen, 1887, cited by Allen Andrews in *The Splendid Pauper*, p. 112.

31 Moreton Frewen to Clara Frewen, cited by Allen Andrews in *The Splendid Pauper*, p. 115.

32 Frewen Papers, Shane book; p. 149.

33 Frewen Papers, Shane book; p. 213.

34 Leslie Papers, NLI, L/1/2; Leonie Leslie to Mrs Clara Jerome, October/November 1886.

35 Leslie Papers, NLI, L/1/3; Leonie Leslie to Clara Frewen, October/November 1886.

36 Leslie Papers, NLI, L/1/3; Leonie Leslie to Clara Frewen, 1886/1887.

37 The Duchess of Marlborough to Jennie Churchill, 24 October 1886, in Peregrine Churchill and Julian Mitchell, *Jennie, Lady Randolph Churchill: A Portrait with Letters*, p. 153.

38 Ralph Martin, *Lady Randolph Churchill, vol. I*, p. 205.

39 Char 28/1/14–16; Mrs Clara Jerome to Jennie Churchill, 6 August 1886.

40 Char 28/1/17; Mrs Clara Jerome to Jennie Churchill, October 1886.

41 Frewen Papers, Shane book; Mrs Clara Jerome to Clara Frewen, 25 October 1887.

42 Henry Labouchere to Lord Rosebery, 25 November 1885, in R. F. Foster, *Lord Randolph Churchill: A Political Life*, p. 217.

43 See R. F. Foster, *Randolph Churchill: A Political Life*, p. 218. He points out that 'giddiness' is mentioned in Peregrine Churchill and Julian Mitchell, *Jennie, Lady Randolph Churchill*, as are other symptoms in Lord Rosebery, *Lord Randolph Churchill*, and T.P. O'Connor, *Memories of an Old Parliamentarian*. There are also various references in Randolph's own letters

to his increasing deafness.

44 See Deborah Hayden, *Pox: Genius, Madness, and the Mysteries of Syphilis*, pp. 310–11.

45 R.F. Foster, *Lord Randolph Churchill*, p. 271.

46 *The Times*, 22 December 1886.

47 Cited by Ralph Martin in *Lady Randolph Churchill*, vol. I, p. 213.

48 Mrs George Cornwallis-West, *The Reminiscences of Lady Randolph Churchill*, p. 143.

49 Ralph Martin, *Lady Randolph Churchill*, vol. I, p. 216.

50 Jennie Churchill to Randolph Churchill, 5 March 1887, in Peregrine Churchill and Julian Mitchell, *Jennie, Lady Randolph Churchill*, p. 162.

51 Jennie Churchill to Leonie Leslie, cited by Anita Leslie in *Jennie*, p. 122.

52 Clare Sheridan, *Nuda Veritas*, p. 63.

53 Moreton Frewen to Clara Frewen, 1888 [?], cited by Allen Andrews in *The Splendid Pauper*, p. 134.

54 Cited by Allen Andrews in *The Splendid Pauper*, p. 134.

55 Cited by Allen Andrews in *The Splendid Pauper*, p. 136.

56 Cited by Allen Andrews in *The Splendid Pauper*, p. 136.

7: THE CHURCHILLS IN AMERICA, PP. 147–175

1 Mrs George Cornwallis-West, *The Reminiscences of Lady Randolph Churchill*, pp. 164–5.

2 Leonard Jerome to Leonie Leslie, 1888, cited by Ralph Martin in *Jennie: The Life of Lady Randolph Churchill*, vol. I, p. 244.

3 Moreton Frewen to Clara Frewen, cited by Ralph Martin in *Lady Randolph Churchill*, vol. I, p. 247.

4 Cited by Ralph Martin in *Lady Randolph Churchill*, vol. I, pp. 274–5.

5 Randolph Churchill to Jennie Churchill, 1890, cited by Ralph Martin in *Lady Randolph Churchill*, vol. I, p. 256.

6 Seymour Leslie, *The Jerome Connexion*, p. 1.

7 Lady Constance Leslie to the Duchess of Marlborough, cited by Anita Leslie in *The Fabulous Leonard Jerome*, p. 277.

8 Leonard Jerome to Mrs Clara Jerome, cited by Anita Leslie in *The Fabulous Leonard Jerome*, p. 298.

9 Eugene Jerome to Clara Frewen, cited by Anita Leslie in *The Fabulous Leonard Jerome*, p. 299.

10 Eugene Jerome to Moreton Frewen, 1890, cited by Ralph Martin in *Lady*

Randolph Churchill, vol. I, p. 261.

11 Leonie Leslie to Lady Constance Leslie, January 1891, cited by Ralph Martin in *Lady Randolph Churchill, vol. I*, p. 261.

12 King Milan to Clara Frewen, cited by Anita Leslie in *The Fabulous Leonard Jerome*, pp. 293–4.

13 Allen Andrews, *The Splendid Pauper*, p. 144.

14 Mrs George Cornwallis-West, *The Reminiscences of Lady Randolph Churchill*, p. 206.

15 Clare Sheridan, *To the Four Winds*, p. 20.

16 Clare Sheridan, *To the Four Winds*, p. 18.

17 Moreton Frewen to Clara Frewen, cited by Allen Andrews in *The Splendid Pauper*, p. 149.

18 Moreton Frewen to Clara Frewen, cited by Allen Andrews in *The Splendid Pauper*, p. 158.

19 Moreton Frewen to Clara Frewen, cited by Allen Andrews in *The Splendid Pauper*, p. 158.

20 Leslie Papers, NLI, L/1/3; Leonie Leslie to Clara Frewen, 1890.

21 Elizabeth Bowen was born in Dublin in 1899, and her family owned Bowen's Court in County Cork. She was, however, educated in England and lived alternately in the two countries throughout her life. Considered one of the finest novelists of the twentieth century, Bowen was awarded the CBE in 1948 and received an honorary degree of Doctor of Letters from Trinity College, Dublin, in 1949 and from Oxford University in 1956. Recently, there has been spirited debate in Ireland over whether Bowen, who was Anglo-Irish and did not support the Irish nationalist movement, should be considered an 'Irish' writer. However, Bowen considered herself Irish and wrote extensively about her Irish childhood and the history of her family.

22 Elizabeth Bowen, *The Shelbourne*, p. 88.

23 Leslie Papers, NLI, L/2/3; Leonie Leslie to Mamie (?), n.d.

24 Seymour Leslie, *The Jerome Connexion*, pp. 8–9.

25 Jennie Churchill to Clara Frewen, cited by Seymour Leslie in *The Jerome Connexion*, p. 9.

26 Seymour Leslie, *The Jerome Connexion*, p. 9.

27 Seymour Leslie, *The Jerome Connexion*, pp. 11 & 12.

28 Seymour Leslie, *The Jerome Connexion*, p. 14.

29 Seymour Leslie to Leonie Leslie, [n.d.], cited by Seymour Leslie in *The Jerome Connexion*, p. 15.

30 Seymour Leslie, *The Jerome Connexion*, p. 12.

31 Clare Sheridan, *Nuda Veritas*, p. 14.

32 Shane Leslie, *Long Shadows*, pp. 16–17.

33 Shane Leslie, *The Film of Memory*, p. 115.

34 Shane Leslie, *The Film of Memory*, p. 116.

35 Jennie Churchill to Randolph Churchill, cited by Ralph Martin in *Lady Randolph Churchill, vol. I*, p. 263.

36 Jennie Churchill to Randolph Churchill, cited by Ralph Martin in *Lady Randolph Churchill, vol. I*, p. 263.

37 Moreton Frewen to Randolph Churchill, cited by Ralph Martin in *Lady Randolph Churchill, vol. I*, p. 261.

38 Randolph Churchill to Moreton Frewen, cited by Ralph Martin in *Lady Randolph Churchill, vol. I*, p. 261.

39 Jennie Churchill to Randolph Churchill, 1891, cited by Ralph Martin in *Lady Randolph Churchill, vol. I*, p. 263.

40 Jennie to Randolph Churchill, 1891, cited by Ralph Martin in *Lady Randolph Churchill, vol. I*, p. 265.

41 Moreton Frewen to Clara Frewen, cited by Ralph Martin in *Lady Randolph Churchill, vol. I*, pp. 265–6.

42 Jennie Churchill to Randolph Churchill, cited by Ralph Martin in *Lady Randolph Churchill, vol. I*, p. 264.

43 Jennie Churchill to Randolph Churchill, cited by Ralph Martin in *Lady Randolph Churchill, vol. I*, p. 269.

44 Mrs George Cornwallis-West, *The Reminiscences of Lady Randolph Churchill*, p. 225.

45 Mrs George Cornwallis-West, *The Reminiscences of Lady Randolph Churchill*, p. 225.

46 Mrs George Cornwallis-West, *The Reminiscences of Lady Randolph Churchill*, p. 229.

47 Mrs George Cornwallis-West, *The Reminiscences of Lady Randolph Churchill*, pp. 220–1.

48 Jennie Churchill to Randolph Churchill, 1891, cited by Ralph Martin in *Lady Randolph Churchill, vol. I*, p. 275.

49 Jennie Churchill to Randolph Churchill, 1891, cited by Ralph Martin in *Lady Randolph Churchill, vol. I*, p. 275.

50 Winston S. Churchill to Jennie Churchill, 6 [?] December 1891, in Randolph S. Churchill, *Youth: Winston S. Churchill 1874–1900*, p. 160.

51 Jennie Churchill to Winston S. Churchill, 7 [?] December 1891, in Randolph S. Churchill, *Youth: Winston S. Churchill 1874–1900*, p. 161.

52 Winston S. Churchill to Jennie Churchill, 24 December 1891, in Randolph

S. Churchill, *Youth: Winston S. Churchill 1874–1900*, p. 169.

53 Winston S. Churchill to Jennie Churchill, 27 [?] December 1891, in Randolph S. Churchill, *Youth: Winston S. Churchill 1874–1900*, p. 171.

54 Winston S. Churchill to Jennie Churchill, 29 December 1891, in Randolph S. Churchill, *Youth: Winston S. Churchill 1874–1900*, p. 172.

55 Randolph Churchill to Winston S. Churchill, 1892, cited by Ralph Martin in *Lady Randolph Churchill, vol. I*, p. 281.

56 Randolph Churchill to Jennie Churchill, 6 October 1893, in Randolph S. Churchill, *Youth: Winston S. Churchill 1874–1900*, p. 214.

57 Winston S. Churchill to Jennie Churchill, 29 October 1893, in Randolph S. Churchill, *Youth: Winston S. Churchill 1874–1900*, p. 216.

58 Lord Rosebery, *Lord Randolph Churchill*, p. 72.

59 Cited by Ralph Martin in *Lady Randolph Churchill, vol. I*, p. 295.

60 Doctors Thomas Buzzard and Robson Roose to Lady Randolph Churchill, 25 June 1894, in Randolph S. Churchill, *Youth: Winston S. Churchill 1874–1900*, pp. 235–6.

61 Ralph Martin, *Lady Randolph Churchill, vol. I*, p. 297.

62 Peregrine Churchill and Julian Mitchell, *Jennie, Lady Randolph Churchill: A Portrait with Letters*, p. 166.

63 Mrs George Cornwallis-West, *The Reminiscences of Lady Randolph Churchill*, p. 233.

64 Mrs George Cornwallis-West, *The Reminiscences of Lady Randolph Churchill*, pp. 232–5.

65 King Papers. This letter from Jennie to Consuelo, Duchess of Manchester, is described in a letter from Clare Sheridan to Anita Leslie, 24 August 1951.

66 Mrs George Cornwallis-West, *The Reminiscences of Lady Randolph Churchill*, pp. 233–4.

67 Jennie Churchill to Leonie Leslie, 4 August 1894, in Peregrine Churchill and Julian Mitchell, *Jennie, Lady Randolph Churchill*, p. 167.

68 Cited by Ralph Martin in *Lady Randolph Churchill, vol. I*, pp. 278–9.

69 King Papers; Jennie Churchill to Clara Frewen, December 1894.

70 King Papers; Jennie Churchill to Clara Frewen, November 1894.

71 King Papers; Jennie Churchill to Leonie Leslie, 31 October 1894.

72 Jennie Churchill to Leonie Leslie, December 1894, in Peregrine Churchill and Julian Mitchell, *Jennie, Lady Randolph Churchill*, p 168.

73 Jennie Churchill to Clara Frewen, 18 November 1894, in Peregrine Churchill and Julian Mitchell, *Jennie, Lady Randolph Churchill*, p. 167.

8: THE FUNERAL TOUR, PP. 176–196

1 Cited by Ralph Martin in *Jennie: The Life of Lady Randolph Churchill, vol. I*, p. 306.

2 Jennie Churchill to Leonie Leslie, 3 January 1895, in Peregrine Churchill and Julian Mitchell, *Jennie, Lady Randolph Churchill: A Portrait with Letters*, p. 169.

3 Clara Frewen to Leonie Leslie, cited by Ralph Martin in *Lady Randolph Churchill, vol. I*, p. 306.

4 Lord Rosebery, *Lord Randolph Churchill*, p. 181.

5 Ralph Martin, *Lady Randolph Churchill, vol. I*, pp. 308–9.

6 *The Times*, 19 April 1898.

7 Ralph Martin, *Jennie: The Life of Lady Randolph Churchill, vol. II*, p. 2.

8 Jennie Churchill to Leonie Leslie, 3 January 1895, in Peregrine Churchill and Julian Mitchell, *Jennie, Lady Randolph Churchill*, pp. 169–170.

9 Moreton Frewen to Clara Frewen, cited by Allen Andrews in *The Splendid Pauper*, p. 177.

10 Moreton Frewen to Clara Frewen, 14 October 1892, cited by Anita Leslie in *Mr Frewen of England*, p. 125.

11 Moreton Frewen to Jennie Churchill, cited by Anita Leslie in *Mr Frewen of England*, p. 125.

12 Jennie Churchill to Clara Frewen, 18 November 1894, cited by Anita Leslie in *Jennie: The Life of Lady Randolph Churchill*, p. 172.

13 Cited by Allen Andrews in *The Splendid Pauper*, p. 178.

14 Cited by Allen Andrews in *The Splendid Pauper*, p. 179.

15 Randolph Churchill to Winston S. Churchill, cited by Ralph Martin in *Lady Randolph Churchill, vol. I*, p. 288.

16 Hugh Montgomery-Massingberd, *Blenheim Revisited: The Spencer-Churchills and their Palace*, p. 116.

17 Clara Frewen to Moreton Frewen, 19 January 1895, cited by Ralph Martin in *Lady Randolph Churchill, vol. II*, p. 2.

18 The Prince of Wales to Jennie Churchill, cited by Anita Leslie in *Jennie: The Life of Lady Randolph Churchill*, p. 176.

19 The Prince of Wales to Jennie Churchill, cited by Anita Leslie in *Jennie*, p. 176.

20 The description is Rudyard Kipling's, cited by Ralph Martin in *Lady Randolph Churchill, vol. II*, p. 9.

21 Winston S. Churchill, *My Early Life: A Roving Commission*, p. 62.

22 The Marquis de Breteuil to Jennie Churchill, cited by Ralph Martin in

Lady Randolph Churchill, vol. II, p. 24.

23 Cited by Ralph Martin in *Lady Randolph Churchill, vol. II*, p. 36.

24 Cited by Ralph Martin in *Lady Randolph Churchill, vol. II*, p. 41.

25 Ralph Martin, *Lady Randolph Churchill, vol. II*, p. 41.

26 Clare Sheridan, *To the Four Winds*, p. 22.

27 Char 1/3/9; Mrs Clara Jerome to Winston S. Churchill, 1893.

28 Leslie Papers, NLI, L/1/9; Clara Frewen to Eva Thompson, 28 March 1895.

29 Leslie Papers, NLI, L/1/9; Leonie Leslie to David Thompson, April 1895.

30 Clara Frewen to Moreton Frewen, 16 April 1895, cited by Ralph Martin in *Lady Randolph Churchill, vol. II*, p. 42.

31 Moreton Frewen to Clara Frewen, cited by Allen Andrews in *The Splendid Pauper*, p. 179.

32 Leslie Papers, NLI, L/1/9; Leonie Leslie to Eva Thompson, 1895.

33 Ralph Martin, *Lady Randolph Churchill, vol. II*, p. 56.

34 Moreton Frewen to Clara Frewen, cited by Allen Andrews in *The Splendid Pauper*, p. 182.

35 Moreton Frewen to Clara Frewen, cited by Allen Andrews in *The Splendid Pauper*, p. 183.

36 Clara Frewen to Moreton Frewen, cited by Allen Andrews in *The Splendid Pauper*, pp. 183–4.

37 Olive Guthrie to Leonie Leslie, cited by Anita Leslie in *Mr Frewen of England*, p. 146.

38 Allen Andrews, *The Splendid Pauper*, p. 188.

39 Clara Frewen to Moreton Frewen, cited by Allen Andrews in *The Splendid Pauper*, p. 193.

40 *The Red Badge of Courage* was considered Stephen Crane's greatest literary accomplishment. It went through two editions in its first year of publication, and by March 1896 it had gone through fourteen printings. In spite of the book's success, Crane's poor business sense and unremunerative contracts with publishers kept him insolvent most of his life.

41 Cora Crane to Moreton Frewen, cited by Allen Andrews in *The Splendid Pauper*, p. 196.

42 Gail MacColl and Carol McD. Wallace, *To Marry an English Lord: The Victorian and Edwardian Experience*, pp. 232–3.

43 Several hundred of these letters were handed over to the royal family at their request on the Duke of Connaught's death in 1942, but they are not now available to the public. They have been viewed by the duke's official biographer, Noble Frankland, but his evaluation and description of the relationship had to be approved by the royal family before publication. This

poses the question of why the letters may not be viewed.

44 Noble Frankland, *Witness of a Century: The Life and Times of Prince Arthur Duke of Connaught 1850–1942*, p. 220.

45 Char 28/62/2; Leonie Leslie to Jennie Churchill, 1897.

46 Leslie Papers, NLI, L/1/9; Leonie Leslie to Eva Thompson, 1895.

47 Leslie Papers, NLI, L/1/9; Leonie Leslie to Eva Thompson, August 1895 (or 1896?)

48 Leonie Leslie to the Duke of Connaught, cited by Anita Leslie in *Edwardians in Love*, p. 208.

9: LOWER JEROME TERRACE, PP. 197–220

1 Winston S. Churchill to Jennie Churchill, cited by Ralph Martin in *Jennie: The Life of Lady Randolph Churchill, vol. II*, p. 62.

2 Jennie Churchill to Winston S. Churchill, 11 October 1895, cited by Ralph Martin in *Lady Randolph Churchill, vol. II*, p. 64.

3 Winston S. Churchill to Jack Churchill, cited by Ralph Martin, *Lady Randolph Churchill, vol. II*, p. 71.

4 Ralph Martin, *Lady Randolph Churchill, vol. II*, p. 74.

5 In 1899, Winston became aware of another author living in America, also named Winston Churchill. He ended any possible confusion by adding Spencer (without a hyphen) to his own surname (*My Early Life: A Roving Commission*, pp. 214–15). He has subsequently become known as Winston Spencer Churchill, or Winston S. Churchill.

6 Jennie Churchill to Winston S. Churchill, 3 March 1897, in Roy Jenkins, *Churchill*, pp. 27–8.

7 Jennie Churchill to the Countess of Warwick, cited by Ralph Martin in *Lady Randolph Churchill, vol. II*, p. 81.

8 Ralph Martin, *Lady Randolph Churchill, vol. II*, p. 81.

9 Winston S. Churchill to Jennie Churchill, 28 January 1898, cited by Ralph Martin in *Lady Randolph Churchill, vol. II*, p. 125.

10 Char/28/152B/145; Winston S. Churchill to Jack Churchill, 16 February 1898.

11 The Prince of Wales to Jennie Churchill, cited by Anita Leslie in *Jennie: The Life of Lady Randolph Churchill*, p. 214.

12 Jennie Churchill to the Prince of Wales, cited by Anita Leslie in *Jennie*, p. 214.

13 The Prince of Wales to Jennie Churchill, cited by Anita Leslie in *Jennie*, p.

214.

14 Mrs George Cornwallis-West, *The Reminiscences of Lady Randolph Churchill*, p. 278.

15 Mrs George Cornwallis-West, *The Reminiscences of Lady Randolph Churchill*, pp. 279–83.

16 Winston S. Churchill to Jennie Churchill, 1 January 1899, cited by Anita Leslie in *Jennie*, p. 226.

17 Mrs George Cornwallis-West, *The Reminiscences of Lady Randolph Churchill*, pp. 279–83.

18 George Cornwallis-West to Jennie Churchill, cited by Anita Leslie in *Jennie*, pp. 219–20.

19 Cited by Anita Leslie in *Jennie*, p. 220.

20 George Cornwallis-West to Jennie Churchill, 13 July 1898, cited in Peregrine Churchill and Julian Mitchell, *Jennie, Lady Randolph Churchill: A Portrait with Letters*, pp. 174–5.

21 George Cornwallis-West to Jennie Churchill, 19 July 1898, cited in Peregrine Churchill and Julian Mitchell, *Jennie, Lady Randolph Churchill*, p. 175.

22 George Cornwallis-West to Jennie Churchill, 1 August 1898, cited in Peregrine Churchill and Julian Mitchell, *Jennie, Lady Randolph Churchill*, p. 176.

23 Ralph Martin, *Lady Randolph Churchill, vol. II*, p. 191.

24 George Cornwallis-West to Jennie Churchill, 14 September 1899, in Peregrine Churchill and Julian Mitchell, *Jennie, Lady Randolph Churchill*, p. 192.

25 *Town Topics*, 25 January 1900, cited by Ralph Martin in *Lady Randolph Churchill, vol. II*, p. 199.

26 Cited by Anita Leslie in *Mr Frewen of England*, p. 152.

27 Leslie Papers, NLI, L/1/3; Clara Frewen to Leonie Leslie, 1899.

28 Char 28/62/2; Leonie Leslie to Jennie Churchill, 1897.

29 Char 28/62/14; Leonie Leslie to Jennie Churchill, 23 April 1898.

30 Ralph Martin, *Lady Randolph Churchill, vol. II*, p. 206.

31 Leslie Papers, NLI, L/1/3; Mrs C. Adair to Leonie Leslie, December 1899.

32 Jennie Churchill to Leonie Leslie, 24 December 1899, cited by Peregrine Churchill and Julian Mitchell in *Jennie, Lady Randolph Churchill*, p. 202.

33 Colonel Cornwallis-West to Leonie Leslie, cited by Seymour Leslie in *The Jerome Connexion*, pp. 54–5.

34 Jennie Churchill to Jack Churchill, 23 June 1900, cited in Peregrine Churchill and Julian Mitchell, *Jennie, Lady Randolph Churchill*, p. 219–20.

35 *Morning Post* and *Daily Telegraph*, July 1900, cited by Eileen Quelch in *Perfect Darling: The Life and Times of George Cornwallis-West*, p. 78.

36 Winston S. Churchill to Jack Churchill, cited by Eileen Quelch in *Perfect Darling*, p. 79.

37 Leslie Papers, NLI, L/1/9; Leonie Leslie to Eva Thompson, 1900.

38 Leslie Papers, NLI, L/1/4; Jack Leslie to Leonie Leslie, 1900.

39 Leslie Papers, NLI, L/1/4; Jack Leslie to Leonie Leslie, 30 August 1900.

40 Char 28/75/8; Prince of Wales to Jennie Churchill (now Cornwallis-West), 12 March 1902.

41 King Papers; Leonie Leslie to Clara Frewen, 3 January 1903.

42 This title was created in 1867 by the Ottoman sultan for the Governor of Egypt, Ismail Pasha.

43 Noble Frankland, *Witness of a Century: The Life and Times of Prince Arthur Duke of Connaught 1850–1942*, pp. 222–8.

44 Noble Frankland, *Witness of a Century*, p. 228.

45 Seymour Leslie, *The Jerome Connexion*, p. 39.

46 See Seymour Leslie, *The Jerome Connexion*.

10: MORTAL RUIN, PP. 221–249

1 Frewen Papers; Clara Frewen to Moreton Frewen, May 1901.

2 Frewen Papers; Clara Frewen to Moreton Frewen, 2 June 1901.

3 Frewen Papers; Clara Frewen to Moreton Frewen, 2 June 1901.

4 Frewen Papers; Clara Frewen to Moreton Frewen, 7 July 1901.

5 Leslie Papers, NLI, L/3/3; Moreton Frewen to Leonie Leslie, 1902.

6 Information on Eton fees provided by P. Hatfield, College Archivist, Eton College.

7 Leslie Papers, NLI, M/8/1; Clare Frewen to Jacky Leslie, [n.d.].

8 Leslie Papers, NLI, M/8/1, March 1902.

9 Leslie Papers, NLI, M/8/1; Clare Frewen to Jacky Leslie, [n.d.].

10 Allen Andrews, *The Splendid Pauper*, p. 199.

11 Leslie Papers, NLI, M/8/3; Hugh Frewen to Jacky Leslie, 22 July 1902.

12 Leslie Papers, NLI, L/5/6.

13 Frewen Papers, Oswald diaries; 6 March 1903.

14 Clare Sheridan, *Nuda Veritas*, p. 40.

15 Clare Sheridan, *Nuda Veritas*, p. 40.

16 Anita Leslie, *Cousin Clare: The Tempestuous Career of Clare Sheridan*, p. 35.

17 Clare Sheridan, *Nuda Veritas*, p. 40.

18 Clare Sheridan, *To the Four Winds*, p. 27.

19 Clare Frewen to Clara Frewen, 8 February 1904, cited by Allen Andrews in *The Splendid Pauper*, pp. 203–4.

20 Clare Frewen to Clara Frewen, cited by Allen Andrews in *The Splendid Pauper*, pp. 204–5.

21 Allen Andrews, *The Splendid Pauper*, pp. 202–5.

22 Leslie Papers, NLI, L/5/17; Hugh Frewen to Shane Leslie, 18 August 1956.

23 Moreton had collected twenty acorns from this venerable oak, under which Queen Elizabeth I had sat to have her lunch over three hundred years previously; the other ten acorns were planted by King Edward VII at Sandringham.

24 Moreton Frewen to Clara Frewen, cited by Allen Andrews in *The Splendid Pauper*, p. 208.

25 Leslie Papers, NLI, L/5/2; Moreton Frewen to Clara Frewen, 15 December 1905.

26 Leslie Papers, NLI, L/5/17; Hugh Frewen to Shane Leslie, 18 August 1956.

27 Leslie Papers, NLI, L/5/2; Moreton Frewen to Clara Frewen, 17 January 1906.

28 Leslie Papers, NLI, L/5/2; Moreton Frewen to Clara Frewen, 19 January 1906.

29 Frewen Papers, Oswald diaries; 17 December 1903.

30 Frewen Papers, Oswald diaries; 22 December 1906.

31 Shane Leslie, *Long Shadows*, pp. 14–16.

32 Leslie Papers, NLI, L/2/2; Mary Crawshay to Leonie Leslie, 6 April 1908.

33 Leslie Papers, NLI, L/2/2; Mary Crawshay to Leonie Leslie, 1909.

34 Frewen Papers, Oswald diaries; 15 April 1908.

35 Frewen Papers, Oswald diaries; 22 April 1908.

36 Leslie Papers, NLI, L/2/2; Mary Crawshay to Leonie Leslie, 6 April 1908.

37 Leslie Papers, NLI, L/2/8; Norman Leslie to Leonie Leslie, 1909.

38 Leslie Papers, NLI, M/1/5; Norman Leslie to Shane Leslie, 1905.

39 Leslie Papers, NLI, N/1/5; Leonie Leslie to Norman Leslie, 1905 [?].

40 Leslie Papers, NLI, L/2/7; Norman Leslie to Leonie Leslie, June 1907.

41 Leslie Papers, NLI, L/2/8; Norman Leslie to Leonie Leslie, 1909 [?].

42 Seymour Leslie, *The Jerome Connexion*, p. 34.

43 Seymour Leslie, *The Jerome Connexion*, p. 34.

44 These letters were returned to George V at his request. Anita Leslie, *Edwardians in Love*.

45 Char 28/75/3; Albert Edward, Prince of Wales, to Jennie Churchill (Mrs George Cornwallis-West), 28 September 1900.

46 Winston S. Churchill to Jennie Churchill (Mrs George Cornwallis-West), cited by Anita Leslie in *Jennie: The Life of Lady Randolph Churchill*, p. 259.

47 George Cornwallis-West to Jennie Churchill (Cornwallis-West); in Peregrine Churchill and Julian Mitchell, *Jennie, Lady Randolph Churchill: A Portrait with Letters*, p. 227.

48 George Cornwallis-West to Jennie Churchill (Cornwallis-West), 8 March 1906, in Peregrine Churchill and Julian Mitchell, *Jennie, Lady Randolph Churchill*, p. 227.

49 Cited by Ralph Martin in *Jennie: The Life of Lady Randolph Churchill, vol. II*, p. 306.

50 Jennie Churchill (Cornwallis-West) to Leonie Leslie, 15 May 1907, in Peregrine Churchill and Julian Mitchell, *Jennie, Lady Randolph Churchill*, p. 228.

51 Seymour Leslie, *The Jerome Connexion*, p. 13.

52 Jennie Churchill (Cornwallis-West) to Leonie Leslie, 14 January 1906, cited by Anita Leslie in *Jennie*, p. 273.

53 Jennie Churchill (Cornwallis-West) to Leonie Leslie, 28 January 1906, cited by Anita Leslie in *Jennie*, pp. 273–4.

54 21 November 1907, cited by Ralph Martin in *Lady Randolph Churchill, vol. II*, p. 313.

55 Jack Churchill to Winston S. Churchill, 2 January 1908, cited by Ralph Martin in *Lady Randolph Churchill, vol. II*, p. 313.

56 Mary Soames, *Clementine Churchill: The Revised and Updated Biography*, pp. 4–9.

57 Cited by Anita Leslie in *Jennie*, p. 279.

58 Cited by Ralph Martin in *Lady Randolph Churchill, vol. II*, p. 319.

59 Winston S. Churchill, *My Early Life: A Roving Commission*, p. 367.

60 Winston S. Churchill to Jennie Churchill (Cornwallis-West), 13 September 1908, cited by Ralph Martin in *Lady Randolph Churchill, vol. II*, p. 320.

61 See Mary Soames, *Clementine Churchill: The Revised and Updated Biography*.

11: THE LAST DUEL, PP. 250–289

1 Clare Sheridan, *Nuda Veritas*, p. 47.

2 Clare Sheridan, *Nuda Veritas*, p. 63.

3 Clare Sheridan, *Nuda Veritas*, p. 65.

4 Leslie Papers, NLI, L/5/17; Hugh Frewen to Clara Frewen, 11 October 1907.

5 Clare Frewen to Hugh Frewen, cited by Allen Andrews in *The Splendid Pauper*, pp. 213–14.

6 Clare Frewen to Hugh Frewen, cited by Allen Andrews in *The Splendid Pauper*, pp. 213–14.

7 Clare Frewen to Hugh Frewen, cited by Allen Andrews in *The Splendid Pauper*, p. 215.

8 Anita Leslie, *Mr Frewen of England*, p. 172.

9 Allen Andrews, *The Splendid Pauper*, p. 216.

10 Frewen Papers, Clara letters; Clara Frewen to Moreton Frewen, 8 April 1908.

11 Moreton Frewen to Clara Frewen, cited by Allen Andrews in *The Splendid Pauper*, pp. 216–17.

12 Frewen Papers, Oswald diaries; 30 April 1908.

13 Frewen Papers, Clara letters; Clare Frewen to Clara Frewen, 20 July 1908.

14 Frewen Papers, Oswald diaries; 25 November 1908.

15 Leslie Papers, NLI, M/8/1; Clare Frewen to Shane Leslie, 6 March 1909.

16 Leslie Papers, NLI, L/5/7; Moreton Frewen to Shane Leslie, 12 January 1909.

17 Moreton Frewen to Clara Frewen, 2 November 1909, cited by Anita Leslie in *Cousin Clare: The Tempestuous Career of Clare Sheridan*, p. 53.

18 Clare Sheridan, *Nuda Veritas*, p. 86.

19 Frewen Papers, Clara letters; Clara Frewen to Oswald Frewen, 5 July 1910.

20 Clare Sheridan, *Nuda Veritas*, p. 88.

21 Allen Andrews, *The Splendid Pauper*, p. 225.

22 Clare Sheridan, *Nuda Veritas*, p. 89.

23 Leslie Papers, NLI, L/5/8; Moreton Frewen to Shane Leslie, 23 January 1909.

24 Allen Andrews, *The Splendid Pauper*, p. 224.

25 The Orangemen Lodges, as they are known, continue this traditional (in Catholic areas, controversial) parade through the towns and cities of Northern Ireland each July.

26 Leslie Papers, NLI, L/3/3; Leonie Leslie to Moreton Frewen, 1912.

27 Cited by Robert Kee in *The Green Flag: A History of Irish Nationalism*, p. 477.

28 Moreton Frewen to Winston S. Churchill, 10 March 1910, cited by Allen Andrews in *The Splendid Pauper*, pp. 225–6.

29 Winston S. Churchill to Moreton Frewen, cited by Allen Andrews in *The Splendid Pauper*, p. 226.

30 Randolph S. Churchill, *Youth: Winston S. Churchill 1874–1900*, p. 445.

31 Robert Kee, *The Green Flag*, p. 470.

32 Robert Kee, *The Green Flag*, p. 475.

33 Published by Edward Arnold.

34 Cited by Eileen Quelch in *Perfect Darling: The Life and Times of George Cornwallis-West*, p. 104.

35 Winston S. Churchill to Jennie Churchill (Cornwallis-West), 4 August 1909, in Ralph Martin, *Jennie: Lady Randolph Churchill, vol. II*, p. 340.

36 Winston S. Churchill to Jennie Churchill (Cornwallis-West), 4 August 1909, in Ralph Martin, *Lady Randolph Churchill, vol. II*, pp. 340–1.

37 Anita Leslie, *Jennie: The Life of Lady Randolph Churchill*, p. 264.

38 George Cornwallis-West, *Edwardian Hey-Days, or, A Little About a Lot of Things*, p. 264.

39 Jennie Churchill (Cornwallis-West) to Leonie Leslie, 27 June 1909, in Peregrine Churchill and Julian Mitchell, *Jennie, Lady Randolph Churchill: A Portrait with Letters*, p. 231.

40 Mrs Patrick Campbell, *My Life and Some Letters*, p. 237.

41 *The Times*, 7 July 1909.

42 Mrs Patrick Campbell, *My Life and Some Letters*, p. 237.

43 Jennie Churchill (Cornwallis-West) to Mrs Patsy Cornwallis-West, August 1910, in Peregrine Churchill and Julian Mitchell, *Jennie, Lady Randolph Churchill*, p. 234.

44 Jack Churchill to Jennie Churchill (Cornwallis-West), 4 April 1911, in Peregrine Churchill and Julian Mitchell, *Jennie, Lady Randolph Churchill*, pp. 234–5.

45 Leslie Papers, NLI, L/4/15; Winston S. Churchill to George Cornwallis-West, 13 April 1911.

46 Anita Leslie, *Jennie*, p. 292.

47 Roy Jenkins, *Churchill*, pp. 201–3.

48 Leslie Papers, NLI, L/4/15; Winston S. Churchill to Jennie Churchill (Cornwallis-West), 13 April 1911.

49 *Daily Mail*, 18 January 1912, in Ralph Martin, *Lady Randolph Churchill, vol. II*, p. 346.

50 *Daily Express*, 27 May 1912, in Ralph Martin, *Lady Randolph Churchill, vol. II*, pp. 346–7.

51 Ralph Martin, *Lady Randolph Churchill, vol. II*, p. 351.

52 Anita Leslie, *Jennie*, p. 295.

53 Jennie Churchill (Cornwallis-West) to George Cornwallis-West, 29 December 1912, in Peregrine Churchill and Julian Mitchell, *Jennie, Lady Randolph Churchill*, p. 238.

54 Moreton Frewen to Clara Frewen, cited by Anita Leslie in *Jennie*, p. 300.

55 Daisy, Princess of Pless, to Jennie Churchill (Cornwallis-West), April 1914, in Peregrine Churchill and Julian Mitchell, *Jennie, Lady Randolph Churchill*, p. 240.

56 Jennie Churchill (Cornwallis-West) to George Cornwallis-West, 4 April 1914, cited by Anita Leslie in *Jennie*, pp. 300–1.

57 Char 28/136/8; Leonie Leslie to Jennie Churchill (Cornwallis-West), Monday, 1914.

58 Char 28/136/7; Leonie Leslie to Jennie Churchill (Cornwallis-West), Wednesday, 1914.

59 Char 28/136/9; Leonie Leslie to Jennie Churchill (Cornwallis-West), Saturday, 1914.

60 Seymour Leslie, *The Jerome Connexion*, p. 37.

61 Seymour Leslie, *The Jerome Connexion*, p. 50.

62 Leslie Papers, NLI, N/1/7; General Sir Ian Hamilton to Leonie Leslie, 26 April 1910.

63 Leslie Papers, NLI, N/1/7; Norman Leslie to Leonie Leslie, 1910.

64 Leslie Papers, NLI, M/1/2A; Leonie Leslie to Marjorie Ide, 1911.

65 Leslie Papers, NLI, L/5/13; Marjorie Ide to Moreton Frewen, 3 April 1912.

66 Leslie Papers, NLI, M/1/2A; Leonie Leslie to Marjorie Ide, 9 April 1912.

67 S.J. Connolly (ed.), *The Oxford Companion to Irish History*, p. 295.

68 Char 28/136/9; Leonie Leslie to Jennie Churchill (Cornwallis-West), 1913.

69 Leslie Papers, NLI, L/5/8; 1913, 1914.

70 Lord Edward Grey to Moreton Frewen, 12 December 1912, cited by Anita Leslie in *Mr Frewen of England*, p. 183.

71 Frewen Papers, Oswald diaries; 10 January 1914.

72 Clare Sheridan, *Nuda Veritas*, pp. 17–18.

73 Leslie Papers, NLI, M/8/3; Hugh Frewen to Shane Leslie, 28 December 1913.

74 Frewen Papers, Oswald diaries; 2 May 1914.

75 Edward Grey, 1st Viscount Grey of Fallodon, *Twenty-Five Years 1892–1916*, vol. *II*, Chapter 18, p.

12: THE LAMPS GO OUT IN EUROPE, PP. 290–318

1 For figures on losses sustained by the aristocracy in the First World War, see David Cannadine, *The Decline and Fall of the British Aristocracy*, pp. 75–83.

2 Char 28/136/11; Leonie Leslie to Jennie Churchill, 14 August 1914.

3 Jennie Churchill to Leonie Leslie, 15 September 1914, cited by Anita Leslie in *Jennie: The Life of Lady Randolph Churchill*, p. 312.

4 Liddell Hart was one of Britain's leading military historians and the author of a number of books, including *The Real War 1914–1916 and A History of the World War*.

5 Leslie Papers, NLI, L/1/13; Leonie Leslie to Kitty Mott, 1914.

6 Leslie Papers, NLI, L/2/8; Norman Leslie to Leonie Leslie, 1914.

7 Later, five brigades of cavalry; by December, there were seven infantry divisions. See David Chandler (ed.), *The Oxford History of the British Army*, p. 211.

8 Paul Kennedy, *The Rise and Fall of the Great Powers*, pp. 256–74.

9 Stephen Pope and Elizabeth-Anne Wheal, *The Macmillan Dictionary of the First World War*, p. 104; see also John Keegan, *The First World War*; Spencer Tucker (ed.), *The European Powers in the First World War: An Encyclopedia*; and Ian Hogg (ed.), *Historical Dictionary of World War I*.

10 Stephen Pope and Elizabeth-Anne Wheal, *The Macmillan Dictionary of the First World War*, p. 111.

11 Leslie Papers, NLI, L/2/9; Shane Leslie to Marjorie Leslie, 23 October 1914.

12 Leslie Papers, NLI, L/2/9; Shane Leslie to Jack Leslie, 23 October 1914.

13 Seymour Leslie, *The Jerome Connexion*, p. 79.

14 It would seem that Sir Jack had settled the estate on Norman before his son's death, presumably in order to avoid death duties, which were dramatically increased in this period. Lloyd George's determination to put an end to the avoidance of death duties by settlement of estates was thwarted by his Cabinet. See Peter Mandler, *The Fall and Rise of the Stately Home*, p. 174.

15 Leslie Papers, NLI, L/2/9; Seymour Leslie to Jack Leslie, 26 October 1914.

16 Leslie Papers, NLI, L/2/8; Norman Leslie to unnamed friend, 1914.

17 Leslie Papers, NLI, L/2/2; Mary Crawshay to Leonie Leslie, 1914.

18 Leslie Papers, NLI, L/2/9; Olive Guthrie to Leonie Leslie, 1914.

19 Leslie Papers, NLI, L/2/9; Elsie Hope to Leonie Leslie, 1914.

20 Leslie Papers, NLI, L/2/9; Shane Leslie to Leonie Leslie, 22 December 1914.

21 Leslie Papers, NLI, M/1/2; Leonie Leslie to Shane Leslie, 27 December 1914.

22 Leslie Papers, NLI, L/2/9; Shane Leslie to Seymour Leslie, 28 December 1914.

23 Leslie Papers, NLI, M/1/1; Jack Leslie to Shane Leslie, 18 November 1914.

24 Leslie Papers, NLI, L/2/9; Paul Kennedy to Leonie Leslie, 25 October 1914.

25 Submarine warfare under the rules of commerce raiding stipulated that submarines must give a merchant ship warning before sinking and make provision for the escape of crew and passengers; 'unrestricted' submarine warfare did not follow such rules, and U-boats torpedoed without warning. This practice could lead to wrongly sinking neutrals. A diplomatic disaster occurred in May 1915 when a German U-20 sank the British liner *Lusitania*, causing the death of 1,201 passengers, including 128 Americans. This incident nearly caused the neutral United States to break off relations with Germany. See John Keegan, *The First World War*, pp. 286–7.

26 Frewen Papers, Clare letters; Clare Sheridan to Oswald Frewen, 2 October 1914.

27 Frewen Papers, Clare letters; Oswald Frewen to Clare Sheridan, 24 February 1915.

28 Clare Sheridan, *Nuda Veritas*, p. 105.

29 Clare Sheridan, *Nuda Veritas*, p. 107.

30 Frewen Papers, Clare letters; Winston S. Churchill to Clare Sheridan, 3 October 1915.

31 Clare Sheridan, *Nuda Veritas*, p. 108.

32 Char 28/136/20; Leonie Leslie to Jennie Churchill, 1915.

33 Leslie Papers, NLI, L/4/5; Henry Clay Ide to Leonie Leslie, 1 August 1916.

34 Mary Soames, *Clementine Churchill: The Revised and Updated Biography*, p. 141.

35 Winston S. Churchill to Hugh Frewen, 16 October 1915, cited by Anita Leslie in *Jennie*, p. 322.

36 Jennie Churchill to Winston S. Churchill, cited by Ralph Martin in *Jennie: The Life of Lady Randolph Churchill, vol. II*, p. 374.

37 Jennie Churchill to Leonie Leslie, 24 July 1914, cited by Anita Leslie in *Jennie*, p. 307.

38 Anita Leslie, *Jennie*, p. 331.

39 Clare Sheridan, *Nuda Veritas*, p. 118.

40 Frewen Papers, Clare letters; Clare Sheridan to Clara Frewen, 1916/17 [?]

41 Leslie Papers, NLI, L/3/3; Moreton Frewen to Leonie Leslie, 1916/17 [?]

42 Char 2/91/15; Clara Frewen to Winston S. Churchill, 20 July 1917.

43 Leslie Papers, NLI, L/5/7; Moreton Frewen to Shane Leslie, 1 June 1916.

44 Leslie Papers, NLI, L/5/7; Moreton Frewen to Shane Leslie, 23 June 1916.

45 Leslie Papers, NLI, M/1/1; Jack Leslie to Shane Leslie, 13 February 1916.

47 Leslie Papers, NLI, M/1/6; Seymour Leslie to Shane Leslie, 2 March 1916.

48 Leslie Papers, NLI, M/1/6; Seymour Leslie to Shane Leslie, 9 May 1916.

49 Leslie Papers, NLI, M/1/6; Seymour Leslie to Shane Leslie, 3 September 1916.

50 Leslie Papers, NLI, M/1/1; Sir Jack Leslie to Shane Leslie, 27 October 1916.

51 Leslie Papers, NLI, M/1/6A; Seymour Leslie to Marjorie Leslie, 23 April 1917.

52 Leslie Papers, NLI, M/1/2; Leonie Leslie to Shane Leslie, 7 December 1918.

53 Winston S. Churchill, cited by Martin Gilbert in *Churchill: A Life*, p. 401.

13: AFTER THE DELUGE, PP. 319–341

1 Frewen Papers, Oswald diaries; 18 January 1919.

2 Moreton Frewen to Clara Frewen, 1919, cited by Allen Andrews in *The Splendid Pauper*, p. 245.

3 Frewen Papers, Oswald diaries; 3 May 1920.

4 Frewen Papers, Oswald diaries; 8 May 1920.

5 Frewen Papers, Oswald diaries; 9 May 1920.

6 Frewen Papers, Oswald diaries; 3 May 1920.

7 Frewen Papers, Clare letters; Clare Sheridan to Clara Frewen, 6 November 1918.

8 Clare Sheridan, *Nuda Veritas*, p. 134.

9 Clara Frewen to Leonie Leslie, cited by Anita Leslie in *Cousin Clare: The Tempestuous Career of Clare Sheridan*, p. 100.

10 Anita Leslie, *Cousin Clare*, p. 100.

11 Rex Wade, *The Bolshevik Revolution and Russian Civil War*, p. 23; and W. Bruce Lincoln, *Red Victory: A History of the Russian Civil War*, pp. 369–71 and 477.

12 Winston S. Churchill, *The Aftermath*, cited by Roy Jenkins in *Churchill*, p. 350.

13 Clara Frewen to Jennie Churchill, 19 September 1920, cited by Anita Leslie in *Cousin Clare*, p. 111.

14 Frewen Papers, Oswald diaries; 21 September 1920.

15 Clara Frewen to Leonie Leslie, cited by Anita Leslie in *Cousin Clare*, p. 111.

16 Leonie Leslie to Clara Frewen, cited by Anita Leslie in *Cousin Clare*, pp. 112–13.

17 Leonie Leslie to Olive Guthrie, cited by Anita Leslie in *Cousin Clare*, pp. 112–13.

18 September 1920, cited by Anita Leslie in *Cousin Clare*, p. 114.

19 Moreton Frewen to Shane Leslie, September 1920, cited by Anita Leslie in *Cousin Clare*, p. 114.

20 Jennie Churchill to Leonie Leslie, September 1920, cited by Anita Leslie in *Cousin Clare*, p. 115.

21 King Papers; Clare Sheridan to Shane Leslie, 11 October 1920.

22 King Papers; Clare Sheridan to Shane Leslie, 17 October 1920.

23 Leslie Papers, NLI, M/8/2; Clara Frewen to Shane Leslie, 28 November 1920.

25 Clare Sheridan, *Nuda Veritas*, p. 205.

26 Clare Sheridan, *To the Four Winds*, p. 149.

27 Leonie Leslie to Clare Sheridan, cited by Anita Leslie in *Cousin Clare*, pp. 134–5.

28 Winston S. Churchill to Clare Sheridan, 27 January 1921, cited by Anita Leslie in *Cousin Clare*, p. 135.

29 Leonie Leslie to Oswald Frewen, cited by Anita Leslie in *Cousin Clare*, p. 158.

30 Leslie Papers, NLI, L/5/10; 10 June 1921.

31 Frewen Papers, Oswald diaries; 19 October 1921.

32 Jack Churchill to Jennie Churchill, 14 February 1914, in Peregrine Churchill and Julian Mitchell, *Jennie, Lady Randolph Churchill: A Portrait with Letters*, pp. 247–8.

33 Jack Churchill to Jennie Churchill, 25 May 1918, in Peregrine Churchill and Julian Mitchell, *Jennie, Lady Randolph Churchill*, p. 261.

34 Seymour Leslie, *The Jerome Connexion*, p. 87.

35 Jennie Churchill to Montagu Porch, 8 March 1921, cited by Ralph Martin in *Jennie, Lady Randolph Churchill, vol. II*, p. 393.

36 Ralph Martin, *Lady Randolph Churchill, vol. II*, p. 394.

37 Seymour Leslie, *The Jerome Connexion*, p. 88.

38 The Duchess of Sermoneta, *Sparkle Distant Worlds*, cited by Ralph Martin in *Lady Randolph Churchill, vol. II*, p. 396.

39 Montagu Porch to Jennie Churchill, 8–13 May 1921, cited in Peregrine Churchill and Julian Mitchell, *Jennie, Lady Randolph Churchill*, pp. 264–5.

40 Montagu Porch to Jennie Churchill, 13 June 1921, in Peregrine Churchill and Julian Mitchell, *Jennie, Lady Randolph Churchill*, p. 265.

41 Frewen Papers, Oswald diaries; 13 June 1921.

42 Frewen Papers, Oswald diaries; 14 June 1921.

43 Correspondence with Violet Pym, Eleanor Warrender's niece, cited by Ralph Martin in *Lady Randolph Churchill, vol. II*, p. 397.

44 Montagu Porch to Jennie Churchill, 25 June 1921, in Peregrine Churchill and Julian Mitchell, *Jennie, Lady Randolph Churchill*, p. 266.

45 Montagu Porch to Jennie Churchill, 25 and 27 June 1921, in Peregrine Churchill and Julian Mitchell, *Jennie*, p. 266.

46 Frewen Papers, Oswald diaries; 28 June 1921.

47 Cited by Anita Leslie, *Jennie: The Life of Lady Randolph Churchill*, p. 353.

48 Frewen Papers, Oswald diaries; 14 June 1921.

14: LAST JOURNEYS, PP. 342–366

1 Frewen Papers, Oswald diaries; 29 June 1921.

2 Winston S. Churchill to HRH the Duke of Connaught, 30 June 1921, cited by Anita Leslie in *Jennie: The Life of Lady Randolph Churchill*, pp. 354–5.

3 Frewen Papers, Oswald diaries; 2 July 1921.

4 Char 1/141/48; Clara Frewen to Winston S. Churchill, 5 July 1921.

5 Char 1/142/61; Leonie Leslie to Winston S. Churchill, 5 July 1921.

6 Char 1/142/100; Clare Sheridan to Winston S. Churchill, [n.d.].

7 Char 1/143/168; George Cornwallis-West to Winston S. Churchill, 1 July 1921.

8 Seymour Leslie Archive, Castle Leslie; Jennie Churchill to George Cornwallis-West, 17 June 1919.

9 Char 1/146; *Daily Sketch*, 30 June 1921.

10 All the American news clippings in this section were taken from a file in Char 1/146.

11 Shane Leslie to Clare Sheridan, cited by Anita Leslie in *Jennie*, pp. 355–6.

12 Ralph Martin, *Jennie: Lady Randolph Churchill, vol. II*, p. 52; also see Char 1/138/98, 99 and 118.

13 Leslie Papers, NLI, L/3/3; Moreton Frewen to Leonie Leslie, 29 June 1921.

14 Frewen Papers, Oswald diaries; 12 May 1922.

15 Cited by Allen Andrews in *The Splendid Pauper*, p. 246.

16 Hugh's share of what he had been promised in return for advancing all the money he had given to his parents.

17 Allen Andrews, *The Splendid Pauper*, p. 250.

18 Frewen Papers, Oswald diaries; 14 July 1923.

19 Leslie Papers, NLI, L/5/16.

20 Leslie Papers, NLI, L5/14; Clara Frewen to Leonie Leslie, 2 September 1924.

21 See Frewen Papers, Oswald diaries, 1924–35.

22 Frewen Papers, Clare letters; Clare Sheridan to Clara Frewen, 1 February 1927.

23 Frewen Papers, Oswald diaries; 14 January 1929.

24 Frewen Papers, Clare letters; Clara Frewen to Oswald Frewen, 8 March 1929.

25 Frewen Papers, Oswald diaries; 18 May 1930.

26 Frewen Papers, Clare letters; Clare Sheridan to Clara Frewen, 15 February 1932.

27 Frewen Papers, Oswald diaries; 25 December 1934.

28 Frewen Papers, Oswald diaries; 20 January 1935.

29 Frewen Papers, Oswald diaries; 22 January 1935.

30 Cited by Anita Leslie in *The Gilt and the Gingerbread: An Autobiography*, p. 48.

31 Nansen won the Nobel Peace Prize in 1922 for his work as High Commissioner for Refugees.

32 Leslie Papers, NLI, L/3/7; Clare Sheridan to Leonie Leslie, 9 September 1922.

33 Leslie Papers, NLI, M/1/1; Sir Jack Leslie to Shane Leslie, 15 June 1922.

34 Leslie Papers, NLI, M/1/2A; Leonie Leslie to Marjorie Leslie, 1922.

35 Leslie Papers, NLI, M/1/2A; Leonie Leslie to Marjorie Leslie, 1922.

36 Leslie Papers, NLI, M/8/3; Hugh Frewen to Shane Leslie, 25 August 1922.

37 Clare Sheridan, *Nuda Veritas*, p. 43.

38 Leslie Papers, NLI, L/3/7; Clare Sheridan to Leonie Leslie, 6 January 1925.

39 Anita Leslie, *The Gilt and the Gingerbread*, p. 77.

40 Anita Leslie, *The Gilt and the Gingerbread*, p. 64.

41 Leslie Papers, NLI, L/4/5; Marjorie Leslie to Leonie Leslie, 19 February 1925.

42 Leslie Papers, NLI, L/4/5; Marjorie Leslie to Leonie Leslie, 11 May 1925.

43 Leslie Papers, NLI, M/1/2A; Leonie Leslie to Marjorie Leslie, 1924.

44 Anita Leslie, *The Gilt and the Gingerbread*, p. 77.

45 Leslie Papers, NLI, M/1/2A; Leonie Leslie to Marjorie Leslie [n.d.].

46 Leslie Papers, NLI, M8/1; Clare Sheridan to Shane Leslie, September 1931.

47 Anita Leslie, *Edwardians in Love*, p. 216.

48 Noble Frankland, *Witness of a Century: The Life and Times of Prince Arthur Duke of Connaught 1850–1942*, p. 372.

49 It bears repeating that Noble Frankland has had access to the duke's letters

to Leonie, which are not available for consultation by the public.

50 Noble Frankland, *Witness of a Century*, pp. 372–3.

51 Anita Leslie, *Edwardians in Love*, p. 217.

52 Anita Leslie, *Edwardians in Love*, p. 217.

53 Anita Leslie, *Edwardians in Love*, p. 218.

15: FOUR ROSES FROM FOUR SONS, PP. 367–382

1 Asquith and Oxford Papers; Leonie Leslie to Frances Horner, 9 November 1933.

2 Leslie Papers, NLI, M/1/2A; Leonie Leslie to Marjorie Leslie, [n.d.].

3 Leslie Papers, NLI, M/1/2A; Leonie Leslie to Marjorie Leslie, [n.d.].

4 Seymour Leslie, *The Jerome Connexion*, p. 154.

5 Seymour Leslie, *The Jerome Connexion*, p. 154.

6 Although Queen Charlotte's birthday was in May, her birthday ball was held in winter, to distinguish it from the parties and pomp surrounding the King's birthday on 4th June. Known as 'the Glorious Fourth', this is still celebrated each year at Eton.

7 Leslie Papers, NLI, L/1/3; Leonie Leslie to Clara Frewen, 21 September 1929 [?]

8 Leslie family archive, CLI.

9 Leslie Papers, NLI, L/4/10; Leonie Leslie to Lionel Leslie, [n.d.].

10 Frewen Papers, Clare letters; Margaret Sheridan to Clare Sheridan, 9 September 1927.

11 Frewen Papers, Clare letters; Margaret Sheridan to Clare Sheridan, 19 September 1927.

12 Frewen Papers, Clare letters; Margaret Sheridan to Clare Sheridan, 25 September 1927.

13 Frewen Papers, Clare letters; Margaret Sheridan to Clare Sheridan, 25 September 1927.

14 Leslie Papers, NLI, M/8/3A; Shane Leslie to Oswald Frewen, 6 October 1932.

15 MI5 file, cited by *Daily Telegraph*, 28 November 2002, and *The Times*, 28 November 2002.

16 Leslie Papers, NLI, M/8/1; Clare Sheridan to Shane Leslie, 10 September 1933.

17 Anita Leslie, *The Gilt and the Gingerbread: An Autobiography*, p. 159.

18 Anita Leslie, *The Gilt and the Gingerbread*, p. 159.

19 Leslie Papers, NLI, M/8/3; Hugh Frewen to Shane Leslie, 21 March 1936.

20 Anita Leslie, *Cousin Clare: The Tempestuous Career of Clare Sheridan*, p. 242.

21 Winston S. Churchill to Clare Sheridan, cited by Anita Leslie in *Cousin Clare*, p. 249.

22 Seymour Leslie, *The Jerome Connexion*, p. 184.

23 Seymour Leslie, *The Jerome Connexion*, p. 184.

24 Leslie Papers, NLI, M/8/1; Clare Sheridan to Shane Leslie, 24 August 1943.

25 Leslie Papers, NLI, M/8/6; Olive Guthrie to Shane Leslie, 29 August 1943.

26 Leslie Papers, CLI; Winston S. Churchill to Leonie Leslie, 1 August 1943.

27 Leslie Papers, CLI; *Irish Independent*, 27 August 1943.

28 Char 1/343; Leonie Leslie to Winston S. Churchill, 5 September 1939.

29 Seymour Leslie Archive, CLI; Shane Leslie to Seymour Leslie, 24 August 1943.

30 Seymour Leslie Archive, CLI; Shane Leslie to Seymour Leslie, 24 August 1943.

EPILOGUE: A BEAUTIFUL AFFECTION, PP. 383–385

1 Cited by Marian Fowler in *In a Gilded Cage: From Heiress to Duchess*, p. 293.

2 Leslie Papers, NLI, L/3/2; HRH Duke of Connaught to Olive Guthrie, 23 January 1935.

A NOTE ON SOURCES, PP. 389–392

1 Mrs George Cornwallis-West, *The Reminiscences of Lady Randolph Churchill*, p. vii.

Bibliography

PRIVATE PAPERS

Churchill Papers, Chartwell Collection, Churchill College Archives Centre, Cambridge (Char)

Frewen Papers, held by Jonathan Frewen, Sussex

Leslie Papers, Manuscript Collections, National Library of Ireland (NLI)

Leslie Papers, held by the Leslie family at Castle Leslie, Ireland (CLI)

Leslie Papers, held by Richard Tarka King, Dorset (King Papers)

Oxford and Asquith Papers, held by the Earl of Oxford and Asquith

Seymour Leslie Archive, held by Jennifer Leslie at Castle Leslie, Ireland (CLI)

MAGAZINES AND NEWSPAPERS

Country Life
Daily Telegraph
Illustrated London News
Irish Independent
Irish Times
Nineteenth Century
Nineteenth Century and After

Northern Standard and Monaghan and Tyrone Advertiser
The Times
Town Topics

MEMOIRS AND AUTOBIOGRAPHICAL WORKS

Balsan, Consuelo Vanderbilt, *The Glitter and the Gold* (New York: Harper & Brothers Publishers, 1952)

Campbell, Mrs Patrick, *My Life and Some Letters* (London: Hutchinson, 1922)

Churchill, Lady Randolph, *Small Talks on Big Subjects* (London: C.A. Pearson, 1916)

Churchill, Randolph S., *Twenty-One Years* (London: Weidenfeld & Nicolson, 1965)

Churchill, Winston S., *My Early Life: A Roving Commission* (London: Eland, 2002; first published 1930)

Clark, Kenneth, *Another Part of the Wood* (London: John Murray, 1974)

Cockburn, Patricia, *Figure of Eight* (Dingle, Ireland: Brandon, 1989; first published 1985)

Cornwallis-West, George, *Edwardian Hey-Days, or, A Little About a Lot of Things* (London and New York: Putnam, 1930)

Cornwallis-West, Mrs George, *The Reminiscences of Lady Randolph Churchill* (London: Edward Arnold, 1908)

Frewen, Moreton, *Melton Mowbray and Other Memories* (London: Herbert Jenkins Ltd, 1924)

Frewen, Oswald, edited by G.P. Griggs, *Sailor's Soliloquy* (London: Hutchinson, 1961)

Fingall, Elizabeth, Countess of, *Seventy Years Young* (Dublin: The Lilliput Press, 1995; first published 1937)

Grey, Edward, 1st Viscount Grey of Fallodon, *Twenty-Five Years 1892–1916, vol. II* (London: Hodder and Stoughton, 1925)

Leslie, Anita, *The Gilt and the Gingerbread: An Autobiography* (London: Hutchinson, 1981)

Leslie, Lionel, *One Man's World: A Story of Strange Places and Strange People* (London: Pall Mall Press, 1961)

Leslie, Seymour, *The Jerome Connexion* (London: John Murray, 1964)

Leslie, Shane, *The End of a Chapter* (London: Constable & Co. Ltd, 1916)

Leslie, Shane, *American Wonderland: Memories of Four Tours in the United States of America (1911–1935)* (Michael Joseph, 1936)

Leslie, Shane, *The Film of Memory* (London: Michael Joseph Ltd, 1938)

Leslie, Shane, *Long Shadows* (London: John Murray, 1966)

Leslie, Shane, *Studies in Sublime Failure* (London: Ernest Benn Ltd, 1932)

Leslie, Mrs Shane, *Girlhood in the Pacific: Samoa – Philippines – Spain* (London: MacDonald & Co., 1943)

O'Connor, T.P., *Memories of an Old Parliamentarian* (London: Ernest Benn Ltd, 1929)

Pless, Princess Daisy of, *Daisy, Princess of Pless: By Herself* (New York: E.P. Dutton, 1929)

Rossmore, Lord, *Things I Can Tell* (London: G. Bell, 1912)

Sheridan, Clare, *Nuda Veritas* (London: Thornton Butterworth Ltd, 1927)

Sheridan, Clare, *My Crowded Sanctuary* (London: Methuen & Co. Ltd, 1945)

Sheridan, Clare, *To the Four Winds* (London: André Deutsch, 1957)

HISTORIES AND BIOGRAPHIES

Andrews, Allen, *The Splendid Pauper* (London: George G. Harrap & Co. Ltd, 1968)

Anon., *America and the Americans: From a French Point of View* (London: William Heinemann, 1897)

Anon., 'The Cunard White Star Line', in *Ocean Liners of the Past* (New York: Bonanza Books, 1979)

Auchincloss, Louis, *The Vanderbilt Era* (New York: Charles Scribner's Sons, 1989)

Bateman, John, *The Great Landowners of Great Britain and Ireland*

(London: Harrison & Sons, 1878)

Beard, Patricia, *After the Ball: Gilded Age Secrets, Boardroom Betrayals, and the Party that Ignited the Great Wall Street Scandal* (New York: HarperCollins, 2003)

Blow, Simon, *Fields Elysian: A Portrait of Hunting Society* (London: J.M. Dent & Sons, Ltd, 1983)

Blunden, M., *The Countess of Warwick: A Biography* (London: Cassell, 1989)

Bowen, Elizabeth, *The Shelbourne* (London: Vintage, 2001)

Brandon, Ruth, *The Dollar Princesses* (London: Weidenfeld & Nicolson, 1980)

Brendon, Piers, *Winston Churchill: A Brief Life* (London: Pimlico, 2001)

Brough, James, *Consuelo: Portrait of an American Heiress* (New York: Coward, McCann & Geoghegan, Inc., 1979)

Campbell, Christy, *Fenian Fire: The British Government Plot to Assassinate Queen Victoria* (London: HarperCollins, 2002)

Cannadine, David, *Aspects of Aristocracy: Grandeur and Decline in Modern Britain* (New Haven and London: Yale University Press, 1994)

Cannadine, David, *The Decline and Fall of the British Aristocracy* (London: Papermac: 1996)

Chandler, David (ed.), *The Oxford History of the British Army* (Oxford: Oxford University Press, 1994)

Charlton, D.G. (ed.), *France: A Companion to French Studies*, second edn (London and New York: Methuen & Co. Ltd, 1972)

Churchill, Allen, *Remember When* (New York: Golden Press, Inc., 1967)

Churchill, Peregrine, and Mitchell, Julian, *Jennie, Lady Randolph Churchill: A Portrait with Letters* (London: Collins, 1974)

Churchill, Randolph S., *Youth: Winston S. Churchill 1874–1900* (London: Minerva, 1991; first published 1966)

Churchill, Randolph S., *Young Statesman: Winston S. Churchill 1901–1914* (London: Minerva, 1991; first published 1967)

Churchill, Winston S., *Lord Randolph Churchill* (London: Odhams Press, 1952; first published 1906)

Coates, Tim, *Patsy: The Story of Mary Cornwallis-West* (London:

Bloomsbury, 2003)

Connolly, S.J. (ed.), *The Oxford Companion to Irish History* (Oxford: Oxford University Press, 1998)

Davies, Norman, *Europe: A History* (London: Pimlico, 1997)

Davies, Norman, *The Isles: A History* (London: Macmillan, 1999)

Duff, David, *Eugenie and Napoleon III* (London: William Collins, 1978)

Echard, William E. (ed.), *Historical Dictionary of the French Second Empire 1852–1870* (London: Aldwych Press, 1985)

Eliot, Elizabeth, *Heiresses and Coronets* (New York: McDowell, Oblensky, 1959)

Ellis, Edward Robb, *The Epic of New York City* (New York: Coward-McCann, Inc., 1966)

Emmons, David, 'Moreton Frewen and the Populist Revolt', in *Annuals of Wyoming*, vol. 35, number 2, October 1963, pp. 155–73

Foster, R.F., *Lord Randolph Churchill: A Political Life* (Oxford: Clarendon Press, 1981)

Foster, R.F., *Modern Ireland 1600–1972* (London: Penguin Books, 1988)

Foster, R.F., *The Irish Story: Telling Tales and Making it up in Ireland* (London: Allen Lane, The Penguin Press, 2001)

Fowler, Marian, *In a Gilded Cage: From Heiress to Duchess* (Toronto: Vintage, 1994; first published 1993)

Frankland, Noble, *Witness of a Century: The Life and Times of Prince Arthur Duke of Connaught 1850–1942* (London: Shepheard-Walwyn, 1993)

French, David, *The British Way in Warfare 1688–2000* (London: Unwin Hyman, 1990)

Gilbert, Martin, *Winston Spencer-Churchill, vol. V: 1922–1939* (London: Heinemann, 1976)

Gilbert, Martin, *Winston Spencer-Churchill, vol. V Companion, Part Three: Documents, 'The Coming of War' 1936–1939* (London: Heinemann, 1982)

Gilbert, Martin, *Churchill: A Life* (London: William Heinemann, 1991)

Gilbert, Martin, *A History of the Twentieth Century, vol. I: 1900–1933* (London: HarperCollins, 1997)

Gilmour, David, *Curzon* (London: John Murray, 1994)

Goubert, Pierre, *The Course of French History* (London and New York: Routledge, 1991; first published 1984)

Haslip, Joan, *The Lonely Empress: A Biography of Elizabeth of Austria* (London: Phoenix Press, 2000; first published 1965)

Hayden, Deborah, *Pox: Genius, Madness, and the Mysteries of Syphilis* (New York: Basic Books, 2003)

Heffer, Simon, *Power and Place: The Political Consequences of King Edward VII* (London: Weidenfeld & Nicolson, 1998)

Hendrick, Burton J., *The Age of Big Business: A Chronicle of the Captains of Industry* (New Haven: Yale University Press, 1919)

Hibbert, Christopher, *Queen Victoria: A Personal History* (London: HarperCollins, 2000)

Hickey, D.J., and Doherty, J.E. (eds.), *A New Dictionary of Irish History from 1800* (Dublin: Gill & Macmillan, 2003)

Hogg, Ian (ed.), *Historical Dictionary of World War I* (Lanham and London: The Scarecrow Press Inc., 1998)

Homberger, Eric, *Mrs. Astor's New York: Money and Social Power in a Gilded Age* (New Haven and London: Yale University Press, 2002)

Hoyt, Edwin P., *The Goulds: A Social History* (New York: Weybright & Talley, 1969)

Hutton, Patrick (ed.), *Historical Dictionary of the Third French Republic 1870–1940* (London: Aldwych, 1986)

Jaher, Frederic Cople, 'The Gilded Elite: American Multimillionaires, 1865 to the Present', in W.D. Rubinstein (ed.), *Wealth and the Wealthy in the Modern World* (London: Croom Helm, 1980)

Jackson, Alvin, *Home Rule: An Irish History 1800–2000* (London: Weidenfeld & Nicolson, 2003)

Jenkins, Roy, *Churchill* (London: Macmillan, 2001)

Judd, Denis, *Empire: The British Imperial Experience from 1765 to the Present* (London: Fontana Press, 1996)

Kee, Robert, *The Green Flag: A History of Irish Nationalism* (London: Penguin, 2000; first published 1972)

Keegan, John, *The First World War* (London: Hutchinson, 1998)

Kennedy, Paul, *The Rise and Fall of the Great Powers*

Kraus, Rene, *Young Lady Randolph: The Life and Times of Jennie Jerome* (London: Jarrolds, 1944)

Lambert, Angela, *Unquiet Souls: The Indian Summer of the British Aristocracy, 1880–1918* (London: Macmillan, 1984)

Lane, David, *Politics and Society in the USSR* (London: Martin Robinson & Co., 1978; first published 1970)

Laver, James, *The Age of Optimism: Manners and Morals 1848–1914* (London: Weidenfeld & Nicolson, 1966)

Lees-Milne, James, *The Enigmatic Edwardian: The Life of Reginald 2nd Viscount Esher* (London: Sidgwick & Jackson, 1988; first published 1986)

Leslie, Anita, *The Fabulous Leonard Jerome* (London: Hutchinson, 1954); published in the United States as *The Remarkable Mr Jerome* (New York: Holt, 1954)

Leslie, Anita, *Mr Frewen of England* (London: Hutchinson, 1966)

Leslie, Anita, *Jennie: The Life of Lady Randolph Churchill* (London: Hutchinson, 1969)

Leslie, Anita, *Edwardians in Love* (London: Hutchinson, 1972)

Leslie, Anita, *Cousin Clare: The Tempestuous Career of Clare Sheridan* (London: Hutchinson, 1976)

Leslie, Shane, *Studies in Sublime Failure* (London: Ernest Benn Ltd, 1932)

Leslie, Shane, *Men Were Different: Five Studies in Late Victorian Biography* (London: Michael Joseph, 1937)

Lincoln, W. Bruce, *Red Victory: A History of the Russian Civil War* (New York: Simon & Schuster, 1989)

Lubbock, Percy (ed.), *The Letters of Henry James, vols. I and II* (New York: Charles Scribner's Sons, 1920)

McAuley, Rob, *The Liners* (Motorbooks International, 1997)

MacColl, Gail, and McD. Wallace, Carol, *To Marry an English Lord: The Victorian and Edwardian Experience* (London: Sidgwick & Jackson, 1989)

McCoole, Sinead, *Hazel: A Life of Lady Lavery 1880–1934* (Dublin: The Lilliput Press, 1996)

Mandler, Peter, *The Fall and Rise of the Stately Home* (New Haven and

London: Yale University Press, 1997)

Martin, Ralph G., *Jennie: The Life of Lady Randolph Churchill, vol. I: The Romantic Years 1854–1895* (Englewood Cliffs, N.J.: Prentice-Hall, Inc., 1969; quotations are taken from the Cardinal edn, published by Sphere Books, 1974)

Martin, Ralph G., *Jennie: The Life of Lady Randolph Churchill, vol. II: The Dramatic Years 1895–1921* (Englewood Cliffs, N.J.: Prentice-Hall, Inc., 1971)

Minney, R.J., *The Edwardian Age* (London: Cassel & Co. Ltd, 1964)

Montgomery, Maureen E., *Gilded Prostitution: Status, Money and Transatlantic Marriages, 1870–1914* (London and New York: Routledge, 1989)

Montgomery-Massingberd, Hugh, *Blenheim Revisited: The Spencer-Churchills and their Palace* (New York: Beaufort Books, 1985)

Montgomery-Massingberd, Hugh, *Debrett's Great British Families* (London: Webb & Bower, 1988)

Mordaunt Crook, J., *The Rise of the Nouveaux Riches: Style and Status in Victorian and Edwardian Architecture* (London: John Murray, 1999)

Morris, Lloyd, *Incredible New York: High Life and Low Life of the Last Hundred Years* (New York: Random Books, 1951)

Morris, Richard B., and Morris, Jeffrey B. (eds.), *Encyclopedia of American History*, 7th edn (New York: HarperCollins Publishers, 1996)

O'Connor, Richard, *Courtroom Warrior: The Combative Career of William Travers Jerome* (Boston: Little, Brown & Co., 1963)

Pakenham, Thomas, *The Boer War* (London: Abacus, 2003; first published 1979)

Perkin, Harold, *The Rise of Professional Society: England since 1880* (London and New York: Routledge, 1990; first published 1989)

Pope, Stephen, and Wheal, Elizabeth-Anne, *The Macmillan Dictionary of the First World War* (London: Macmillan, 1995)

Quelch, Eileen, *Perfect Darling: The Life and Times of George Cornwallis-West* (London: Cecil & Amelia Woolf, 1972)

Quetel, Claude (translated by Judith Braddock and Brian Pike), *The History of Syphilis* (Baltimore, Maryland: The Johns Hopkins

University Press, paperback edn, 1992; first published 1986)

Ramsden, John (ed.), *The Oxford Companion to Twentieth Century British Politics* (Oxford: Oxford University Press, 2002)

Rhodes James, Robert, *Lord Randolph Churchill* (London: Ebenezer Baylis & Son, 1959)

Rhodes James, Robert, *The British Revolution: British Politics 1880–1939* (London: Methuen & Co. Ltd, 1978)

Rosebery, Lord, *Lord Randolph Churchill* (London: Arthur Humphreys, 1906)

Rosenbaum, Robert A., and Brinkley, Douglas (eds.), *The Penguin Encyclopedia of American History* (Harmondsworth: Penguin Reference, 2003)

Rubinstein, W.D. (ed.), *Wealth and the Wealthy in the Modern World* (London: Croom Helm, 1980)

Sandys, Celia, *Chasing Churchill: The Travels of Winston Churchill by his Granddaughter* (London: HarperCollins, 2003)

Schlereth, Thomas J., *Victorian America: Transformations in Everyday Life, 1876–1915* (New York: HarperCollins Publishers, 1992)

Schneer, Jonathan, *London 1900: The Imperial Metropolis* (New Haven and London: Yale University Press, 1999)

Seward, Desmond, *Eugenie: The Empress and her Empire* (London: Sutton, 2004)

Shukman, Harold (ed.), *The Blackwell Encyclopedia of the Russian Revolution* (Oxford: Blackwell Reference, 1988)

Soames, Mary, *Clementine Churchill: The Revised and Updated Biography* (London: Doubleday, 2002; first published 1979)

Stead, William T., *The Americanization of the World or the Trend of the Twentieth Century* (New York and London: Garland Publishing, Inc., 1972; first published 1902)

Thompson, F.M.L., *English Landed Gentry in the Nineteenth Century* (London: Routledge & Kegan Paul, 1963)

Tucker, Spencer (ed.), *The European Powers in the First World War: An Encyclopedia* (New York and London: Garland Publishing Inc., 1996)

Turner, John (ed.), *Britain and the First World War* (London: Unwin

Hyman, 1988)

Vanderbilt Jr., Cornelius, *Queen of the Golden Age: The Fabulous Story of Grace Wilson Vanderbilt* (New York, Toronto and London: McGraw-Hill Book Co., Inc., 1956)

Vickers, Hugo, *Gladys Duchess of Marlborough* (New York: Holt, Rinehart & Winston, 1979)

Wade, Rex, *The Bolshevik Revolution and Russian Civil War* (Westport, Connecticut: Greenwood Press, 2001)

Wasserstrom, William, *Heiress of all the Ages: Sex and Sentiment in the Genteel Tradition* (Minneapolis: University of Minnesota Press, 1959)

Wecter, Dixon, *The Saga of American Society: A Record of Social Aspiration 1607–1937* (New York: Charles Scribner's Sons, 1970; first published 1937)

Weymouth, Lally, *America in 1876* (New York: Random House, 1976)

Index

Letters are indexed selectively under the name of the sender.
Abbreviations have been used as follows:
CH = Clara (*orig.* Clarissa) Hall (*later* Jerome)
CJ = Clara (*orig.* Clarita) Jerome
JJ = Jennie Jerome
LJ = Leonie Jerome
RC = Randolph Churchill

8; friendship with Jennie Lind 8; rumour of Minnie Hauk's parentage 8–9, 91; birth and death of Camille (third daughter) 9, 18; extravagant lifestyle 10–11, 12–13, 14, 18, 22, 47; birth of LJ (youngest daughter) 11; friendship with Fanny Ronalds 12–13, 31, 210; and Adeline Patti 13; legendary generosity 17–18; daughters' education 21–2, 29; letters 49, 50, 59, 120, 124, 135–6; JJ's marriage 49–50, 55–6, 60–1; marriage settlement 51, 57–9, 112; financial problems 89, 112, 147–8; liking for Moreton Frewen 94, 98; ill health 111, 112; LJ's marriage 120, 135–6; financial provision for daughters 136, 145, 147–8; Clara and new will 145; last years and death 151–3

Jerome, Leonie ('Sniffy'; 'Tante Leonie'; youngest daughter of CH; *later* Leslie) character and personality xvi, 75, 98–9, 111, 135, 158, 373–4, 384–5; marriage to Jack Leslie xvii–xviii, 88, 111–23, 158; relationship with sisters xviii, 105, 115, 149, 242; childhood and education 11, 20–1, 111; love of riding 20, 75; musical ability 20, 29, 75, 111, 122, 129, 166, 219, 385; boarding school 39, 75; doomed romance with Charlie Fitzwilliam 99, 100–2; pursued by Freddie Gebhard 100; letters 101–2, 112–13, 114, 137, 161, 195–6, 240–1, 267, 279, 282–3, 284, 298, 317–18, 328, 331, 364, 372; fondness for nephew Winston 111, 151, 381–2; eldest son John Randolph (Jacky; Shane) 128, 129, 234–9, 282–5; Norman Jerome (second son) 128, 240, 280, 294–5, 297–9; love of Glaslough 129, 158–61; financial problems 136–7, 143–4, 257, 285, 369; Seymour (third son) 151, 161–3; death of CH and will 183–5; enjoys society life 190–1; close friendship with Arthur Duke of Connaught 191–4, 195–6 & n, 216–17, 242, 365–6; Lionel (youngest son) 195; JJ's marriage to Cornwallis–West 214,

216; tour to Egypt and India 217–19; Clare's debut 228; death of JJ 340–1; relations with Marjorie (daughter–in–law) 373–4; death and bequests 381, 382 *see also* Glaslough; politics, Irish
Jerome, Mary (sister of Leonard) 2
Jerome, Samuel (paternal great–grandfather of Leonard) 2
Jerome, Timothy (paternal great–great–grandfather of Leonard) 2
Jerome, Travers (nephew of Leonard Jerome) 351
Jocelyn, Lieutenant–Colonel John Strange 87
Jung, Sir Salar 132–5, 143

Kamenev, Lev Borisovich 325, 327, 328
Keith, Dr Thomas 171
Kenmare, Earl of 116
Kennedy, Paul: letter 299
Keppel, Violet 277
Keppel, Mrs Alice 245
Kerry, Countess of 295
Kevenhuller (acquaintance of JJ) 56
Keyes, Commodore Roger 300
Kinsky, Count Charles 104, 123–4, 133, 149, 151, 165, 166, 173–5, 277
Kintore, Earl of 178, 187
Kipling, Rudyard 250
Kitchener, Lord 202, 218, 291
Knollys, Francis 50, 61

Labouchere, Henry 139–40
Lane, John 205
Langtry, Lily 95, 96, 148
Lansbury, George 274
Lavery, Sir John 358
Law, Andrew Bonar 266–7
Le Temps 36
Lee, General Robert E. 15
Leinster, Duke of 116
Lenox Hotel (NY) 152
Leslie, Anita (granddaughter of LJ): writings 18n, 77–8; comment on Jack Leslie 88; and LJ 111, 228, 242, 365–6, 373, 377;